# A Sow's Ear

*Digressions and Transgressions
of a Gay Humanist*

A. Ian Fraser

For Ambrose

# CONTENTS

# Preface

Ian Fraser's life is an extraordinary one by any standard. Here is a man who sprang into the world in West Africa and landed in Indianapolis by way of Jamaica, Scotland and England. At every stage of his long and well-lived life, he has met with colorful events, cultivated relationships with fascinating people and made generous contributions to his community and world. From the minute I met Ian in 1996 I was captivated by the man and his story. When I compared his path to my own upbringing in rural Indiana, his life seemed so different, so exotic – and yet there were themes in his life that felt familiar to me, as they would to most gay men.

It was Judy O'Bannon who introduced me to Ian in 1996 when she was the 'second' Lady of Indiana. I had just graduated from Purdue University and was working in the Lt. Governor's Office and Judy was able to understand how much I would benefit from meeting a man like Ian. She thought he might become a mentor to me and she was absolutely right. She had no idea what that introduction would do to my life. We bonded with each other instantly and his impact on my life was immediate and absolute. It wouldn't be an exaggeration to say that it was Ian who taught me how to be a man of the world, how to be a successful professional and how to be an energetic participant in important social and community causes. Since getting to know Ian, I haven't taken any important personal or professional decisions without consulting him.

For me, one of the most inspiring dimensions of Ian's life story is his lifelong commitment to his partner Ambrose. As you read this book, you will be inspired by the pure and honest love and commitment these two men share. Their love and devotion to each other has been an inspiration to countless friends, gay and straight. Ian and Ambrose recently celebrated their 60th anniversary and, at the party, friend after friend remarked on how they consider Ian's and Ambrose's relationship the standard for evaluating the success and quality of other committed relationships. At a time in which the right of same-sex couples to marry is being debated in state legislatures, the U.S. Congress and the Supreme Court, Ian's and Ambrose's story of commitment and fidelity takes on a special relevance. If an opponent of marriage equality should happen to read this book, I suspect he or she will want to reevaluate their position on that important social question. On a personal level, I too have entered into a committed relationship with the love of my life and I have no doubt that the courage to do that came, in part, from the wholesome example Ian and Ambrose gave us.

I've always known how lucky I am to have had the privilege of knowing Ian Fraser. I use stories from his life to illuminate issues in my own and I've always taken a lot of pleasure in passing on those stories to other friends. I always hoped that Ian would find a way to make the stories of his remarkable life available to others and now he's done just that in this delightful book.

May this book and especially the life it describes inspire you and may Ian's example help you shape your own life in the way it helped shape mine. May it further the argument that love is not defined by courts or church but by the honor with which two people who love each other cherish and cultivate their commitment.

Thank you, Ian, for capturing and telling your story so well. May you continue to touch the hearts and souls of countless others as you've touched the lives of so many of us for decades. Thanks for a story well written and a life well lived.

Ryan L. Messer

## Introduction and Acknowledgments

Among my papers is a letter dated January 7, 1904, written to my grandfather from his grandfather. The writer, about to celebrate his ninetieth birthday, was sharing his pent up experiences and his hopes for the future of his successors. The world seen through his eyes is very different from the one that welcomed me a mere twenty five years later. Now, as I grow ever closer to Great-great-grandfather's age, I realize that our world has changed more radically than his ever did. With each passing decade, the pace of that change has accelerated.

It was about ten thousand years ago that agronomy gradually replaced hunter-gathering and families began to build towns and villages for mutual well-being. Apart from occasional blips, human development was so gradual that generations would come, and go, believing in the status quo. Then, just a hundred years before I was born, an engineer, by the name of George Stevenson, invented the "Rocket." At a maximum speed of twenty eight miles per hour, that railroad steam engine traveled faster than anybody had done before. Courageous early passengers wondered if our bodies could withstand the shock. When cars followed, a few decades later, British law required that a man must walk in front of the vehicle, for safety's sake, waving a flag. My Grandmother remembered those days. She also remembered another man planting a flag on the moon. Now, fifty years after Granny's death, I am writing these words while seated at her desk.

For a long time, I resisted adding yet another autobiography to the zillions already out there. As a man of modest means, and abilities, what possible interest could my story have for any but my nearest and dearest? Many kind friends felt otherwise and encouraged me to write this book. Ina Mohlman was among the first. The scales were tipped in February 2012 by a letter I received from Herb Budden outlining four distinct audiences, other than friends and family, who might take vicarious pleasure in reading about my journey through life. Though my friend Herb had no hidden agenda, the timing of that letter had the desired effect. Ambrose Smith, my faithful partner of sixty years, was rapidly failing. I sorely needed something to take my mind off the inevitable. Maybe, I did have a tale worth sharing.

I well remember the time that Queen Mary, Grandmother of Queen Elizabeth II, asked why a van was parked in front of Marlborough House, her London home. When informed that men were there to install a telephone, she had them dismissed with the remark, "Can't people write letters anymore?" As for me, I was much impressed with the arrival of rotary dialing. Today, most people have never used such a device. With technological breakthroughs occurring almost daily, I would like to think that the story of a colonial child, born between the two world wars, who is still around in the second decade of the next century, has lived through a time of unprecedented change and has a story that warrants recording.

Throughout this book, there are stories about some of the countless people who have touched my life in one way or another. To the best of my knowledge, all the events happened as I describe them. As many tales occurred long ago, and the people involved are no longer alive, my memory is entirely responsible for their accuracy. In the case of those still around, I take this opportunity to thank you all for correcting or corroborating my account. Among those who have helped in this way are Rick Cohen, Sally Reel, Ben Solomon, Barbara O'Keefe, Nancy Butler, Mary Jo Showley, Allene Doddoli, Annette Kaufman, Pam Bevan, Helen Armstrong, Matthew Tivy, Bill Grimes, Doug Shoemaker, Patrick Hayes, Ed Kelley, Judy Waugh, Steve Wright, Mel Meehan, Leila Holmes, Sterling

Zinsmeyer, Louis Bixenman, Josh Kantor, Linda Wittkowski, Peter Sehlinger, Ellen Lee, Carol Linné, Philip LeBas, Barbara Michael, Tom Beczkiewicz, Raymond Leppard, Billy Vantwoud, Vanessa McCaffrey, Bob Schloss, Patti Rodriguez, Jacqueline Lorber, James Irvine Robertson, Miranda Cutler and my sister, Sheila Fraser Derfler.

When it came to transferring the manuscript into a word processor, I receiver invaluable assistance from these technically savvy people; Herb Budden, Ian Cutler, Ryan Messer, Jimmy Musuraca, Sandy Smith, Jenny Ross and Ernie Ospina. Thank you all. Before going to press, our dear friend, Brad Luther is working on layout, illustrations and the jacket design. Without all this help, and input, this project would never have come to fruition. A special thank you, to you, Brad.

Above all, I am forever indebted to Herb Budden without whose ongoing encouragement this story would have remained untold. He, Bonnie and their daughter-in-law, Alice, devoted countless hours making sense of my scribbles to create a first draft. Herb has helped me every step of the way with his technical knowledge and, as an English teacher, with his gift of drawing my attention to the most egregious literary shortcomings in the kindest possible way. Please accept my totally inadequate thanks.

I know there are others to whom I owe gratitude for bringing information to my attention. If I have failed to mention you, please forgive me and attribute the gaff to senility rather than malice. Finally, dear readers, I take full responsibility for any, and all, mistakes whether of fact or spelling to be found between the covers. I sincerely hope they are few.

# Chapter One
## *African Beginnings*

Following a protracted confinement, I entered the world on March 27, 1929 at Achimota, Ghana, some six miles inland from the coastal capital, Accra. In spite of my mother's protestations to the contrary, the attending midwife was convinced that I would be black. From all accounts, I was the first white baby to be born in that part of the world. A possible explanation for my pallor and blue eyes lies in the fact that I was conceived on the Isle of Skye off Scotland's west coast.

My father, Alastair Garden (Sandy) Fraser and my mother, Phyllis Isobel (Phil) Walton, had married at Achimota in September of 1927. At the time, Dad was twenty-five and Ma was twenty-one. They would have married sooner but for her Aunt Eddie, who was known to her charges as "Teedie." Here an explanation is in order.

My mother, the youngest of three children, was born in the city of Ranchi in western Bengal province, India. Her father, like most of her family, was "Indian Army." The circumstances of both her parents' simultaneous deaths, when Ma was only three, are as murky as the water of the lake beside their house. Tradition has it that they went out in a boat and drowned. Uncle "Grum" Walton, an Indian Army colonel, was Ma's mother's fraternal twin. As he and his wife, Teedie, were the closest family in India, they adopted Fred (ten), Dorothy (seven), and Phil (three) and changed their name to Walton from Savie. Uncle Grum and Teedie had two children of their own, Ben and Esther, to whom they were devoted. It seems that Teedie resented being landed with three orphans and took her frustrations out on Phil. Ma was a pretty child with long wavy brown hair which Teedie used to tie her to a chair.

At some point, in their childhood, it was decided that all five children should finish their education in England where assorted friends and relatives could be called upon to check on them while Grum and Teedie were in India. As they attended boarding schools, most of the time they were considered in safe hands. Ma was sent to Sherbourne Girls School where she excelled in all sports. Mary Fraser, Dad's younger sister, was also there. She and Ma became friends and soon Ma was invited to Mary's home for a vacation where she met Dad. To hear her tell it, it was love at first sight! She was thirteen, and he just about to leave Rugby School for Oxford University.

Dad's parents lived in Ceylon. Alexander Garden (Alec) Fraser had been principal of Trinity College, Kandy, since before the First World War. In 1924, at the urging of Sir Gordon Guggisberg, Governor of the Gold Coast (later Ghana), he began planning for the school which came to be known as "Achimota" along with Dr. Emmon Kwegyir Aggrey. It opened in 1927. Dad, having graduated from Queen's College Oxford in 1924 had already been training, in Ghana, since October of that year. Teedie refused to allow Phil to marry until she turned twenty-one, hence the Achimota wedding in 1927.

I remember very little of my early life in Ghana. Every year we would sail on a small ship to England for three months. Most of the time there would be divided between London and Newcastle. Chipstead is a southern suburb of London where deaf Uncle Joe (Oldham) and Aunt Mary (Mag) lived in their spacious arts and crafts Dial House amidst antiques and hushed sobriety. She was Grandfather's only sibling. After their mother died, their father, Sir Andrew Henderson Leith Fraser, had married again. From that union there were three sons, but no love seems to have been lost between the two families. During these English leaves we would spend much of the time at the Dial House before touring around to visit other relatives, especially Aunt Nina, an unmarried great aunt, in Newcastle. She was a younger sister of my grandmother, Beatrice Annie

(Bea) Fraser, nee Glass. She was a sweet and gentle lady with a charming house and garden. Usually, we traveled around England by train, but one year we bought an old Morris convertible with a large tear in the roof for fifteen pounds. It did us proud.

The voyage between England and West Africa took two weeks and was a far cry from a twenty-first century cruise. Most cabins had a small porthole for a window and four bunk beds. All doors had a high threshold that had to be stepped over. Each hallway had one or two bathrooms and arrangements had to be made with the cabin steward for a bath. The bath was filled with salt water, but the steward brought a ewer and basin with fresh water so that you could soap your body first.

My most vivid memory, from those years, was the arrival of the ship in Accra. As the country had no deep-water port, the ship would drop anchor some three miles off shore, whereupon huge canoes would be rowed out to collect all the passengers, luggage, furniture and whatever else the ship had brought. The sea was invariably rough so the passengers would sit on deck to await their turn in the 'mammy' chair. It was a topless wooden crate with an entrance gap on the side. Inside were two benches facing each other to seat a maximum of four adults. Ropes attached to the top four corners joined with a ring that hooked onto a winch or crane. Once you were seated, the "mammy" chair would be lifted up, swung over the side of the ship, and lowered until a mass of glistening black arms deftly pulled it into the bowels of the heaving canoe. The passengers would then be helped out and over sundry benches to a seat between rowers. This exercise would be repeated until the canoe could no longer accommodate more passengers at which point it would be rowed toward the beach and another canoe would take its place alongside the ship. Bringing the canoe onto the beach required great skill. The oarsmen would come in on the crest of a wave, jump overboard, and run up the beach pulling the boat behind them. Then with much laughter all the passengers would be safely helped from the prow with the aid of steps, to terra firma. On one such trip, my grandmother had brought a small piano that fell into the sea as it was being lowered into a canoe. She always traveled with her slope-top mahogany desk that fortunately did not suffer the same fate and ultimately she left it to me.

## Chapter Two
### *Chipstead*


Tsetse flies and malaria-carrying mosquitoes were an ever-present danger in West Africa. By the age of four children could no longer be confined indoors where screens and netting offered some protection. Consequently, once that age was reached, the British shipped their erstwhile bundles of joy back to Britain to be cared for by relatives. In my case, I was sent to live with Auntie Mag and Uncle Joe in the Dial House, Chipstead.

By this time, my sister Sheila was due to be born in four months. A sickly baby she proved to be so my parents had much more to worry about than how Ian was getting on in England. I had been christened in the Church of England as Alastair but, for some unknown reason, I've always been called by my middle name. At the age of four, I understood little of what was happening to me.

Auntie Mag was elderly and childless but with a matched pair of Scotch terriers instead. Uncle Joe was almost always closeted in his study-cum-library writing scholarly ecclesiastical books or working on The Christian News Letter, of which he was the editor. His occasional foray into levity took the form of malapropisms. A memorable example is when I asked, "Uncle Joe, what is an antimacassar?" With barely a pause, he replied, "There's Auntie Mag ask her."

Bishops and other distinguished prelates were frequent guests for meals or to stay. C.F. (Charlie) Andrews who had been Gandhi's close friend since South African days visited on more than one occasion. He had a long, smelly beard, no change of clothes, and traveled with nothing but a battered briefcase full of whatever manuscript he was currently writing. I was terrified of him. Auntie Mag, in a futile attempt to allay my fears, told me of a miracle which this man of God had performed. Once, in India, he had come across an abandoned, starving baby. Beneath his flowing beard, milk flowed from his hairy chest so that he successfully suckled the child. Far from reassuring me, this unlikely story agitated me to the point where I became inseparable from Rag-a-bag-a-duster, my enormous stuffed rabbit.

My mother returned to England to give birth to Sheila. My first sibling soon developed a sinister-looking tumor on her back, which called for surgery. For obvious reasons, her first-born received short shrift during these anxious months. It will come as no surprise when I say that I became incorrigible. Dear long-suffering Auntie Mag did her best to humor me. At breakfast, for example, the sideboard would be laden with a dizzying selection of porridge and cereals from which I was invited to choose. Scanning the lineup I would select an absentee, such as Grape Nuts, and throw a tantrum when the maid failed to find any in the larder. By tomorrow, when they had been added to the selection, I would refuse them. A sandpit had been installed beyond the tennis court for my amusement. When I heard that a VIP dinner party was in the offing, I buried all the silverware in it.

Auntie Mag resembled nothing so much as a Pre-Raphaelite painting with masses of straw-colored wavy hair parted in the middle and with a bun at the back. She took cold baths daily. Her hands were chapped and blue. She wore a rope of huge amber beads that hung down to below her waist. Crewelwork was her hobby, so examples of her handiwork could be found throughout the house on biscuit-colored linen bedspreads and curtains and on the seats of her Queen Anne chairs.

In spite of fulltime servants and a spacious residence, in the garden, for the housekeeper's family Auntie Mag was eccentrically frugal. The string from every incoming parcel was carefully untied, neatly "butterflied" and sorted for size. She had made several embroidered linen sacks to store the various gauges of string for future use. When the mail arrived twice daily, the envelopes were slit at one end for re-use. The perforated white edging from sheets of postage stamps was kept in a box for the purpose of re-using envelopes or for any job that today would be solved with Scotch tape. One day, when all adults were absent, I used up her supply of stamp paper by sticking it all over the priceless furniture.

In a vain attempt to civilize me, I was sent to a day school called "Sunny Corner." When Auntie Mag arrived to collect me, a scene of horror unfolded before her eyes. Through a window she saw that I was proving the despair of a teacher who was attempting a dancing class. My partner was screaming bloody murder as I was prancing about stamping on her toes. Sunny Corner was history.

A few months after my fifth birthday, I found myself in a dormitory full of boys in a school called "The Wells House" on Epsom Common. The next twelve years of my life would be spent in boys' boarding schools. One night, a teacher woke us all up to watch a big fire that we could see through the window. Next morning we learned that had been the Crystal Palace. One teacher believed in gnomes. He used to take us into the woods and fields of bracken in search of the elusive chaps. Once he spotted one, we'd all creep quietly behind him. Because only very good boys can see gnomes, we none of us wanted to admit that the little fellow who was being inspected by the teacher was invisible to us. I spotted a bit of flattened grass where a gnome was sitting, so the teacher spoke to him and he kindly allowed me to pick him up, but very gently. He was lighter than any feather but I was a happy camper that day.

## Chapter Three
### *Newbattle Abbey*

1935 was a good year for me. Grandfather, having nearly died of tropical diseases in Ghana, took early retirement. He had been born in Scotland in 1873 and was educated at Merchiston Castle School in Edinburgh. Over the years he and Philip Kerr, the Marquess of Lothian, had become friends. Blickling Hall, a splendid Jacobean pile in England, was Lord Lothian's principal residence, though he had two others in Scotland. He decided that Newbattle Abbey near Dalkeith some six miles south of Edinburgh, would make a superb adult education center, and Alec Fraser was his choice to take it over and start such a project. Granny and I had always shared a special bond so the millstone was removed from Auntie Mag's neck, and I moved into Newbattle.

For me, Newbattle was a dream come true. It had started as a Cistercian Monastery in about 1200. To this day, most of the lowest level of the house dates from the 1220s, including a 200-foot long crypt. The ancient family chapel contained a school of Botticelli Madonna and child tondo, above a lovely alabaster altar and the font in which Mary, Queen of Scots, and my sister Mary were both baptized.

Most of the house is eighteenth and early nineteenth Century. When we lived there it contained a fine collection of Italian Renaissance and Baroque paintings and sculpture. The immense drawing room has been described as among the grandest rooms in Scotland. Among other treasures displayed beneath the Italian painted ceiling is an enormous equestrian portrait of King Charles I by Van Dyck. Carvings by Grinling Gibbons grace the dining room, which also sports a magnificent plaster ceiling, as does the lovely L-shaped library with another Van Dyck portrait over the fireplace mantel. Our private drawing room had a domed ceiling crisscrossed with gold ribs, framing raised stars, against a sky blue background. The Louis XV suite of furniture was gilded with pale blue striped satin upholstery. The room contained a bay window overlooking the formal Italian gardens with its pairs of fountains and tall sundials. At the end of the gardens, beyond the clipped hedge, stood the oldest and largest beech tree in the world. Sadly only some offspring survive today. In that drawing room, Granny held court.

One day, the Duke of Kent (Queen Elizabeth's uncle) came to visit. Grandfather and the other gentlemen bowed before shaking his hand. For a stout lady, Granny managed a more than passable curtsy. As I was wearing my first kilt, I outdid the old lady with a gracious sweep to the floor, and ended by kissing the handsome gay Duke's hand, to the horror of all.

My Aunt Jean, at nineteen, was the youngest of their five children. Her bedroom was two doors down the hall from mine. She had been invited to Buckingham Palace to be "presented" to the King and Queen (George V and Queen Mary). She was required to wear a white satin gown with a train attached to the shoulders. Her blonde hair was arranged with veiling down the back and three ostrich feathers to give her an extra foot of height and as an appropriate symbol of deference to the Prince of Wales. For weeks she had practiced dressing up and walking about balancing books on her head while I watched transfixed.

If my memory serves me right, Newbattle Abbey was nestled in about 125 acres. The main entrance is through handsome gates flanked by a pair of battlemented cottages. A straight tree-lined drive of about a quarter of a mile leads to a turnaround in front of the front door. To the right of the house a stone colonnade protects the formal gardens and leads the eye to the babbling Esk River. Across the river is a high bank with extensive woods. Following the river, well beyond the formal gardens, you come to an old Romanesque bridge.

One tree had weeping branches all round to the ground. It was my secret house. However, Ma was back from Ghana for her twenty-ninth birthday so I surprised her with a party in it. She said that it cheered her up, as she was feeling very old. Soon she left again. As the taxi pulled away, she handed me a small gift to distract us both from crying. Granny said, "Go on, open it and see what it is." Grandfather, whose sense of fun I always abhorred, waited till I lifted the lid, then shouted, "Watch out! It might bite!" I flung it away screaming and thus smashed my first watch.

Mostly, at Newbattle, I played by myself. There were dungeons and spiral staircases hidden behind secret panels to be explored. The so-called Chinese bedroom and dressing room contained furniture with secret compartments. I was allowed to ride my tricycle around the house. I did so to excess. A large lion with gaping jaws was a triumph of taxidermy, but it scared me. One day, I took my courage in both hands, climbed onto the lion's plinth and put my head into its jaws. I hadn't noticed Grandfather nearby. Needless to say, he let out a blood-curdling roar that nearly gave me cardiac arrest.

Before closing the Newbattle chapter, I must mention Lord Lothian, without whose generosity, none of this would have happened. He was what would be euphemistically known as a "confirmed bachelor." We took to each other right away. On one of his visits, he was getting outfitted for the aborted coronation of King Edward VIII. He had several titles, one of which was Earl of Ancram, which entitled him to wear a splendid jeweled belt. Evidently I was enamored of that particular item of his regalia for he gave it to me. When I pranced into the drawing room to show it off to Granny, she was not amused, and I was made to return it. In its place, he gave me a bronze medal that had been presented to him a couple of years earlier by the French government for his services to art and architecture. That I still have.

Chapter Four
*Munro College, Jamaica*


When Grandfather retired from Achimota, he was succeeded by Canon Harold Grace. Dad was a housemaster with ambitions to follow the tenure of Grace as principal. As he had had no teaching experience outside of Ghana, he looked for a job that would prepare him to return to Achimota. The post which he accepted was as principal of Munro College in Jamaica. Finally, our nuclear family could be reunited.

We were to sail from Liverpool, with all our furniture and a new Buick, in the middle of December 1937. Auntie Nina was to accompany us for two or three months. Unfortunately, by the time we boarded the overnight train at Newcastle for Liverpool, it was evident to all that I was suffering from a full-blown case of mumps and should have been forbidden from setting sail. After Dad had spent some time closeted with the ship's captain, it was agreed that I was to board ahead of the other passengers and was to remain a stowaway confined to our cabin throughout the two-week voyage. My quarantine was to expire the day we were due to dock in Kingston. In retrospect, my incarceration seems unnecessarily Draconian in view of the fact that neither Sheila nor eighteen-month old sister Mary came down with the affliction. On arrival in Kingston, we were scheduled to stay a few nights with the Governor and his wife at King's House, their gracious residence set in lovely gardens at the end of an avenue of royal palms. When His Excellency heard about the mumps, which neither of their young sons had had, we were disinvited and instead drove a hundred unpaved miles to Munro.

Munro College is the only boys' school in the West Indies that is a member of the British alliance of "public" schools, such as Eton, Harrow and Rugby. It is roughly in the middle of Jamaica some twelve miles inland via a treacherous road, on top of a 2000-foot mountain in the parish of St. Elizabeth. Malvern, the nearest village, is four miles away. From our house, we had a view to the south over the Caribbean Sea to a horizon sixty miles distant. The sunsets were spectacular. That having been said, the school that Dad inherited was a disaster in more ways than one.

The buildings were all extremely old and, without exception, in deplorable condition. In the two-story headmasters' house, for example, the bedroom ceilings would separate by one or two inches from the top of the walls whenever there was a wind that was most of the time. It was probably the worst of the campus buildings and we were soon evacuated while it was bulldozed to make way for a delightful four-bedroom, two-bath replacement.

Far more serious than the decrepit buildings was the hostility between staff and students. The previous headmaster, who had recently died in surgery, was a fierce and much loathed disciplinarian known as "Wagger" on account of a riding crop which served as an ever-present reminder of who was boss. Such affection as he had for living creatures was reserved for his horse, so no sooner had he been carted off to the hospital than some of his abused students cut out his horse's tongue! The previous year, a teacher from Chicago who had recently joined the faculty, vanished without a trace from his room one night. A month or so later, a crate containing putrid human remains and addressed to Chicago was discovered on the Kingston wharf. So far as I know, that crime has never been solved.

Vera Moody was on the board of Munro College in Jamaica. As a result, we got to know her soon after our arrival on the island. Her husband, Dr. Ludlow Moody, was a leading physician in Kingston. Their only child, Pamela, was a student at Munro's sister school, Hampton. She was an excellent student who studied violin from an early age and ended up as a brain surgeon at Kidderminster in England. She was two years older than I. Vera's brother, Norman Manley, was to become Jamaica's first prime minister. His wife Edna was an internationally acclaimed sculptor, and their son Michael, who also became prime minister, was at Munro with me.

As a child, Vera had shown outstanding musical gifts and had won a scholarship to study piano in St. Petersburg, Russia. There, among her fellow students, was Vladimir Horowitz. Her studies came to an abrupt halt with the 1917 revolution and she was lucky to escape to England. That country, of course, was over two years into the First World War, and finding a passage home to Jamaica was out of the question. She found employment however, teaching piano at Prior's Field School for girls. Among her students was Prudence Bateson, whose son, Ambrose, was to become my lifelong partner.

In Jamaica, the Moody's soon became our closest friends. We would often stay with them at "Tremain," their spacious home situated in the Kingston suburb of Half-Way-Tree. Being a classically trained pianist, Vera had a fine grand piano that was always kept well tuned. Many famous pianists such as Claudio Arrau, Benno Moiseiwitsch, and Artur Rubinstein would break into their concert tours between North and South America to stay with the Moody's and practice on her piano.

All the rooms had French doors giving onto wide verandas that wrapped the house around on three sides of both the main floors. Whose idea it was, I don't know, but one night via the interconnecting veranda, I found myself at eleven years old, in Pam's bed all agog to have my first sexual experience. She was already thirteen, but as I was pre-pubescent, there was no danger of an unwanted pregnancy. A year or so later, I tried it again, but by then, Pam had wised up and I was told in no uncertain terms to pull up my pajamas and beat it!

At Dunn's River Falls there was a guesthouse with a cottage in the garden. Each summer, we would rent the whole place for a month with the Moodys. Dr. and Mrs. Moody slept in the main house along with Pam, Sheila, Mary and me. Mom and Dad had the cottage. On arrival, the first order of business was to construct an eight-foot square bamboo raft. Dad and Dr. Moody would make it out of two or three-inch thick bamboos tied tightly together three layers deep with the center layer at right angles to the other two. The house was on a promontory looking across to the beach and falls but, between the house and beach were thick mangroves into the sea so the shortest way from the house to the beach was by water. There was a small rowboat that took the four grownups and picnic supplies. We four kids traveled by raft attached to the boat's stern. Today, Dunn's River Falls is a seething mass of sweating humanity. In those days, we were almost invariably on our own.

Barely one hundred yards from shore is a coral reef just inches below the surface of the water. One day, my mother swam out to it and sat on a sea urchin. They have long, brittle, black needles. She swam back bleeding and in considerable discomfort. Modesty, rather than Isobel, should have been my Mom's middle name. Her one-piece thick black woolen-skirted bathing suit under normal circumstances suited her perfectly. But that day was different. From the halter neck to the south end of her bleeding bottom it all had to be rolled down while Dr. Moody found a candle. As Mom mooned us all on the beach, the doctor let hot wax drip on her bottom to slowly, but agonizingly draw out the black spines to be removed with tweezers. I believe that was the first and last time that Mom swam out to the reef.

One year we were at Dunn's River just after I had had my appendix removed and I was not yet allowed to take exercise for fear of reopening the wound. Pam was a good swimmer so she swam about with me hitching a ride from her shoulders. In shallow water, we came to some partially submerged rocks. I was just about to put my foot on one when an octopus with a large, menacing eye slithered onto it. Forget about rupturing my incision, I high-tailed it, screaming all the way, back to the beach.

Twenty years later, Ambrose and I had been staying in Kingston with Vera Moody when we were invited to visit the Ashenheims at Ocho Rios. While there, we were told that an English writer by the name of Angus Wilson had bought the Dunn's River Guest House. As we had known Angus Wilson when we lived in London, we showed up there one afternoon just as an immaculate white-clad butler arrived on the lawn carrying a silver tray of afternoon tea. The gentleman at the table turned out to be a different Angus Wilson. Nevertheless, he greeted us warmly and we were entertained with tea and a tour. Soon the cottage disgorged two women houseguests who joined us. One turned out to be Monica Baldwin, who had escaped from a closed-order nunnery after half a lifetime as a nun and had recently published an autobiography called "I Leaped over the Wall." She was the daughter of Stanley Baldwin, who had been a British prime minister. With her was her lover, Ruth Arbuthnot.

The following year, Vera Moody came to stay with us in Indianapolis. Clowes Hall was under construction, so we took her to a symphony in the Murat Temple. She had recently been in England where she had stayed with my parents. During the hush when the lights are dimmed, in anticipation of the conductor's appearance, she turned to me and said, "Your father wants to know if you are homosexual. Are you?" "Yes I am," I whispered in reply. "So what on earth do homosexuals do?" she asked. Fortunately the conversation stopped at that point as Izler Solomon arrived at the podium.

My father, along with the majority of the British who belonged to his class, was convinced that sparing the rod spoilt children of either sex, and clearly the anarchy among the boys at Munro was to be attributed to lack of consistent corporal punishment. This failure was to be rectified right away.

All two hundred boys at Munro were boarders who ranged in age from eleven to eighteen. Hampton, the sister school for girls, headed by the sanctimonious Miss Rainforth was about six miles distant from Munro. Chaperoned girls, fully clad in unassailable uniforms, were brought to the Munro chapel for my father to administer Holy Communion on appropriate feast days. That was the closest that any of the boys got in the way of a whiff of skirt. Is it any wonder that homosexual behavior was rampant? Is it any wonder that I was unhappy to find myself not yet nine years old, as a boarder forbidden to visit our house or my mother, some hundred yards distant.

Almost every shortcoming resulted in a whipping which was variously known as a "caning" or "six of the best." Dad believed it should be administered with a one-half inch diameter bamboo cane on a bare bottom with the recipient touching his toes. To this day I remember the sound of the whoosh through the air before the agony started. The punishment was always preceded by Dad telling me that this was going to hurt him more than it hurt me, a fiction I never for one moment believed.

Mr. Dunlevy taught football and geography. One day, when he asked for our geography homework, almost all of us had failed to complete it. Mr. Dunlevy had left his cane in the "masters' office." I was ordered to fetch it, but I'd had enough. I sneaked around the back of the buildings and took off running. Deep in the woods beyond a native settlement, lower down the mountain, I found a suitable tree where I hid all day. That evening, a search party found me. I was taken home and locked in my room. There I remained imprisoned for weeks because I would not agree to return to school. Meanwhile, my grandparents arrived from Newbattle for a visit. Even Granny was not allowed to speak to me, though she would write loving notes and slip them under my door.

Finally, Dad took me into his office, told me that this childish behavior was to stop, immediately, and that I was to walk straight back to my dormitory and report to my housemaster. I left his office, turned away from the school buildings and took off running. This time, the alert was sounded and I was caught by our gardener, but I had won. Grandfather convinced Dad that, at nine, I was two years too young to be at Munro. Next term, I was sent to Mandeville, thirty miles away to attend DeCarteret, an elementary boys' boarding school for about sixty pupils.

## Chapter Five
### *From Jamaica to England*


My principle memory of D.C., as DeCarteret was called, was of the horrific toilets. The multi-holer shack was situated in the grounds and, depending on the wind direction, could be easily detected from the schoolhouse. A row of ill-fitting doors each opened to reveal a decaying wooden bench with a twelve-inch circular hole cut through it. The dark pit below was of considerable depth judging from the delayed time between a missile's dispatch and the sound of arrival at its repulsive destination. As we were small boys, most of us could climb through the hole onto a narrow ledge that was free of all but the most explosive deposits. This ledge ran the length of the building enabling agile kids to perpetrate unmentionable horrors on developing genitalia. Never having been amused by scatology, my time spent in these outhouses rank among my most unpleasant memories.

After two years at D.C., it was time for me to return to Munro. Though I didn't like it any better the second time around, I was mature enough to tolerate it. At least it had indoor flushing toilets.

While I had been away at DeCarteret, Dad had taken holy orders as a priest in the Anglican Church. Henceforth he was to be known as the Reverend A. G. Fraser, Jr. as grandfather was also ordained. I was soon taught the Catechism and, in due course, confirmed. My parents were much relieved as I had written from DeCarteret that I would like to become a Roman Catholic. The suggestion had horrified them to the extent, as I soon discovered, that of all offensive four-letter words, "Pope" was possibly the worst. Needless to say, at that age, my understanding of religious cults was virtually non-existent.

However, a couple of boys in my dormitory were Roman Catholics with rosaries, and I wanted some beads too!

During the vacations at home, I spent most of my time painting and drawing. For a small oil painting, of the view through some wind-swept casurina trees, I had won a prize encouraging me to devote myself to art. The headmaster's house contained a large gramophone and a collection of records. There were highlights from Gilbert and Sullivan operas, patriotic British numbers, some early popular songs such as "Red Lips-Kiss My Blues Away" along with a motley assortment of classical music. My favorite was Stravinsky's symphony for wind instruments. Most of the records rotated at seventy-eight revolutions per minute. A few were one-sided and revolved at eighty. Those ones had their labels hand-typed. In any case, each record only lasted three or four minutes before it had to be turned over, or changed, and the machine re-wound and the needle replaced. Beethoven's Fifth Symphony, I recall, was on twelve sides of six twelve-inch shellac records.

When I wasn't painting, practicing conjuring tricks or listening to music, I liked to explore nearby caves on my own. Sheila is four and a half years younger than I and Mary was younger still. They had always lived with Mom and Dad. They shared a bedroom, a nanny, and a nursery where they ate separately from us. All in all, I interacted very little with them. The Second Master, Mr. Wiene and his wife lived about a mile away from Munro. They had a charming house full of antiques and collectibles and she was quite a good watercolor artist. They had no children and made me very welcome whenever I rode my bike over.

Three miles beyond the Wiene's house was the village of Malvern. It had a tennis and golf club where my parents played most afternoons. Across from the clubhouse lived a glamorous divorcee called Dorothy Watson, who was an outstanding tennis player. There was gossip that she and Dad were having an affair. Though she did nothing to allay suspicion, he vehemently denied any dalliance whatsoever.

Colonial life was rather different from life as it's lived today. The five of us and the white nanny lived in the headmaster's house. Connected to the house on one side was a garage with Dad's dressing room above. That, in turn, was connected to an older building that had its own outside staircase. It consisted of two large rooms. Downstairs was Dad's secretary. It functioned as the main school office and contained classroom supplies. Dad's office was upstairs, the scene of many a whipping. On the other side of the house a breezeway connected a large pantry to the outside kitchen where meals were prepared over wood-burning stoves. Behind the kitchen was a range of dilapidated rooms for the servants as well as a stable for the horses and my donkey. The gardener took care of the animals and the car as well as the garden. Mom worked beside him as she was a keen gardener. The indoor maid waited table, washed dishes and made all the beds. Another maid did all the heavy cleaning and the laundry. Then there was a cook and, so far as I remember, there was a scullery maid.

First thing in the morning we were awakened by the maid bringing a cup of tea and some fruit, often a peeled orange on a fork, to us in bed. After breakfast, Mom would meet with the cook to discuss the day's menus and dispense the requisite ingredients from her locked storeroom. She also carefully measured out rice and red peas for each of the servants' meals. Once a week, the ice truck came from Kingston to deliver a large block of ice into our icebox. It also brought a full stem of bananas that hung in the breezeway for anytime snacks. Once the servants had been given their orders for the day, Mom did the flowers. We always had at least one vase of fresh flowers in each room while the drawing room had several. All the vases would be brought into the pantry and emptied out. Mom would then deftly sort the quick from the dead before heading into the garden in search of fresh bouquets. No sooner were the flowers done than the gong would sound for elevenses. All meals, including elevenses, were heralded with a gong. Elevenses took place in the drawing room and consisted of a cup of tea and some sweet cookies. Between elevenses and lunch, Mom would usually garden or bake cakes and scones for afternoon tea. After lunch we'd have a rest and Mom would knit, do embroidery, or make clothes for Sheila and Mary. Before or after tea, there would be golf or tennis at the club. Then it was back home for drinks on the veranda at sundown before dressing for dinner. Sheila and Mary, following their supper in the nursery, would be tucked into bed. I stayed up for dinner but would be dispatched as soon as the meal was over. We ate everything that was put in front of us, or we would get the half-eaten dish returned cold, for completion at the next meal. Once in bed, Mom would come into my room to say prayers and kiss me goodnight. One children's prayer that we recited nightly contained the line, "Pity my simplicity." Not having seen it in print, I read the line as, "Pity mice in Plicity!" Where Plicity was, I had no idea, but it clearly fell into the same category as Hell. To complete our household, we had a pair of blue Persian cats and a fox terrier. At one time, I also had a pair of very affectionate doves. Except for goldfish in the pond, that almost rounds out our menagerie.

Dad decided that I should learn to ride a horse. With that goal in mind, one was saddled up and I was put on top. On Dad's advice, my steed and I took the path down the mountain to the school's playing fields that were overlooked from our veranda. No sooner were we on the level than the horse broke into a full gallop from a careful walk without so much as a nod to trotting, let alone a canter. At the end of the field was a large pile of rocks and stones that is exactly where the horse decided to dump his terrified passenger. I came to in the school's sickbay where I remained bedridden for a couple of weeks with a painful back. Once on my feet, Dad had good news for me. A full-sized horse he declared was too large, so he had bought me a donkey. Needless to say, the vendor had not informed Dad that the animal was very old. No amount of cajoling could persuade the jackass to take me further than the next tuft of edible grass. Finally I dismounted and, in the vain hope that he would understand my agenda, I got behind him and pushed. The ancient donkey had had enough. With his antepenultimate breath he sent me flying backwards with a kick to the solar plexus. While recuperating from this second disaster, I prayed fervently to God to spare me any more equestrian experiences.

God, of frequently limited mercy, heeded my prayers for the next decade. However, in 1952, at twenty-two, I was dating Ambrose in London. His family lived outside the little town of Calne in Wiltshire. There I was bidden for the weekend to meet them all and hopefully make a good impression. Louise, the younger of his two sisters at eighteen, already taught riding, and Ambrose was a good horseman. When she ran into their drawing room to seek help with collecting the grazing horses, as it was time for them to be stabled for the night, Ambrose and I promptly volunteered. In the field were five horses with loose bridles, but otherwise naked. Louise picked up the bridle of one, hopped onto his back and trotted over to another, grabbed the second bridle and without further ado they trotted off down the lane. Ambrose effortlessly followed his sister's example. The remaining horse was clearly mine. He was still busy eating grass when I tried to mount him. He didn't look any larger than the other four but, for some reason, I couldn't figure out how to get up there. From my admittedly limited experience, horses come equipped with stirrups and other things to pull on. This one merely offered a mane and a tail. Recalling my Jamaican donkey, I steered clear of the rear end. The mane proved my salvation, though I'm not sure the horse approved. Once I was mounted and properly facing the right direction, the horse spotted his pals at the far end of the lane and decided he could catch up more quickly without any encumbrance. I was unceremoniously thrown to the side of the road. The impact, it later transpired, had fractured a vertebra.

Meanwhile, I dragged myself into a chapel and lay down on a pew. That's where Ambrose found me. By the time we returned to the house, my misfortune was the cause of general hilarity. Prudence, Ambrose's mother, knew how to save my back from stiffening up. I should get the lawn mower and mow the tennis court. Even pulling the starter for the engine was torture. Once in gear it went at a good clip with me running behind. After each length the mower had to be swung around for the return trip. By the time I crawled into bed that night, I couldn't recall ever having enjoyed myself less. At least I had learned an important lesson. My life as a jockey was over. But I digress.

In September 1939, Britain had declared war on Germany. Dad wanted to enlist, but was told that his job was too important and he was to remain in Jamaica. He did so until the end of the war by which time he had missed his opportunity to return to Ghana. I thought I was physically fine, but my parents detected a slight limp that Dr. Moody confirmed so that it was deemed necessary for me to see a specialist at Oswestery orthopedic hospital in England.

During the summer of 1942, a camouflaged ship put into Kingston harbor bound for Liverpool. I had just recovered from chickenpox in the nick of time to board it armed with a medical prescription for Oswestery and the promise of attending Gordonstoun School. The voyage took six weeks! First we went to Santiago de Cuba before clinging to the Florida coast all the way up to New York. There we dropped anchor beside the sunken hull of the *Normandie*. After several days in New York we set sail with a small convoy north to St. Johns, Newfoundland. There we waited another few days while an enormous convoy was assembled. From Canada we slowly made our way toward Greenland as we had to travel at the speed of the slowest ship. Finally, we left the convoy at full speed down the Irish Sea into Liverpool.

Chapter Six
*Gordonstoun*


Suddenly I was in England in the middle of the Second World War.

Things were grim. Once we had cleared customs, I bought a train ticket to London. It was to depart about midnight, so I had a miserable dinner at the Adelphi Hotel and sat there to await the train. At Paddington next morning, I was met by great Aunt Ethel Luxmore. In point of fact, she was no relation. She was a girlhood friend of Granny's. She lived in Gloucester Square in dignified, if fading, elegance with very little to eat. At night she patrolled rooftops as a volunteer fire warden to alert the fire station as to where a bomb had landed. In those days there were raids nearly nightly. I stayed with her overnight.

Next day Aunt Ethel took me to Harrods where we were to meet the McKay's for lunch. Auntie Mary McKay was Dad's sister, so the Reverend Canon Roy McKay was my uncle by marriage. Ann, their daughter, was four months older than I, and Jeremy, her brother, was four years younger. Of my grandparents' fourteen grandchildren, Ann was the eldest by four months with me being next as the eldest grandson. She was already a published author. Without adult input, at the age of twelve, she had written a novel and mailed the manuscript with a covering letter to Collins, the London publisher. They followed up because they didn't believe it could be the work of such a young child. Furthermore, with paper in short supply during the war years, very little was being published. The book, *Riddleton Roundabout*, concerned inner city London children being evacuated to a rural village along with the inevitable conflicts and adjustments involved in the new reality. It was published in 1942 when Ann McKay was thirteen, but on the dust cover it said she was sixteen. When I arrived to stay, Ann had started writing a history of Russia! So far as I know, that project didn't get very far.

The McKay's were to be "in loco parentis" while my parents were in Jamaica. They lived in Goring-by-Sea, near Worthing, on the south coast of England. By the time I moved in with them, the "buzz-bombs" had started. They were flying bombs that sounded like a two-stroke motorbike. When the engine stopped, they usually coasted down into power lines, trees, houses, or whatever, before exploding. However, some of them were designed to drop straight down. The Germans sent them over at roughly five-minute intervals nightly. As Goring was in one of the flight paths, once the sirens sounded, we would all huddle together in a closet under the stairs to await the "all clear."

If Goring was boring, Gordonstoun was anything but. It had been the brainchild of Kurt Hahn in Germany. His friend, Prince Max von Baden, had given much of his schloss on Lake Constance for Hahn to found a school for European aristocracy. It was called Salem. In 1933 Hitler rounded up the Jewish staff, including Hahn, and incarcerated them. Following concerns expressed in the British Parliament, Hitler released them and they fled to England along with a number of students. One of the students was Prince Philip, who was destined to marry Queen Elizabeth II. On arrival, they were befriended by Lady Gordon Cumming. She had an estate in Morayshire near Elgin in the north of Scotland. The main house was called Gordonstoun, which became the name of the new school.

At first, the staff and nearly all the boys were German. Gradually that changed. Soon the school was attracting the middle class as well as the rich and famous. It was said that when you were fired from Eton or Harrow you could always find a welcome at Gordonstoun. Soon after World War II started, the British put an air force base near the school. Naturally that put the school in the path of danger from enemy raids. Lord Davies, a big landowner from central Wales, had both his sons attending Gordonstoun. He generously offered Plas Dinam, his stately home, and Bronierion, the dower house, to accommodate the school throughout the war years.

By the time I attended Gordonstoun it was well established in Wales. To get there, we took an overnight train from Paddington. The train was cold, pitch dark and we had to change twice before arriving at the little village of Llandinam in Montgomeryshire. How our luggage and bicycles arrived simultaneously is beyond me. I was to live in Bronierion, a large mansion on a hill north of the railway station. The gardens contained some of the finest wellingtonian trees on the planet.

The first night, no sooner had I climbed into my dormitory bed than Kurt Hahn burst in to greet me. It was the start of an unhappy relationship. He was a large, tall, bald man with piercing eyes. His head tipped forward as his very thick neck contained a metal plate. It had been medically inserted following sunstroke during his student days. He held the world record for standing high jump and considered all kinds of sports and athletics to be of the utmost importance in the formation of manly characteristics. He spent an inordinate amount of time investigating ongoing reports of homosexual activities throughout the school. Such crimes were punished with a good thrashing and removal to another dormitory. His own sex life remains a mystery. He certainly never married and, so far as I know, he never had a lover. He was born Jewish, but converted to the Church of England.

Outward Bound, which ended up going global, was Kurt Hahn's creation. The first one was at Aberdovey on the coast of Wales. It was about forty miles west of the transplanted Gordonstoun School. Offering a month-long training course, it aimed to toughen up boys and to teach them self-reliance. Soon after my arrival in Llandinam, I was dispatched there for a course. Some of the month was spent at sea in Cardigan Bay aboard the *Garibaldi* or the *Prince Louis*, two antique sailing vessels that could each accommodate twelve students. This Outward Bound Sea School also had an obstacle course that could have doubled for circus trainees. There were swinging trapezes, and high poles to be walked across. Most scary of all was a fourteen-foot wooden wall. We had to run up to it, jump and two teachers would catch us and throw us up to grab onto the top where we swung our legs over, let ourselves down until we were hanging from our fingers. Then we had to push off and jump down.

Hahn had persuaded Grandfather to be on the staff of Aberdovey Outward Bound. Newbattle Abbey had been commandeered by the army as an Officers' Headquarters soon after the start of the war. After a time in Jamaica the grandparents had returned to England at the same time as I. Grandfather and Kurt Hahn had a long-standing friendship and held each other in high esteem.

In Aberdovey, my grandparents settled into a small hotel on the waterfront called The Penhellig. As my time with the McKays in Goring had proved less than stellar, I was to spend my first vacation from Gordonstoun at The Penhellig with them. The only available bed in the hotel was in a twin-bedded room that was taken by Lt. Philip Robertson Fortay. Being a pedophile, he was delighted to have me as a roommate! At fourteen, I had already enjoyed the occasional schoolboy dalliance, but that was my first adult encounter, and very frankly, I enjoyed it. Years later, Philip Robertson Fortay was to play a significant role in my destiny.

Farther along the waterfront on the Dovey estuary was a handsome four-story house. It had recently been bought by Dr. Guido Regendanz for his wife Elsa and their three children. Guido and my grandfather had become drinking buddies and I was soon introduced into the household. In less time than it takes to tell, they became my adopted family. Lisabella was stunningly beautiful and three years older than I. Guido Jr. was my senior by a year, and René was a year younger. Both boys were attending Westminster School that had been evacuated from London to someplace east of Wales. Elsa Regendanz took me to her heart. They had original paintings by Renaissance masters as well as by such varied artists as Vlaminck, Corot, Courbet, Camille Pissarro and Vincent van Gogh. Many of the works of art were German as the Regendanzes themselves were German. They had escaped from there in 1933. Old Guido was an international lawyer and had been in the Weimar government. Among other real estate, he owned German railroads, the knowledge of which proved invaluable to the British government. They had lived in Dahlem, a Berlin suburb, and their house had been designed to surround a magnificent organ where their friend, Albert Schweitzer, often performed. The Regendanzes had invested money in Richard Strauss when he was impecunious. For all I know, their heirs may still be getting royalties from his music. With help from the American ambassador, they got to England in 1933 along with most of their treasures. They bought a lovely house in East Sheen, London, on the edge of Richmond Park, where I had my own room for many years. Early on in the war, a bomb fell in their garden, blowing out the windows and bringing down ceilings. As it was impossible to have the house repaired in wartime, they moved to Aberdovey.

René Regendanz became the nearest thing I've had to a brother until his death in 2011. He had a skiff with two rolling seats that we would row all over the Dovey Estuary, steering clear of amphibious craft preparing for the D-Day landing in Normandy. In the hills above Aberdovey, were a number of abandoned mines to be explored. Some of them still had rail lines and miniature cars for moving ore about. We would push a car uphill before jumping on for the ride back down. We enjoyed exploring the countryside on our bikes and climbing about ruined castles and churches.

After Westminster School, René studied farming in Chelmsford. Before becoming a farmer in England, old Guido sent him to a farm in Kenya for a year of practical farming. What Elsa didn't know was that he would be living with Ingeborg Lazansky who, under a different name and location, had had a long steamy affair with her husband. Omi wrongly believed that all ties had ceased to exist. Not so. Guido Regendanz was a member of the Royal Automobile Club on Pall Mall from where he continued to collect and mail many a love letter. This Countess Lazansky had two daughters. One was a ravishing beauty. Today she is the Dowager Countess of Cawdor. The other has a heart of gold. René fell in love with Mechtild, who, after his return to England, wrote to him "care of Ian Fraser." This ploy merely postponed the inevitable and eventually Elsa had to accept the fact that her youngest, and favorite, child was marrying the daughter of her mortal enemy. Happily, in the end, Omi grew to love Mecht and their three beautiful daughters. René bought Corkwood Farm, Iden, near Rye in Sussex, where he farmed successfully for over fifty years.

On the morning following my meeting with my new headmaster, matron outfitted us in our school uniforms. The storeroom housed used uniforms of all sizes. The government strictly rationed new clothing, so uniforms had to be recycled. During the daytime we wore navy blue knee-length socks, shorts, shirts and long-sleeved pullovers. From tea till bedtime, the uniform was the same except for the color, which was a pale blue-gray. As luck would have it, my uniform turned out to be "hand-me-downs" from Prince Philip. In those days, a firm called Cash manufactured nametapes for parents to sew onto garments. Mine were labeled, "Philip of Greece." Had I realized what the future had in store for him, I would have kept at least one item. Oh well!

Gordonstoun, in my day, had less than two hundred students. We were all male boarders spread between several houses as far as four miles apart. We had bicycles to converge on Plas Dinam for classes and sports. Life was Spartan. We slept in dormitories of various sizes from about four to ten per room. An assigned student would run round the halls shouting, "Ten to eight, time to get up!" In our bedside locker would be shorts and tennis shoes that we donned before assembling outdoors in a line-up, come rain, snow, or shine. Shirtless and sockless we were led off on a run of about half a mile. Back at the house we had cold showers, dressed for the day and made our beds. Muesli with chopped fruit was a breakfast staple. Then we biked over to Plas Dinam for morning prayers and classes that followed the British public school curriculum.

About eleven, we stopped for an hour of physical training. En mass we did pushups and various other exercises. Then we were divided into small groups for such things as javelin, discus, or shot put, hurdles, sprinting, half-mile and two-mile runs, long and high jump, or the obstacle course, which was much like the one at Outward Bound. Following P.T. we took another cold shower before the next class. After lunch we did sports and battle enactments for an hour followed by our third and final cold shower leading up to tea and more classes before dinner. After supper we had time to catch up with homework, letter writing, and our personal training plan.

Where Gordonstoun differed from other schools was over a virtue known as "absolute honesty." We kept our own grades and most punishments were unsupervised. For example, if you walked into class or the dining room a moment after the second gong had sounded, a teacher would say, "Fraser, you're late, take a number one or maybe a number two or three." Those punishments involved a walk to various landmarks, and back, to be taken before the 8:00 a.m. morning run. It could be done anytime during the following three days, but it was up to the miscreant to be awakened in time to carry out the assignment.

The "Training Plan" we kept in our notebook by our bedside. We were obliged to fill it in daily. We would check off a list of things that we were supposed to do on our own, such as five pushups, sixty rope skips, teeth cleaning twice, etc. Mine had a couple of extra items as a result of my evaluation at the hospital in Oswestry that I had visited by train shortly after arriving in Wales. One of the growing points in my hip had been damaged, possibly from my riding accident, but more likely from when I had jumped out of a window at the age of six. Back at school, I was to be fed grated raw carrots twice daily and do a number of stretching exercises while lying on the floor. This remedy evidently worked, as I don't limp anymore. Once in a while, the housemaster might come round and ask to see your Training Plan. Failure to have it up to date was taken very seriously as was any lying.

Weekends were my salvation. Saturday mornings were devoted to individual projects that had to be approved by the housemaster. Mine was a German surrealist painter called Dr. Meisner. My major project was to create a papier-mache topographical map of Lladinam and surrounds based on a twenty five-inch to the mile ordinance survey map. It never got finished. From lunch on Saturday till supper on Sunday we could do what we liked so long as we informed Dr. Meisner and promised not to change our plans. I had a little tent and would go off on my bike exploring byways and lonely trails. I always went alone. In the hills I came across a lake called Tal-y-llyn, fed by an overgrown stream at one end and with a boathouse at the other. Inquiring at a nearby farm, I learned that it belonged to a Mr. Hamer who had a small hardware repair shop in the town of Llanidloes that was about ten miles distant. When I ran him to ground, he kindly gave me the key and instructions. The boathouse had a mattress and blankets for me to sleep, and underneath was a little rowing boat for exploring the lake and stream. Mr. Hamer never asked me questions. I could go there with his permission and key any weekend I wished. I always left the boat properly secured and the boathouse shipshape before I locked up and returned the key.

Half a century later, Ambrose and I revisited my old haunts. At the Llanidloes town hall, I found a photo of the late Mr. Hamer who had, at one time, been a much-loved mayor of the town. His daughter, we were told, was a Member of Parliament and wouldn't return from London until the next week. At least I had the opportunity to leave a letter for her attention to tell her what her father's trust had meant to a teenager named Ian Fraser.

I made no lifelong friends at Gordonstoun. While at school, my buddy was Duncan Grant. Like me, he enjoyed climbing about on ruins. From some high vantage point he'd spot something on the ground and bet me that he could piss on it. I no longer remember which of us could pee the farther, but I do remember when the wind returned the compliment. He was a baronet, which, in the British class system, is the lowest rank to have a hereditary title.

Among the titled students in my house was Lord Carnegie. He was the son of the Duke of Northumberland and had come to Gordonstoun after Eton expelled him. It seems he had a penchant for practical jokes. On one occasion he planted weeds all over the carefully manicured cricket pitch during the night before the Eton versus Harrow match. What happened on that occasion I do not know. However, ere long, the royal family was to attend a service in Eton chapel. He thought it would be funny if the organist couldn't play the correct notes. With that in mind, he removed a restraining strut and rearranged a number of pipes. Unfortunately, in his haste, he forgot to reinstall the strut with the result that when the organist struck the opening chord, a bunch of pipes cascaded down causing thousands of pounds worth of damage and narrowly missing the man's head. That very day was Carnegie's last, at Eton.

In my day, at least half the teachers had been with Hahn since Salem. Frau Lachman taught music. She had been first chair of a major German orchestra when she escaped to England with nothing but her fiddle and her young daughter Ruth. She did her best to teach me piano and would pull my slightly webbed fingers apart till I screamed. There was a school orchestra, but a serious shortage of printed music. As a result, every concert featured Schubert's Fifth Symphony. I joined the madrigal singers. During the summer months we would sit on the lawn of an evening singing unaccompanied rounds and numbers peppered with "Hey nonny-nonnies." Mr. Burkhardt was a closeted gay. He had a spinet in his room that he would use to accompany me as I attempted the singing of songs by Schubert and Wolf. I was always comfortable with him and looked forward to our evenings together. My favorite teacher was Lore Colden. I really don't know what her subject was. I never had her as a classroom teacher. I think she instinctively recognized me as a fish out of water. Like several of the other members of the staff, she had escaped from Germany with her daughter Barbara and very little else. She treasured some drawings by an artist called Kowalski and, to this day, I have three that she gave me. Years later, when Barbara married, Ambrose and I were included in the wedding party.

My *bête noire* was Kurt Hahn. I dreaded running into him anywhere. "Ian, my man, what are you doing?" "I'm on my way to math class, sir." "Are you absolutely certain that that is where you are going at this moment?" "Yes, sir." "I expect the truth at all times. Is that perfectly clear?" "Yes, sir." "Then go to your class right now, and don't be late." "Yes, sir. I mean no, sir. Thank you, sir." Mind you, I had proved a bitter disappointment to him. As grandfather's grandson he had planned for me to end up as the school's Guardian, or head boy, but from the very first "gay" dustup, it was clear that was not going to happen. Try as he might, he could see none of the qualities in me that he idolized in Grandfather.

Oddly enough, despite the bond between them, Hahn, who had a pronounced German accent, had no understanding of British humor. One day he said to Grandfather, "Please explain to me, Alec, why they always try to sell me two tickets when I go to take the train." "Well," said Grandfather, "what exactly do you say to the clerk at the ticket window?" "I just say, 'to London.'" Being German, the emphasis was on the first word. "Oh, dear me, no," said Grandfather, "you should say, '*for* London.'" According to Grandfather, he never understood why the clerk tried to charge him for four tickets.

The war in Europe ended while Gordonstoun was in Wales, so it was safe to return to Scotland. While we had been his guests, Lord Davies had died of cancer. Even worse, both his sons had been killed in the war. Lady Davies mourned alone in a cottage adjacent to the Plas Dinam estate. Not only had she lost the three people she loved most but, to add to her misfortune, with her youngest being the first to go, triple death duties left her almost destitute.

The move was to be made during the eight-week summer vacation. Along with many of the boys, I volunteered to spend the holidays helping in Scotland. Builders were working on vital repairs. Gordonstoun House had been badly damaged by fire. The building next to it is called "the round square." Many great houses in Scotland have a large square stable building built around a courtyard that would serve to protect the cattle in winter, or time of war. Traditionally, that building is always called "the square." The story goes that when the laird was planning the Gordonstoun square, the devil came to him in a dream and warned him that his wife would become his victim in a corner of the building; hence the only round square. Today it houses the library and classrooms. After several years of total neglect there was much clean-up to be done. All the bicycle paths were knee high in weeds and the long lake was a perfect mess. We all worked hard and, by the time all the boys arrived for the fall term, the place was in pretty good shape. By now I was sixteen and had decided that this should be my final year.

I lived in Duffus House that was about a mile along the bike path to Gordonstoun House. Now that we were back in Scotland we were given classes in Scottish country dancing. Many of us had kilts and sometimes we would make a noisy and colorful sight dancing on the flat roof of Gordonstoun House. I soon discovered that I had what it took to become a good dancer and I thoroughly enjoyed it. When it came to other physical activities I wasn't much good. I was best at long distance running and fast walking. While at the Outward Bound Sea School, I had broken a record for my age group in the five-mile walk. Beyond that, my sporting prowess is pitiful with the exception of bike riding. I rode everywhere. I even rode from Gordonstoun, in Scotland's far north on the Murray coast to Goring-by-Sea, in Sussex, a distance of about 700 miles.

Soon after the return of the school to Scotland from Wales, Kurt Hahn prevailed upon the grandparents to relocate to Lossiemouth, a village about six miles along the coast from Gordonstoun. Every day, a car was sent to bring Grandfather for talks with Hahn and members of the staff or to conduct services. Invariably, the car was late. Now my grandfather was not so much a stickler for punctuality as an eccentric who was known to show up hours early. If you were their houseguests he would bid you good night with the promise of waking you up at 7:30 a.m. with a cup of tea. As likely as not, the unsolicited cup would be delivered with a hearty "Good morning, breakfast is nearly ready" at six or even earlier. In spite of endless hours silently devoted to his devotions, his temper was uncontrollable if he was kept waiting for even a few minutes. In short order, he told Hahn where to stuff his car and the old man bought a motor bike. He'd never ridden one before so it's hardly surprising that he soon had an accident. The result was a truly messed up pelvis and femur that were poorly repaired with metal pins. He never walked properly again though he and Granny continued to travel the world for several years. He died in 1962 at 88 to be survived by Granny, who was his senior by six months, for another decade.

I recall visiting my Grandmother in Newcastle, where she began and ended her life. She was in her late 90s, blind and bedridden, but she was content. As a child she had memorized reams of poetry including the entire *Canterbury Tales*, which she would recall, with fresh insight and pleasure, as she lay awake. "My life has been fascinating," she told me. "When I was a girl, the busses were pulled by horses yet I've lived to see a man walk on the moon." In 1899, she was one of very few women with a degree from Cambridge. Her goal was to be a missionary in East Africa. She had already met Grandfather at a church missionary society conference and he had preceded her to Uganda. Early in 1900 she set sail, unsuitably clad, in a rat-infested ship bound for Mombasa, some 800 miles from her destination of Mengo, Uganda. From Mombasa, there was a railway for a short distance but, with only native tracks, most of the journey was done on foot with porters carrying the luggage and setting up camps at night. Happily, she kept a journal, which was subsequently printed. In Mengo, now a suburb of Kampala, she married and gave birth to my father in 1902, and also my Uncle Andrew a year or so later. But I digress.

# Chapter Seven
## *The Edinburgh College of Art and Architecture*

By the time I left Gordonstoun, in 1946, Dad had returned from Jamaica in search of a new job. He was to start as deputy Director of Education in Nyasaland, later Malawi, where he would live in the town of Zomba for the next nine years taking Mom, Sheila and Mary with him. Once that assignment was settled, Mom got the movers organized in Jamaica and soon she and the girls were back in England.

Following twelve consecutive years of boys' boarding schools, it was finally decided that I should be allowed to leave Gordonstoun at 16 ½ instead of returning for my final year because I had already passed my college entrance exams. But no, I could not study fashion design in London. How about "architecture" in Edinburgh?

Ian Rutherford, Dad's best friend and my godfather, was an Edinburgh lawyer. He and his wife Mary had no children. They volunteered to have me live with them. Their flat was the top floor of Number 2 Darnaway Street, in the New Town, overlooking Herriot Row Gardens. Farther along Herriot Row was the architectural firm of Gordon and Day. Esme Gordon agreed to take me into the firm for a year's apprenticeship. War veterans had applied for, and received, all available freshman student openings at the Edinburgh College of Art and Architecture for that year. I was to be admitted, full time, the following year. Meanwhile, during my apprenticeship, I was enrolled to take evening courses at the college.

Ian and Mary Rutherford were very good to me. I was treated as an adult. They gave many formal dinner parties in which I was always included. Uncle Ian taught me my capacity by letting me get drunk. Winter was the season for parties and elegant balls. They frequently took place in the sumptuous Assembly Rooms on George Street. I landed a lovely half-French, half-Scottish girlfriend called Yvonne Gilan. She danced beautifully and did me proud at every social event. Some thirty years later, Ambrose and I were vacationing on the west coast of Scotland with my cousin Sandy Irvine Robertson who was in the wine business. We spent one night at the Summer Isles Hotel. The hotel's owner was a longtime pal of Sandy's. He came over to greet us, looked at me and said, "I know who you are. You stole my girlfriend, Yvonne Gilan. I never loved anybody the way I loved her and you stole her from under my nose." What could I say?

The Rutherfords made sure that I had tickets for the opera and all the best concerts at the Usher Hall and would take me to dinner at the DeGuise or the Café Royal where I developed the champagne taste from which I have never recovered.

I was introduced to a man called Frank Govan and his wife Muriel. They belonged to the We Free Church and encouraged me to join. However I had already joined the youth fellowship at the Anglican church of St. John 's at the west end of Princes Street. Though the Rutherfords took a jaundiced view of all religions, they encouraged me in the family faith. One Sunday, following evensong, our minister was meeting with the youth in the church hall discussing dogma. He had just explained that, in order to enter the Kingdom of Heaven, one must be baptized with water and the Holy Spirit. "Wouldn't a sinless baby go to Heaven if he or she died before the rite could be performed?" I asked. "Alas, no," he replied. That was my moment. I got up and walked out and as far as I recall, have never said a prayer since.

I've read a lot about religions in my life but, I confess that I find the whole concept of gods and an afterlife absurd. Frank Govan's beautiful younger sister, Sheena, had a very different view. Not long after my defection, she declared that God had chosen her to stand in for Jesus for an imminent second coming. In no time she had rounded up a dozen male disciples who left their wives and families to follow her. They became known as "The Nameless Ones" and for a couple of months, the news reporters had a field day as one angry wife after another set off in hot pursuit. Somehow, Sheena had acquired a fast boat to accommodate the thirteen of them as they bolted from one Hebridean island to the next. Needless to say, they were eventually caught and following the inevitable recriminations, the episode finally fizzled out.

Frank and Muriel Govan had five children, the second of whom, Douglas, was my age and studying accountancy. He became my best friend. We biked and pitched our tent all over Scotland in all kinds of weather. One time we happened on a McBrayne's ferry at Kyle of Lochalsh bound for Stornoway on the isle of Lewis and Harris. There a couple called Muir ran the County Hotel. Florence and Rosemary were their young and attractive daughters who were to play an important part in my future. The night of our arrival was a Saturday so the girls whisked us off to the weekly dance. Later, back at the hotel they snuck us into the kitchen and fixed us a full Scottish breakfast.

Stornoway, with ten thousand inhabitants, was the largest town in the Hebrides. Herring were plentiful, so all along the waterfront there were smokehouses turning the catch into kippers. The other major industry was Harris Tweed. Most of the islanders lived in crofts where they had sheep and wove the tweed on home looms. The cloth would be collected weekly to be washed and finished in Stornoway. Florence was the principle source of island information as at eighteen she had her own beauty shop in the middle of the main street. Outsiders were led to believe that nothing happened on the Sabbath, apart from interminable kirk services. All the houses had their curtains closed and no shops, cafes or bars were open. There was no traffic and the streets were deserted. However, behind drawn blinds, many people, we soon discovered, doffed their Sunday black and settled down to a good game of poker liberally lubricated with a bottle or two of single malt scotch.

Back in Edinburgh I had joined the Royal Air Force Auxiliary and was learning to fly tiger moths. They were virtually crash-proof biplanes that cruised at about seventy knots an hour. I continued flying throughout the two years that I was studying architecture.

During my apprenticeship I had a couple of memorable assignments. The first was in St. Giles Cathedral on the High Street. Esme Gordon had won a competition to design the organ. I had to make measured drawings of the bay in which it was to be housed and of the ancient columns which were to flank it. As everything was hand carved and nothing was at right angles, it proved to be much more challenging than I had expected. The other assignment involved going down to the border town of Hawick with one of the office draftsmen. There we worked for about three weeks at the Braemar Woollen Factory. They were about to install a number of new fast knitting machines and conveyor belts which called for various alterations to some of the buildings. The business had long been housed in a ramshackle collection of sheds. The whole place should have been bulldozed and replaced with a modern structure. However, in those early post-war years, new building permits were not being issued.

Towards the end of my first year with the Rutherfords, Mary's mother, Mrs. Morrison, fell gravely ill. She lived, with her unmarried daughter Betty, in a spacious Georgian house in Inveresk, a village above the town of Musselburgh. It is about seven miles from Edinburgh. Ian and Mary Rutherford spent most nights there while I stayed in the Darnaway Street flat. After Mrs. Morrison died and after I left Edinburgh, they sold the flat and moved permanently to Oak Lodge, the Inveresk house, and built another one next door for Betty. The road outside their house is of Roman origin. The property across the street still has a Roman bath in the garden. One time, following a stay with the Rutherfords, at Oak Lodge, Uncle Ian drove me to Edinburgh's Waverley station to catch a night train to London. That night he had a fatal heart attack. Mary didn't give me the news for two weeks as she knew I had planned a trip to Europe and didn't want to spoil my fun. When she eventually died she left me some money that I spent on a lovely three-pedestal antique Sheraton-style dining table that could comfortably seat twelve. For many years Ambrose and I strove to serve the quality of dinners that I first learned to appreciate when I had lived with them.

The big annual event at the Edinburgh College of Art and Architecture was a winter ball called "The Revels." Every year a theme would be decided upon and design competitions would take place to determine how the various halls, within the building, should be decorated. During the final two weeks of the semester, all the students would help in the transformation. The enormous two-story high sculpture court was always the main ballroom. One year, when the overall subject was *Alice in Wonderland*, the sculpture court was brilliantly altered to look like a miniature room. For several years after I left Edinburgh, a vanload of us would head north from London for The Revels.

Soon after getting to know the Govans, I met Philip Robertson Fortay (the pedophile) in their house. He turned out to be a relation and, as it happens, both Douglas and I had been molested by him. Shortly thereafter, Frank Govan was sent to Germany for Command Control in the British Sector. Meantime, during a visit to the Regendanz's in London, I had become friends with Helge Ringsdorf. She was a young niece of Guido's, from Bad Godesberg, who was staying with them to learn English. She invited me to stay with her in Germany.

The summer was 1947. Douglas and I decided to hitchhike our way around Europe. Five pounds was all the money allowed to be taken out of Britain per person per year. Even in those days it amounted to no more than twenty dollars. Never mind, we packed our backpacks with cans of sardines and other iron rations. We put on our kilts and boarded the ferry for the three-hour crossing from Dover to Ostend, Belgium. Two or three cars were on the deck. One had a bumper sticker saying "American Consulate Stuttgart." Inside was a couple locked in lovemaking from which they surfaced as we bumped against the dock on arrival. We then asked them for a lift. They would take us, they said, but only as far as Brussels where they planned to spend the night. With that we settled into the back seat.

We learned they were Mormons from Salt Lake City, Utah. Our total ignorance was exactly what they had hoped for. We were soon the proud possessors of the Book of Mormon and various tracts of which they seemed to have in abundance inside the trunk. They had several small children back home and, after another stop for gas, we had pictures of them too. We were much impressed with their stories of Joseph Smith, the angel Moroni and the "golden tablets" and did our best to conceal our lingering doubts. Apparently we did a commendable job for they decided to treat us to dinner, in Brussels, and then to drive through the night toward Stuttgart.

On arrival at the chosen restaurant, as Mrs. 'Mormon' stepped out of the car, a man on the sidewalk opened his flies and waggled his erect penis at her. The shock sent her jumping back into the car and we took off for another restaurant. At about 5 a.m. the next morning the Latter Day Saints let us out on the shoulder of the autobahn. We had about half a mile to walk into Bonn. Apart from being the birthplace of Beethoven, it was known for little else. It would be a number of years before it would become the capital of West Germany. As dawn broke we wandered about the town. There were quite a lot of bombed out buildings, but compared with the City of London it had fared quite well. We discovered that Germany had an electric articulated tram system that was inter-urban. It travelled down the middle of streets with the final destination posted on the front of the front carriage. We boarded the tram for Bad Godesberg and learned that a five-pfennig note was all it cost for the few miles involved.

The Ringsdorf home turned out to be positively palatial with gardens, and a swimming pool, sweeping down to the Rhine River. We arrived in time for breakfast and were made to feel thoroughly at home. Helge and her father lived alone in the mansion. We never saw the old man and shortly after our visit, he died. Alex Werth was dancing attendance daily. He was the manager of Ringsdorfwerke, which was the major industry of Bad Godesberg. As a child in Berlin he, and his younger brother Hubert, had been adopted by Guido and Elsa Regendanz.

Both Guido and Omi had been married previously. From her World War I marriage, Elsa had two daughters who had become part of the Regendanz household following her remarriage. Elsa herself was one of six beautiful daughters born to a wealthy Hamburg industrialist by the name of Englebrecht. He had amassed a world-class collection of German drawings, and prints, a few of which I now possess. Guido Regendanz had eloped with one of Omi's sisters and married her against old Englebrecht's wishes. Unfortunately, she died during her first pregnancy. Finally, in 1923 he married again, this time to Elsa, his deceased wife's sister.

During World War II, Alex and Hubert Werth, along with Schpatzi and Irmi, the girls from Omi's first marriage, remained in Germany. In due course, Alex married Irmi and, by the time Douglas and I reached Bad Godesberg, they were living in a small new house with their three children, Felein, Geli and Alexander. Though we were only eighteen, we soon figured out that Alex and Helge were having an affair. It distressed me considerably because Irmi was a wonderful person with three delightful children. In retrospect, we know that he was bad news. He eventually wound up behind bars convicted of a number of serious white-collar crimes. While we were staying there, he plied us with a seemingly endless supply of a champagne, white wine and fruit concoction called "boehler."

We took the tram into Cologne to go sightseeing. It was the first German city we visited that had been almost obliterated by the allies. The cathedral was standing though the nave had lost its roof and vaults. We climbed up inside of one of the spires to look out on a city of rubble in every direction. Douglas went running about, exploring every medieval nook and cranny while I looked out over the desolation crying like a baby. I think it was the contrast between the reality of the destruction and the courageous determination of the people to rebuild that moved me so. At street level, the city looked almost festive. Eight-foot high wooden fences had been erected around every block to hide the mountains of rubble. On the sidewalks, in front of the fences, vendors had set up trestle tables to sell their wares and people were decorating the fences with pictures and balloons. Most of the cities we visited were at least as devastated as Cologne. In Munich, we found a cheap room in the middle of town where we couldn't sleep a wink. Under the glare of overhead lights, clearance and rebuilding work was going on 24 hours a day while, back in England, the workers were settling down for a nice mug of tea. We visited Berchtesgarten where we took an elevator inside the mountain to visit the ruins of Hitler's "Eagle's Nest."

Frank and Muriel's house was in Dortmund so, naturally, we spent a good deal of time with them taking day trips to the nearby ruined cities of Essen, Duisburg and Dusseldorf. Travelling in our kilts proved to have been a wise decision. Hitchhiking, we could be spotted half a kilometer away. People always stopped for us if they liked the Scots and spoke English. We hardly ever had to walk far before we were offered a lift. When we weren't staying with friends or family we used youth hostels. Most of them were basic and unmemorable, but after visiting the Romanesque monastery of Maria Laach we came to Coblenz where the Mosel river joins the Rhine. At that time, the old castle was being used as a hostel. We enjoyed that place so much that we stayed two nights.

At last, the time came for us to head back to Scotland but first, we had to see Paris. We were walking along the road near Laon when a young Parisian, driving a convertible, stopped to pick us up. It was a picture perfect sunset as we drove into the city. Our new acquaintance couldn't have been kinder. He drove us all over the place. What a contrast to the ruined cities of the Ruhr. Dazzling fountains seemed to be on every corner. I had never seen such beauty. Finally, with advice on what we should see in the city, he dropped us off at a hostel at Place des Ternes, near the end of Avenue Wagram.

The next evening we were standing in line at the Marigny Theatre in the hopes of being given returned tickets for the ballet when we were approached by an elegant, and highly perfumed, lady. Handing us her card, she offered us a paid job for *Elle* magazine. We were to report to the office the next day at noon. Our five pounds having been all but spent, the timing couldn't have been better. On arrival next day, we were shown up some stairs where we sat in a hallway watching scantily clad models dart in front of us as they hurried between studios for photo shoots. In due course, Madam of last night appeared and we were herded into a vehicle with photographers, a model and one or two others. Then we were off to the Gare St. Lazare. Finally, all became clear. That was the year that Dior had invented the "A" look. The model's "A" look coat was in a bold tartan plaid. We were duly arranged on an island in front of the station. The model stood in front while wads of tarlatan were stuffed beneath her top coat to make it stand out like a capital A. Standing behind her, we were wearing our kilts, examining a map that we held between us. The resulting photograph was to grace the cover of *Elle* a couple of months later. When the shoot was over we were paid in francs. I think we got 10,000, which was about the same as the five pounds with which we had started. Then we all repaired to a café for a drink. Everybody ordered Pernod. Though neither Douglas nor I had the remotest idea what Pernod was, we decided to have the same. We had both grown up eating licorice, so we happily imbibed a couple of drinks in short order. The rest of our time in Paris remains a blur, though as we departed for Calais, I determined to return soon.

# Chapter Eight
## *The Regent Street Polytechnic*

Back in Edinburgh I was seriously questioning my future in architecture. I loved all the design projects including models and renderings of imaginary buildings but I had not expected that so much in the way of mathematics would be required. Even at Gordonstoun, I had failed algebra. Now I was wrestling with the incomprehensible. Having completed my first full year at the College of Art and Architecture, I decided to do my military service while I rethought my goals.

Having done well as a tiger moth pilot, I volunteered for the Royal Air Force in the misguided assumption that I'd soon be flying fighters or bombers. A secondary consideration was the blue-gray uniform with its "Glengarry"-like cap. I had a neat wave of hair that made me feel quite dashing as it flowed out from under it. In addition the color of the uniform almost matched my eyes. In any event, my time in service was a far cry from what I had anticipated.

Following a couple of months of basic training, I was assigned to a camp called Padgate where I spent the entire time doing clerical work in the library. It is located near the dreary town of Warrington but not too far from Liverpool where four little boys were growing up to be known as The Beatles. I went into Liverpool frequently, as I was fascinated by two mammoth cathedrals that were under construction. The Anglican one was two-thirds finished and was a modern adaptation of the Gothic. The Roman Catholic cathedral, on the other hand, was to be neo-byzantine. Roughly one-third of the crypt had been built. Had it been completed as planned, it would have rivaled St. Peter's in Rome with regard to size. In the end, the expense proved too much. The multi-domed plan was abandoned in favor of a much smaller central planned contemporary design.

Most weekends, I went to London to the Regendanz's at The End House. By then Omi was often on her own. Lisabella, who was fluent in French, German and English, had taken a job in Cairo as a translator. There she frequented the Gazira Club where she rubbed shoulders with King Farouk and met her first husband, John Warren. Young Guido was serving in the army and René was studying farming. Old Guido spent every winter in Palm Beach, Florida. For tax purposes, he spent less than six months in Britain each year. When he was home, he had his own room where he slept all day, came down for dinner and then returned to his room to read and work all night. Every night he would drink a couple of bottles of Rhine wine while chain smoking. His nickname was "Schnapsy." There was little love lost between Omi and Guido, but he was very good to me. I was always welcome in his smoky room where he plied me with wine sage advice and, quite often a generous tip. Most days, from dawn till dusk, Omi tended her beautiful garden and an enormous collection of rare and exotic cactus plants. Classical music was always being played wherever she was and, at weekends, we'd visit art galleries and attend concerts together. She had superb taste and was my much-loved mentor. In February 1990 I arranged for my classes to be covered in Indianapolis so that I could attend her hundredth birthday. By the time I reached London, however, she was gone.

My stint in the R.A.F. gave me time to plan what to do next. As soon as I was discharged, I explored London art schools and settled on the Regent Street Polytechnic, which is affiliated with London University. I signed up for the Commercial Arts Studies program. From the End House, East Sheen, it was too long a commute so I rented a room in Pembridge Gardens close to Notting Hill Gate station. The street was filled with boarding houses. They tended to be dark and gloomy and most of them had a sign in the ground floor window saying, "Room to let...no Coloureds or Irish." My room, at number 19, had been a conservatory in its heyday. From the front hall, carpeted stairs went up to a landing with two doors off it. To the left was a bathroom with a sign that read, "Tenants are respectfully requested to refrain from dropping anything into the W.C. calculated to cause a blockage." The other door involved a step up into my room that took the form of a Victorian glasshouse, supported on columns, above the garden. The glass door and walls were hung with green velvet curtains to afford privacy while the overhead glass had been painted white. At the end of my bed was a small gas ring so that I could boil an egg or make tea. The landlady wore whalebone corsets that creaked audibly as she navigated the staircase landing. When the sun shone, which was seldom, my room was a furnace, but at night it could be perishing.

From Pembridge Gardens, I could walk through Kensington Gardens to the Royal Albert Hall in half an hour. If I arrived at the box office just before the concert, there were often free returned tickets to be had just for the asking. There were world-class concerts to be enjoyed almost every night of the week. When I wasn't Scottish dancing, I took every opportunity to hear great music. One evening, as I was standing at the box office, a gentleman offered me the seat next to him. I learned that he was the music critic for a newspaper and that he always had an extra seat in the stalls. All I had to do was to meet him, punctually, at the appropriate entrance and it was mine. As a musicologist, he took an avuncular interest in my education and suggested I try out for the London Philharmonic Choir. He knew Frederic Jackson, the choirmaster, and kindly put me in touch with him. My voice was totally untrained and poor, but there must have been a serious shortage of basses, because, following a brief audition, I was accepted.

During the next two or three years I was to perform under the baton of some of the most famous conductors of the day including Sir Adrian Boult, Sir Thomas Beecham, Edouard van Beinum, Victor de Sabator and a number of others. Concerts were in the Albert Hall as the Festival Hall had yet to be built. Rehearsals were generally held in Westminster Cathedral Hall. One time, I must have been one of the last to leave a rehearsal for, when I stepped outside, there was Sir Thomas standing alone looking skyward. I said, "Good night, sir." "No, don't go yet," he replied. "Just look at that marvelous sky and breathe the evening air. It's too lovely an evening not to savor it awhile." We stood side by side for several minutes looking at the stars in silence until his chauffeur arrived and we parted. At the time we had been rehearsing the Mass of Life by Delius. After singing the agonizingly beautiful phrase, "Draw the tear of endless grief," which is scored for the bass section, he stopped us. "Gentlemen," he said, "the significant word is 'tear', not 'beer'." Another time he regretted he would not be with us for the following rehearsal because, as he explained, he was to be a guest at the upcoming wedding of the year.

The Earl of Harewood, who had started the annual Edinburgh festival, was to marry the lovely Marian Stein, daughter of the music publisher. Benjamin Britten had composed original music for the occasion. "I feel I ought to attend the ceremony," Beecham said. "if only to hear what kind of music Mr. Britten has written for a marriage of two people of the opposite sex!" Most of the choir greeted his remarks with gales of laughter while I squirmed.

On another occasion we were rehearsing Britten's *Spring Symphony.* It calls for a small boys' choir. Sir Benjamin was listening in the balcony. So far as I remember the conductor was Sir Malcolm Sargent. At any rate, following one of the treble bits, he turned to say, "Ben, how are the boys?" "Just lovely," he replied, to hoots of derisive laughter. I was mortified. Britten had already been living with Sir Peter Pears, a distinguished tenor for a number of years. As lifelong companions they were gays to be emulated, not castigated.

With gay marriage gaining worldwide acceptance, it's hard to remember just how serious a crime homosexual behavior was in pre-Alfred Kinsey days. When Queen Victoria read the proposed anti-sodomy laws, she had them altered before signing. They had been written to apply equally to men and women, but she had women removed because, so far as she could tell, there was nothing that women could do to each other of a sexual nature! For men, it was another story altogether.

They say, "It takes one to know one." Homosexuals are born with "gaydar." With rare exceptions all gays were closeted and none that I knew lived with another man. People picked each other up anonymously for furtive trysts and hoped that the pick-up wasn't an undercover policeman. If it was, jail and exposure in the papers was all but certain. There was even a code language starting with the word "gay" which to heterosexuals meant "cheerful." Even "camp" had only the original meaning as far as the straight population was concerned. In mixed company one could say, "so-and-so is friends with Mrs. King," to point out a suspected gay. Apart from the obviously dangerous pastime of "cottaging" which meant getting sex in public toilets, there were a number of gay clubs such as *The Rockingham.* A secret password was all that was needed to gain admission. Once inside, there was drinking and dancing with the opportunity to flirt and make a date. Wealthy gays would throw house parties, which proved to be an excellent way to meet new friends. I soon had a large circle of gay friends but made sure that there was no overlap into my everyday life.

Towards the end of my choir days, we recorded Bloch's *Sacred Service* with the composer as conductor. It was one of the earliest recordings to be made at thirty three and a third disk revolutions per minute. The new technology meant that up to half an hour could be enjoyed without turning the record over. Soon thereafter the old five-minute shellac disks were no longer manufactured. They were replaced by thirty threes for all classical music and by seven-inch diameter forty fives for pop. Marco Rothmuller was the cantor for the *Sacred Service.* He ended his distinguished career as a professor of voice at I.U. Bloomington, Indiana.

Three Albert Hall concerts which I attended during those years are memorable for different reasons. One time the orchestra was to play Beethoven's *Leonora III* overture that calls for an off-stage trumpet solo. The hall has a top gallery above the balcony which, except during the Promenade Concerts, is never used. On that evening, the conductor put the trumpeter up there. His solo entry was magnificent and all eyes turned up in admiration. A minute or so into his performance a screaming note was sounded as guards rushed in to wrestle the instrument away from him. They had mistaken him for some sort of a lunatic exhibitionist. Alas there was damage to his instrument and he was too shaken to try again, so to this day that performance is unfinished.

Another time I was there to hear the Sibelius *Violin Concerto*. The soloist was a young French woman by the name of Ginette Neveu. She had suddenly taken the musical world by storm and little wonder. I think I was on the edge of my seat the entire time. Never had I witnessed such ferocity as she brought to the first and last movements or such heartrending beauty in the second. There were moments when she spread her bent legs so far apart that I quite expected her skirt to rip. Shortly after that concert she was killed in a plane crash along with her gifted violist brother Jean and two irreplaceable Stradivarius instruments were destroyed. That disaster had a profound effect on the musical world. For years thereafter, many musicians refused to fly. Once, in the 1980s I was wandering among graves in the Pere Lachaise cemetery in Paris. I noticed an old lady putting fresh flowers on a tomb. As she left, I saw that it was the tomb of Jean and Ginette Neveu. The old lady was probably their mother. One can hardly imagine the grief she had lived with for so many years.

The third concert which has remained with me was given by an exotic Peruvian singer by the name of Yma Sumac. She performed with a full orchestra dressed in blazing costumes and crinolines that covered half the stage. She had raven hair and was flawlessly beautiful. She claimed to be reincarnated from the ancient Incas as the "Xtabay." Whatever the facts of her origins might be, there was no disputing her astonishing voice. She could soar effortlessly through more than four octaves without changing gear. The music she sang was said to be Incan passed down to her through Atahualpa, the last Incan king. If you suspect me of exaggeration, please listen to a recording of her voice.

It wasn't long before the novelty of living in a greenhouse palled. Deciding that Chelsea was more to my taste I resolved to move there after spending the Easter vacation in Paris.

I don't recall how I met Pat Meaney, one of two male dancers at the Lido, a nightclub on the Champs Elysées in Paris. He was French Canadian, about thirty, good looking and sophisticated and, best of all, smitten with me. Catherine Trevil was the chanteuse at the Lido. The rest of the cast consisted of a couple of stuntmen, a conjurer, and, of course, the Bluebell girls whose frequent costume changes dazzled me. Each exotic outfit seemed to be more amazing and imaginative than the last. It was *de rigueur,* of course, to make sure all breasts were fully exposed at all times. I got to know all the high-priced prostitutes who sat at the bar waiting for a john. Pat would arrange with the barman to keep me happy with champagne. When the show finished at about 2:00 a.m. we'd go with Catherine, or some other friends, to have a meal before returning to his flat. We'd sleep till about noon. On Sundays we went to the Longchamp races, in the Bois de Boulougne, where he taught me how to place bets. Before I returned to London

Pat signed a contract to be a dancer in Tessie O'Shea's summer show in Blackpool, England. Naturally, I joined him there during my vacation and was spoiled rotten by Tessie. Catherine Trevil remained a friend for many years but, by the end of the Blackpool summer, the Pat Meaney affair had run its course.

At 39 Poulton's Square, I settled into my first Chelsea home. My landlord Richard Cox was an actor and theatrical director. His stage name was Rupert Scott to avoid the diminutive of Dicky Cox! His fey but lovely wife Monica Merlin was an occasional actress but a full time eccentric spiritualist. She was tall, very thin and usually dressed in pastel shades of floor-length chiffon with a flower in her upswept hair. Often, at night, we would see her communing with the moon while dancing gracefully around a large witch's ball in the garden. We all had the use of the kitchen. Along with my room and a coal shed under the sidewalk, that was the extent of the lowest level of the house.

Classes at the Poly were exciting and I soon made friends, some of whom have lasted all our lives. It seemed as though all our generation were into Scottish Country dancing. Several of us from the Poly attended classes taught by a no-nonsense instructor by the name of McDonald Murray. I took extra lessons from Justin House who was an expert in Highland exhibition dancing. Soon I was performing Sword dances, Ghillie Callum and the Highland Fling at West End balls and teaching classes at the English Speaking Union in Berkley Square. One evening, during recess at the English Speaking Union, a few people suggested that I start my own Scottish dancing club. They would sign up there and then to pay for it. That suggestion coincided with my graduation from the Polytechnic where a notice board carried job openings.

Barbara Brook Displays was looking for a designer. Mrs. Brook had a tiny but delightful house at 7a Pont Street Mews, just behind Harrods. An interview armed with my portfolio secured the job. I was to design window displays for travel agents and the head offices of airlines, rail lines and shipping lines. Altogether, there were some two hundred London offices to be serviced. She was a chain-smoking glamorous woman who was seldom without a gin and tonic. She could be great fun, but if your work fell short of what she had in mind her neck and face would turn scarlet and the cursing could be devastating. She had an uncanny ability to build her invectives to a climax. An example of a typical tirade is as follows. "That backdrop is not the color I wanted. I distinctly told you that it was to be the color of the abrasion on the toe of my shoe. Don't you listen to anything you're told? What the bloody hell's the matter with you for Christ's sake? I'll tell you what's the matter. You're a perishing half-caste bastard son of a third class scrofulous Chinese sea-cook. That's what you are. And furthermore, you'd better get that color right before you go home or I'll have your bleeding guts for garters. Now come on, Riff (her toy poodle), we're going home before I really say what's on my mind." With that she'd scoop the dog up and head off in her convertible sports car. Fortunately, her fiery temper was short lived, and though she never apologized, she would invite you over for drinks and then take you out for a delightful dinner.

Her workshop was on Lilley Road. There were two carpenters and a painter. Next door was the studio where Bert Sampson was the manager. He was a master at hand lettering in any size or script. I was the designer. Daily, at noon, a woman came in to cook us lunch which we all ate at a table in the studio. Barbara had employed her daughter, Pam, for office work. She would use her mother's phone to set up seasonal exhibit changes at the various agencies around London and schedule the routing of the Barbara Brook Displays van for the following day. Barbara was a superb salesperson. She would sell my designs to the agency's head honchos. Many of the designs had moving parts which had a nasty habit of going wrong at the least opportune moment. Taking the backs out of office windows, during the business day, could be thoroughly disruptive for the staff, but Barbara was the consummate charmer on these occasions.

On February 6, 1952, I had just arrived for work when Omi phoned to say that the King had died. I called Barbara, who told me to hop a bus immediately and come to her house. In the meantime, she phoned a store called Rubans de Paris to buy their entire stock of black and purple silk and velvet in both yard goods and ribbon. As soon as I arrived, we jumped into her car and ran all over town buying every available scrap. Soon we were pulling out all our colorful displays to be replaced with somber black and purple installations surrounding a beautifully framed photograph of George VI. According to protocol, these windows had to remain *in situ* for the six-month mourning period.

As her business was expanding, Barbara had hired another designer. Older than I, he had served in the navy during the war. His name was John Beckford Silvanus Bevan, but known as Jock. He was living in the home of his maiden aunt Cathy who had lived many years in China where she had acquired a choice collection of porcelains. Jock proved to be a brilliant designer, which I wasn't, with the result that I began to spend more of my time installing windows and getting to know Pam, who was forbidden by her mother from mingling with the employees. But I digress.

The Six Bells is a large pub on the King's Road, Chelsea, with a spacious hall above. The Spongs agreed to a modest rent so long as I allowed a half-hour intermission for the dancers to descend for a pint or two. The arrangement worked perfectly to everyone's advantage for the next six or seven years. Soon there were so many beginners showing up each week for Scottish Country Dancing that I rented another hall for a different weeknight in the Chelsea Community Centre. There I taught the basic steps.

In the misguided notion that all I needed was a good woman to turn my sex life around, I started dating Joy De Pledge. She was the young talented pianist who played for Iain McDonald Murray's classes. I had known her for some time. She had even been my date on a trip back to Edinburgh for The Revels. At the time, we certainly thought we were in love but, just at the moment when we became engaged, my parents returned from East Africa with Sheila for a protracted vacation. They took rooms near Paulton's Square. No doubt I was pleased to see them after so many years, but the pleasure proved short-lived. I had not lived with them since I left Jamaica at age thirteen. Even now, though I had turned twenty-one, Dad tried to run my life. Every day when I returned to Paulton's Square from work, I would find my parents and Sheila in my room. Dad would be reading and smoking while Mom and Sheila were doing crochet, knitting or some other kind of handiwork. They disliked Joy and made no secret of it. I was totally indifferent to the fact that my fiancée had a strong London accent, that she had been a foundling of no known parentage, and had what was euphemistically referred to as "a touch of the tar-brush." Apart from rather protruding buck teeth, I thought she was flawless. A few chilly encounters with my family however, and Joy was gone. She met and married a jeweler in Croydon, and I never dated a woman again.

A week or two after the De Pledge debacle, Dad told me to get permission from Mrs. Brook to leave work an hour early, on Friday, as we were to catch a train to Droitwich, near Worcester, for the weekend. Evidently, he had arranged for the four of us to stay with the grandparents who had recently bought a house there. "I don't need to leave work early," I said, "because I'm going to Winchester." Dad looked thunderstruck. "To Winchester? What in heaven's name are you going to Winchester for?" "To see the cathedral," I replied. "Nonsense," he said, "you can go to Winchester another weekend, but this weekend we're all going to Droitwich, and you're going to take a portfolio of your work to show the grandparents." "For once, Dad," I said, "you're wrong. You three are welcome to go to Granny and Grandfather's, but I'm going with Desmond to Winchester." With that, I walked out of the room and went up to Desmond's room.

Desmond Tivy was a year older than I. He was studying to become a doctor and we had become good friends through our shared love of classical music. He was in the midst of an internship at Charing Cross Hospital where he would arrange for me to sit in the gallery while he was assisting in operations. His mentor, a Mr. Thomas, had been one of the surgeons involved in removing one of the late King's cancerous lungs. His father was deceased. Tan Tivy, his mother, taught piano at the remarkable artistic community of Dartington Hall, near Totnes in Devon. Several times he took me there to spend a few days in that idyllic setting listening to music and meeting many creative artists in sundry disciplines. It was there, in fact, that he met Janet, a voice major, who decided to jump ship and marry Desmond instead. I was honored to be their best man and Ambrose was an usher.

For the weekend of the Droitwich controversy, Desmond had planned to study for some looming examinations but gladly agreed to accompany me to Winchester instead. That weekend was bliss. We had a wonderful time exploring Winchester together but, best of all, I knew that I had finally broken free of the shackles of parental control.

At work, Jock Bevan and I became firm friends and decided to get a party together, including Pam Brook and my sister Sheila, to spend Easter weekend in Paris. Before we left, Jock and Pam had barely met, but by the time we returned, they were joined at the hip. When, soon after, they announced their engagement, Barbara didn't know what had hit her. She knew nothing of the Paris trip. She soon faced reality, however, and paid for a wonderful wedding. The bride and groom honeymooned in Barbizon, south of Paris. They were supposed to stay for a week. In fact, they returned after three days having run out of money, and Pam was pregnant. When Barbara found out, her totally unreasonable anger was out of control.

When Pam was born, Barbara was living, during her brief marriage, in India. At the time, she had a tiger cub. Of her two dependants, she much preferred the cat and was miserable when she was forced to return to England with Pam instead. Having spent half her life denying motherhood, she was in no mood to become a grandmother, so she shot herself in the foot by firing Jock. Working for Barbara Brook was never dull.

Just as everyone remembers where they were when hijacked planes destroyed the World Trade Center, so too do they remember the first time that they saw Patric O'Keeffe. In my case it was on the occasion of Colin's christening at The End House. Colin was the son of Lisabella and John Warren. After the war, John had landed a job with Adprint, a London publishing company. Patric O'Keeffe was designing book jackets for the same company, and had been invited to the party. I had never seen anybody who looked remotely like him. In that suburban setting he was as dazzling as a tiara in a bowl of Irish stew. One time, at the theater, he happened to be seated in front of Hermione Gingold. When she saw him, she turned to her companion with the remark, "Must have fallen off the stage!" That afternoon, his suit was of black velvet to match his dyed hair and hairpiece. His shirt, pocket handkerchief and carnation boutonniere were pink. His tie and waistcoat were made out of gold embroidered, lavender silk, sari material from Benares. To top it off, he wore lavender gloves and carried a silver mounted black Malacca cane. I was soon to discover that he regularly went to work similarly attired. Like a moth attracted to light, I spent the afternoon with him and afterwards we took the bus together back to London. His flat, near Marble Arch, was unbelievably over-decorated in a style that was widely known as O'Keeffe Baroque. Beyond the bizarre, however, he turned out to be both gifted and highly entertaining. He was destined to play a singular role in our lives for many years to come.

Like many professional Irishmen, his name was his trump card. Both grandparents on his mother's side were thoroughly English as was his accent. His paternal grandmother was Spanish. Though Patric was born in Cork, he moved to England as a baby. His mother produced three daughters, at three year intervals. Thirteen years after the third girl's arrival, Patric, a tiny baby appeared. According to him, the doctor remarked that of the two, the afterbirth looked the healthier. However, a shoebox lined with cotton wadding proved to be a perfect incubator. As a child he must have been over-awed by the giant of Cerne Abbas. His mother's home at Piddletrenthide overlooked that vast naked pre-historic monument with its intimidating twelve foot long erection, visible to this day, for miles around. While his poor mother had to look at every penny twice, his spendthrift alcoholic father remained in Ireland driving around Dublin in a horse drown carriage waving graciously to all the pedestrians in the mistaken belief that he was a Spanish grandee.

Patric was brought up in a convent of French nuns who prayed in vain that he would become a saint. What he gleaned from that upbringing was a vast knowledge of religious iconography. One of his hobbies was the making of remarkably convincingly fake icons and byzantine ivories. That he was artistically gifted may be partly due to having a grandfather who was the successful Edwardian painter, John Leverson-Lunn.

From his job at Adprint Patric became the art director for the London office of Raymond Loewy, the French designer who is best known in the United States for his streamlined Pennsylvania Railroad trains and the 1947 Studebaker. Finally he became European Art Director for Unilever International Packaging Design. He loved jewelry, especially cabochon stones, and wore papal sized rings on most of his manicured fingers. In spite of his outré appearance, he was a serious scholar with a photographic memory of the printed word. When asked a question, his voice changed and there would be a distant look in his eyes and he would answer as if reading the pertinent page of a book. Among other interests, he immersed himself deeply in Jungian psychology and its connection to mythology, which led him to collaborate on two books with Patricia Dale-Green, "The Cult of the Cat" and "The Cult of the Dog."

As well as the name "O'Keeffe" he inherited the Irish gift of the gab and an enviable sense of the ridiculous. He could mimic accents in several languages and his stories, always told with a straight face, could be guaranteed to reduce any listener to gales of helpless laughter. In 1969, under the auspices of the Temple Gallery he, along with a small group of art lovers, travelled to Russia. Here are a few excerpts from a letter which he wrote to us following his return to London.

*The Hotel Russia in Moscow has 6000 rooms, 500 more than the Conrad Hilton in Chicago. It is managed with all the 'know how' of a small English seaside boarding house. Very American in design within the rooms, some teak wood and tasteful 'Schmaltz', but with a bugging device on the wall between the beds. It is in fact a status symbol and makes one feel most important. However, I was scared that I might talk in my sleep and say things that one's supposed to suppress, so I made a cotton cone and clamped the resulting pad over it each night and attached it to the wall with Scotch tape.*

*The restaurant service is comparable to that offered by the British post office. It takes 3 ½ hours to get a meal in Moscow's best restaurant in the Hotel Metropole. People have been known to drop dead of starvation between courses and their bodies found lying stiff between the aisles and under tables.*

*We joined a 3/4 mile queue to look at Lenin in his tomb - which is de rigueur if one hopes to have a trouble – free visit. Red guards are so thickly standing at attention with razor-edged bayonets that one could do without a shave beforehand.*

*Russian puritanical prudery would make your sainted mother feel like a brazen wench! Huge muscle bound statues stand at the end of every prospect, avenue and street, all nailed with a bronze fig-leaf.*

*As in all totalitarian or police states, one can walk around all night without being molested by pestering pimps or tarts. The most oppressive personality we had was a Russian born woman called Lady Maria St. Just, the sort of Knightsbridge type who can take anything and create utter confusion in short order. She spoke tsarist Russian and had a father who had been murdered by the Bolsheviks. Her original name was Suranov and was the great granddaughter of a dwarf- like general, who, dressed up as the god Mars stands in the middle of a bridge in Leningrad. She resembled him to the last degree both in physique and nature.*

*The Trans-Siberian train which took us from Moscow to Leningrad is all plush, carved mirrored glass and mahogany - with aspidistras in vases along the corridor. Blinds are locked down to prevent one from taking pictures of the passing scenery in the dark! Across the blinds cherubs disported themselves with Russian propriety, locked in patterns of lace.*

*Lady St. Just wanted to see her parents' house near Tzarskoe Selo, so we hailed a taxi. When the driver asked why we had no 'Intourist Guide" St. Just flared up so he made a phone call. Her indiscriminate conversation in Russian and English sealed our doom. The road was cordoned off by police and more Red Guards with those infernal bayonets. "All climb out." There follwed a long interrogation. Lady St. Just raved in Tsarist Russian. When asked what her husband does for a living she said, "Nothing. He sits in the House of Lords and war may break out if we are threatened in any way!" It was evident that we did not make a favorable impression but the bayonets were put down and eventually we were let through. Tzarkoe Selo proved a dream. The Palace was built by Rastrelli with additions by George*

*Cameron who also built the Pavlosk Palace nearby. It was here that the Tzar was imprisoned by the Menchoviques under Kerensky. The Empress loved Parma violets and had them supplied all year round. All her apartments are pale lilac as she loved that color.*

These excerpts illustrate his singular ability to deflate pomposity with barbed wit. Following early retirement, he moved to Indiana where he died in 1997 at the age of eighty four.

The enormous popularity of Scottish Country Dancing throughout Britain in the years following World War II may seem inexplicable today. In fact, there was little to celebrate at that time. Nobody had much money. Clothing and food continued to be rationed and very few people owned a car. In London, most young people with jobs lived in a rented bed-sitting room with one gas ring for cooking, and a shared bathroom. Nobody we knew had a television set. Scottish Country Dancing was inexpensive, fun, good exercise and, above all, a perfect way to meet and make friends. Almost all the couples we knew who married, after first meeting at Scottish Country Dancing, never divorced. Even during the summer, when dancing was in recess, the members would have parties and get-togethers.

## Chapter Nine
### *Life Begins with Ambrose*


One of my fellow students at the Regent Street Polytechnic was Philip Le Bas, who went on to make quite a name for himself as a super-realist painter. Along with his elder sister, Yanie, and a younger brother, Michael, he regularly attended my classes. He also went, on a different week night, to the Chelsea Reel Club, a rather more formal venue. There he met Ambrose Smith who was also a Poly student, although his classes were on another floor of the building as he was majoring in Chemical Engineering. He brought Ambrose to the Six Bells one night in February or March of 1952 and, within weeks, we were dating. Ambrose William Halliburton Smith and I were to become a lifelong couple.

Apart from both being gay, we had much in common. We were both first born and each of us has two younger sisters. We are just under four months apart in age. Ambrose entered the World on July 19, 1929. In the British class system, our parents clung to similar values. His parents, Frank and Prudence, sent him off to attend an elementary boys' boarding school when he was nine. His secondary education was at St. Edward's School in Oxford, another boys' boarding school. In those days, about five percent of British children attended boarding schools. We were both brought up firmly rooted in the Church of England but, by the time we met, we were agnostics. Frank Smith was an architect and Prudence had been studying architecture when they met each other. Grandpa Smith had been a very successful architect in London where he was known for his bank buildings and theatres. Although Ambrose became a chemical engineer, he was at heart a frustrated architect. We shared a love of classical music,

Scottish Country dancing and gourmet food. At the same time, we had our differences. I knew nothing about chemical engineering or any other kind of engineering for that matter, and he knew little about my work.

At the time we met, I was already employed by Barbara Brook and Ambrose was eighteen months away from his degree. He was living with Norah Thomas, an elderly second cousin in Earl's Court, about three miles from Paulton's Square. She was an excellent cook, having spent most of her youth in Italy and France. She cooked for Ambrose always, and for me, whenever he brought me by. We both enjoyed Norah's food for the stomach but the food of love we shared in Paulton's Square.

Dicky Cox, my landlord was an incurable romantic. He owned a small house at the end of a cul-du-sac called Bywater Street, off the King's Road near Sloane Square. As one stood on the King's Road one could see two shops flanking the entrance to Bywater Street, both of them by appointment to the Royal Family. On the right was Aage Thaarup, the Queen's milliner and, on the left, the Royal plumbers since Queen Victoria, Thomas Crapper and Sons. The upper half of Dicky's house, number 25, was soon to be available for rent so he offered it to us. As Ambrose was still dependent on his parents, he had to clear the matter with them. Although they finally agreed, it was not without misgivings. Norah provided not only room and board but she could report back to the parents if their son was partying when he should have been hitting the books.

Calne, in Wiltshire, where his parents and sisters, Charlotte and Louise, lived is about 100 miles west of London. I had visited them a few times and, on the whole, met with their approval. Needless to say, they were oblivious to our relationship. We could, they decided, be roommates at 25 Bywater Street and Ambrose would be given some money but nothing more until he accounted for every penny spent. From that moment on, he became our bookkeeper.

We moved in on September 10, 1952 and have always acknowledged that date as our anniversary. Like most central London houses, the first floor was up a flight of steps from the street with a perfectly habitable floor below. Those two floors, with the exception of the front hall, which we shared, were rented by Tom and Mimi Gourlay. He was a war veteran and had overlapped with me at the Edinburgh College of Art and Architecture from where he had graduated as an architect. Mimi was his lovely young wife from Philadelphia, Pennsylvania. The rest of the little house was ours.

Stairs from the hall led up to the bathroom, off the landing, and then up again to two rooms. The large front room was the width of the house and overlooked the street; it doubled as our bedroom and drawing room. The smaller back room had a single bed, for show, and a dining table. Up another flight of stairs was a bright and airy kitchen overlooking rooftops. It was our first chance to decorate, which we did with a vengeance and at minimum expense. The front room we did in duck egg blue with a tomato soup ceiling. We closed in the spaces above a pair of closets flanking the fireplace with frames covered in opalescent plastic. Behind the plastic were concealed lights placed behind cutouts of fish. This gave the effect of a pair of aquariums.

If memory serves me right, we painted the walls yellow in the back room with a very dark ceiling. Thanks to a display supplier of Barbara's, I had acquired a large number of colored, transparent glass balls of many sizes from half an inch to four inches in diameter. With nylon thread and pins, we suspended them in a great cosmic sweep from above. The smallest ones almost touched the ten foot ceiling with gradual lengthening of threads till the four inch balls were low enough to touch.

The piece de résistance, however, was the staircase. At a sale we had found two carpet remnants. One was black, the other cherry red. Even together they were not long enough to carpet the stairs. We therefore painted all the risers white to match the walls before cutting the carpet in to short pieces sufficient to cover each tread and its nosing. Then we alternated the colors with the result that, from above, the steps alternated between black and red but from below they were black, white, red, white, black, white etc. At Sanderson's wallpaper shop we found a dizzy-making tartan plaid paper with a lot of red in it. It was to do the ceiling above the staircase. If any other evidence were needed, such a choice should make it absolutely clear that we hadn't the faintest idea what we were getting into. Neither of us had ever hung paper before, let alone on a ceiling. Old London ceilings tend to be uneven under the best of circumstances. Add to that the problems of a ceiling that curves and twists above the turns of a staircase and you begin to see the picture. It obviously hadn't occurred to either of us that (a) paper does not mold to changing contours and (b) you can't erect a ladder on stairs. Be that as it may, we'd bought the tartan paper and a tartan ceiling we were determined to have. With the aid of such things as telephone directories piled on a step to bring it level with the one above we ultimately triumphed. Matching the pattern as it turned corners, proved impossible. A friend of ours had a nearby lampshade shop specializing in flock lampshades. He kindly gave us a box of offcuts. We chose all the colors that were in the tartan and cut out flock disks of random sizes to stick onto the white walls of the staircase. Whether our friends were pleasantly impressed with our efforts, or not, I can't say. Judging from overheard comments, they were certainly astonished.

Ambrose soon became my right hand in Scottish Dancing. We had to carry a case of records and a record player with us. He would keep the books, collect money from the dancers and issue receipts. After dancing finished, we often were invited to go back to somebody's room for a drink or we would invite people back to us. Of the two hundred or so people in our register, a core number became lifelong friends. For years after we moved to the States there would be parties for us whenever we visited the UK.

For the most part, we were consumed with work during the week, Ambrose completing his degree, at the Poly, and me, working for Barbara Brook. One morning, after working at her house, I enjoyed an entertaining lunch hour. Harrod's was Britain's largest department store boasting that it carried almost any retail item imaginable including both domestic and exotic live animals. An article on the subject in one of the London newspapers had caught my attention. Among the more unusual available items listed were chastity belts. My curiosity whetted, I entered the emporium to check them out. Barbara's house, in Pont Street Mews, was almost next door to the southwest corner entrance. It happens to lead into the men's department. As I surveyed a sea of bowler hatted mannikins in pin striped city suits with furled umbrellas, I sensed that this was not where chastity belts would be found, so I headed in the direction of Ladies Lingerie. A beautifully coiffed assistant stiffened and regarded me with ill-disguised disgust when I mentioned the object of my quest. While I apologized for suggesting that such a barbaric item might be found among her silk and lace unmentionables, I added that I had been assured of its availability by the London press. Without cracking a smile, the enameled face recommended the hardware department on the lower level. At least, the assistant down there thought my request was funny, but no, they didn't stock such an item. If, on the other hand, the newspaper I had read was correct, then he had two suggestions to make. First, I should check at the Information Desk on the ground floor in the escalator lobby. Then when I'd made my purchase, I should return to him to buy one of his tamper-proof locks! The friendly lady I consulted at the Information Desk was being asked this question for the first time. Nevertheless, she took my request in stride and, adjusting her reading glasses, opened a large tome and turned pages till she came to the "C's."

Running her finger down past "chaplets," "charcoal" and "chargers," she stopped at "chastity belt," looked up brightly and said, "You'll find them on the fifth floor in the Hospitality Shop!"

About the time we moved into Bywater Street, official mourning for the late King George VI came to an end. I was instructed to be careful to box up all the black and purple and to label each box with the information for which windows and in which agents' office it had been installed. When I asked,"Why?" Barbara said, "Queen Mary will be next so we can get double mileage out of this lot." Queen Mary was George VI's mother, a splendid old lady known for wearing a toque on top of her hairpiece, heels that resemble tiny toilet pedestals, a bust that appeared to be fused into a single entity with innumerable strands of pearls starting with chokers and ending with ones to her waist. She never appeared outdoors without a furled parasol. Though she had lived in England long enough to speak the language fluently, she preferred her native German. This hardly inspired affection among the British during hostilities. Marlborough house, her home on the Mall, was deemed unsafe in 1940, so her Majesty, and her household of krauts, were evacuated to Badminton house. The patriotic staff quit. Throughout her long life, when it came to valuable *objects d'arts*, she was relentlessly acquisitive. Her aristocratic acquaintances knew to hide everything of value whenever Queen Mary visited. She wasn't a kleptomaniac, but she would drop hints ceaselessly about her desire to add that jewel encrusted snuff box, or vinaigrette, to her collection until her hostess agreed to part with it.

We were in full spate working on decorations for Queen Elizabeth's coronation when, as Barbara predicted, Queen Mary died. This time, official mourning was to be three months which was a relief as, had she survived another month, or two, the coronation would have had to be postponed.

While London was being transformed with temporary triumphal arches, and miles of tiered bleachers draped with patriotic bunting for the anticipated festivities, we were creating appropriate window displays. We were making models, or cutouts, in assorted sizes, of household cavalry, gentlemen at arms, drum majors, heralds, pages and guardsmen in bearskins along with other colorful regimental types and mythical animals, such as the Queen's beasts, particularly the lion and the unicorn. This work required a certain amount of research because the figures had to be correct in every detail. For example, we would paint the uniform to show the figure wearing all his medals and decorations. However, he must be shown wearing the requisite minimum. An extra medal might narrow the field of say a yeoman of the guard to one individual and that was not permitted. Inspectors checked all installations to make certain that the highest standards of accuracy and decorum were maintained.

As coronation day drew near, Barbara Brook threw financial considerations aside and rented a spacious room, with a balcony on Piccadilly, overlooking the parade route. She invited us to join her. The day chosen was June 2nd, 1953. Almost every major politician and aristocrat from the four corners of the World had converged on London for days, if not weeks, of magnificent parties and balls leading up to the solemn, time-honored service in Westminster Abbey. Radio broadcasts would describe the scene within the Abbey as the event was not to be televised.

The great day, weather-wise, sucked. It was miserably cold with steady rain falling from leaden skies, when we awoke, and it remained that way all day. Nevertheless, we did our best to dress up for the occasion. My outfit was commensurate with the national colors of red, white and blue. White socks matched my shirt. I had a new bright blue gabardine suit to go with my blue suede shoes. I wore a red bow tie and carried a matching silk handkerchief to wave at all the people in the carriages. The police had cleared the streets of all traffic. Hardy souls had been camped out on sidewalks for weeks. About 6:00 a.m. Ambrose and I set off, on foot, from Bywater Street. By the time we had threaded our way through the throngs of happy citizens to our Piccadilly destination it was nine o'clock. Barbara, and some of the party were already there breaking out the first bottles of champagne. We very soon lost track of the number of toasts we drank to the Queen's good health, and long life, or the number of times we stood to attention for the National Anthem being played on the radio over loudspeakers.

At one point, the interminable Coronation broadcast was interrupted for a news brief. Sir Edmund Hillary, aided by his Sherpa, had conquered Everest – the first person to ever do so. Finally, the moment we had all waited for came as marching bands heralded the start of the magnificent procession. I had no idea that there were so many landaus or splendid horse-drawn carriages on the planet. Owing to the relentless rain, all but one landau had its top up. In the open one, soaked to the skin sat the vast Queen of Tonga, having the time of her life nearly upsetting the vehicle as she bounced about waving and blowing kisses to adoring fans on either side of the street. She was dressed in a long magenta-colored gown and from the top of her head sprouted what looked like two long chopsticks. At a conservative three hundred plus pounds on a six foot two inch frame she presented an unforgettable image. Unfortunately, she had to share the landau with the Sultan of somewhere or other. He was a shrimp of a man in white with a white turban. Soaked to the skin, he looked utterly miserable. As the procession passed one of the reviewing stands, someone asked Noel Coward who it was sitting with the Queen of Tonga. "Her lunch," he replied.

From her arrival in England she became an instant hit and a popular calypso topped the charts. Some of the words ran more or less along these lines: - "In the Pacific islands of Tonga, they make their people stronger. It can rain or storm or squall, but they don't feel nuttin' at all. The Queen of Tonga came to Britain from far away. That loveable Queen of Tonga came to Britain for Coronation Day." Although it happened some 60 years ago, it's still remembered by this writer as if it were yesterday.

London used to be infamous for its fogs, or more correctly, smogs. While we were living on Bywater Street, we experienced the last one. We had gone to spend the weekend with Ambrose's family in Wiltshire. On Sunday evening we were returning on the train from Chippenham. Well before reaching Paddington, we were brought almost to a standstill by thick smog. What should have been a two hour journey took at least twice that. On arrival, we took the tube to Sloane Square which is about a mile from Bywater Street. Emerging from the underground station, it was so thick that you couldn't see your hand if you stretched your arm out. We felt like blind men slowly groping our way along the King's Road with scarves over our noses. Even with that protection, our nasal passages were soon jet black. Worst of all, we had left a window open. While the fog wasn't as dense in the house as it was outside, it had left a black oily coat over everything, including the walls and ceilings. Only items in drawers or closed closets were spared. Cleaning bills decimated our finances. At least we survived which is more than can be said for many senior citizens or people with bronchial problems.

To understand what caused the smogs, you need to know that London lies in an artesian basin. Much of the cooking and most heating were done with soft coal. Generally, the smoke belching forth from millions of chimney pots would dissipate in the atmosphere. Occasionally, the weather would have an inversion bringing the smog back down. Fortunately that smog was the trigger that made Parliament take action to ban the burning of soft coal. Foggy London town now only exists in songs.

Saturdays were reserved for domestic chores and fun. Armed with a shopping list and some strong bags, we'd walk down the King's Road to the World's End pub checking meat, egg and vegetable prices at every market stall before buying our groceries on the return trip. En route we would often see famous theatre people such as Dame Sybil Thorndyke, her husband Sir Lewis Casson, Joyce Grenfell, Margaret Rutherford and Peter Ustinov or familiar eccentrics like Quentin Crisp or Virginia Dawn. That section of King's Road between Sloane Square and the World's End, is the main street of Chelsea, traditionally the Bohemian or artistic, heart of London.

In those days, Quentin Crisp was an artist's model with dyed red hair and toe nails to match. His fame as the author of "The Naked Civil Servant" was still in his future. The same could be said for his other writings and films. New Yorkers remember him, in later life, fully made up with purple hair and black fedora mincing down Broadway politely acknowledging anybody who stared. That he obtained a resident's visa from the United States Embassy, in Grosvenor Square, is remarkable in view of his reply to the interviewing official who asked if he was a practicing homosexual. "Of course not," he answered, "I'm perfect." We barely knew him in London, though he was a good friend of Virginia Dawn who played an important, and ongoing, part in our lives.

The name, Virginia Dawn, was her own invention. She was a French night club chanteuse from Paris who escaped to London with her mother when France fell to Germany. During the war years she was a popular singer at the Prince of Wales Theatre. Soon afterwards she fell on hard times and frequently had to beg for rent money. Her problems were twofold. In her late forties, playing the sex kitten no longer worked and whenever she did secure a gig she was unfailingly late, often by more than twenty four hours. In a word, she had become unemployable. This was a tragedy as she was multi-talented. She was a gourmet cook and baker. She could draw and paint anything and make fabulous clothes without a pattern. Her wallpaper and fabric designs were truly inspired. With her gifts, she should have made a fortune, but her failure to make deadlines proved to be her Achilles' heel. Her two mongrel terriers, Patsie and Gigi, lived forever. I believe one died at 19 and the other, marginally younger, shortly thereafter. The secret of their longevity, she believed, was raw garlic of which her handbag contained a plentiful supply. Even the blind knew when Patsie and Gigi were in the neighborhood. Once I had my shop, I employed her whenever I could even though her unreliability was a constant bone of contention. She painted delightful turbaned blackamoors on our dining room wall.

Though the circumstances of Virginia landing a temporary job as a seamstress are obscure, this true, but improbable, story bears repeating. A sailor, whose name I've forgotten, spent the war years plying between England and South Africa. With the termination of hostilities, he found himself with a sizeable nest egg and being entrepreneurial, sought a lucrative way to invest. On Lower Sloane Street was a handsome deconsecrated church which had been used throughout the war as a distribution center for government food and clothing coupons. He bought it, installed a pair of large sculpted hounds on the west steps, and renamed it St. Christophorus Kynokephalus Ancient Catholic Church. In less time than it takes to tell he was the Bishop and his large circle of cute boyfriends held lower ecclesiastical titles. What differentiated the Ancient Catholics from other sects, depended not so much on its gay curia as on its embrace of the animal kingdom. Animals, he preached, have a collective soul which ensures that if they come to service with their owners, a place will be found for them in Heaven. This blissful news resonated with many a wealthy widow who had a pet or two. Not to be outdone by the plumage of Brazilian macaws, Virginia set about designing and making exotic robes and miters for the bishop and all his acolytes.

Dicky Cox was in a play called "Teahouse of the August Moon." The cast included a live goat which joined the motley assortment of animals and their doting owners at Sunday services. As the congregation and donations soared, Virginia was employed to make altar frontals and various seasonal specific albs, capes and just about anything else. In appreciation for all her hard work, the bishop invited her to a summer barbeque at his home. The place turned out to be a mansion, with a swimming pool, in Kingston on Thames. Not bad for a rating who thought out of the box!

Probably the most colorful King's Road friend of ours was Roy Alderson. Nobody could outdo Roy when it came to *trompe l'oeil*. His vehicles were a bicycle and an old London Taxi. The former he painted to look as if it were made of bamboo and the latter was all pink quilting and silk fringe with oval Wedgewood plaques in the middle of the doors. His King's Road shop specialized in Victoriana, but with a Roy Alderson twist. For the Coronation, he enthroned a moose head attached to a magnificently gowned female figure in his shop window. The antlers were dripping with chandelier crystals. On the head was a jeweled crown. Along with ropes of pearls the model held both orb and scepter. As with his taxi, painted quilting was a specialty. Such items as black metal Victorian coal scuttles would wind up as if they were made of quilted satin. Chests of drawers would look as though garters and other unmentionables had not been fully shut in. Almost everything in his shop had some inspired Alderson alteration.

Above Roy Alderson's shop was his astonishing home. One flight up brought you to the main floor which, in reality, consisted of a large L-shaped room. However, on arrival, guests would enter a lovely rectangular drawing room with windows onto the King's Road. Between the windows, and on the other three walls were fake, but totally convincing Corinthian columns and between the columns, on the wall opposite the windows, were niches containing marble busts. It was all done in *trompe l'oeil*. When Roy was ready to serve dinner, the entire wall would roll up like a blind and we'd enter the dining room with no sign of a table. The three genuine walls and the ceiling were covered in real trellis with bunches of glass grapes hanging from an artificial entwined vine. The wall at the far end of the room had an arch cut in the trellis through which one could see formal gardens with fountains, statuary and topiary stretching into the distance. Below the trellis, on the side walls were banquettes.

Once we were all seated, Roy would push a button. We'd all look up to see the ceiling trellis open up so that it folded down against the side walls above our seats. Then supported by pulleys attached to all four corners, the dining table, fully set for dinner would slowly descend. Once down, those of us sitting at the corners had a job to do. We would pull down the legs which had been folded up against the underside of the table. Then Roy would push the button again to settle the table on the floor and to facilitate releasing the pulley hooks from the four corners. Finally, the reverse electric button would be pushed to send the pulleys skyward followed by the concealing trellis while we lit all the candles and started hors d'oeuvres.

From that point on, dinner deteriorated. All dishes had to be passed down and collected by the two people at the drawing room end of the table. The stack of dishes would then be carried up to the kitchen on the floor above. This involved about 30 steps as Roy had sixteen foot ceilings. As long cocktails hours usually preceded these dinners it was a rare and happy evening when the stairs survived without so much as a single casserole being dumped on them.

Formica was new in those days. It was made by hot-pressing many sheets together. Roy would paint sheets with fruit, flowers or whatever, send them to a factory and have them fused onto a fake wood or marble product. The resulting Formica he would use for garden furniture. We still have a philodendron table which he made for us.

London, like major cities worldwide, celebrated New Year's Eve like no other. The largest indoor party, held annually, was the Chelsea Arts Ball which took place in the Albert Hall. There is a removable floor that covers the oval arena and stalls to the outer wall of the lowest tier of boxes thus creating arguably the world's largest dance floor. The ball was a costume party for at least ten thousand people with a spectacular parade and prizes for imaginative outfits. As it was sponsored by the Chelsea Arts School, it should come as no surprise that a number of artists' models could be counted on the turn up as Greek and Roman deities or as Adam and Eve before they discovered fig leaves. We never attended that affair as it always coincided with Bunny Roger's costume ball to which we were invited.

Bunny Roger and his brother shared a large house on Walton Street, Knighsbridge. For their New Year's Eve ball, they would have most of the furniture put into storage to make space for some four hundred costumed dancers to do everything from the Charleston to Scottish reels. There was a sweeping staircase from Bunny's bedroom into the ballroom. Guests would be invited for 8:00 p.m. and festivities would be well under way when about 9:30 or 10:00 p.m. the band would suddenly stop, a fanfare would sound and in a blaze of sequins and ostrich plumes, Bunny would descend the stairs for his grand entrance. One year, he dressed as a camp version of Hyacinthe Rigaud's portrait of Louis XIV down to the red platform heels. That year I made us up to be a couple of cotton pickers. I bought green and white checked gingham for Ambrose and blue and white for me. That made us each bib overalls. We found matching checked gingham framed dark glasses and straw hats trimmed with gingham ribbon. Our costumes were cute but reasonably restrained which was just as well in view of the fact that word of the affair had leaked to the press. Droves of paparazzi were in the street as we arrived. I remember Terrence Rattigan's boyfriend was wearing a wisp of open-work string netting which left nothing to the imagination. The next morning the newspapers had a field day. One headline simply read "A Queer Party." As Bunny always wore makeup, even at work, he was very well known, but he got warned by the police to watch his step following that unsolicited notoriety.

A well-known story concerns his arrival back to London after a weekend, suitably clad, in the country. From the station he hailed a cab to return home. When the driver spotted Bunny, through the rearview mirror, powdering his nose he said "I guess you'll be pinning on a diamond brooch next?" "You silly man," Bunny replied, "One never wears diamonds with tweeds!"

As an arbiter of taste, Bunny was *nonpareil*. At the time, He was the haute couture designer for Fortnum and Masons. He was also a dress designer for Hardy Amies, who did most of Queen Elizabeth, the Queen Mother's evening gowns. I believe that his father was a successful Aberdonian tycoon. He was knighted and, I dare say, was more than a trifle chagrined to have produced two effeminate sons.

When Ambrose graduated from the Regent Street Polytechnic, he found employment with the Morgan Crucible Company in Battersea. Meanwhile, following Jock Bevan's dismissal, Barbara Brook had hired a pair of somewhat undesirable gay lovers who soon had her where they wanted her and I wanted out. Old Guido Regendanz gave me the financial start I needed to open a small business. In short order, I acquired a twenty-one year lease on a shop with the building above, at 502 King's Road. The top floor had a family of tenants who could not be evicted though they proved no trouble and paid a modest rent. The shop had most recently been a bakery. The basement had to be cleared of vats of rancid yeast and other things of an indeterminate nature.

Ambrose had always been good at carpentry so, with me as his gofer, we worked for about six months to get the place up to snuff. It was a corner premises on Slaidburn Street where there is a slight kink in the King's Road, making it visible well ahead of the bus stop. While the shop itself faced King's Road, the long frontage including a garage door was on Slaidburn Street. From an exhibition which had recently closed at Olympia, I acquired hampers full of fire retardant fabrics in pale blue and gold as well as vast quantities of white spun glass. All of this would be incorporated in the décor. The shop would sell handcrafted contemporary furnishings.

I had a welder who worked for me. I designed metal tables, chairs, stools, and such things as lamps and magazine racks. The metal forms were spray-painted matt black and then caned. Most of the cane work I did myself. Chairs would then have foam rubber cushions covered in bright colored felts. I also sold glass, handmade ceramics, weavings and rugs and greeting cards. With the aid of people like Virginia Dawn, we undertook decorating jobs.

The shop was called quite simply "Ian Fraser." A side door, on Slaidburn Street, led into a lobby and staircase to the two upper floors. Above the shop were two rooms. The larger one we rented to Pussy and Pixie. They were lesbians. Pixie's real name was Jocelyn Scott. She had been a fellow student of mine in Edinburgh. In a nearby studio she painted china before re-firing it for sale. Her most famous client was the Duchess of Gloucester for whom she decorated a dinner service. They don't come much butcher than Pixie. When they visited us, years later in Indianapolis, Mrs. Clowes (a grande dame) invited us to dinner. For the occasion Pixie reluctantly agreed to wear a skirt but we were never forgiven. Pussy's real name was Josephine Jarrett, so to many people they were "Jo" and "Jo." Unlike Pixie, she was fat and giggly. She wore dresses and lipstick, worked for the railroads by day and played in amateur theatricals at night.

The other room we rented to Rosemary Muir from Stornoway on the Hebridean island of Lewis and Harris. She was encouraged to come down to London by her elder sister Florence who used to fly down to visit us from time to time. Rosemary was an excellent secretary and found employment with the advertising manager of Fortnum and Mason's. A Welsh boy, by the name of Tudor Davies, while doing his national service in the navy, had been stationed in Stornoway. There he met and started dating Rosemary. By now he was working towards a law degree in Birmingham, so he would come down and stay with us for weekends. He and Rosemary soon started making very saleable wooden trays with tiles so, along with everything else, "Ian Fraser" carried "Tudor-Rose" products.

The shop had a very high ceiling. From a pole along the middle we draped spun glass to the top of the display shelves which gave the effect of being in a shimmering marquee. Behind the shop and beneath Rosemary's room was the kitchen-dining room. Ambrose built a large sweeping counter through 90 degrees which enclosed the kitchen with a hinged section. We all shared the kitchen and sat on stools to eat, drink or visit. I had a large roll-top desk in that room enabling me to work there while watching the shop.

To look professional, I decided that I should type bills and business letters so I consulted Rosemary. "Oh," she said, "There's a new Italian portable typewriter just arrived at Fortnum's which I can get at a discount and, I believe, it would suit you perfectly." For about seven pounds, I became the proud possessor of an Olivetti Lettera 22. Rosemary taught me the correct fingering which I've used ever since. Apart from new ribbons, from time to time, that typewriter stayed with me and worked like a dream for over fifty years. When the Museum of Modern Art in N.Y.C. had its re-opening a few years ago, there, at the top of the grand staircase, was an identical typewriter! Today, mine is in the collection of the Indianapolis Museum of Art.

From a hallway behind the shop, there were stairs down to a lower level. One could also continue back through a drawing room and beyond it, to a bathroom. There was an exterior door from the bathroom into a walled-in courtyard. Off the courtyard, to the left, one could go down steps to our bedroom. Exiting the bathroom to the right, you'd first come to the garage with a shed-cum-studio to complete the property.

Patricia Allman-Smith had been a fellow student and dancer at the Poly. At parties, we used to do sing and dance numbers together. She was a print major and on graduation, had bought an antique etching press. It was large and heavy and she had no place to put it. Our shed turned out to be ideal and in lieu of rent, she would help out in the shop.

Under the shop, was a large room with our bedroom off it. From a central disk, we radiated spun glass to create a false ceiling with cascading spun glass, held back by gilded cherubs, to frame our bower. The big room became a pirate's cave and soon thereafter the subject of a newspaper article. Chicken wire tacked to wooden struts made the cave's framework which was then coated with *papier maché* before painting. Where there was a blank wall, we created a hole in the cave so Jock could paint a view out to sea with the pirate ship and pirates here and there, including two that looked like Ambrose and me. Barbara had given us an old steamer trunk full of antique parasols, dresses and heaven knows what, so it all fitted right in and proved the ideal setting for many a party.

On one occasion, we threw a party for Virginia Dawn, who was turning fifty. Barbara Brook was sitting down nursing a gin and tonic when Virginia whirled past. She was jitterbugging and narrowly missed knocking Barbara's glass, with a flying breast, as she had discarded her bra. Looking up with a jaundiced eye Barbara remarked "Did you say her name is Dawn? My dear, Dusk would be more suitable."

With the opening of the shop we discovered multi-tasking as a way of life. Ambrose had a nine to five engineering job with the Morgan Crucible Company. He walked to work in about twenty minutes as it was just across Battersea Bridge. Some sort of anthracite rods seem to have been a byproduct which the company was happy to give us. Ambrose's parents had kindly given us a splendid tiled Dutch stove, and anthracite, which burns with a minimum of ash or smell, was exactly the right fuel. A metal disk in our sidewalk gave access to a coal cellar to store the fuel. Voila! At least we had that problem solved.

Rats were another matter entirely. London's sewer rats are the size of cats and a lot smarter. Suddenly, we were overrun. A phone call to Chelsea Town Hall produced a gentleman who introduced himself as the "Rodent Officer." That there must be a break in a city sewer he acknowledged right away, but to locate the rats' point of entry into our premises proved more of a challenge. *Papier maché* caves along with false ceilings and walls could conceal innumerable rat holes. He had a field day trapping them by the dozen. There was no end to the supply of replacements. Eventually they were traced to a hole in the coal cellar. Once the entry port had been sealed, the rodent officer succeeded in catching all but one enormous wily rat. He had found a safe hiding place by day but we could hear him all over the place once we'd gone to bed.

One night he landed on the spun glass false ceiling of our bedroom. We woke up to find him overhead bouncing about like a kid on a trampoline. Ambrose unsheathed the sword which I was in the habit of using for sword dancing and started leaping about stabbing at wherever the rat landed next. Though it was an exercise in futility it was fun to watch the penis of a naked man snapping about hither and yon regardless of the carefully choreographed leaps of its owner. The next day, the officer proposed a plan to which we agreed. He would put a large piece of brown cardboard on the kitchen counter, with a very sticky substance spread in the middle. He explained that it would attract the rat, who would be stuck, unable to move, and would then try to push off with his mouth. From that point on he would never be able to eat again. Our job was to fold the cardboard over him and quickly put him out of his misery with a hard hammer blow. My courageous knight agreed to the *coup de grâce*. Hardly were we abed when all hell broke out in the room above. Rushing upstairs we found that the rat had escaped but not before getting the cardboard off the counter and upside down onto the carpet. Neither we nor the nice humanitarian rodent gentleman succeeded in running the miserable creature to ground so eventually, we got on with our lives.

Fast forward a couple of weeks. There was a movie showing that Ambrose and I wanted to see. While we were all in the kitchen fixing our various dinners we told Pussy and Pixie our plans. Thinking we'd be gone for several hours, they planned some sort of fun and games of their own. When we reached the cinema, there was an endless line up of people waiting for that movie and the collective wisdom was that there were already too many for the next showing so we went home. What a sight greeted our eyes. In the drawing room were Pussy and Pixie stark naked with their arms around each other wailing and shaking like contiguous bowls of jello. They were against a wall facing a curio cabinet which was set catty-corner. The cabinet stood about four feet high. In the corner behind it cowered the elusive rat. Spikes of the now hardened glue stood up all over his emaciated body. My job was to pin the animal from above with my sword. Ambrose then eased the cabinet away from the wall prior to delivering the fatal hammer blow. I have no idea what movie we planned to see but that evening's dénouement is forever.

One day Daphne Govan appeared on our doorstep. She was the younger sister of Douglas, my friend from Edinburgh days, whose family belonged to Scotland's We Free Christian church. No Vogue model was more beautiful so of course she was welcome to stay as long as she liked especially as she enjoyed both cooking and cleaning. It took us a couple of months to realize that she was pregnant. It had happened, we subsequently learned, on a barge in Paris. No, she couldn't tell anyone in the family. That is why she had come to us in London. As Chelsea Town Hall had solved the rat problem, we turned to them again. This time we were referred to a home for unwed mothers in North London. Needless to say, she was a good six or seven months into her pregnancy without seeing a doctor. The North London home turned out to be her salvation. She delivered there, put the baby up for adoption and returned to her unsuspecting family in Scotland. In due course, she married a Norwegian and for all we know still lives in that adopted country.

Equally unexpectedly Robin Bevan walked into my shop. He was a doctor and Jock's younger brother. On vacation in England for six weeks, he had been, for the past three years, tending the natives on a remote island in the Solomons. On the way home he had stopped off in New Zealand, bought a practice in Queenstown, where he would be returning by ship six weeks hence. He had been referred to us as we had at least one hundred nubile young women attending my dancing classes and he needed a wife to take out with him. Clearly, there was little time to be lost. Without a moment's hesitation we had the answer. He should come to the Scottish dancing tomorrow evening. We would introduce him to the Crickmay sisters, Jo and Sue. Sue, the younger, was rather plain with several unattractive moles, but Jo was stunning and a beautiful dancer. What's more, she had just finished a relationship with a young doctor so Robin could catch her on the rebound.

The next evening Sue Crickmay was a no show and the dazzling Jo failed to dazzle Robin. In fact, none of the ladies that night appealed to him. Pam came to the rescue with plan number two. An ad appeared in *The Times* for a doctor's secretary in New Zealand. Pam and Jock had produced Katie and had bought the studio of the fashionable portrait painter

James Gunn, at the end of Pembroke Walk, just off Edward's Square. There she interviewed all the applicants and short listed them for Robin's consideration. How many Robin talked to is anybody's guess but not one turned him on despite the fact that after three years on a desert island he must have been thoroughly horny! Barely a week before his ship was due to sail he met and instantly fell in love with a girl he met at a cocktail party. Incredible as it may seem it was Susan Crickmay. He cancelled the ship and booked a flight which allowed for an English wedding and still got them to Queenstown to open his practice on time.

I recall the first time that Jock and Pam invited us to dinner in the James Gunn studio. *Comme d'habitude,* we were punctual and Pam was running late. When she opened the front door she was wearing an apron and explained that she must get straight back to the kitchen as she was in the middle of a soufflé. With that she spun round naked as a jay bird save for the skimpy apron.

Clearly, having a garage at 502 King's Road called for a car. Catherine Scott-Moncrief, Jock's aunt, had one that she was prepared to sell for sixty pounds. It was a 1934 four door Austin. Even though I had no idea how to drive, Ambrose did, so we bought it. We headed out of town, to Calne, for the dual purpose of showing it off to Ambrose's parents and to be in a safe place to give me driving lessons. Unfortunately, my cocky chauffeur was stopped by the police for making an illegal turn in Marlborough. That misdemeanor led to a court appearance because we hadn't yet secured title to the vehicle. Squeaky clean Aunt Cathy was summoned to vouch for my man. What the penalty was, I forget, but the chastening worked. That was Ambrose's first and only time in the dock.

1934 Austins would challenge most modern drivers. In the first place, it takes two people to make it start. The driver fiddles about with a couple of knobs on the dashboard called "choke" and "throttle," neither of which have anything to do with criminal intent. At the same time, he has to work one or two of the pedals while the other person stands in front of the car with a large key to wind it up. That can take a long time, especially if the engine gets flooded. This car had five gears to go forward and one to reverse but, every time you changed gear, you had to do what's called a double declutch. This involved pumping one of the pedals twice in sync with the gear change. Between the front and rear doors the jamb contained the turn signals. In England they were called trafficators. They took the form of little arms with orange lights which jumped out of the appropriate side. We soon traded it in for a new Ford van which was both easier to drive and doubled as a delivery vehicle for the business.

Coffee bars were springing up like mushrooms all over London. They tended to have a tropical theme with palms, bamboo and exotic birds in cages. My wrought iron and cane stools fitted right in. Especially popular were ones designed with a leaf shaped seat. Being new in business, I underpriced everything and underestimated the wear and tear that restaurant furniture receives. The result was that my biggest seller proved to be a money loser so I needed other irons in the fire.

Whenever I could get Virginia Dawn to show up we did decorating jobs together. In the shop she had painted a screen with colorfully beguiling eighteenth century-style blackamoors as an advertisement for her creative abilities. One of our first commissions was for my parents. Dad had finished his work in Nyasaland and returned to England as overseas secretary to the YMCA . He and Mum had bought a rambling old farm house in a village called Robertsbridge in Sussex. The grandparents sold their house in Droitwich and planned to have a three room flat in the parents' house. With that in mind, Virginia and I descended on my parents for a week of painting and hanging wallpaper. We did a good job and everybody was pleased with the results. Mum and Dad however, didn't know what to make of Virginia. At the dinner table she had a habit of getting up and doing French cabaret numbers by the likes of people like Charles Trennet and Jean Sablon. She would slip her dress off one shoulder and display her cleavage as she crooned around the back of our chairs flirting all the while with even a hint of lap-dancing. There was a gentleman friend of my parents from New Zealand who was staying with them. He became the object of much of her attention to his acute embarrassment and her delight.

A more creative job was for our friend Hillary James. He was opening a French restaurant in Pimlico to be called "La Bicyclette." We decorated it in the period of bustles and penny-farthing bicycles (the kind with a huge front wheel). Soon after it opened, we were dining there when Ambrose went to the rest room. It was at the top of a flight of stairs that went straight up from the restaurant. We had attached a long coatrack to the wall at the bottom of the staircase. Being winter, it was fully laden with coats of all descriptions. When Ambrose emerged, he tripped and flew head first down the stairs, hit the coatrack which parted from the wall and he landed unscathed on a soft bed of coats!

At the barber's shop where we regularly had our hair cut, they asked if I would mind having my hair styled in one or two different ways to be photographed for publicity purposes. I was flattered and as there was a small payment, I readily agreed. Recognizing another source of income, I signed up with a modeling agency. They were happy to have me but renamed me Alek Francis. In no time I was an extra in a couple of movies out at Ealing Studios. I was also in a few commercials. It was boring work. Most of the time I sat or stood waiting to be called and the pay hardly warranted the effort, so I soon quit.

We worked very hard without a vacation for a couple of years. For public holidays, like Christmas and Easter, we usually visited our respective families. Robertsbridge had not been a success. The Grandparents had gone off to Ceylon for an extended trip and my parents bought a smaller house in Chaldon, near Caterham, in Surrey. It was certainly a much simpler commute to Dad's London office. Sometimes, I would go to Calne with Ambrose and sometimes he would come with me to Chaldon. Never was our relationship with each other discussed with either family.

Our gay London friends belonged to a separate and secret world. Sometimes things happened which I knew about and which made the paper but felt I shouldn't share for fear of opening a can of worms. An example concerned our friend Cecil Gould. He was deputy director of the National Gallery and keeper of the Italian paintings. We were frequent guests at his flat in South Kensington where he would have gay parties for thirty or forty people at a time. Through him we got to meet interesting writers, scholars and show people. While browsing in a junk shop, he spotted a grimy painting which he bought for four pounds. When cleaned, it turned out to be by John Constable, one of England's most esteemed landscape painters. Cecil had bought it because he recognized that the picture included a corner of Constable's mother's house. I forget what it subsequently fetched at auction but it was enough to warrant a newspaper article. In retrospect, it seems absurd that I wouldn't discuss that story with my parents but my two lives were tightly compartmentalized and so they remained.

Ambrose and I were warmly welcomed when we visited each other's families, where it was understood that we were roommate friends. We couldn't possibly be more, because neither of as behaved like loose-at-the wrist screaming ninnies. Every sane person knew that that is the way all homosexuals acted.

One of the Mitford sisters had a cottage for rent in the northwest Scottish village of Ullapool. We took it for a month. Charlotte, Ambrose's elder sister, had recently married Grant Beswick. They stayed there for the first two weeks, and handed it over to me before they headed south. The next day, Ambrose and Barbara Brook arrived with Riff, the miniature poodle in Barbara's convertible. To honor the country and in an effort to cut back on her excessive gin consumption, she arrived with a case of scotch. The four of us spent the next fortnight thoroughly enjoying ourselves in a haze of inebriation except for Sunday. As everything was closed for the Sabbath, Barbara, in a rare display of domesticity, did some laundry. She hung it on a line behind the cottage to dry. You don't provoke the Highland natives in a such a way. We were lucky that we were punished lightly by having all the items merely ripped off the line and thrown in the mud. It proved a salutary lesson of God moving in mysterious ways Her wonders to perform.

## Chapter Ten
### *The Last of England*

In early September 1956, Patricia and I were just finishing up a cane furniture order when Philip Robertson Fortay rushed in. What was I doing for the next six weeks? Well, I was shop keeping, that's what. It soon developed that he was currently involved with a travel agency in Berkeley, California called "Stop Tours." American customers would sign up for six-week European tours, by car, with driver/guides. Philip provided the drivers. This was the tail end of the summer tourist season. There was only one carload left, and he had a problem. The driver was a student at Cardiff University and the school year was about to start. Philip was desperate for a replacement driver, so would I do it? Patricia pointed out that September was always a slow month, and she would gladly mind the shop, so I agreed. Could I pack in twenty minutes because there was train leaving in an hour? I rushed about like a chicken with its head off and almost forgot my passport.

Philip drove me to the station and gave me the tickets I needed for the three trains and boat which I would need to get to Genoa. I arrived about midnight. There I was met by the Cardiff student with a large Cadillac who drove me around hairpin bends down the coast road to Rapallo. On the way, he informed me that he had started the tour with three elderly ladies and had told them that by breakfast they would be in new hands. At the hotel he gave me the tour money, the daily itinerary, plus tickets and vouchers for the next five and a half weeks. He also gave me a list of shops where I would get a commission on purchases. "If you know which side your bread's buttered, don't let them shop anywhere else," he advised. Then, having given me the car keys, he grabbed his things and was gone.

At 8:00 a.m. I looked down a flight of stairs into the lobby to see my charges looking up expectantly. I smiled and waved and started down the stairs as I overheard one say, "Is that little boy our new driver?" They had no idea how utterly ignorant I was. I had never been to the places we were about to visit. I had never driven on the right-hand side of the road, nor was I familiar with an automatic shift or, for that matter, an American car. Least of all was I familiar with the American language. After breakfast, when one of them asked me to open the trunk, I looked around wanting to be helpful, but they only had suitcases. Whose idea was it, I wondered, to call a car's "boot" a "trunk?"

That first day was a nightmare. We were soon in the Italian countryside with Mrs. Mitchell from San Francisco in the front beside me. I discovered right away that she held the other two ladies in contempt. Her late husband, she confided, had belonged to the Bohemian Club, a fact intended to impress me. She always wore a hat with a nose veil. She next informed me that as soon as it was convenient, we should stop as she needed to "pick a wildflower." To this day, I've never heard such nonsense. She needed a pee. Well, of course I stopped when I spotted a clump of flowers and suggested this was as good a place as any. She was not amused. Soon we were passing Carrara. "What in the world is up there?" I was asked. "Just an early snowfall," I nonchalantly replied. Day one had been an unqualified failure, and I vowed to do better in future.

Fortunately, the ladies were in the habit of retiring as soon as dinner was over, enabling me to study the guide books, to prepare for the following day. Soon we were all having a good time. Mrs. Mitchell, at sixty seven, was the youngest. At every tourist site, she would have me buy her a postcard which she wrote to herself in San Francisco. In the backseat were two old friends from Shelbyville, Indiana. Bernice McLane, sixty nine, was a Jewish widow. She and her late husband had had a dry goods store on the main square. Whenever there was a K.K.K. rally in town, she knew who they were from the shoes, which she had sold them. One night, when we were in Stressa, she whispered that she'd like me to meet her, for a drink, after dinner. Over the nightcap, she handed me a little gift which I was not to mention to the others. It was a nutcracker made to look like a shapely pair of women's legs! From then on, we had a special bond.

Prudence Douglass, seventy one, turned out to be a true soul mate. Her hair was almost indigo blue, held in place with a band of fabric to match her dress. All her dresses were made from the same pattern. They had Peter Pan collars, short sleeves, a loose, rather low belt, and they buttoned all the way down the front with large, mother-of-pearl disks. They were invariably made of Egyptian cotton printed with sprigs of flowers. To counteract the drooping lines of her face, she wore upswept glasses. She was a well-read and highly opinionated Democrat. Up to the Great Depression, she had been a farmer's wife to her husband Bernie. Then, during the McNutt administration, she went to work in the Indianapolis statehouse checking all the bills for clerical errors or ambiguity of meaning. She was so good at her job that she survived every Republican administration and finally retired in her eighties. Though she was a militant atheist, she was the organist at the central Shelbyville Methodist Church. Sometimes she needed to be nudged out of a racy novel when the congregation was ready for the next hymn. At forty, she produced Anne, her only child. Anne became home furnishings editor for the Chicago Tribune, where she met and married John Bayless, who was the Tribune's international editor. They produced their only child, Martha, when Anne was forty. Last I heard, Martha, armed with a Ph.D. and no husband, is a professor at a university in Oregon. Prudence Douglass became a tremendous influence in our lives.

Before leaving London for this European adventure, Ambrose and I had already given serious consideration to the idea of emigrating from Britain. The so-called "brain drain" was in full spate, with Canada, Australia and New Zealand being the usual destinations. However, young Guido Regendanz had gone to New York to work for the wine importing firm of Sichel and Sons. He let me know that they needed designers and that, if I were to join him, he could get me a job.

If there was one thing that all three of my ladies agreed on, it was that I should emigrate to the states. Mrs. Mitchell advised San Francisco, where all her highly influential moving and shaking friends would take me under their collective wings. Bernice and Prudence favored the eastern seaboard or the Midwest. I listened to all their advice without tipping my hand in any direction.

Towards the end of the trip we were in Lucerne, Switzerland, and all three decided to splurge on cuckoo clocks and watches so I steered them to a shop on my list. Once I had returned them to our hotel with their loot, I hightailed it back to the shop where my commission enabled me to choose a fine watch for Ambrose. The six weeks concluded in Paris. Ambrose came over from London for the last couple of days there. We dropped the ladies off at Orly airport, for their flights home, before we headed to Amsterdam to return the car.

Hardly had the ladies returned home than a letter arrived from Prudence suggesting that I move to Indianapolis. When I replied, I pointed out that, delightful as that sounded, I had no intention of emigrating without Ambrose and that neither of us could do so without promise of a job. Her next letter bore good news. Mrs. Gauspohl Baier of the Gauspohl Baier Travel Agency had a husband who was looking for somebody to work in his furniture store with the aim of becoming its manager. Mrs. Baier would be writing to me. As for Ambrose, there was a manufacturer in Indianapolis called P.R. Mallory Co. which might be a possibility. She enclosed their address. Before long I had a firm offer of employment with Mr. Baier and Ambrose, after being wined and dined by a Mallory representative, who was in London on business, was also offered a job.

When we told people in London that we planned to move to Indianapolis, almost nobody had the faintest idea where it was. Somebody even said, "There's no such place. You must mean Minneapolis?" Even the 500 Mile Race was unknown in England. Once we mentioned that it was near Chicago, they were horrified. Everybody knew that there were so many massacres in that city that the streets were rivers of blood. As for Indianapolis, if there really was such a place, did the natives live in wigwams?

Prudence kindly sent us all the materials she could get from the Chamber of Commerce plus some picture postcards. The latter were printed on a linen-like material in impossible colors. One was of Butler Fieldhouse, which, for all we knew, was an outsized barn. Another depicted the Merchants National Bank building at Washington and Meridian streets. At nineteen stories, it was Indiana's tallest building. We found the information fascinating, if somewhat confusing and at times, alarming. We learned, for example, that the city of 400,000 had forty theaters and over four hundred churches! Theaters, we later discovered, were movie houses, but surely the numbers must be reversed. Even London didn't have four hundred churches, and the ones it did have were mostly empty. What on earth could a small town like Indianapolis be doing with so many? Then there was a postcard depicting the First World War memorial. It appeared to be a grandiose attempt to reinterpret the mausoleum of Halicarnassus, one of the seven wonders of the ancient world. The Chamber of Commerce information, on this vast pile of vaguely Hellenistic masonry, contained the statement that the room for the flag, which is within the monument "is widely recognized as the most beautiful room in the world!" We were so excited at the prospect of seeing this masterpiece that we could hardly wait for our arrival in the Hoosier capital. At this point, I must digress once again.

As I tried to imagine the breathtaking beauty which awaited us, I was reminded of another room, equally praised for its surpassing beauty. The room to which I refer is known as the "Double Cube." It is the state drawing room in Wilton house, near Salisbury, England. Its dimensions are said to be thirty feet wide, thirty feet high and sixty feet long. On my first visit, I had a question for the guide, because at the top of the walls there is a bold cornice. Above that the wall curves up a few feet to a flat ceiling. Was the thirty foot measurement taken to the cornice or all the way up to the ceiling, I inquired. Many people ask that question, I was told, and the answer was that it was just to the cornice. "In that case," I replied, "the end wall must be square, but to me it looks oblong." The patient guide explained that the acknowledged perfection of the room's proportions gave an oblong illusion to the square. There being no point in arguing any further over a matter of fact, I waited till I got home before writing a polite letter to the Countess of Pembroke, whose home it is.

After praising the beauty of her famous drawing room, I suggested that perhaps our guide was mistaken and that the thirty foot measurement might be to the flat ceiling rather than to the cornice. I received a reply from Lady Pembroke's secretary informing me that this supreme masterpiece by Inigo Jones, England's first Renaissance architect, had been measured many times and the guide's information was correct. Had the letter ended there, I might have let the matter rest but, it didn't. It went on to point out that the room is full of priceless antique furniture. Moving it to erect the necessary scaffolding to reach the ceiling was out of the question.

My second letter, which explained how to measure the height without moving any furniture, received no answer. I mentioned that I had taken a walk in the garden, after touring the house. In a small shed by the Palladian bridge, I had noticed bundles of bamboo canes and twine. I suggested that half a dozen canes would suffice. Somebody could overlap the ends and bind them with twine till you reached the ceiling. Then by measuring from your hand to the floor and adding that to the length of the combined canes, you would have the answer.

A few years later I had occasion to revisit Wilton. Another guide quoted the familiar measurements of the double cube room, so I asked to which point the height is measured. "Funny you should ask," she said brightly. "We always believed it was to the cornice, but, a few years ago a rather unpleasant visitor made such a fuss that we had it remeasured. It's thirty feet to the ceiling." My failure to keep a straight face throughout the rest of the tour prompted her to say that I seemed to have much enjoyed myself. So I confessed to being that difficult tourist.

Having been raised in the sincere, if misguided, belief that everybody in the world was British or wished they were, it came as a shock to discover that Ambrose and I were not alone in our desire to flee the motherland. Red tape on every hand smothered initiative, producing a climate of lethargy and pessimism throughout the country. Only my mother, whose peripapetic life had been spent largely in remote outposts of Her Majesty's Imperial realm, visualized a rose-covered house in suburban England as the nearest thing to heaven on earth. Sister Mary, having turned twenty one, was about to marry Oliver Robinson, a marine she had met in East Africa. He would father all her children. They were headed for a posting in the Far East. Sheila was completing her nursing training at Edinburgh's Royal Infirmary. From there she was off to work in New Zealand. When Jock and Pam heard our plans, we were instructed to look for a job for Jock in Indianapolis so that they too could join the exodus. My grandparents, having just returned from trips to Ceylon and Ghana had been won over to "Moral Rearmament," a cult offshoot of the Oxford Movement, founded by a Dr. Frank Buchman. They informed me that they would be leaving soon for a conference at Moral Rearmament's world headquarters on Mackinaw Island, Michigan. Indeed, they would be there before we reached Indianapolis. However, before they departed, my sainted grandmother was given a severe rebuke by their council. It seems that one of their pious members had caught a glimpse of Granny wearing an apron which bore the lascivious slogan, "Kiss the Cook."

While in the midst of our predeparture sale, Ethel Luxmore, Granny's old friend, dropped by. "Your grandmother informs me that you're moving to Indianapolis. Is that true?" she asked. "Yes," I replied in astonishment. "Have you actually heard of the place?" "Oh! Yes," she informed me. "My old friend, Miss Marguerite Dice, lives there. She and I took a government course together, at the University of Chicago, in about 1900. We've kept in touch by letter ever since. I'll let her know that you're going to be there." Now we had something else to look forward to. But first we needed permanent visas and green cards for the United States.

In those days there were quotas for each country with percentages supposedly based on the current American racial mix. Sixty percent of Americans were believed to be of British ancestry, so more than half the annual quota was set aside for the Brits. Ambrose was welcomed with open arms because, in general, the British had such a jaundiced view of the U.S.A. that few of them applied for visas. Though I was as British as Ambrose, I found myself sidelined to a sub-Saharan quota because I had been born in Ghana. A year later, when Jock and Pam Bevan joined us they came over on the Burmese and Indian quotas respectively to reflect where they had been born.

We booked our passages, from Southampton to New York on a ship called *Italia.* It was small, old and slow belonging to a company called Home Lines. Departure was set for July 12, 1957 which left little time to prepare. A giveaway sale at the shop got rid of the stock. However, there was not sufficient time to sell the remaining seventeen years of my lease. A lawyer friend, Tommy Franklin, undertook that chore following our departure. In the end I recouped the money that I had paid for it four years earlier so I saw no reason to complain. Nevertheless, had I known what Chelsea Town Hall had in mind, I would have hung on to the empty property for the next two years and wound up with a nice little nest egg. In 1959, the municipality paid 60,000 pounds to the new lease holders in order to bulldoze the place and thus straighten out the kink in the Kings road. On the other hand, I've never been good with money and probably would have invested the lot in a Ponzi scheme.

We turned over the running of the Scottish Country Dancing Club to our friend Meg Holt. She ran it for a couple of years before handing the reins to Yanie Le Bas and Ann Wells. They continued for a few more years but, eventually, it had run its course. Before our departure, they had a big party for us and we were presented with a canteen of Swedish stainless steel cutlery.

Despite taking seventeen pieces of luggage, we left the house fully furnished. We even left most of the pictures on the walls and all the appliances as they wouldn't have worked in the States. On departure day, a number of friends came to Waterloo station to see us off, including Desmond Tivy. Barbara Brook had brought Patric O'Keeffe to say farewell and, as the train pulled out, she said, "Mark my words, Patric, Ian won't rest until he's got Desmond to move to America." What made her say that, I don't know, because it most certainly wasn't on my agenda. All the same, a few years later, after his mother died, Desmond wrote to us in Indianapolis to ask what we knew about Pittsfield, Massachusetts. The hospital there was looking for a doctor. The timing was perfect. We were about to leave by car for Cape Cod and Pittsfield was hardly out of our way. We took pictures and sent off such material as we could gather for their information. Soon Desmond, Janet and their four small children moved permanently to the United States.

We celebrated Ambrose's twenty eighth birthday two days out from New York. The ship had a small swimming pool where I swam daily and became friendly with a guy from Connecticut who was about our age. One day, he asked me if I would mind if he gave me some advice. "Please do," I said. "Well, it's your swim suit," he replied. I was flummoxed. It was a typical blue European swim suit. As politely as he could he pointed out that there was a visible bulge in my crotch. Well, for Christ's sake, what else would you expect unless I was emasculated? He drew my attention to his own outfit, which had so much material that I had wondered if he was wearing the lower half of his mother's costume. My first lesson in American prudery had been learned.

## Chapter Eleven
### *Early Days in Indianapolis*

It was barely daylight when we steamed into New York after our nine day crossing. Ambrose and I were on deck to watch the Statue of Liberty emerging from the mist. Once we'd cleared immigration and customs, we managed to get all our luggage to Grand Central Station. While one guarded the luggage, the other went in search of lockers to store it all. Then with just a suitcase each, we took a train to Croton on the Hudson where we were met by Barry and Mimi Gourlay. They had had the lower half of the house on Bywater Street. By then he had been an architect in New York for a couple of years. They had driven to the station in their large convertible armed with iced martinis to sustain us during the three minute drive to their mansion. For the next week we were spoiled rotten. Each morning we would go into Manhattan with Barry so that we could do all the sights while he was at work.

Soon it was time to head for our new life in Indianapolis. We traveled there by train, leaving Grand Central one afternoon to alight at Union Station around 11:00 a.m. on July 30, 1957. Mrs. Baier, who had promised to meet us, was not there. Following a phone call we took a cab to their house on Fall Creek Parkway where she awaited us. A good-looking woman of fifty seven, it soon became obvious who wore the pants in that childless home. We were instructed to put all of our luggage on the front porch. Included were eight heavy cases of shellac gramophone records. They were soon rendered unplayable as a result of the blazing sun.

From a tropical outfitter in London, we had bought linen suits which proved no match for the heat and humidity of a Hoosier summer day. Apart from the Downtown department stores of Ayres, Blocks and Wasson's, central air-conditioning was almost unknown. Very few people even had a window air conditioner. Accepted wisdom was that, by day, the house was sealed up with draperies closed to keep out the heat. Then, before going to bed, windows were opened and a powerful extractor fan was turned on in the attic, to draw in the moist, but marginally cooler, night air. Mrs. Baier had booked accommodation for us in the home of a neighbor but, for some reason, we were not to be taken there till after dinner that night.

Meanwhile, as Mr. Baier was at work in his furniture store, she would take us out to lunch. We could all three fit in the front seat of her car. Our destination turned out to be a drive in opposite the Fair Grounds on 38th Street. It was called "Merrill's Hi-Decker." Mrs. Baier handed the telephone to us to order what we wanted but the menu might as well have been written in Chinese for all the sense it made. Anyway, before long, a young lady came out with a tray of food, which hooked on to the partially raised car window. This was Merrill's first venture into the catering business. Over the years he was to become one of the biggest players in the State's food industry. As a retiree, he and his wife traveled with me on a trip to Spain where we found much to reminisce about. That day, Mrs. Baier took us in behind the scenes to see the operation. On account of the heat, the back door was open. Merrill, his white chef's hat yellowed with sweat, was shooing flies off hamburgers as they circled on a conveyor belt awaiting buns. I was glad that we'd eaten as I could not put cow dung out of my mind.

Next stop was our first introduction to a supermarket. We trailed behind while Mrs. Baier dropped this and that into a bascart. Then, it was back to their house to await Mr. Baier's arrival around 5:30 p.m. There was to be an outdoor pig roast that evening at the Athenaeum Club, of which they were members. That was scheduled for later. Meanwhile, there was much to be discussed. Tomorrow, being Sunday, Mrs. Baier inquired after our church affiliation. When we said, "None," she smiled brightly and said that in that case we would go with them to the Methodist Church. By refusing, I realized we had got off to a rocky start. We were way off base in our assumption that church had something to do with God. Far from it. They went there to fraternize with all their business associates. Mrs. Baier, we soon learned, had been married to a Mr. Gauspohl whose business had been an up-market luggage store located on the Circle. Following his death, she had continued with the Gauspohl Travel Agency. Mr. Baier, who she subsequently met and married, had been a furniture buyer for Marshall Field department store in Chicago. Why he was fired from there, I don't know, but she underwrote the Gauspohl Baier Furniture Store. Gauspohl we were informed, is pronounced "Gospel" and Baier is pronounced "Bare," so their advertisement always announced, "It's the Gauspohl truth and the Baier facts."

Once we met Mr. Baier, we discovered that we were mistaken in thinking that Indianapolis was a six syllable word. From his mouth, between spitting tobacco juice, it was "Naplis." He was never without a cigar of which three inches was always sopping wet inside his mouth. In a word, I found him repulsive.

A vertical flood at 5:30 put paid to the Athenaeum Pig roast so we were to dine at the Columbia Club, on the Circle, instead. When we got into Mr. Baier's trashy vehicle for the drive downtown, I politely mentioned that I was looking forward to seeing his store. "Sure," he said, "it's on the way so we'll stop and have a look around while Mrs. Baier talks to Ambrose in the car."

He and I entered the dimly lighted premises on Vermont Street. It was full of cheap, garish furniture dumped anywhere it happened to land. In Naplis, I learned folks don't hold wid all dat hiflootin stuff. Next, I was steered through the back where furniture was prepared for delivery and into a grimy restroom where I suddenly feared for a fate worse than death. Out of the medicine cabinet, he produced a bottle of hooch, unscrewed the cap and took a long swig before wiping it off on his sleeve and handing it to me to do likewise. After my little sip, he downed a good deal more while telling me that I was his pal and not to breathe a word to Mrs. Baier. At any rate, I was relieved to discover that my boss was an alcoholic rather than a rapist. A couple of high balls at the Columbia Club and Mr. Baier was a menace. As he and I were on the same side of the table, Mrs. Baier was oblivious to the movements of her husband's roaming hand as he explored the upper reaches of the miserable waitress's thigh. Dinner, when it came, consisted of vast steaks on toast. Having been taught to eat everything on my plate, I found that meal was a challenge.

At long last, the time had come to see where Mrs. Baier had arranged for us to sleep. But first, it was back to their house to collect the luggage. One look and we realized that, whatever had survived the blistering heat had been drenched. We were assigned to the attic of the old Duisenberg mansion on Fall Creek. Our landlady pointed the way up. By the time we'd lugged all seventeen pieces up the various staircases we were exhausted. A couple of roll-away cots had been set up among typical attic clutter but neither the heat nor the roar of the fan could prevent us from sleeping soundly. As the final day of July dawned, we wondered if we had made a ghastly mistake in leaving Britain. Could Oscar Wilde have been right when he said that the USA was the only country to go from barbarism to decadence without an intervening civilization? Fortunately we kept our feelings to ourselves or we might have been on the next train back to New York.

It was clear that the Duisenberg attic could only be endured for a few days so, thanks to the Sunday paper, a map and a notepad we checked out the rental ads. Used, as we were to European cities, we decided to live as close to downtown as possible. There was a sizeable hotel-cum-apartment building on Pennsylvania St. at Vermont called the Essex House. It bore a large neon sign to announce itself but, for some reason, the first two letters had a nasty habit of going out altogether leaving the "sex" part pulsating. Ambrose would check it out on Monday morning while I was being initiated into my new job. They had no vacancy but a smaller apartment building, at 402 North Delaware, had a one bedroom available for ninety dollars a month plus five dollars for a window air-conditioner. We took it. Lacking any furniture, it was Gauspohl-Baier to the rescue. Apart from a rather pretty walnut coffee table, the choices were grim. We bought the minimum. A bed and chest of drawers for the bedroom. An innocuous metal and Formica dinette set for the kitchen. An off cut of carpet for a living-room rug and two sixty five dollar sofa beds covered in gray toweling with lurex gold thread. A couple of end-tables in limed oak with lamps and we called it "home."

Ambrose contacted Mallory's and discovered that his job was to start next Monday. That suited us fine as we needed wheels. We found an honest used-car dealership on East Washington Street where they not only fixed us up with a low mileage 1951 Power Glide Chevy but they could issue driving licenses, no questions asked. Now we were all set and could drive down to Shelbyville to meet with Prudence and Bernice and get to know Bernie Douglass and their circle of friends.

Prudence drove a large, very old car and as she seemed to shrink more every week, she looked through, rather than over, the steering wheel. Inexplicably, her reverse hadn't worked for years so it was vital that she park on the street, at the corner, or just shy of a hydrant, so that nobody could park in front of her. She never had it fixed. Once a year, a painter would be summoned to give a quote for the exterior painting of their gingerbread cottage. She never had that done either because the sum quoted would pay for a trip to Europe or Africa which seemed like a more sensible deal. With each passing year, the painting quotes escalated which was great as it enabled

Prudence and her daughter, Anne, to go on ever more exotic safaris. She was passionate about cats but was nearly mauled on one expedition when she beckoned with a "kitty, kitty, kitty" to a hungry lion.

One of Prudence's friends was particularly interesting to us. Her name was Kathryn Turney Garten. She was a very good looking old lady with a commanding presence who lived in a house full of books at Beverly Shores on Lake Michigan. She made her living, she said, by lecturing on books to people who were too lazy to read. During the year she ordered all the New York Times best sellers. Then during the summer she would read them all, usually lying out on the beach in front of her house under a large umbrella. She would select the twenty most promising books to re-read so that she would know every detail of the contents. Finally she would go to New York to see all the new Broadway shows and plays before sending out her list of Fall/Winter lecture offerings to book clubs throughout the states. As well as the twenty books and the latest New York theatre, she always offered the story of the Bible. As she said to us, " I can tell you everything you need to know in one hour from Genesis to revulsions." In Indianapolis she used to give her talks in Ayres auditorium downtown next to the famous Tea Room. She was beautifully turned out, wearing an elegant hat and with a large silk or chiffon handkerchief attached to one of her rings. Always remarkably animated, she walked about the platform telling the story while the audience's eyes would drift into a trance following the fluttering fabric.

No sooner had we settled into 402 North Delaware Street, than we received a welcome note from Aunt Ethel's old acquaintance, Marguerite Dice. She was still at her summer home in Michigan but, on her return to Indianapolis, she'd write again. True to her word, we were invited to Sunday lunch. Her comfortable home was on the west side of Washington Boulevard in the 3600 block. The house still stands though, following her death in the nineteen sixties, it was turned into an office building.

Miss Dice was probably about eighty at the time, had never been married, but had long kept house for her uncle, Judge Dice who had died some years earlier. In appearance, she could easily have stepped out of a painting by Grant Wood. Her spotless clothes were well-starched, and she wore her straight white hair in a bun on the top of her head. She may have powdered her nose, but otherwise she eschewed makeup.

After inviting us to sit in a couple of chintz-covered chairs, she repaired to a rocker that might have been custom made to measure. The customary pleasantries completed, and our sherry glasses topped up by her houseman, she wasted no time in cutting to the quick. How fortunate we were to have left Britain in the nick of time. Our mystified expressions called for clarification as obviously Parliament was shielding the population from the facts. Didn't we know that the Communist takeover of the British Isles was to all intents and purposes a done deal? The news stunned us. Indeed we had not heard anything about it until that very moment. "In that case," she said, "maybe you haven't heard the truth about the president, either?" "Are you talking about President Eisenhower?" we asked. "Yes," she replied. Then she slowly rocked forward and nearly inaudibly whispered, "He's pink." "Pink!" we echoed, "Do you mean he's a Communist, Miss Dice?" A sad nod was all she could muster. Where on earth had we been these past few years? Such alarming news had made us wonder if we were living in a parallel universe.

Once seated at the dining room table, she embarked on a rambling grace that implored God to enlighten all the benighted politicians in Washington while thanking him for Senator Capeheart. In view of the fact that her prayer was directed at God, it really didn't matter that we knew nothing about any of these miscreants, or for that matter, the good senator.

As food arrived, she said that she liked having people to lunch on Sundays and that we could expect another invitation soon. In former times, she explained that she never had guests over on a Sunday because she would be attending church services. However, one by one the churches had been taken over. Taken over by what was far from clear but, when you're a guest of Alice in blunderland, you don't ask too many questions. At any rate, since all churches had evidently strayed from the paths of righteousness, Marguerite Dice conducted her own services at home.

We did elicit one bit of information which we would promptly act upon. In the auditorium of the War Memorial, a long established series of chamber music concerts was about to begin a new season. Known as The Ensemble Music Society, it continues to this day to bring Indianapolis' audiences the finest musicians from all over the world. Nowadays the concerts are held at the Indiana History Center. We became subscribers right away. We might have balked at the venue had we known that the great singer Marian Anderson, who had been scheduled to sing there, was barred from entering when she turned out to have brown skin!

Having gained Miss Dice's approval, we were soon invited to a second, and I may say final, Sunday lunch at her home. This time we were being introduced to four new people. Dr. Gatch was a highly respected surgeon. At this stage of his life, however, he could barely manage the war memorial steps. Next year, he died. Mrs. Gatch was Canadian, a handsome old lady and very charming. Susan Ashby was their daughter. Their son-in-law, Bob Ashby, completed the four people we were to meet. The Ashbys were both valuable supporters of the Indianapolis Museum of Art, and its predecessor, the John Herron Art Museum. Bob was one time chairman of the board. Susan served as a longtime docent. Years later, when I had a museum office, there was a twelfth century Madonna and Child sculpture standing in the gallery close to my door. Working at my desk, I could hear Susan Ashby with a class of small children say, "No, no, not that Madonna. This is a Christian lady!"

Up to the occasion of our second luncheon with Miss Dice, Ambrose and I had never heard of John Birch. We soon discovered that within weeks, Marguerite Dice would be hosting a two-day symposium for a Mr. Robert Welch and eleven like-minded men, from other states, to found the secretive John Birch Society. Unfortunately, shortly before she died, Miss Dice destroyed all her papers. The membership of the J.B.S. was kept secret, but its aim was to disrupt the Communist takeover of the U.S.A. Though they maintained a phone number for some thirty years, like many another crackpot organization, it slowly withered on the vine.

Growing up in a family of Colonials, I had always known that the color of a person's skin was neither more nor less important than the color of their eyes. It didn't take long, however, to discover that most Hoosiers had a very different take on the matter.

Our first black friends were John and Annette Green. He ran an office cleaning company and she was an elevator operator at the Banner Whitehill Furniture store. A nicer and more loving couple would be hard to find. When we first got to know them, they were bubbling over with joy as they had just adopted a little boy called Tony. John had a sister, Louise, who worked at the Ft. Benjamin Harrison Finance Center, a military building second in size only to the Pentagon. Her husband, Wallace Waugh, was a barber. The Waughs had three perfectly delightful, fun loving daughters, Judy, Dixie and Benji. Like teenage girls everywhere, they knew all the latest dances and spent an inordinate amount of time teaching Ambrose and me the right moves. Though we lacked talent, they never lost patience with us. Both families took us to their hearts and ere long we were all best friends. Soon Jock, Pam and their children were being included in Green/Waugh parties.

In 1959, Jock's sister, Helen, an elementary teacher in England, came to visit for four months. It turned into four years. Trinity Episcopal Church, at 33rd and Meridian Streets, was planning to open a private elementary school. The head rector, Father Lynch, would be in charge. Once she had met Helen Bevan, Edith Clowes recommended her to Rev. Lynch. He employed her to be the first and only teacher for 1960. From then on, there would be one new teacher hired each year till all the elementary grades were covered. The school was to be called St. Richard's and, with advice from the Royal College of Arms, Jock designed the emblazon. The first year would only have a first grade, open to all qualified children.

Helen was busy in the church building signing up parishioners' children and making all necessary preparations for the school's fall opening. Annette Green asked me if Tony would be eligible. After a test, Helen happily enrolled him. A few days later, Father Lynch was scanning the expected pupils' names when his Episcopal eyes spotted the name Tony Green with an address on Northern Avenue. "Is that child a Negro?" he asked. "Yes, I think so," Helen answered uncertainly. "If he is," said God's spokesman," we can't accept him." Fortunately, there was to be a board meeting that afternoon, so the matter would be dealt with then. At the meeting, Helen made it clear that, if Tony was denied admission, St. Richard's would be opening without her. After much discussion, the board decided that a maximum of ten percent of the pupils could be Negro, as that would reflect (wrongly in fact) the city's ethnic makeup. Tony was the only black child that year.

We counted Reg and Mary Bruce among our friends. Reg was our doctor. He was black. Mary, his wife, was white. Their three young children were Mary Ann, Nancy and Reggie. As the school grew, much to Father Lynch's chagrin, so did the number of black pupils. Mary Ann Bruce was enrolled and doing very well when Helen got a call from Mary Ann's mother. Nancy was in another school where she was having serious problems, so please could she transfer to St. Richard's? Normally children were not admitted in mid-semester but, under the circumstances, Helen agreed to take her in.

It didn't take long for Lynch to spot an unfamiliar black face, and Helen was in trouble. "Call that Mrs. Bruce right now from my desk and tell her to pick up her child immediately," he ordered. From his perspective, Helen had committed two crimes, the justified one of admitting a student midterm without his permission, and the unjustified one of boosting the number of Negro enrollees to over ten percent. The total absurdity of his argument becomes clear when you look at Mary Ann and Nancy's parents. Dr. Reginald Bruce was lighter skinned than many white people I've known, and his wife Mary, was white. A reasonable person would calculate that their children were three quarters white and one quarter black, which would have brought the total percentage of blacks to below ten. Prejudice, of course, ignores facts, so Helen was fired.

Allen Clowes was having a New Year's Eve party. Among the guests were his neighbors, Sandy and Carol Holliday. Everybody was having fun and dancing so I asked Carol for a dance. She declined. A few weeks later we were together again being entertained by Tamara Jacques when Carol Holliday turned to me and said, "I'm sure you've been wondering why I refused to dance with you at Allen's party?" Frankly, I hadn't given the matter a moment's thought but, rather than disappoint her with the truth, I tilted my head inquiringly. "Well," she said, "perhaps it's just me, because I'm from Virginia, but just before Christmas, I saw you kissing a colored woman, and after that I couldn't bear to have you touch me." The picture which she conjured up of me as a passionate heterosexual, with a taste for miscegenation, caught me completely off guard. So I said, "Where did this happen?" "You attended the Nativity play that the children put on at St. Richard's when a colored woman came in and you stood up and kissed her," Carol replied. "Oh! My goodness," said I with relief, "that was Annette Green." "You mean you know her?" Carol's astonishment was palpable. "Yes, of course I know her. She and her family are friends of ours, and her son Tony is a pupil at the school. Surely you don't think I'm in the habit of kissing strangers?" I inquired. In fairness to Carol, she eventually recovered to such an extent that, as the years rolled by, she would greet me with a kiss.

Eli Lilly and Company was responsible for attracting a number of distinguished black families to Indianapolis, a few of whom became our friends. In particular, we enjoyed and grew to love two of the wives. One was Bernice Fraction. Once seen, never forgotten. She was as black as a Masai, stunningly beautiful, and multi-talented. She had one of the finest soprano voices of the twentieth century; it was widely acknowledged that if she had put her career ahead of her family, she would have had starring roles in the Metropolitan Opera. Her laughter sounded like a peal of enchanting bells. She could draw, paint and make anything, including her gowns. All her clothes made the most of her shapely breasts and cleavage. Suddenly, she was diagnosed with breast cancer, which entailed a radical mastectomy.

The day after surgery, Ambrose and I visited her in Winona Hospital. She was sitting up in bed, a white bow in her hair, making fashion sketches. When we asked to see what she was drawing, she showed us a design for a gown up to her neck in front, but plunging in the back so far that there was a hint of buttocks cleavage. She laughed as she showed it to us while remarking, "There's more to Bernice than one missing titty!" Tragically, the cancer returned and she died with so much unfulfilled promise.

Another memorable and much loved black wife was Blanche Ferguson. Apart from skin color, she could hardly have resembled Bernice less. When Bernice made an entrance at any gathering, it's safe to say that she turned every head in the room. Little old Blanche, on the other hand, would scuttle in like a mouse. Awkward and graceless, I doubt she had anything much in the way of manual skills. A husky voice and cough betrayed a lifetime of smoking. What she had was a wonderful mind. She was widely read, a brilliant conversationalist, and gifted teacher. Her youth had been spent in New York City, where she developed a deep appreciation of the Harlem Renaissance. When we first knew her, in the early 1960s, she was writing a biography of Countee Cullen, a black poet who died in 1946 at the age of forty three. We'd never heard of Countee Cullen. Blanche suggested we read some of his writings. We did, and one of his poems so impressed me that I've always remembered it:

> *Once riding in old Baltimore*
> *Heart filled, head filled with glee*
> *I saw a Baltimorean*
> *Keep looking straight at me.*
>
> *Now I was eight and very small*
> *And he was no whit bigger,*
> *And so I smiled, but he poked out*
> *His tongue, and called me "Nigger."*
>
> *I saw the whole of Baltimore*
> *From May until December,*
> *Of all the things that happened there*
> *That's all that I remember.*

Ambrose's research proved interesting. He was designing capacitors for the space program and presenting papers at Electrochemical Society Conventions. Gauspohl-Baier Furniture turned out to be almost as bad as I had feared. On the plus side, we went up to the Merchandise Mart in Chicago on a couple of occasions and stayed at the Palmer House. Round the corner from that hotel is the Prudential building, at forty two stories, then the city's tallest. I was much impressed with the furniture showrooms in the Merchandise Mart and looked forward to the day when I could deal with products of that quality. At the same time, I felt an obligation to the Baiers who had sponsored me sight unseen. I decided to stick it out for six months.

Meanwhile, I checked out the competition. By far the largest furniture store in the state was Banner Whitehill. It was built in the English Tudor style, complete with fan vaulting, and was located on Meridian Street, across from Ayres. Unfortunately, it has long since been bulldozed and replaced with a multi-story parking garage. In those days it carried everything, except the highest end merchandise, on seven floors which included carpeting, drapery and decorating departments. One interview with the personnel manager and I could start as a salesman as soon as I liked.

As the Baiers paid me bi-weekly, I gave two weeks notice when the six months expired. Mr. Baier went ballistic. I could not quit. It was out of the question. Mrs. Baier wouldn't permit it, etc., etc. Being the end of the day, I walked out saying, "I'll see you on Monday." By the time I got home the telephone was ringing. The infuriated man never wanted to see me again. He never did. I dropped my keys through the mailbox and started at Banner Whitehill on the next Monday. Mr. Baier died soon after.

Banner Whitehill's organization and code of behavior were new to me but had to be learned fast. I was one of about twenty salesmen and saleswomen. Near the lighting department were three cubby holes, each of which contained a decorator. Beside the manned elevators, on the first floor, were the cashiers in front of more cubby holes. This lot contained credit officers. Just inside the main entrance stood elegant Julie at a podium on which rested a list of all the salesmen. When customers entered, they would be asked if they would like help. If the answer was yes, the next salesman would be called and a check mark put against his or her name on the list as it worked in strict rotation. Selling, as we did, entirely on commission, it was up to each of us to make the most of every opportunity. In a worst case scenario, on arrival at the floor displaying the sought after furniture, the customer realizes that she left all the dimensions at home along with color swatches so she won't waste my time! When that happens, all you can do is say how delighted you were to meet her and, as you give her your business card, assure her that you'd very much like to look after her when she returns. Meanwhile, of course, you've got some nineteen salesmen ahead of you before you get another chance at a customer. After a while, with luck, customers walk in and ask for you or, better still, phone in to confirm a sale or add to an order. In that case, the salesman maintains his "in line" position.

One of my first lucky breaks was a young couple buying a houseful of furniture. They needed everything including carpets and draperies. For the customized draperies, I split my commission with one of the decorators. There was no problem with any of the special orders so my commission, on that sale, more than covered my $300 monthly draw. Oddly enough, James Kittle, the young husband, went into the furniture retail business himself and has become remarkably successful.

Mrs. Clowes, a wealthy widow of whom you'll be hearing much at a later date, phoned me. An advertisement for a set of porch furniture, on sale at Banner Whitehill, had caught her eye. Her friend, Mrs. Adams, who lived on Watson Rd., was having a birthday on Thursday, so please would I make arrangements to have a set delivered to her, with appropriate birthday wishes, on that day and just send Mrs. Clowes the bill. As the call came on a Monday, it should have been a slam dunk. It was not. When I took the completed form back to the credit department, it transpired that she didn't have a Banner Whitehill account so I should phone her to come to the store to apply for one. She didn't want to open an account, I explained, just send her a bill and she'll mail in a check. Not possible, I was told. The only way Mrs. Clowes could avoid a credit application would be to take delivery of the furniture C.O.D. Fearing an impasse, I picked up the paperwork and took it into Mr. Musselman's office. He was the chief financial officer. As the porch set amounted to less than a hundred dollars, I offered to have it put on my account. That wouldn't work either as employees got a twenty per cent discount so buying for friends was not allowed. After some humiliating groveling, he agreed to let me fill out a credit application on behalf of Mrs. Clowes with the caveat that I was responsible for the debt in the event that she stiffed the store. Next was the problem of delivery. Banners only delivered to the northeast quadrant of Indianapolis on Mondays so Mrs. Adams would have to wait till next week. Taking a copy of the delivery receipt, I walked to the warehouse to discuss the matter with Elmer Chance, the head honcho. He was a prince and helped overcome more than one pitfall. Without his intervention Mrs. Adams would have to sign a receipt with the price of the merchandise on it. Also, the furniture itself would have been delivered four days late for her birthday with the price tags attached to all five pieces. Saint Elmer fixed the paperwork while I removed the tags and he personally delivered the cane set on the Thursday using his own pick up. As that porch furniture was a "lead" item, my commission was less than two dollars. In effect we were penalized for selling lead merchandise which carried a very small markup. The idea was to draw in customers with a bargain and then sell them something better.

An old lady walking slowly with two sticks bought an inexpensive occasional table. For some reason, the scheduled delivery wouldn't work for her so I offered to put it in my car and drop it off on my way home. She was delighted. Her rental flat had seen better days and it was obvious she was living in straightened circumstances. However, she insisted that I take an old Chinese bowl as a "thank you" for delivering the table. It remains with me as one of many priceless memories.

Another snapshot is of Mr. Greenbaum. He was a fellow salesman who, like me, had emigrated to the US in his twenties. Some thirty years my senior, he hailed from a village near Lille in Northern France. One morning we headed simultaneously into adjoining cubicles in the men's room. The stalls had the usual partial partitions. I was mystified when, moments later, his feet disappeared from view apparently without opening his door. Having first checked to make sure that his head hadn't risen over the top of the partition, I ventured, "Mr. Greenbaum, are you there?" which he promptly affirmed. Realizing that his evident lack of feet had elicited my curiosity, he explained that having grown up squatting to defecate over a hole in the floor he could only perform by standing on the toilet seat!

When Winthrop Rockefeller came into Banner Whitehill to see Harry Schacter, the owner and CEO, Mr. Bultman, a salesman, offered to escort him to the seventh floor office. En route, the elevator stopped to collect Mrs. Landis, another salesperson. Bultman said, "Mrs. Landis this is Mr. Rockefeller." "Yeah right," she replied, "and I'm Mrs. Astor!" Mr. Miller, another of my colleagues, was incredulous at my naivety in believing that the Russians had photographed the back of the Moon from a satellite.

Fred Thomas, the buyer for kitchen appliances and dinette sets, became a very close friend until his early death from bladder cancer. His partner Alfie joined him in death of a heart attack less than a year later. They were each around fifty years old and you guessed it, smokers.

Everybody liked young Mack Polhill. He was carpet buyer, a recent employee and an even more recent, bridegroom. The entire Banner Whitehill family was invited to their Louisville wedding. Weeks later, Mack collapsed. An open heart operation was needed and so was blood. Ambrose and I organized the "Polhill Plasma Party" which did much to bring the Banner Whitehill employees together for a worthwhile common cause.

Broyhill, a family owned furniture manufacturing company, offered a reward to the top salesman of their brand over a period of three months. As ours was said to be the seventh largest furniture store in the nation we embraced the challenge and won. Rowena Landis won by a wide margin with me second and elderly Mr. Judson third. The three of us were flown in a corporate plane to Lenoir, North Carolina, to be entertained by the Broyhill family and to tour the factory. It was Mr. Judson's first plane ride. He was a menace from the start. No sooner were we airborne than he was in and out of his seat like a jack-in-the-box alternately pestering the pilot and the hostess. Once settled in our hotel a limousine came to take us to the senior Broyhill's mansion in the mountains to have cocktails and watch a spectacular sunset. By the time we reached their country club, for dinner, it was plain to see that Mr. Judson couldn't hold his liquor and had already imbibed too much.

Young Mrs. Broyhill had been crowned Miss North Carolina some two or three years earlier. She was at one end of a table for about twelve of us with her husband at the other. The first course was oysters on the half shell. As I don't care for either animals or fish that are still quivering, I left mine untouched. Evidently, Mrs. Broyhill didn't care for them either but, in her case, she surreptitiously wrapped them in a large white napkin and set them aside. Meanwhile, in a loud inebriated voice Mr. Judson was telling a scatological story that had something to do with a parrot in a toilet bowl. No sooner had his tale concluded, to thundering silence, than he picked up a wine cork, blackened it in a candle flame and lurched at Mrs. Broyhill grinding the hot black coal into her cheek. While some of us wrestled him away, somebody else grabbed a napkin to help clean her up and the oysters flew everywhere! I did my best to make amends by encouraging future customers to buy Broyhill furniture but to no avail. We were never invited back!

Living in downtown Indianapolis turned out to be quite unlike what we expected. At 5:00 p.m. the population fled, and soon you could fire a cannon down any street with no chance of hitting a living soul. A Sicilian restaurant called DeBiase stayed open until eight or nine. You could smell garlic all over downtown but, other than that, you were on your own.

There was a sleazy theater on Illinois Street, called The Fox. Few people patronized it which was just as well because it was difficult to find two adjacent seats in reasonable condition. If you sat carelessly, you were liable to impale yourself on a wayward spring or even crash to the floor. We paid our dollar and went there once. One act was memorable. The lady undressed behind a fan till all that remained were two chains around her neck. The *piece de résistance* was accomplished when she hung one chain on each breast nipple and rotated her shoulders till they spun like windmills in opposite directions. Male anatomy doesn't permit us to attempt such a feat but I still wonder at the imagination and practice involved in perfecting such an act.

There was a bar called The Famous Door where a monumental black lady called Ophelia sang and held court. In spite of a generous belly and watermelon breasts she had no trace of an ass. She was as flat behind as if she had been rearranged by Lizzie Borden's axe. Her favorite song was a raunchy number called "Nuts" that she delivered wandering about the establishment while emphasizing the lyrics with obscene gestures. Another lady with a special talent plied her trade in a Capitol Avenue nightclub called The Venus Fly Trap. Her name, surely invented for stage purposes, was Lotti the Body. She was thoroughly curvaceous. No doubt her striptease titillated most of the males in the audience but, to grinding music, what she did once her clothes were off was what impressed us. The lights went out to be replaced by ultraviolet

120

ones. Then she would turn her back to the audience to reveal a pair of luminous rubber gloves one attached to each cheek of her bottom. She had developed her posterior muscles to work independently and so subtly that the gloves seemed to take on a life of their own. After keeping us all in fits of laughter for some time she would squeeze and release her cheeks together in such a way that the gloves appeared to clap.

A bar in the flatiron building on Massachusetts Avenue, boasted an ancient Native American pianist. In spite of her emaciated appearance, she could crank out jazz and the likes of Scott Joplin uby the hour. For the price of a beer, one evening, we discovered that she had appeared before Queen Victoria in Buffalo Bill Cody's Wild West Show.

There must have been a gay bar downtown but I don't remember any from the 1950's. So far as I recall, not even The Unicorn or Our Place go that far back. Betty and Darlow's was a Lesbian bar on South Alabama Street. It was eventually knocked down and absorbed into the Lilly complex. We were having a drink in there one night when a fight broke out. Evidently, some girl had been poaching on another's territory. What started with some name calling soon escalated into a wild melee, only terminating when the largest of these bruisers grabbed a pair of legs and dragged her screaming victim to the door and flung her into the street. Not long after that, Betty and Darlow, who had been a couple, split up. Darlow kept the bar on Alabama Street and Betty bought a house on Central Avenue that had both gay and lesbian drag shows.

On Sunday afternoons, gays would flock to a rambling old house off Greasy Creek Road in Brown County. It was the home of a free-wheeling fag-hag called Marian DeTrey. A short wooden bridge linked her forested homestead to the road. A dozen or so cars could find parking spots between abandoned cast-iron cauldrons, wagon wheels and other assorted junk scattered about her yard. Later arrivals parked along the road. The door to the house was always left wide open to allow

Marian's family of cats, chickens and a goat freedom of movement. No reservations were required but everybody contributed something to the evening, usually in the form of wine or beer, plus a five dollar charge for the pot luck dinner. Sometime in the past, interior walls had been removed to create a large irregular space with a noticeably uneven floor. Behind a counter was the wood-fired range, with Marian stirring an enormous pot of the evening's surprise. She was a tiny woman with long chandelier earrings pierced through paper-thin lobes. The cigarette attached to her lower lip never dislodged as she cackled her greeting to each new arrival. Peanuts in their shells, along with raw vegetables and dip were usually set out by early arrivals to ensure that they were enjoyed by us rather than the goat that often had to be shooed off a table. Hampers full of old clothes and hats were there to encourage everybody to turn the evening into a creative costume party. With music blaring, a log fire burning and liquor flowing, Marian's Sundays were the gay's panacea for Monday's straight-jacket.

On 16th Street, just east of Herron, a London style coffee bar opened offering guitar music and ad hoc poetry reading. Almost any evening one would find Joanie Johnson *in situ*, in The Bird Cage. At 23 she was already famous. Once seen, never forgotten. She had very short blond hair and a round pretty face. Her makeup was unique. Apart from heavy mascara and a black line around her eyes, she powdered her face snow white. It was impossible to gauge how many hundreds of pounds she weighed because all except her head was contained within a black floor length tarpaulin. Being far too large for any chair and too heavy for a sectional or sofa she always sat on the floor. Though beautifully spoken and sweet natured, she was permanently homeless, usually sleeping under goods wagons in a railroad siding. Most days, she sat wherever she happened to be, armed with a sketch pad, ink and watercolors, painting a never never land filled with beautiful children dancing joyfully.

If she liked you, she would open her portfolio and give you lovely paintings by the dozen. If she didn't, her tiniest scribble would be absurdly priced.

Invariably, at the annual Talbot Street Art Fair she had quantities of paintings stacked on a folding table. I remember a lady who said that she was looking for something that would compliment her persimmon davenport. "How much?" she asked, holding up a picture that emphasized the color she was after. "Forty dollars and eleven cents," came the reply. "Why the eleven cents?" enquired the mystified lady. Joanie drew her attention to a large leather bag with two flaps. "The dollars go in that side and the change goes there," said Joanie matter-of-factly. So far as she was concerned, no further explanation was needed.

What happened under a freight car one cold winter night is anybody's guess but, the following fall, except for a tiny penis, Joanie Johnson had cloned. For the next decade, Indianapolis watched the boy grow daily less distinguishable from his mother. What ultimately became of him, I cannot tell. Sadly, Joanie succumbed to diabetes at an early age.

Indianapolis, in the late 1950's bore little resemblance to today's city with its four to five-fold population increase. The morning radio was devoted largely to what was trading in the stockyards on Kentucky Avenue next to the *abattoirs* and meat packing plants. Trains were constantly in and out of Union Station. I believe there were nine daily commuter trains to Chicago. President Eisenhower had started an interstate system of roads but that was still pie in the sky as far as Indiana was concerned. The main road from New York to California included Washington Street in downtown Indianapolis.

A modest strip mall had been built in The Meadows on 38th Street, and a larger one, to be called Glendale, was under construction but not enclosed, as we know it today. However, both Ayres and Block planned to open their first branch stores at Glendale. Up to that point, the department stores were all one-of-a-kind and family owned. Lyman S. Ayres was a very large store. There were eleven floors above ground and a lower level that was three times the size. Their Christmas windows, and those of Block's, would annually attract hoards of tourists from the surrounding counties. The store carried almost anything you could think of including pharmacy, books, yard goods, gourmet foods and European imported antiques and old master paintings. We made friends with Bill Ratcliff, elegant and suave, who was the buyer for that department. His other half, John something or other, was head of Ayres display department and, once Jock had sent him samples of his work, we were all set for the Bevan family to come from England.

Block's made delicious handmade chocolates and had a French bakery department where one could buy authentic croissants and brioche. In short, if you wanted the best of almost anything, you had to shop in downtown Indianapolis or go to Chicago or New York. The city market was full of ethnic produce. The stalls were run by the descendants of the original stall holders dating back a century. The market as it stands today is only one third the size that it was in the 1950s. The larger part had some kind of convention facilities above it called Tomlinson Hall. That whole section burnt down in about 1960.

Another treasure lost to fire was the Test Building. It was located on the south side of Washington Street just East of Meridian. Its several floors were of iron grillwork and the elevators were cages. The building was full of old world trades people. Whatever needed fixing you could be sure of finding the necessary artisan in the Test Building, watches, clocks, porcelains, shoes, copper and silver, or alterations to clothes and Lord knows what else was to be found there.

The Marrott at Meridian and Fall Creek was the largest hotel. What few other hotels there were were down town. The Claypool, The Lincoln and The Greylyn have long been demolished. The Canterbury, by another name and The Severin, now much enlarged, were both there. The bus station was a large open shed on the north side of Market Street between Illinois and Capital. There were no parking garages, unless you count a tiny one, within a building on the Circle, which claims to be the World's oldest. The English Hotel and Theater, on the northwest Circle quadrant had been demolished before we appeared on the scene. The splendid French neo-Baroque courthouse would soon be history. Fortunately, I had a sketchbook in which I recorded a number of buildings before the wrecking ball struck.

Lyman Bros. was an art store on the Circle with an upper level for painting and sculpture restoration. The restorer was a muscular young man of Greek extraction called Paul Spheeris. He believed that he was a reincarnated Chinese Emperor. His father had been a professional wrestler with a traveling carnival. Childhood had been spent traipsing about throughout the South where he absorbed a varied education. With large jug ears, a Pinocchio nose and upturned half-moon mouth, without any make-up, he resembled nothing so much as a circus clown. Though he could draw or paint anything, his chosen subject was male pornography. So skilled was he in that particular genre that you'd swear that the outsized genitalia depicted were actually throbbing.

Paul, and his long suffering friend, Andy Filchak along with his Buddha-like mother, and innumerable cats, lived in a tiny mud-floored shack just south of 64th Street. It could only be reached by way of a dangerously rickety footbridge over a creek. The shack was mainly furnished with oriental curio cabinets composed of little drawers filled to capacity with Chinese nephrite bowls, buckles, scepters and other treasures. He was usually to be found holding court dressed in imperial robes. Somewhere he had acquired a small Japanese tea house and had it erected some fifty feet from the shack. Given half a chance he would subject you to an endless tea ceremony while you sat miserably uncomfortably on your heels.

At his parties, which were large and frequent, he always seemed to come up with a flock of geisha women who could be counted on to keep pouring liberal amounts of sake. On one occasion a whole lot of sailors, en route to wherever, were grounded overnight in Indianapolis so Paul, never one to waste an opportunity, trucked them out for a party. While many transient visitors have found Indianapolis unmemorable, I'm confident that every last one of those Tars will carry memories of the affair to his grave.

Though he had minimal formal training, Paul Spheeris was fearless when it came to restoration. The most delicate and challenging of problems he tackled with gusto. Mrs. Booth Jameson who was the widow of Booth Tarkington's nephew and president of the Women's Alliance at the Herron Museum of Art had a sixteenth century panel painting attributed, at that time, to Hans Holbein the Younger. The subject was Henry VIII's son Edward. When Jo Jameson brought it in to Lyman's it was a disaster. What had caused the problem, I don't know, but the entire panel was a mass of paint blisters of various sizes. Unfazed, Paul made a map of the blisters which he transferred to the back of the panel. Then, armed with a hypodermic filled with glue, after securing the panel on to an easel, he penetrated every blister from the back and deposited a bead of glue therein. Finally he put the panel into a heavy rubber bag from which, with the aid of a vacuum machine, he extracted the air. I watched fascinated and by golly, when the panel re-emerged, the paint surface was perfectly smooth. I saw the painting recently and was told that it's never needed treatment since. Paul Spheeris later became first conservator at the Herron Museum of Art where he also doubled as Oriental curator.

## Chapter Twelve
### *Becoming Hoosiers*

Almost from the moment of our arrival in Indianapolis, The John Herron Museum of Art became our oasis of choice. Each year they had at least one major exhibition, as well as other openings and lectures to attend. Wilbur Peat, the longtime director, spoke eloquently and always lectured in a tuxedo. The museum, though small, had been purpose built in 1904. The collection was modest, which is probably just as well in view of the fact that there was no climate control. The Italian primitives were displayed upstairs in an east gallery where the thermometer frequently registered a hundred and thirty degrees.

The first unforgettable lecture we attended was given by the aging Frank Lloyd Wright. Though he'd lived much of his life in and around Chicago, he'd never been to Indianapolis. On arrival, he was given a tour of the city. While viewing the War Memorial, it was explained that the two churches flanking it on the west and east would soon be removed to allow for the completion of the landscaping and steps. "Why?" asked the famous architect," I suggest that you leave the churches exactly where they are and remove that monstrosity between them!" The much loved, but recently demolished, English Building, on the circle, had been replaced by a J. C. Penny store. That new building was almost universally despised. Having toured the wonders of the Hoosier capital, Lloyd Wright pronounced Penney's to be the best bit of architecture in town. The shock of all that he saw a mere hundred and eighty miles from Chicago may well have precipitated his death a few months later.

It's safe to say that, though Frank Lloyd's lecture produced a standing room only audience, my sparsely attended first talk, which occurred about the same time, was more favorably received. I had been asked to give a talk comparing English taste in interior decorating with that of Indianapolis; a trite and trivial subject to be sure but, in hindsight, the start of a long and wonderful relationship.

Early friends were Gerhardt and Anne Weunch. He was an Austrian pianist with a strong resemblance to Schubert. Anne was a violinist from Florida. She met and married Gerhardt while they were both students in Texas. Now they had their first jobs teaching at Butler University. Mrs. Robertine Daniels owned a large clapboard house in the eighteen hundred block of Pennsylvania Street. She offered to rent it to them for fifty dollars a month. They suggested we share it. Even with heating it should work out no more than a hundred dollars per couple so, after four months in our flat overlooking Roberts Park church on Delaware, we moved. The house had a working elevator with a quarter size reproduction of the Venus de Milo on its roof. Though we shared the kitchen, the whole place was so spacious that we never got in each other's way. Butler colleagues and other musical friends would come over to visit and make music. Soon we had a new circle of friends including Izler Solomon, the conductor of the Indianapolis Symphony Orchestra. While sharing the Daniels' house Anne delivered a son, their first baby. Eventually they settled on an appropriate name but, in the meantime, he was known as "Sputnik" in honor of the recently launched Russian satellite. We only shared that house for the winter as the Bevans were due in March.

We had become friends with Fred Thomas, buyer of appliances and kitchen furniture at Banner Whitehill. He had an apartment in The Meadows, a large complex on East 38th Street commonly known as "Diaper Downs" because of the large population of young families. Each building had twelve two-bedroom apartments, four per floor. There was an available apartment on the floor above him and another in the adjacent building. We rented both and moved in to await the Bevans. Jock and Pam arrived with Katie aged three and a half, and Simon, eighteen months. Just as we had, eight months earlier, they came by boat to New York followed by train to Indianapolis. The Meadows was a good starter home for them and suited us fine. Freddie Thomas turned out to be a wonderful friend. He drove a convertible, and loved children. Every Sunday morning Katie and Simon would rush over to wake Freddie who would take them for a ride and breakfast. It was sad day when he was transferred to Muncie to be manager of the Banner Whitehill store there. Jock and Pam, however, would put the children on the bus in Indianapolis bound for Muncie for magical week-ends with their beloved Freddie.

We all became friends of the Freihofers. Walter Freihofer had recently retired from a bakery business. Along with Big Mama, his Virginia wife, he had moved in to an apartment next to ours. They had five delightful grown up children, all of whom were married and starting families. Their youngest son, Reno, a lawyer, lived in the next building with Joanie, his wife, and infant Sally. The Freihofers exemplified everything good and wholesome about Midwesterners. They were very family oriented with a welcome-to-all cottage on Lake Wawasee. All the children were taught to say "yes Sir" or "Mam" to grownups, and to give a helping hand whenever it was called for. Family get-togethers in the next door apartment were common, and we were not only invariably invited but always treated as family. During the first year that we lived there, we had several visits from British friends and relations including Dad, both Ambrose's parents and my Uncle Roy and Aunt Mary. The Freihofers were wonderful to all of them.

Every summer, in a field between the Meadows apartments and the Meadows Shopping Center a marquee would be set up for theatrical productions. It was Allen Clowes's first venture into the role of impresario. The offerings were mostly tried and true comedies with a semi-retired

Hollywood star bought in as the lead. We were regulars. At Butler University there was a large outdoor summer theatre next to the Fieldhouse. It was called "Starlight Musicals" which leaves any explanation superfluous. The shows there were generally sold out but seldom did they hold any interest for us. On the other hand, Butler also hosted a summer series of chamber concerts in the Holcomb Gardens on a terrace attached to the pavilion from where the carillon is played. Led by Eric Rosenblith, first chair of the symphony, the players were orchestra members along with Dorothy Munger, a pianist. The group had an official name but was commonly known as the "Citronella Series" as the humid night air was heavy with that mosquito repellant.

Of course we'd heard of people dying, the newspapers carried obituary columns every day, but they were other people, not anybody you knew. True, the last of Ambrose's grandparents had died but that was when he was a child. All our parents and siblings, uncles, aunts, cousins and even my grandparents seemed indestructible. While still in our twenties death was not on our radar. Like many Brits, we had read "The Loved one," a novel based on the American way of death, by Evelyn Waugh. However, it seemed so preposterous that we didn't take it seriously. All of that was about to change.

When Uncle Roy and Auntie Mary arrived for a visit from England, we inquired as to any sightseeing requests they might have. Number one, we discovered, was to experience a funeral home as such places don't exist on the other side of the Pond. I should explain that the Right Reverend Canon Roy McKay was the head of the BBC religious programs so any new angle on the hereafter was grist to his mill. Having often driven past Broad Ripple's Flanner and Buchanan Funeral Home, we repaired thence. On entering, we were quietly greeted by an impeccably, if soberly, dressed gentleman who was duly impressed to make the acquaintance of so august a man of God as Uncle Roy. An imposing man, Uncle Roy not only looked convincingly ecclesiastical but spoke in measured unctuous tones that, for me at least, conjured up visions of a pulpit in Westminster Abbey. The gentleman, we learned, would be delighted to show us around and answer questions. We gathered that respectable Americans don't die, they merely "pass" or, to be precise, "pass on." Furthermore, by the time they'd undergone the Egyptian treatment, followed by an extensive workover at the hands of Fanner and Buchanan's skilled cosmeticians, the beloved corpse was sure to look better than anybody could ever remember it looking in life. Soon we were upstairs in spacious and tastefully furnished viewing rooms. That day, there seemed to be a dearth of bodies, which was just as well in view of the fact that none of us had ever clapped eyes on a dead human being and now didn't seem to be an appropriate moment to start. After explaining the customary arrangement of a fully or half open coffin which he called "a casket" he enthused about two recent "viewings" which had been unusually lovely.

The first concerned the "passing" of a beautiful four year old girl. Rather than boxing her up, the bereaved parents arranged to have her sitting on a bench in front of the window surrounded by her dolls overlooking children playing in Broad Ripple Park. The second was an older lady who had been a noted hostess and socialite. In her case, Flanner and Buchanan had done an exemplary job of seating her, elegantly gowned, at a respectable facsimile of a Louis Quinze *bonheur du jour,* quill in hand, writing a thank you note. I dare say that, at least some of what we had seen and heard that day became material for future BBC broadcasts.

Hardly had the McKays departed for England than tragedy struck. Answering a knock at our door, we found Walter Freihofer ashen faced. Big Mama, sixty seven, had just died. She had suffered a massive heart attack and died before the ambulance reached the hospital. Within the hour, the Indianapolis children and their families were in the apartment next to ours. We opened our door to make room for everybody. Jane Gray, their eldest child and only daughter, lived with her doctor husband and family in Connersville. She arrived red eyed and deeply distressed but unaware that worse would soon follow when her young daughter would be hit by a car and killed crossing 38th Street by the Fairgrounds. Now it was back to Flanner and Buchanan for the real thing.

After it was over, Mr. Freihofer chose to grieve alone and refused invitations to eat with us. However, in anticipation of a trip to visit young Walter, the son in Michigan, he gave us a set of keys to collect his mail and put it in his apartment. It was a Saturday, six weeks later. I had a customer at Banner Whitehill when I was called to the phone. It was Ambrose. Finding the Freihofer mailbox full, he had taken the mail in to their apartment to find old Walter Freihofer, sixty eight, dead. He was sitting in his chair, a book on his lap and his pipe on his chest. He'd been dead for days. Poor Ambrose only managed to get ahold of Cecil Freihofer by phone. He became hysterical. Two sudden deaths, in six weeks, in a family with so much love was truly a low point for us so early in our lives. From then on, we never lost touch with Reno, more correctly William, or Bill, and Joanie and their brood of wonderful children. For many years it was a tradition to drop by their home on Christmas Eve to have a drink while helping decorate the tree.

Before closing the chapter on Flanner and Buchanan, I'm reminded of a still unsolved mystery which, I believe, dates back to the nineteen twenties, or thirties. A distinguished German female scientist had come to Indianapolis to do research. She found a downtown carriage house in which to live and soon met, and fell in love with, Mr. Flanner's daughter Janet. Such a liaison was clearly not what the Flanners had in mind for their daughter. When the German lady failed to show up in the lab, one morning, police were notified and her carriage house was found empty but for a bloody bed. To this day no trace of her has been found. However, Janet Flanner left

Indianapolis never to return. She became a writer and settled in Paris for many years as correspondent for the New Yorker magazine. For many years, under the *nom de plume* of "Genet," she wrote Letter from Paris, for American consumption.

Not long into our tenancy, we crossed swords with the Meadows Management. Our cleaning lady, Katie Winston, used to bring her tiny daughter to work and install her in a play-pen outside our living-room window. When informed that this practice must stop immediately, I asked why in view of the fact that such a set-up was a common sight throughout the complex. Evidently Katie and daughter were the wrong color. Well, speaking of color, that order was a red rag to a bull. We knew that Indianapolis was rife with segregation, but the Meadows had been government funded which, in theory at least, made discrimination illegal. The row that Ambrose and I made in the office could be heard well beyond its four walls. In the end, we got our way but we never felt at home in the Meadows after that especially as the Bevans, who were about to have an addition to the family, had moved into a larger place. Before moving out, they also had a run-in with the management.

There was a play-pool behind the building where Simon, along with other neighborhood kids, was splashing about. Suddenly an infuriated mother was banging on Pam's door. She was so apoplectic that she was almost incoherent. Simon was naked! "Yes, I know" said Pam, "it's hot." Clearly, the gravity of the situation had entirely escaped her. It was bad enough that Katie, aged four, was running around topless but that a two year old, not even circumcised, boy should be in the pool in the altogether was, if not criminal, certainly unforgivable. Just as well that they had given notice that they would be leaving at the end of the month.

In the summer time, we loved to swim. The best and most convenient pool was Broad Ripple. We only swam there once because it was "whites only." Instead, we joined the jolly masses at Westlake where we could swim and picnic till dark and then enjoy an outdoor movie.

Dad visited us for the second time while we lived in the Meadows. His first visit had been some two months after our arrival from England when we lived at 402 North Delaware Street. As overseas secretary to the YMCA, his job brought him to the states every couple of years so he would always arrange to take a short vacation with us. No doubt he was doing his best to build a relationship with me but, in all honesty, he was far more comfortable with Ambrose. We had so little in common that, in order to avoid confrontation, we never discussed anything of consequence. Sadly, the same can be said for all my immediate family. As her first born, my mother loved me dearly and I did my best to reciprocate but failed to make a very good job of it. With a four and a half year gap between my birth and that of Sheila we never became close especially as Mary was less than two years younger than Sheila. The one thing that we all shared was to have been born and brought up in a colonial family where lack of stability is the norm.

Ambrose comes from a much more settled background. Apart from childhood holidays in the Scottish borders, he'd always lived within a hundred miles of London until he met me. I felt more at home with his family than with my own.

We were in the Meadows the first time Frank and Prue Smith came to stay with us. Frank was international secretary to Alcoholics Anonymous so ere long, he and Prue made friends with a motley group of Hoosier ex-drunks. In no time their pals included several movers and shakers and, at a special ceremony, they were presented with the "keys to the city of Indianapolis" by the Mayor. After that visit, they were scheduled to return to England on a ship sailing from Savannah, Georgia. With that in mind, on the advice of Prudence Douglas, we set off to vacation in the Cape Romaine Wildlife Refuge.

Slightly north of Charleston S.C. there is a guest house, on Bull's Island, in the heart of the protected area. To get there we took a lonely road till we reached a telephone box. A call to the guest house produced a boat to take us there. Meanwhile we parked our car in a field at the water's edge. On arrival we were greeted with the news that we might be in for a hurricane. Our two anticipated days turned into six. Fortunately, the house survived but the surrounding forest was decimated. Once it was all over, we donned special mosquito proof clothing and set forth to inspect the damage. The tractor, that we were supposed to ride on, had an air intake that quickly clogged with so many mosquitoes that it broke down. Thankfully, on returning to the mainland, the car was unscathed and Ambrose's parents managed to get to their boat on time.

A letter from Cecil Gould, in London, informed us that he was soon to embark on a lecture tour to the States and that the Herron Museum of Art, Indianapolis, would mark the midpoint of the trip. Having done similar tours before, he found fawning matrons anathema, but nearly impossible to escape. He would love to stay with us but please protect him from that monstrous hoard of women.

Our phone rang. A voice said, "This is Mrs. Clowes." "Good evening, Mrs. Clowes." I replied. "Mr. Peat informs me that Mr. Gould is to be your house guest when he lectures at our Museum. Is that so?" Yes indeed." I said. "Well, in that case, may I invite you both to dinner before his lecture?" "That's very kind of you," I spluttered, "but he will be tired from all his travels so we plan a quiet dinner here." After a prolonged pause, she said, "Do you know who I am? This is Mrs. George Clowes." "Oh! Yes indeed," I answered, "Ambrose and I were thrilled to see your wonderful collection of old masters on display at Herron in the fall." "Well," she asked, "don't you think Mr. Gould would like to see the paintings?" "He'll be with us for a few days," I said, "so I wonder if it would be possible to visit your house one day, without disturbing you, to have a look around?" It was agreed that I should phone her after his arrival and, hopefully, he would agree to a visit which would include afternoon tea. In the event, that's what we did and so I met Mrs. Clowes for the first time. As a grand dame who had been an arbiter of good taste in Indianapolis, who knew and was known by absolutely everybody who was anybody she was at a loss to figure out where I'd sprung from.

A few weeks later, John Stegeman came to stay with us. He was scheduled to give a lecture, at the Herron Museum, on Sir Joshua Reynolds, eighteenth century British portraiture being his specialty. Like Cecil, he was a friend from London days, now Director of the Montreal Art Museum. Another call was initiated by Mrs. Clowes. She very much hoped that Mr. Stegeman was less skittish about accepting invitations than Mr. Gould, and would we all dine with her before his lecture? After all, I had probably noticed her lovely painting of Mrs. Thomas Watkinson Paylor, by Sir Joshua, hanging over the dining room mantelpiece? Indeed I had and yes we would.

Not long after John Stegeman's visit, a third call from Mrs. Clowes invited me to tea to meet her son, Allen. They had a proposal to make. Dr. Clowes, who had died eighteen months before, had set up a Clowes Foundation which included an endowment and most of the collection of paintings. It transpired that the family was on the horns of a dilemma. Mrs. Clowes was in no mind to part with the paintings. The IRS agreed that she could keep them on condition that she pays inheritance tax. As most of them had been acquired very reasonably during the depression, their value had so much appreciated that she couldn't afford the tax. The only acceptable course of action would be to open the house, to the public, on a regular basis. This is where I came in.

Westerley, the Clowes home in Golden Hill, would be open to the public one afternoon a week. I would guide people around telling them about the paintings, furniture and artifacts and answering questions. As there were no signs to welcome people and the only publicity was by word of mouth, we had very few visitors. That suited me to perfection as I could devote my time to reading and studying the files. The few visitors which we had were asked to sign a guest book for tax purposes. At the end of the first year, the IRS was quite put out by the dismal showing. Unless we could show a marked increase in attendance either the collection would be forfeited or inheritance tax paid. From then on, we opened two days a week and I recorded radio commercials to invite people in. That was a turning point. Soon, we had so many people coming to visit that I began to train extra guides, the most faithful of whom was Diana Jackson, heavily pregnant with her second son Craig.

Diana was beautiful. See had a swanlike neck and was remarkably erudite with a penchant for poetry. At the same time, when it came to understanding the male libido she was singularly naive. Not only was her highly respected, financially astute husband having an affair with a male beautician, but her joyfully anticipated son was destined to be gay and totally immune to the infallible courses of counseling inflicted upon him. Today he lives happily with his long term companion in California.

All in all 1960 was a year to remember. Having a secure part time job with the Clowes Collection, coupled with saved commission money from my job at Banner Whitehill, I was able to attend Butler University. With allowances made for my London diploma I could get a teaching degree in eighteen months. All my relations seemed to have been in education or the church. Since the latter, in my opinion was a con game, I settled for the former and became a Butler student bicycling daily to Jordan Hall for classes.

Much else was happening at the same time. We had decided to rent half a double on the south side of Fall Creek Parkway just east of Delaware Street but, before moving, we invited Allen and Mrs. Clowes to dinner as we had been their guests on a number of occasions. On account of the Avondale Summer Playhouse, in the marquee, they knew where the Meadows apartments were located and were probably curious to see what kind of dwellings people in straightened circumstances inhabited.

We had done our best to turn what was, frankly, a sow's ear into some semblance of a silk purse. Ours was the only apartment in a complex of six hundred with window boxes. Working at Banner Whitehill, I had been able to secure pieces of furniture, after a final reduction, with an employee's discount. Our prize purchase was a so-called "party set" made by the Heritage Company. It consisted of a fifty four inches round cherry table with a central marble inset. It was lower than a dining table but higher than a coffee one. With it came four armless upholstered chairs with cabriole legs. They doubled as sitting-room chairs. While the nation's supply of plastic was being diverted to the manufacturing of hoola-hoops for kids, fondue parties were the latest adult craze and "party sets" such as ours were designed with that purpose in mind.

Unable to compete with the customary elegance of a Westerley dinner party we would introduce the Clowes' to immersing cubes of steak into a fondue pot kept boiling in the table center, above a flame. Ramekins of sauces, such as béarnaise, were to be on the table within reach. As each person had his or her own dish of raw meat with a few color coded skewers it was nobody's fault but your own if your beef was either overcooked or still quivering. By way of dessert we had decided to serve *crêpes Suzette*. With that in mind we had invested in an electric skillet complete with a thermostat in the handle. To allow maximum time for socializing, we would prepare the crepes before our guest's arrived. They could be kept warm in the oven. The grated orange rind and Cointreau sauce would be heated at the last minute. Needless to say, with preparations taking longer than Tante Marie's cook-book had indicated, we were not only running late but, in all directions at once like beheaded chickens, without noticing that the stick of butter was sitting in the lidded skillet set at maximum heat. A sheet of flame greeted us as the lid was removed and within seconds thick smoke filled the apartment. We could hardly breathe and our eyes were burning when, punctual to the minute, our guests arrived. Mrs. Clowes, soon to be nicknamed Duchess, was serenely gracious and declared our fog-bound apartment "charming." Half an hour with the aid of a fan, plus opening the windows, returned the atmosphere to a tolerable level and the evening was declared a somewhat qualified success.

Allen and his mother were much involved in plans for a concert hall in memory of Dr. Clowes. By locating it on the Butler University campus, rather than downtown, it would be possible to finance the project with private donations. First, and foremost, it was to be the home of the Indianapolis Symphony Orchestra. Dr. Clowes had helped in the orchestra's creation, many years earlier, with Ferdinand Schaefer as conductor. He had been chairman of the board during Sevitsky's tenure, as second conductor, and was instrumental in saving the Maestro's life, at a concert, shortly after the latter had initiated a torrid affair with the harpist. Mme. Sevitsky, an opera prima donna in her own right, having discovered the infidelity, was attending the concert seated next to Dr. Clowes in their regular box in the Murat Theater. While her philandering husband was on the podium, she produced a pistol out of her handbag with the intention of terminating his transgressions abruptly, and permanently. Fortunately, a glint of steel caught the good doctor's eye and his swift response allowed the concert to reach its scheduled conclusion with barely a noticeable blip. John Johanson and Evans Woollen were the chosen architects for Clowes Hall. Jock Bevan would design beautiful brochures for the grand opening. When not

139

being used for symphony concerts it would be used for Broadway shows, ballets and operas with Allen as impresario.

In order to gauge what kind of plays would attract the public, Allen Clowes bought an old movie house, on Central Avenue and Fall Creek Parkway North Drive. It was called the Zaring Theater. Travis Selmeier, Jim Stehlin and Jim Wills were hired to build a stage and dressing rooms to adapt the vaguely Egyptian looking building for its new use. They did such an excellent job that they became permanent fixtures not only at the Zaring but later at Clowes Hall. Allen and his crew managed and manned the theater throughout its two year life. One year they ran it as a repertory theater presenting a variety of popular shows from drawing room comedies to Sandy Wilson's musical *The Boy Friend.* This last, required our services as we still talked English English rather than the Hoosier version. The other year, we enjoyed a variety of imported shows often starring big names such as Tallulah Bankhead, Agnes Moorehead and Dame Judith Anderson who gave a riveting performance of Medea. Above the box office lobby was a lobby with a bar. It was open before and after the show as well as during intermissions. We had regularly changing art exhibitions on the lobby walls and all the art was for sale. The Clowes attic contained an abundance of unwanted pictures which had once been hung around the house, in the days of comparative penury, before insulin put El Grecos and Rembrandts within reach. We only sold a few pictures out of the Zaring but, at that point, every penny raised was being funneled into the Clowes Hall building fund.

Another event, to occur in 1960, was the addition of baby George to the Bevan family. He was born at Coleman Hospital, in Indianapolis, where Pam described the treatment they received as "barbaric" and vowed never again to face a confinement in the United States. Having delivered her first two children in England she had grounds for comparison. At that time, the US had the highest number of deaths per hundred thousand births in the industrial world. Even more alarming, Marion County, where Indianapolis sits, had the highest number of infant deaths of any county in the country.

In order to assimilate and become comfortable in our new life, we stayed stateside for nearly three years. True, the previous Christmas and New Year we had gone to stay with Vera Moody in Jamaica, but we had not visited England in spite of much urging to do so. That summer we made a trip to Britain and Denmark, armed with eight millimeter Kodak movies which we had taken, and carefully edited, to make Indianapolis appear only marginally inferior to Paris. The Monument with its cascading fountains, and pot-bellied bears, had a certain charm especially when shown against a background of the Columbia Club and Christchurch Cathedral. Likewise University Square with Stirling Calder's enchanting fountain of dancing children was lovely, when filmed through flowering trees towards the Athletic Club. Of course one always had to pick up scads of old newspapers and a medley of other discarded junk before shooting and, even then, it was hard to avoid the hobos flaked out on rusty benches.

We decided against filming any part of War Memorial Plaza. In those days, it boasted nary a tree nor a blade of grass. From the War Memorial to the Public Library, it was one vast soul-destroying sheet of crumbling concrete on which were a couple of decommissioned tanks along with a few old anti-aircraft guns. I rather think there was an old fighter plane as well but I can't be sure as I've devoted half a lifetime trying to wipe the depressing scene from my memory.

A second movie of suburban Indianapolis had been far less of a challenge. Some of the loveliest gardens in the city were annually on show during the first weekend in May. The event raised money for Park School for boys, which was soon to be joined to Tudor Hall, a private girl's school. Perhaps the most impressive garden belonged to Nicholas Noyes on Sunset Lane. The forty acre estate had vistas down to the White River that put us in mind of the landscaping of Capability Brown. There was a bucolic lake fed by a babbling stream running through an herbaceous rock garden.

The Holcomb garden, today an estate of houses and condominiums, was even larger if considerably less tasteful. It contained a ravine which was described as a Japanese garden. True, it boasted an assortment of temple lights, vases and Buddhas, with the odd bamboo fountain and some bonsai trees, but no attempt had been made to tame the indigenous plantings. Truly shocking, however, was a small contemplative circle where one could sit. Mr. Holcomb called it his "World Garden." When he traveled, he took a small pick axe which he used to smash off bits of famous landmarks such as Britain's Houses of Parliament, Notre Dame, in Paris and the Taj Mahal etc. All this ill-gotten loot would wind up cemented into his "World Garden" with little bronze labels to identify the item's provenance. To quote W.S. Gilbert, "I've got a little list of society offenders who might well be underground and who never would be missed." He's definitely on my list in spite of the gifts of a carillon and observatory to Butler University's campus.

So impressed were our English friends with our documentaries, that we soon had a steady stream of them coming to see the place first hand. Patric O'Keeffe came, loved it and kept coming back. The same is true of Ann Wells and Yanie LeBas. We've long since lost count of the number of times they've been over to vacation with us. Pussy and Pixie came once, the former with an open mind but, the latter to find fault with everything. She even complained about the arrangement of clouds in the sky! We took them all over the place including New Orleans. The "Big Easy" might have been seen as having a modicum of charm had we not spotted a man, just as we entered the French Quarter, who locked eyes with butch Pixie and followed it up with an obscene gesture. Patric, on the other hand, had a rather less jaundiced first impression.

On arrival he was immediately accosted by a man who greeted him as follows. "Hi, gorgeous! I'd like to help you get the wrinkles out!"

All our European visitors found Indiana's drinking laws quite ludicrous. If you bought a beer in the supermarket and the teller was underage she would have you lean across the counter to push the appropriate key. Then you had to sack the item yourself as if it were radioactive. Nobody was allowed to stand at any bar that sold alcohol. If the bar had stools, men could sit on them and order a drink which had to be consumed while seated. However women could not sit on bar stools. If there were tables and chairs, women could sit there and order a drink but if a man at the bar wished to join the lady, he could only do so by leaving his drink where it was to be delivered, in due course, by the bartender. These, and other seemingly preposterous laws, seem to me to be the product of a general psychosis brought about as a result of being the only country on Earth with no clear nationality. Let me explain.

If you're from Australia you're Australian, from Finland you're Finnish or from Lebanon you're Lebanese, but you're nothing at all if you're from the United States. Many citizens claim to be Americans. Of course that's true, but it hardly describes their nationality in view of the fact that the same holds true of all inhabitants of the double continent from Cape Horn to the Bering Straits. After all, Brazilians, Canadians, and Mexicans are just as American as citizens of the United States.

This brings me to the serious problem of Hoosieria, the country that never was. Every Midwesterner knows that citizens of the great state of Indiana are Hoosiers, not Indianans. To date, nobody is certain why that should be, even though scholarly research into its etymology has been ongoing for at least a century. Rather than re-hash theories of its origin, let's discuss pronunciation. The word is pronounced "WHO shur" and the state they inhabit is pronounced "INdeeANuh."

Two twentieth century British Prime Ministers, Winston Churchill and Harold McMillan had mothers from the United States. In the latter case, she was from Greencastle, Indiana, where her father had been instrumental in founding Depauw University. When Mr. McMillan flew in to be feted and honored, in the best tradition of Hoosier hospitality, Ambrose and I, carrying little Union Jacks, joined the greeters. The tiny Indianapolis airport, then known as Weir Cook, was his point of arrival. Down the aircraft steps and onto the red carpet the honorable Prime Minister walked up to a podium, set up with microphone, to greet the expectant crowd. Having failed to do his homework, he succeeded in putting both feet in his mouth during his opening sentence to whit: I am simply delighted to be here in " INdeeAREnur" as I myself am half "WHOzeeARE." The welcoming committee broke into gales of laughter leaving poor Harold to wonder if perhaps his flies were open to reveal tartan boxers!

Nineteen twenty five saw the start of The Hoosier Salon, an annual juried art exhibition. It was modeled on the French traditional Salons. In all probability, the average Frenchman is no better educated than the late Prime Minister with regard to the niceties of Mid-Western usage. However, on reading the printed word, a French speaker could be forgiven for pronouncing "OOzeeAy," which in conjunction with "salon," sounds authentic. Pronounced "Whoshur," it might be more appropriately paired with "saloon!"

The exhibitions favored representation art, and were held in the auditoriums of Ayres and Blocks. There was a permanent office and small gallery in the ill-fated Test Building. I know something about these matters because, about 1963, I became "Art Critic" for a monthly magazine called The Indianapolis Downtowner. I continued in that role until publication ceased five years later. The managing editor was Gene Slaymaker, a well respected local radio and TV anchor. His wife Martha was a gifted artist. We still own one of her earliest paintings, traded for a window air-conditioner. Researching monthly articles rapidly expanded our circle of friends and acquaintances. I'm forever in Gene's debt for his trust in me and for giving me the freedom to explore whatever avenue caught my youthful imagination. But I digress.

No sooner had Jock and Pam bought an old farmhouse at 4949 N. Illinois Street, than Pam found herself pregnant again. Recalling the horrors of Coleman Hospital, careful planning was called for. She would return to England with all three children for a year. Jock, who was now self-employed doing architectural renderings, would remain in Indianapolis in their house and we would share it. Rather reluctantly we terminated our half double rental on Fall Creek. It had been a great house for parties and for enjoyable walks along the river bank. The first time that Mrs. Clowes visited, she returned to the sitting room following a necessary trip to our barely adequate bathroom with the encouraging observation that we had a bath just like Mrs. DuPont's! Somehow, I suspect she had stretched the truth to a considerable extent. I dare say that Mrs. DuPont's tub stood proud of the floor, on cast iron ball and claw feet, but very much doubt that hers lacked most of its original enamel or was equipped with mismatched old taps and a perishing rubber stopper. Anyway, move we did.

The Bevan house was ours to share with Jock for all of 1961. Right off, we realized what a sensible move we had made. It was a mere five minutes by bike to Butler University and even less to School 86 where I was about to do my student teaching under Ida Lobraico, a dearly loved elementary art teacher. Under her watchful eye, I learned more about interacting with students in a few weeks, than in all the college education courses combined. Day one she took me into a fourth grade class. Each kid had made a picture which had been taped to the chalk board and I was to choose the "best" one. This was not what I wanted to do, but do it I must, so I spent much time admiring sundry qualities in each work and saying that I would love to choose all of them. Finally, the rubber had to hit the road. I selected one to the obvious delight of the artist amidst a sea of disappointed classmates. Would that it had been the end of the assignment... but no. Miss Lobraico asked me, as an art critic, to explain what made me choose that particular work. "Well" I said, "it's about as fierce a lion as I've ever seen in the zoo." "It's not a lion" wailed young Roddy Usher, "She's my pussy cat."

Roddy was the youngest of Rod and Alice's four children. He grew up to be an Eli Lilly executive. His mother is a gifted artist in several media though she's best known as a sculptor. The family has been lifelong friends. While their children were still young, Rod, a professor of history at Butler, got a sabbatical to do research at the British Library. Westminster Abbey was under restoration at the time so Alice took the opportunity to carve a stone finial for one of the transepts. We still have, and treasure, a bronze female torso which she created some fifty years ago.

What had been nicknamed "Clowes Hole" was beginning to shape up into a multipurpose performing art center. Once the workmen had packed up for the day, we made a habit of inspecting the latest bit of construction. On the day that the official cornerstone laying was to take place, several well intentioned friends had sent corsages to Mrs. Clowes. Not surprisingly, they were a motley collection of freesias, roses, or whatever else the good folks had deemed appropriate. To avoid hurting anybody's feelings she alighted from her Austin Princess limousine, for the dedication, wearing the lot. Had they not been pinned all over the upper front of her coat, she might well have been mistaken for a floral delivery person.

On several occasions, during that year, Jock flew to England to check up on Pam and the children. During one such absence, Vera Moody was to come and stay with us from Jamaica. She notified us that her flight from New York was due to arrive at twelve noon. Sure enough, there was a scheduled flight that did just that so we met it at the airport. As she wasn't on it, and another flight was due in about three hours, we had lunch and read the paper, without going home, in anticipation of her coming on that one. When she still hadn't shown up we returned to the house to find her sitting in the garden, with her luggage beside her, reading a book! Having looked up Indianapolis on a small globe, she figured that it was a suburb of Chicago. Once at O'Hare, she got a taxi but, when the driver saw the address, he advised her to take another plane!

During her visit, we were invited to dinner at Westerley by Mrs. Clowes. The Duchess later confessed, to us, that Mrs. Moody had turned out to be one of the most delightful and erudite ladies she had ever met, but that she had been quite concerned beforehand because it was the first time she had ever entertained a colored person!

Clowes Hall opened in 1963. It was the only theater of its type, in the States, to be built, since Lincoln Center in New York City, and as such, grabbed national attention. We enjoyed three days of opening festivities including the world premiere of a work created around Dr. Clowes' initials, G.H.A.C, by Bernard Heiden. Unfortunately, the Austin Princess chose to misbehave on the grand opening night, while the event was receiving national television coverage. Just as the Clowes party stepped out of the limousine, it suffered an intestinal problem and dumped all its oil there and then. In other respects, the whole affair was widely applauded and the Metropolitan Opera chose the venue for six weeks of rehearsals and performances for the Traveling Company.

Among the first year's offerings was Verdi's opera *La Traviata.* The famous European designer Rolf Gérard was to do the sets and costumes. This involved his spending several weeks in Indianapolis where he was housed in the Lincoln Hotel, downtown. As a life-long friend of the Regendanzs, we were alerted to his imminent arrival and warned that he was apt to be vague and had hardly ever set foot outside a major city. He was certainly a nervous nelly and never seemed to know which of his several languages he was currently speaking. He found the city thoroughly confusing and not a little frightening so he was most appreciative of our help. At the Plaza, in New York, there were letter slots in the hallways for sending mail. The Lincoln lacked that convenience along with almost everything else that he was used to. Outside his room was a noisy air-conditioning unit from which the management had to retrieve a number of his letters which otherwise might have caused a fire and, in any case, stood no chance of reaching their destination. The sidewalks presented hazards at every step. Bits of concrete jutted out, at all angles, from random chuck-holes. The cracks sprouted knee-high weeds. The only place to have a half way acceptable meal was the King Cole restaurant. It was below ground on the east side of Meridian Street at the Circle. While the food and drink were less than stellar, the ambience was reassuringly womb-like. With few working street lights and with nobody but criminals in the streets at night, the two block walk to the King Cole presented poor Rolf with an almost insurmountable problem. All three of us were greatly relieved when his Metropolitan work was done. Now he could return to his secluded Avenue Foch home in Paris.

With Clowes Hall open, performing arts offerings in Indianapolis improved almost overnight, and we were able to enjoy a wider spectrum of shows than ever before. One Broadway show was cancelled when Herman Krannert, who was on the board, heard that it involved nudity so the defunct Circle Theater was re-opened for *Hair*. Another event was to showcase an up and coming young singer called Barbra Streisand. Allen Clowes invited us to go as the sale of tickets had been pitiful. We arrived to find the Hall nearly empty so we sat near the stage. With a bar stool as her only prop, she sang in her inimitable sultry way which evidently delighted the sparse young audience. By intermission, the three of us had heard enough and departed never expecting to hear her name again, but then that was a couple of years before *Funny Girl*. Flanders and Swann came, touring with their British *farrago* called *At the Drop of a Hat*. The next day, they came to tea with Mrs. Clowes. Afterwards, I took them on a tour of the collection. They were not only very knowledgeable about almost all the artists but they were astonished that such treasures had found their way to Indianapolis.

After a recital given by the distinguished pianist, Arthur Rubinstein, he was invited back to Westerley for refreshments. As it was about 10:30 p.m. Mrs. Clowes had arranged for the help to leave a cold snack on a tray for the old gentleman. He never ate before concerts, so he was hungry. When the plate which was put beside him in the library disappeared in the blink of an eye, Mrs. Clowes asked him if he would like some more. "That depends on what's for dinner," he said. Nothing had been planned, the help had long since departed, and neither Allen nor his mother knew the first thing about cooking, so Ambrose and I headed to the kitchen while the great man ploughed through a fine bottle of Lafitte. In due course we produced a steak and presumably something to go with it. Evidently it was to his liking for, as far as I recall, nothing was left on his plate. Among the interesting things we learned was that he always traveled with his own two pianos. One he had just played. The other had gone to his next destination to be tuned prior to his arrival.

Recalling that evening, reminds me of a story which I heard the Duchess tell on more than one occasion. The family was at Woods Hole for the summer as usual. Professor J.B.S. Haldane, the eccentric evolutionary biologist was there so he was invited to lunch. Being both an atheist and Marxist, and as Mrs. Clowes understood little of his scholarship, conversation was a challenge. As guest of honor, the butler, Clarence, brought in the fish for the professor to help himself first, which he did. He lifted the entire fish, which had been intended for all of them, on to his plate. Fortunately, another one was in the pantry in case anybody wanted a second helping. While Clarence was out of the room, collecting the second fish, the Duchess made desperate small talk in the hope that Haldane would fail to notice his gaffe. She needn't have worried. He was busy wolfing the lot, with obvious relish, blissfully unaware of the shortfall he'd caused. "Next time you're in the States please bring your wife to visit us," she said. "Oh no," he replied, "she will never come back here. You see she can't stand the dreadful American food!" What he thought of her food is not recorded but, soon after that visit, he went permanently to India, took Indian citizenship and became a vegetarian. Asked a question concerning the possibility that there is a creator, what might be uppermost in the creator's mind? He replied, "An inordinate fondness for beetles." Forgive the pun but that ought to give one food for thought. After that unfortunate luncheon, Mrs. Clowes always had the help offer her the food first so that any uninitiated guest could observe how they were expected to behave when their turn came.

This brings me to the subject of establishment dinner parties. With minor adjustments, most of them followed the same format. One would arrive around 6:30 p.m. Most hostesses hired Ernie as bartender giving one a curious sensation of déjà vu. As the WASP guest list varied little, Ernie, knowing everybody's favorite tipple, had their drinks ready by the time the maid had hung up their coats. The length of time allowed for preprandial drinking varied depending on the venue. At Westerley, half an hour was allotted. At that point, Irene would enter the library and say, "Madam, dinner is ready." If you hadn't finished your drink, you were invited to bring it to the table. There you looked for your place card before pulling out the adjoining chair for the lady assigned to sit next to you. It was a rare occasion that failed to have equal numbers of men and women. Equal numbers were invariably invited and, as Mrs. Clowes told us, "once you've accepted an invitation you show up unless you're dead." Before sitting down, it was as well to make a mental note of who was sitting on the other side of the table as many a hostess had such an enormous floral centerpiece that it totally eclipsed several of one's fellow guests. Once seated, the first order of business was to admire the beautiful plate in front of you, for in a moment a black hand camouflaged with a Mickey Mouse glove would exchange it for a cheaper one. Depending on one's hostess, it was often a good idea to have your drink topped up, en route to the dining room, as many houses only served water or iced tea with dinner. Those who offered wine often stretched a single bottle to a dozen glasses. Apart from Kurt and Kitty Pantzer, those who did serve wine were as likely as not to serve an inappropriate one at the wrong temperature. The help served all the women first, beginning with the oldest dowager. Ambrose has always maintained that the real reason for this curious practice is that men like to have their food hot, noting that in polite society, nobody starts eating until everybody has been served.

At old money dinner parties the hostess was seldom concerned with dietary considerations as the guests were never Jewish, Muslim or, heaven forbid, touched with a tar brush. Peculiar to the Clowes household was the dessert ritual. It required each guest to be alert to the possibility of imminent social disaster. The help would place a dessert plate, on which sat a cut glass finger bowl of water, with a flower in it, in front of each person. Between the bowl and the plate, there was a doily of exquisite Brussels or Venetian lace. For guests unaccustomed to this formality, the possibilities could be daunting. Should one raise the bowl, with both hands, to quaff, and, if so what about the flower? Some are edible but others, like certain mushrooms, can be fatal. As one's table setting usually included a dessert spoon and fork, the unwary guest could be forgiven for spooning the water up like soup. As perfume was added to the water, it might well turn out to be an acquired taste. In fact, the diner was expected to remove both doily and bowl and place them on the table. In theory, one could rinse off a finger or two that might have come in contact with sauce or gravy from the previous course but, if you did so, great care should be taken to avoid splashing condiments or guests. Many people failed to address the problem until the help proffered dessert. At that moment, a knee jerk reaction could spell trouble. Failure to move the doily, along with the bowl, and you might wind up with a mouth full of mousse flavored lace!

At almost all the thirty or forty establishment homes the dinner party formula from cocktails through coffee and liquors, in the drawing room, to the fond farewell around 10:00 p.m. was highly predictable. The one exception was Liz Fortune, a rotund and raucous grand dame from Texas. She, and her late husband, Pete, had built the house with entertainment in mind. The forecourt was flanked by a pair of pavilions which were connected to the main house by sweeping colonnades giving rise to the suggestion that it would serve as the Vatican filling station. Whereas most hostesses limited dinner parties to twelve people, with Liz, forty or more was not uncommon. Apart from a fountain, her spacious front hall was nearly devoid of furniture so it could comfortably accommodate half a dozen circular tables. She and Pete had bought an enormous and splendid old Paris dinner service. In some sizes she had dishes for as many as sixty people. Every piece contained a different French mythological scene. Priceless as it was, it was always used for dinner parties. Whenever it was remarked upon she would say, "It belonged to Princess Mary." When asked, "Which Princess Mary?" she'd reply, "The French one!" Her Houston decorator's name was Otto Zenke and her fountain of historical misinformation could be reliably traced to him.

From Colnaghi's gallery, in London, she and Pete had acquired a large Roman male torso, provenance Leptis Magna.

It was installed on a plinth at the end of a hallway. At a dinner, which Liz gave, to honor John Walsh, the new director of the Getty, at Malibu, we were enjoying cocktails when she steamed up to him saying, "Ah! Mr. Walsh, do come with me. I want to show you my torso. I'm told that it's a heroic size, but you can judge that for yourself when you see it!" The poor man was terrified.

Her cocktail hours had a habit of lasting for several, and many a guest was three sheets to the wind well before dinner appeared. On one such occasion, several guests were thunderstruck to see a stark naked man walking past the window for a skinny dip in the pool. By the time he emerged, all the guests were watching. One look and my suspicions were confirmed. It was Ambrose!

Mind you, a previous incident beside Liz Fortune's pool had shocked me more. A few of us were sitting under an umbrella at a glass topped table enjoying a refreshing drink when a large lady joined us. "I'd like you to meet Josie Orr," said Liz. "Her husband Bob is our new Lieutenant Governor so they've just moved here from Evansville." Introductions complete she sat down next to me and her knee touched mine. As soon as I shifted my position, her knee followed and pressed mine hard till I was forced to look her in the eye. Without any preamble she leaned in close and whispered, "I don't have any underwear on!" Now I've always prided myself on having a fairly good memory but, in this case, I have no idea how I handled the situation. That she was eager for something became abundantly clear, a few weeks later, when she plopped down next to me on a sofa and wasted no time in reaching for my crotch. After Bob Orr's term as Governor he was appointed Ambassador to Singapore. There, Josie's behavior became so scandalous that she had to be flown back to the States.

At a summer barbeque given by Liz Fortune, the company with the cooking equipment was late. I spotted Mrs. Bowman Elder, at almost a hundred; she was the younger sister of

Evelyn Bartlett who, until she died at a hundred and nine, was the last inhabitant of the historic Bonnet House in Fort Lauderdale, Florida. Madeline Elder said, "Ian, do you think we're ever going to get something to eat or should I go home and make myself an omelet?" Next moment, I saw her seated with a plate on her lap sawing away at a chicken breast. "Well done!" I said. "How I wish it were!" she replied.

The Duke, and most recent Duchess, of Bedford arrived for two nights. I was selected to dance attendance throughout their visit. They were staying at the Essex House which, if possible, had less to recommend it than the Lincoln. They were in town to show slides of and speak about, Woburn Abbey, their stately home in England. The purpose was to attract much needed tourists. The Duke, to the manor born, was pleasant enough. His new wife was French, rude and demanding. The Hoosier matron who was currently president of the Women's Club sponsoring the Murat lecture, planned to take us out to dinner, that first night, to Woodstock Country Club. However, after one look at our hostess, the Duchess informed me that she planned a *malade imaginaire*. Their suite sitting room was filled with TV equipment and reporters. The Indianapolis Star had sent a pitifully timorous girl to interview this dragon.

To set the scene, the Duchess accepted the offer of some coffee. No sooner was it delivered, than she demanded, "Do I look like a truck driver?" to which the intimidated girl replied, "Why no Ma'am." "So why is my coffee in a mug?" After this inauspicious start it was downhill all the way. Her ladyship said that she and the Duke enjoyed discovering new restaurants while touring the country. "Do you and the Dook like Eyetalian food?" the neophyte asked hopefully. To this young reporter, the reply of the Duchess was both rude and incomprehensible. She said, "Perhaps you consider Italian food haute cuisine, but we don't." In a final desperate effort, the wretched girl asked Lady Bedford if they planned to have children? "What a ridiculous question," she replied. "Look at me. I'm forty seven, for Christ's sake, and thoroughly rusty!"

Having refused the President's dinner invitation, they dined, on my advice, at the King Cole. There some fawning diner, at a nearby table, recognizing them, put his plane and villa, on an island south of Puerto Rico, at their disposal! The next morning the Duchess told me that they planned to take up his offer next month. When I took them over to the backstage sitting room that had been set aside for them at the Murat theatre, we discovered that a dog had recently defecated in the middle of the rug. Seldom have I been happier to conclude an assignment than I was when they departed the following morning.

## Chapter Thirteen
### *A Home of Our Own*


As the time approached for Pam to give birth to Jessica, in England, we needed to plan another move. Having had six roofs over our heads in less than five years we decided to buy a house. Next door to Westerley was a charming one with a three acre garden separated only by the Spring Hollow Creek from the Clowes'. Mrs. Clowes urged us to buy it especially as the Ball family was prepared to let it go very inexpensively. We were sorely tempted but, when Ambrose did the math, we would have to do without annual trips to Europe. That seemed too high a price to pay.

We had become friends with Everett and Alexia Martin who had a pleasant four bedroom house at 3678 N. Delaware Street. For the previous couple of years, we four had shared a box at the Murat for the Symphony concerts, often preceded by delightful dinners at their house. They had moved to Indianapolis from New York City soon after we did. Everett had a job with a moving company and she had ideas well above her station.

To hear her tell it, her parents thought she was nuts. They had her institutionalized until she was thirty. Once released, she went to live in Paris where she worked for an up market decorating firm and met Everett, who was visiting France. Her maiden name was Samarin. She claimed Russian ancestry, which judging by the drama and threats of suicide in her life, may well be the case. She designed and made couture gowns and anything else with fabric such as draperies and upholstery. Throughout the house she had created curtains and hangings for every room. Sadly, she was a spendthrift. Alexia would think nothing of spending the morning at Ayres ordering everything from dinner services to several hats at a time, extravagances which Everett's salary couldn't support. The solution, she decided, was for Everett to find a job back in New York that would underwrite her lifestyle. To cut a long story short, they rented a mansion on long Island and we bought 3678 North Delaware Street in move-in condition. It was to be our home for the next twenty five years.

To coincide with moving into our first home, I applied for American citizenship. It seemed like a good idea. While working for my Butler degree, I had taken American history from Professor Emma Lou Thornbrough, an inspiring teacher who had now, along with her sister Gayle, became a friend and mentor. She sponsored my application and accompanied Dad and me to the Federal Building on the day I was to be accepted. Having answered all the test questions to his satisfaction, the examiner checked the forms I had filled out. He found an error. "I think you checked the wrong box here," he said and pointed out that I had marked that I would not bear arms. "That's right," I replied, "I'm not prepared to bear arms." He asked me if I had religious objections to doing so because that would be acceptable. Being an atheist, I couldn't claim that. Then he asked me how come I had been prepared to bear arms for the United Kingdom but balked at doing do for the United States. I answered by pointing out that I had been a thoughtless teenager at that time but now, as an adult, I could never bring myself to kill a fellow human being for political reasons. The friendly examiner really wanted to pass me so he tried one more idea. Now that I was over thirty, I was too old to be called up for military service so he suggested that either I check the "agree to bear arms" box or mark my reason for not doing so as "religious." Deciding that perjury would be a mistake, I waited another thirty years, before applying again for citizenship, by which time the requirements had changed.

To celebrate the achievement of my Butler bachelor's and the start of a new career as a tenure track teacher in the

Indianapolis Public Schools system, Mrs. Clowes presented me with an impressive set of the heaviest quality aluminum pots, pans and casseroles. We used it for years in blissful ignorance of its manifold health risks. If this book contains too many errors, please remind me, in the likely event that I will have forgotten, to lay the entire blame on carcinogenic cookware.

Life was good in Camelot, though events in Dallas would soon bring a reality check. In London we were merely plankton in a vast ocean but here in Indianapolis we were beginning to feel like gold-fish in a pond. Following symphony concerts, there were often parties to which we were invited. The Slaymakers were giving such a party after a concert starring David Oistrach. At the time, he was Russia's most celebrated violinist. With the Iron Curtain in place, few Russians were allowed to travel unescorted for fear of embarrassing defections of the Rudolph Nureyev variety. Mr. Oistrach was on his own when Martha came over to us to ask if we would drive him back to his hotel as he was tired. On the way he chatted in passable English about his flat in Moscow, his family and country dacha, but I wasn't paying much attention. An inner voice was saying, "Ambrose and Ian are you aware that unbeknownst to the Kremlin you've taken their prized virtuoso hostage along with his priceless fiddle?"

Among our first musical friends were the Indianapolis Symphony Orchestra conductor and his second wife. Izler Solomon's first wife had died shortly after they arrived in Indianapolis in 1956. Mrs. Goodman, an important symphony supporter and incorrigible busybody produced Betty as a replacement. Within months, Izler had gone from a life of tranquil domesticity into totally unfamiliar territory. Betty was a stunningly beautiful blond from Arizona. In their garden she had a swimming pool which she kept heated to one hundred and ten degrees Fahrenheit throughout the winter.

At post concert parties, she would herd her more adventurous guests into the dining room where a pile of towels awaited. There, reduced to birthday suits, she'd briefly open the French doors so that we could run the few steps through the snow into the pool. Meanwhile Izler and their more inhibited guests concluded the party in the drawing room. Outdoor swimming in zero weather could be challenging as one is obliged to keep most of one's head out of the water to minimize the risk of drowning. My ears were always first to feel the cold, like my hair, they soon iced over once you broke the surface. When news of the polar swimmers reached the drawing room, a tray of paper cups of booze would be assembled and some brave guest suitably muffled and gloved could be relied upon to keep us sated. By the time the last of the swimmers had reentered the dining room, the "establishment" guests had gone home and Betty was all set for body painting! I have to admit that Ambrose and I chickened out at that point. As this book is limited to my memoirs, I will refrain from reporting on any grand finale gossip.

Every Easter, Betty Solomon had an egg painting party. Bowls of fresh eggs and paint boxes would be distributed around the house and every guest was expected to paint at least one egg. She explained that you must take care not to crack the egg and eventually, within a year or two, the contents would dry up and rattle about inside the shell. As she did this annually, she knew what she was talking about. The drawing room contained several vitrines and a large, glass-inset coffee table all filled with painted eggs. An artist friend of hers had painted a rhea's egg, as a gift. Holding pride of place, she had it standing in the middle of the sofa table looking as impressive as anything in the Romanov Collection. Unfortunately, the artist had varnished it. One night Izler and Betty were awakened by a loud explosion downstairs. A putrid smell invaded the entire house. The egg's central drawing room location insured that miniscule particles of its contents penetrated every nook and cranny. Though the Solomons continued to live in the house while the room was cleaned and redecorated it was not weeks but months before the smell was completely eradicated. My intimate knowledge of that incident was brought about because I had arranged to bring my Wood High School students to meet the Solomons and see the egg collection. By the time their house was rehabilitated, the semester was over.

I realized, in a quasi apocalyptic flash, that only in a place like Indianapolis would we have such diverse opportunities. We were so fortunate to have wound up here. It was about then that a head hunter had the offer of a job, for Ambrose, with Texas Instruments. His salary would have had a big boost and he would soon be climbing the corporate ladder. In addition, with my teaching degree, I would be a shoe-in for a job in Texas. It took very little soul-searching, however, to turn the offer down. In spite of all its drawbacks, we had fallen in love with Indiana, in general, and Indianapolis, in particular. That love was beginning to be reciprocated. This was truly our home and the place where our expanding circle of friends lived.

Butler University, my recent alma mater, was one of only three universities in the country to grant degrees in dance. Consequently, the city has long been known for both classical ballet and modern dance troupes. Before being fully absorbed into Butler, the Jordan College of Dance was located at Washington Boulevard and 34th Street. I forget David's last name, but I see him still in British grey flannels and blue blazer. He had arrived at about the same time as we. In England, he had been a dancer with Sadler's Wells but retired early with a damaged Achilles tendon. He was on the Jordan faculty as was the venerable Margaret Saul, a renowned British ballet teacher.

Harry Schachter, from Louisville, had acquired Banner Whitehill, through a bank take-over, shortly before I started working there. It was not long before both he and Mrs. Schachter were finding greener pastures. Evelyn Schachter and Margaret Saul became a couple while Harry fell for a red headed knockout half his age. The writing was on the wall

160

before I left to attend Butler. Harry sold accounts receivable, emptied the registers and bolted to England with his mistress and whatever he could lay his thieving hands on before the authorities could catch up with him.

David, who was gay, had been friends with a lady called Mary Foreman in England. Before marrying, she had been a Thynn (i.e. from the family of the Marquess of Bath). Like many English aristocrats, she had teeth only marginally better arranged than the spikes on a barbed wire fence. After one had recovered from the initial visual shock, she was interesting and delightfully witty. David brought her to Indianapolis to escape an abusive relationship. Since World War II, during which she was in the Land Army, she had earned her living as Girl Friday to two high profile gay men. One was Ram Gopal, in those days the most famous Indian dancer in the world.

Ram came to Indianapolis where he gave a riveting performance in the Herron Auditorium. At a Meridian Hills Country Club dinner given in his honor, the polite conversation had centered upon regional differences in Indian music and dance. During a lull, Ram Gopal decided to scuttle Hoosier respectability once and for all. Sitting across the table was a man who'd sooner die than have anybody spot a chink in his heterosexual armor. Out of nowhere, Ram asked him, "Tell me, darling. Do you prefer men with, or without, hairy chests?" All eyes turned on the dancer's victim as the poor guy, turning red, spluttered an incoherent answer.

Mary Foreman's other London boss was the fashionable portrait photographer, Anthony Armstrong Jones. Though gay, he soon recognized which side his bread was buttered. Being good at his chosen profession, he got royal commissions and married the Queen's sister, Princess Margaret. Officially, the princess had only been in love once before. His name was Group Captain Peter Townsend, equerry to her father, divorced and nearly twice her age. In fact, long before the Townsend affair, she had been mentored by Princess Marina of Greece,

161

considered by many to be the best dressed woman in Britain. What was not generally known was that she was a lesbian. Marina was the widow of Margaret's youngest uncle, the gay Duke of Kent, whose hand had received a kiss from my tender lips in Newbattle Abbey. The Duke, incidentally, had been killed in a plane crash early in World War II. When the dowager Duchess of Kent recognized gay tendencies in Princess Margaret she introduced her to Sharman Douglas, the lesbian daughter of the US ambassador to Great Britain. Wind of the affair, soon reached Buckingham Palace and the unfortunate Douglas girl was promptly shipped back stateside.

This brings me to the ever popular, and intriguing, subject of human sexuality. So much has been written on the subject that you may be forgiven for thinking that there's nothing further to be discussed. What is more, I have no qualifications to justify my opinions. At the same time, as a gay man, well into his ninth decade, my perspective, on the matter, may differ from the norm. Let me begin by quoting an anonymous limerick.

A lesbian girl from Khartoum
Took a nancy boy to her room.
When they got into bed
She turned and said,
"Who does what and by which and to whom?"

Whatever absurd ideas such an unlikely liaison may conjure up, at least we should credit the Sudanese lady with an excellent command of English grammar.

Overwhelming evidence supports the theory that homosexuality has always existed throughout the animal kingdom rather than being an exclusively human condition. Nevertheless, since the Middle Ages, until quite recently, people have generally either condemned or shut a blind eye to homosexual practice. Dr. Alfred Kinsey at Indiana University, in the nineteen forties, went a long way towards shining a light on this formerly taboo subject. The Stonewall riots, thirty years later in New York, insured once and for all that the genie could no longer be returned to the bottle. Now, with public opinion moving in favor of same-sex marriage, the time seems ripe for this subject to be discussed freely and openly.

When it comes to falling in love, the animal kingdom is overwhelmingly attracted to the opposite sex. For obvious reasons, this is just as well. At the same time, a small minority are only sexually aroused by their own sex. It's certainly not a matter of choice. Another significant minority are bisexual. They should not be confused with homosexuals, who marry, may or may not have children, before recognizing their true sexual identity. These latter, usually divorce and, hopefully, find lasting happiness with a same-sex partner. Bisexuals, for the most part, cherish a partner of the opposite sex but find dalliances with their own sex hard to resist. Ambrose and I know, or have known, a number of people who fall into this category. For them it is important not to be found out for fear of wreaking the carefully maintained illusion of normal respectability. Many a spouse has departed this world in blissful ignorance. We gays seem to possess a sense that heterosexuals lack. For want of a better term, we call it "gaydar." Without having to exchange a word, our bisexual friends know that Ambrose and I are aware of that urge in them. I'm reasonably sure that a few of our bisexual friends never actually act out their homosexual fantasies. In any case, I have no intention of outing anybody from their chosen closet. If I do discuss anybody's affairs, the matter is so widely known that no trusts have been broken.

We've seen enough permutations of human behavior that nothing surprises us anymore. I admit to a mental block when it comes to transgender issues. Having known and liked several transgendered people, I'm deeply sympathetic to their situation. The problem, from my perspective is one of identity. Though I'm attracted to my own sex, I have no difficulty understanding heterosexuality. What baffles me is the question of who could be attracted to a transsexual. The matter being unresolved in my mind, let's move on.

Without exception, all our closest heterosexual friends are totally comfortable with homosexuals. With them it's a non-issue. Likewise, all our gay friends feel the same way about straights. Ambrose and I have never been drawn to mincing ninnies or the militant kind who eschew normal society. Before we all came out of the closet, most people thought that gays fell into one or other of those categories. In fact, they are the exception rather than the rule. Another unfortunate misconception is that gays are likely to be a menace in military showers. Almost never has that been the case. Even when a gay is tempted, gaydar saves the day. The old saying, "It takes one to know one," is really true. Nor is it the case that we are child molesters. A few are but overwhelmingly child molesters are heterosexual.

Dull as it sounds, we generally fall in love with people who share our values, are of much the same socio-economic background and are close to us in age. That having been said, gays have problems, some of their own making, that complicate their lives. In the straight world, when a financially successful man marries an attractive younger lady, the union is likely to meet with general approbation. The same is seldom the case in gay society. The kept young man is not treated with the same respect as his lover. That particular malaise can be traced back to childhood, usually well before signs of sexual orientation appear. Boys don't cry, they take care of girls and will grow up to be pillars of society with a lovely doting wife and children. While I'm not suggesting that such expectations are explicitly taught, our entire way of life, toys, clothes, haircuts, hobbies and sports foster such an outcome and devoted children don't want to disappoint their parents.

A case in point, involves the eldest son of our friends, Desmond and Janet Tivy. They were blind to any signs that

Matthew might not have inherited his parents sexual orientation, especially as he was developing with all their hoped for virtues. Classical music was always within earshot and living, as they did, next to Tanglewood, the Summer Festival was an exciting part of life. Desmond was doctor in residence for the Boston Symphony Orchestra and Janet ran the V.I.P. tent. Young Matthew could not only recognize the music coming over the airwaves but identify the orchestra and conductor responsible for the performance. His mother was a good cook and baker so, while his younger brothers, Robbie and Chris, were out playing ball, Matthew was helping in the kitchen. He would become a chef. To that end, he studied with some of the best in the business both here and in Europe. Not only did he become an outstanding chef but, with his musically attuned ear, he became fluent in French and Spanish.

From his parent's point of view, the capstone to his future promise of success was when Matthew and Jenn married. They settled in New York City where Matthew built a growing reputation in a variety of well known restaurants. Several months into their marriage, I recall asking Desmond how it was working out. "Just fine," he said, "they're totally joined at the hip." What none of us knew was that, devoted as he was to Jenn, the sexual spark wasn't there. Matthew was on the psychiatrist's couch. I have no doubt whatsoever that Matthew wanted to make a success of his marriage both for his parent's and Jenn's sake. After about six years, they admitted defeat and divorced. Jenn married an Englishman and Matthew became godfather to their first child. Keith Jameson Richard, a gifted tenor, headed for roles at the Metropolitan Opera, became Matthew's lover and soul mate. They were a perfect couple. The chef had finally found happiness so off to Massachusetts he went to bring the glad tidings to his parents. Far from sharing his joy, they were horrified. I'm sure they believed that their love for their son was unconditional but it was not. The son they believed in was actually a figment of their imagination.

Knowing that Ambrose and I were his parents' oldest friends he assumed, wrongly as it turned out, that his sexuality would be no more of an issue than ours. Matthew Tivy, as good a son as any parent could wish for, was crushed.

Back in New York, he let us know his feelings. With his permission, we wrote to his parents. Matthew, we pointed out, was by no means the first son to do everything possible to meet with parental approval by getting married in the belief that by tying the knot with a wonderful woman, he would permanently banish homosexual desire. As a doctor himself, Desmond should have known that there is no cure. Like skin color, it can not be changed, with the possible exception of Michael Jackson! In fairness to Janet and Desmond, they soon did a complete volte face and were soon thrilled to have Keith in their family. In the fall of 2012, after fifteen years together, they married.

Though unknown at the time, the Episcopal Church in Indianapolis had its fair share of sexual problems. The charismatic dean of the cathedral on the Circle was Paul Moore, on his way to becoming suffragan Bishop of the National Cathedral in Washington D.C. and, from there, to be Bishop of New York with St. John the Divine as his seat. At six foot seven inches he was an impressive figure. He arrived in Indianapolis with his beautiful raven-haired wife Jenny and their nine children. That he was a liberal, deeply concerned with the plight of inner city blacks, was well known. Jock and Pam were smitten. He was to become godfather to their son George.

The Columbia Club, which is next door to Christ's Church Episcopal Cathedral on the Circle, used to be a Republican stronghold. Ambrose and I were sometimes invited to functions there, when extra men were required to even up the sexes. Among the dowagers at one such function was a certain Josephine Latham. As the band struck up a sufficiently stately fox trot, I asked her to dance. With her cane hooked over her arm we slowly shunted backwards and forwards while she enthused about her wonderful son. He was headmaster of a prestigious Episcopal school in New England. Earlier that day, The Indianapolis Star had carried an announcement that Bishop Paul Moore would be in the city, next week, to give a talk. I therefore asked Mrs. Latham if she planned to attend the lecture. Though the band played on, our dance ended abruptly. She stood back and eyed me if not with contempt certainly with suspicion as she said, "I most certainly will not be attending. That man's a liberal. He's got money and should know better!"

No sooner was Moore consecrated Bishop of New York than he began to justify Mrs. Latham's suspicions. He ordained the first two female priests into the Episcopal Church. They both started their ministries in Indianapolis. That was an appalling affront to the traditional church but worse was to come. He ordained a man who admitted to being a practicing homosexual. Invited to be on the Today Show, he pointed out that, in every other respect, the new priest was suitable for ordination and that there were already many gay priests. They were closeted. If you're going to have homosexual priests anyway, do you prefer to have them honest or dishonest? Put like that, his point was well taken.

When Moore retired, he wrote an autobiography. He had grown up amidst such affluence that when they traveled the world they had three planes, one for the family, one for the servants and one for luggage. The embarrassment of riches had led him to God who changed the course of his life. God failed to check the manuscript's accuracy. Shortly before he died, Paul Moore sent for his eldest daughter, Honor, who is a writer. He gave her access to his secret stash of photographs and love letters. Not only was he bisexual, he had enjoyed a full lifetime of male lovers. After her father's death, Honor Moore published a more truthful biography called simply The Bishop's Daughter. To paraphrase the well known saying, "God moves in a mysterious way Her wonders to perform."

Chapter Fourteen
*A School Teacher*


From my perspective, Wood High School was the most exciting Indianapolis school in which to teach. As luck would have it, I would have to wait a year before that school had an opening for an art teacher. Meanwhile, I was given a split assignment. Two days a week I was to teach at Shortridge Junior High. The other three days, I was at School 78. That was an excellent learning experience for me. At Shortridge all the students were seventh and eighth graders. I had my own art room with display cabinets and bulletin boards to exhibit students' work. In the hallway, outside the art room, was an extensive gallery of original art by most of the best Hoosier old masters. I would arrive early to set up the various classes I would be teaching that day. Double periods were the best. Everybody had time to get fully involved in his or her project. Most classes were only forty minutes long. By the time thirty or forty students had got their materials organized, and clean up allowed for, there was only about twenty five creative minutes.

The day President Kennedy was assassinated I was in the middle of a class at Shortridge. The principal got on the loud speaker to tell us what had happened. Then he switched over to the radio broadcast so that we could listen to the shocking events as they unfurled. It took a few minutes for the gravity of the situation to fully sink in but, once it did, nobody said a word and most of the students began to sob or put their heads down on the table. It was obvious that there would be no more work done that day so I spent my time quietly putting supplies away. That day brought the halcyon dream of Camelot to a screeching halt. I'm not sure that, as a nation, we have ever fully recovered from the horror of that day. For those of us who lived through it, it remains as vivid a memory as if it happened yesterday.

At School 78 I taught grades two through six. In every way, the experience was markedly different from Shortridge. To begin with there was no art room. There was a supply storage room with a cart. I would load it up with whatever was needed for the day. I wheeled the cart to whatever classroom I was to teach in next. None of the rooms contained a sink so nothing could be washed up. Every classroom was the jealously guarded preserve of the "homeroom teacher" who could be counted on to return for a thorough inspection as soon as the bell rang. Mess-free lesson plans were, without a doubt my biggest challenge. At the same time, those young kids were a joy to be with. They seemed to rise to whatever the occasion demanded. I can't recall a single discipline problem in School 78. When the bell rang for recess, the kids lined up in silence, before quietly walking through the halls, down the stairs and out to the playground. At Shortridge, when the bell went, the noise was deafening.

Teaching is no sinecure but it has its rewards, not least of which is a three month summer break. For me that meant Europe. I usually went for two months. Ambrose was allowed two weeks paid vacation. He often took another week or two and, as luck would have it, Mallory's paid him anyway. He would join me at some point half way through the summer.

After my first year of teaching, I signed up for a summer school at Indiana University in Bloomington to begin work on a Master's degree in art history. I did six hours of post graduate courses every semester in the evenings. In those days, before IUPUI, all applicable courses had to be taken in Bloomington. That involved about two and a half hours round trip driving plus three hours of lecture. Generally, I could get away from my school teaching by about four in the afternoon, grab a bite and get to IU in time for a six to nine class. While it was a tiring schedule, I thoroughly enjoyed my courses and got to know interesting fellow students and brilliant, if sometimes eccentric, professors.

One such professor was Bertrand Davzac. His father who was chief executive of the French Gas Company had a difficult time understanding Bertrand's fascination with medieval art. I had Davzac for several courses and seminars including one on the art of Cluny. Meanwhile, his own Ph.D. had dragged on for so many years that Columbia University threatened him with expulsion from the program unless he completed his thesis in short order. With that in mind, he invited about eight of us students to spend the summer in Paris. Part of the time was to be spent studying ecclesiastical buildings in the Ile de France for which we'd receive credit. The rest of the time we would be examining Carolingian manuscripts in the Bibliothèque Nationale to help him complete his thesis. His work was concerned with stylistic influences to be found in a particular ninth century manuscript. We were all issued with the requisite documents to allow us free access to the reading room of the department of manuscripts. There we would order several incunabula at a time. We discovered that in the eighteenth century the French Government had rounded up the ancient manuscripts from Abbeys and Monasteries throughout the country. This resulted in making the Bibliothèque Nationale by far the largest collection of such treasures on earth. With the exception of a few priceless works such as the "Ebbo Gospels" we could handle anything we wanted. Bertrand had given us each a list of related works to examine and make notes for him to use. As far as I can remember, I was assigned works done in monastic scriptoria in, and around, Tours.

With Professor Davzac we could expect a chaotic summer school and we were not disappointed. We had expected accommodations in the United States pavilion in the Cité Universitaire but, as they weren't ready for us, we stayed in the Hôtel du Vieux Paris also known as "The Beat Hotel" from the

170

days when William Burroughs, Allen Ginsberg and others had lived there. In fact Burroughs had written several novels while living there including Naked Lunch and Soft Machine.

We arrived just after Madame Rachon retired. She had been running the Vieux Paris into the ground for thirty two years. The new owners Monsieur and Madame Laigle, saved the place from complete collapse. They replaced the six Turkish toilets with seated pedestals. All six toilets were accessed off the spiral staircase which ran through the six and a half above ground floors. The basement is of Roman origin and the next five floors are seventeenth century while the top one and a half are from the eighteenth. The doors of the toilets opened outwards, a hazard to people exiting the convenience as well as to anybody on the staircase. Each door was the width of three steps, none of which was at toilet floor level, so one had to decide on which of the three to alight. The length of one's legs could be the deciding factor. Though the staircase spiraled, it was elliptical. A further problem was that all the steps sloped away from the wall towards the central elliptical well. Fearing total collapse guests tended to cling to the wall, oblivious to the more immediate danger of being hit by a toilet door. Not only were the stairs dangerous but less than a minute elapsed before the timer on the light switch expired leaving one to grope for the next landing, where there was another one.

The hotel had about thirty rooms. Only one had its own bathroom. There were three shower rooms which could be reserved at the front desk for an extra charge. Over the next thirty years Ambrose and I stayed there many times. Once, we got the room with a bath. The faucets were so corroded that when fully opened the stream of water could fairly be described as a string of beads. By putting the plug in, before going to bed, there were a couple of inches of cold water in the tub next morning. The Vieux Paris had three virtues. It was dirt cheap. It has a fabulous location, 9 Rue Gît-le-Coeur, on the left bank just west of Place St. Michel, and Madame Laigle is a treasure. In about two thousand the hotel was renovated at considerable expense. An elevator was installed and the number of rooms halved. Today it's an expensive little boutique. Ambrose and I dropped in fairly recently to check it out and were surprised to be warmly greeted by Madame Laigle.

For our 1964 summer school with Bertrand Davzac we all arrived on staggered flights. When I reached the Hôtel du Vieux Paris, I learned that one of our fellow students had arrived with acute appendicitis. He had been rushed to the Hôtel Dieu on the Ile de la Cité for an emergency operation. He made a full recovery but wasn't able to participate, in our seminars, for two or three weeks.

As a member of the Shlumberger family, Bertrand, his lovely Egyptian wife, Shihira and their little son Karim had the use of a splendid eighteenth century Hôtel Particulare next door to the home of the French President. Meeting there for classes was always a treat. Not only could we count on delicious goodies from Shihira but, more important, Professor Davzac would be there. Having spent half my life in academia, I've met my fair share of absent minded professors, but Bertrand Darzac was in a class by himself. One morning he went off with Karim, aged two, in the car, stopped to fill up with gas and drove off without his son. What with one thing and another, he didn't return home for several hours. It wasn't until Shihira informed him that he had taken the boy in the morning that he realized what he'd done. On another occasion he told us to take a train, the next day, to Soissons. He would meet us at 10:00 a.m. at the west front of the cathedral. He was a no show. When we confronted him, instead of confessing to the obvious truth, he claimed to have overslept, so, instead of arriving late with abject apologies, he rolled over and went back to sleep.

One of my fellow students was Mel Meehan. We already knew each other quite well as we had taken several courses together and were destined to have a lifelong friendship. At the time she was dating Tom Solley. He was finishing up an art history degree at Bloomington. Before long, he would become director of the Indiana University Fine Arts Museum. While we were in Paris, Tom was traveling all over Europe. Mel would join him, wherever he happened to be, at weekends. When summer school ended, Mel met Tom in London where they married. She had acquired a new Mercedes which she left in my care. Along with Bezie Droege, a mutual friend, we took the car to Rotterdam and shipped it back to the States where Mel collected it.

Bertrand Davzac had a sabbatical following our departure, to finish his dissertation for Columbia University. On his return to Bloomington, in the spring, he arrived with a decidedly dubious story. In New York, they had stayed with friends for a few days. Getting ready to depart for Indiana, he loaded up the car before going in to say, "Good-bye" to their hosts. However, he forgot to lock the car. On returning, he discovered that his thesis had been stolen! Fortunately he's related to the De Menils. The last time I heard of him, he was curator of the De Menil Collection in Houston, Texas.

For my second year of teaching, I lucked out. I was to become a full time art and humanities teacher at Harry E. Wood High School. I would remain there for eight years. Prior to my going to Wood, the building had been Manual High School. When Manual moved south into a new facility, the old school buildings, on Meridian Street just south of downtown became available and Dick Emery pounced. He was an impressive figure of a man, a dedicated educator with missionary zeal. In fact his parents had been Christian missionaries in West Africa. They had got to know my parents when they had been traveling there on the same ship. On a visit by Dad, to Indianapolis, shortly after I started at Wood, he and Dick Emery had much to talk about.

The near south side of town, at that time, had a large population of very poor people who had moved there from Kentucky and Tennessee in search of work. For the most part they were neither bright nor ambitious. Mr. Emery wanted to change all that and, as he invariably refused to take no for an answer, the school board turned over the old Manual building to him so that he could create a school to meet the needs of the neighborhood. Recognizing that most students would never attend college, he offered a number of trade training courses to supplement the traditional curriculum. For the boys there was automobile service, and repair, in a fully equipped shop. There were courses in woodworking and the building trades. We had professional looking beauty and barbers' shops and a large home economics department. Known to students and faculty as "Big Daddy," Emery hand picked his teachers and made it his business to visit the students' homes to assess their needs.

I particularly remember an incident during my first semester. The students had been working on an assignment and I was calling them up, one at a time, to discuss progress. When I called one young man he looked at me and told me to "Fuck off." I said, "Excuse me. What did you say?" "You heard me. Fuck you." There's a first time for everything and this was certainly one such occasion. The entire class had heard the exchange. I knew that on my reaction depended the future of my relationship with them. I stepped over to my desk, wrote an account of what had happened, sealed it in an envelope addressed to Mr. Emery and took it over to the boy in question. "You may leave the class now," I said, "and I would like you to take this to Big Daddy in his office." Fortunately, the boy did as requested. Later, I went to see Mr. Emery to discuss the situation. I was not prepared for what he told me. The boy was one of five children to a single mother. All six lived in a ramshackle garage with a dirt floor and no heating. There was little food and they slept on piles of old newspapers. Rather than punish the boy, Dick arranged for him to go to the cafeteria every morning, before school, to join some fifty other students in similar straightened circumstances, to get a full free breakfast paid for by Mr. Emery. Of all the wonderful things I learned from Big Daddy, compassion was the most valuable.

One of my duties was to be a homeroom teacher. Each morning about thirty students came to my classroom for various announcements and roll-call. An IPS form arrived in my mail box. It was to be completed, by me, each semester and returned to the Board of School Commissioners. I was obliged to inform them how many of the students were white, black or native American (in those days few Mexicans had yet reached the Hoosier state). I had been around the block often enough to have filled out many personal forms demanding such information. I've never discovered what the recipients made of my invariable reply of, "origins unknown." In this case, I decided that my poverty stricken charges, in all likelihood, knew even less than I do on the subject. I therefore informed the class, who for the most part considered themselves "white" that I would tell the school board that all thirty of them were "black." Once I had quelled the indignant protests, I made them two promises. First, I would change the tally for any student who could convince me that he or she had no black ancestors. No one took me up on that challenge. Second, I promised that next semester the same thirty students would all appear on the form as "white." I did as promised and still await any feedback from the Indianapolis Board of School Commissioners!

For the most part, the teachers at Wood were good people and very dedicated. A few of them became friends for life. Rick Cohen taught English and Spanish. He was a keen thespian involved in both school productions and the Civic Theater which is the longest lived amateur theater in the United States. Lacking a car, he sometimes he got a ride with me and, before long, I would get to know his closest family. I say "closest" because, of all the people we know, none has a longer Indianapolis connection than Richard Cohen. His first family house stood on the ground where the Indiana State House stands today! We only overlapped for a couple of years at Wood because Rick went to Mexico in pursuit of another degree and, of greater importance, to meet and marry Rachel. In due course, they produced Marcus and Nick. Now they are grandparents. Rick had one sibling, a sister who died young in a hot-air balloon accident. Of all our friends, Rick and Rachel are the only ones whose date of marriage we know. They share September the tenth with us.

Mary Jo Showley taught music. She had been a voice major at Indiana University. At school concerts, she would conduct the choir. After a tour of duty, her husband, Jack returned from Vietnam. Mary Jo left Wood to start a family. They complemented the Cohens by producing two daughters. Ivy appeared first. When number two arrived, one Christmas Eve, they claimed ignorance of the popular carol and named her "Holly." Jack is a superb dentist. Once he had established himself in Indianapolis, Ambrose and I went to him. Hailing from England, which boasts some of the world's worst dentists, and no fluoride in the drinking water, our mouths were declared disasters and in need of immediate attention. Jack replaced every filling with gold inlays of such impeccable quality that they continue to impress all our subsequent dentists.

The Showleys bought a boat and beach house on Longboat Key, in Florida. For nine years, we were there, as their guests, every Thanksgiving for about a week of sailing and having fun. Unfortunately, Jack celebrated their silver anniversary by dumping his lovely wife in favor of, you guessed it, his dental assistant, Sharon. For better or worse, they're still married while Mary Jo has made a career for herself selling real estate.

Carolyn Fay, taught English. A couple of years after I started at Wood, she took a year off to join her husband in the Far East. Alas, it didn't save her marriage and she wound up raising Anne and William on her own. Later she met Providence Benedict who has proved to be an enriching lifetime partner. Carolyn and I were friends when we taught at Wood and later when we both transferred to Shortridge.

Mrs. McCracken taught French. She had a promising student who, along with a brother, was in an impossible home situation. "Lisa and Ted Stone have got to be rescued" she told me, "and I need your help." She took Lisa to live with her, Ambrose and I took Ted. I think it was only for one semester but it's hard to imagine that kind of unsupervised arrangement being sanctioned today.

High school cheerleaders are girls, or are they? At Wood they were all boys. I remember three who all went to an early grave. Lester went first. Like the other two, he was effeminate and a victim of bullying. Going downstairs, some kid banged him on the head, from behind, with a dirty rake. It poisoned him. He died at nineteen.

Richard Hostetler had a very low IQ but was generous to a fault. He liked to hang around my classroom to help with cleaning up or whatever jobs I might have. His father worked in a factory so Richard managed to land a job there as a janitor. Every Christmas, he would drive up to our house with a car full of gifts. Not only had he spent far too much money but there was seldom anything either to our taste or usable. The one thing that we still use from all Richard's gifts is a crock pot.

His mother needed to talk to us, he said, because he had contracted AIDS. Thus began the ghastly, and inevitable, decline in the days before the disease was understood. The only thing that could be done was to give him blood transfusion. He loved to attend ice-hockey games at the Coliseum, so on the day of a game he would have a transfusion which would afford his emaciated body a few hours of tolerable health. The final two, or three, months he was in Methodist Hospital having transfusion with ever increasing frequency. His doting mother was at his bedside all day and every day. Ambrose and I tried to visit regularly to help comfort Mrs. Hostetler as Richard's father refused to have anything more to do with his son. One evening, Richard said he'd had enough transfusions. By then, even his mother agreed that he'd suffered enough. Within a couple of hours, as we sat around his hospital bed, holding hands, he died. We stayed in touch with his mother until she died about fifteen years later. Richard was her only son.

Billy Peed, the third cheer leader, was one of seven boys and five girls. All of them were Wood students at one time or another. Their father was scraping a living as a handy man. We hired him to replace a pair of French doors with sliding ones. When they didn't work properly we discovered that he'd hung them upside down. Of the twelve siblings, Billy alone went on to college. He was a freshman at Indiana University, in Bloomington, when I got an hysterical phone call from him begging me to meet him at the bus station downtown. He was in such a state, when I picked him up, that I brought him back to our house, put him in one of the guest bedrooms and hoped that he would get himself under control by the next morning. In due course, the story emerged. He had made a sexual overture to his room-mate who promptly went ballistic and, in no time, everybody was jeering at him. The result was that he ran away vowing never to return. The problem was more than Ambrose or I was able to handle. Gene Bennett, a closeted gay, had headed up the "slow learning" program at Wood. Though he and I had never had much reason to interact, now seemed the moment to do so. Billy was in no state to leave our house so I asked Gene to come over to see if he could calm him down. Whatever wise council he gave had the desired effect. Within a week, I was able to drive Billy back and settle him into a different dormitory room. He finished his first semester without any "F" grades but decided to leave Bloomington.

For better or worse, we took him in while he signed up for courses at IUPUI, the Indianapolis campus. At first all went well but it wasn't long before an incident occurred that made us wonder if he was going mad. We were asleep, when Billy rushed into our room to ask what had become of a letter he had been typing. Naturally, we said that we didn't have the foggiest notion. He accused us of stealing it! When he'd finally left us in peace, we decided that enough was enough. He must either go back to his family or find a rooming house. He did the latter, but not for long. It was a bitterly cold night. We were in the middle of dinner when Billy appeared shivering. He had just flung his landlady downstairs and broken her arm! Needless to say, we fed him and notified the police that he was at our house. He subsequently spent some time in the Marion County Jail. A court ordered evaluation revealed that he was bi-polar. He did eventually graduate but he never held a job for more than a couple of weeks. We visited him in hospital just before he died of AIDS.

Big Daddy asked Mary Zenor and me to start a program for at risk students to be called "humanities". It was limited to twelve students per semester. The idea was to open the eyes of these culturally deprived students to the endless possibilities of the wider world. We would meet together in a conference room for free ranging discussions on a host of subjects and ask for student input on what programs and field trips would interest them. For the most part, we signed up students who chose to be in the program.

There was a fifteen year old boy who had caught my eye in the school hallways. He always looked furtive and walked about with his head down. He had a spotty complexion and wavy unkempt blond hair. No other boys at Wood had long hair. His clothes were old and worn and included a khaki jacket, covered in symbols, and a rabbit's foot. Above all he was

179

a loner. Once I had discovered his name I went to the office to pull up his records. He lived with grandparents. Until grade six he had had excellent grades and his IQ was estimated at a hundred and thirty. From Junior High on he had been in decline. Now his grades were mostly "Fs" and he was absent more than half the time. From that moment, Steve Wright and I have been part of each other's lives, sharing a special bond.

When I broached the subject of his being in the humanities program, he was less than enthusiastic. However, he agreed to attend one session to see what it was like. When Mrs. Zenor asked for student suggestions, Steve said, "Let's all get down on the floor and fuck!" As Mrs. Zenor was clearly speechless, I said, "Steve, your suggestion might be appropriate under certain circumstances. Trust me on this one. The school board would never sanction such a thing on school property so I suggest that you make a more acceptable suggestion." Whether he had another idea, I don't remember. However, there was a look in his eye that said, "Fraser's not the stuck up prude I had expected. Maybe, just maybe, I can trust him." He stayed with the humanities program which opened his eyes to a host of possibilities.

Richard Lugar was Mayor of Indianapolis. He invited us to his offices to hear about his job and to ask him questions. We visited the Carmelite Monastery on Cold Springs Road to learn, from the lips of a nun, concealed behind black drapes, what it meant to be totally cloistered. Of course that was before Vatican II.

A field trip to sit in on an eighth grade class at Park Tudor, an expensive private school, was an eye opener for the Wood students. They couldn't get over the fact that the kids never spoke until called upon to do so or their respectful way of addressing the teacher. The class we attended was discussing a story they had read. The teacher was following up by asking what single thing they would choose to buy that would make their neighbors jealous. All hands were raised and a boy was asked what his choice would be. When he said, "A tennis court" several hands were lowered. The next day, our students couldn't believe that answer and that several other students would have given the same one. When Mary Zenor and I put the same question to the Wood students most agreed that a Cadillac convertible would top the list!

We went to the City Market and bought things they'd never eaten to be cooked by the home economics students at Wood for our lunch the following day. A two night field trip to Chicago was a high point during one semester. We stayed at the Palmer House where we were treated to a behind the scenes tour which included the presidential suite, the creation of ice sculptures and the bakery where they were making proper French croissants.

I doubt if, even in their wildest dreams, our students thought they would fly, but fly they did. They sold popcorn, around the school, to raise money. Big Daddy went to talk to Lilly's. Next thing we were sent to Washington D.C for three days in a corporate jet. The last night there we went to a good restaurant in Georgetown. Escargots were on the menu. I ordered a dozen and told the students that they could order whatever they wanted for a main course provided they tried a snail first. Every student did as requested, with mixed criticisms, and afterwards we splurged on superb steaks. As the sizzling platters arrived, Steve Wright turned to me and said, "In my opinion, Mr. Fraser, this calls for a bottle of Chateau Neuf du Pape!" It was an inspired suggestion but as I was the only adult, sadly, it was another of his ideas that had to be tabled.

Steve had just finished his junior year. I was completing paper work at the desk in my class room when he walked in and flung down his report card for me to see. He'd missed more classes than he had attended. His appalling grades reflected that. "So," I said "I'm not surprised. Are you?" "Mr. Fraser, I want to go to college," He said. I told him that with his accumulated GPA college was out of the question. He sat down and we had a long serious talk. That he'd had a terrible home life was evident. He'd almost died with a drug overdose which he described to me in frightening detail. With no love at home he'd had a number of girlfriends and at least one child to show for it. His room was a broom closet under the stairs in his grandparents' house. He had a sister but she lived elsewhere. As he poured his story out, I recognized that, with just a little help, he could make something of himself. I was particularly impressed with his honesty. He always tells the truth no matter how painful it maybe.

After much discussion, I made Steve an offer. Next year would be his last in high school. He must not miss a single day of school or be late for his first class and he must get straight "As." If he managed that, I would go to bat with the administration at Indiana University to get him admitted. To help him stick to his side of the bargain, he had a phone by his bed which I would use to give him a daily wake-up call. When we looked over the classes that he needed to take, he said he couldn't possibly get an A in history because the only teacher who taught that course didn't know his stuff. I knew the teacher in question and had no doubt that Steve's assessment was correct. He agreed to keep his opinions to himself in his history course and to do his best to regurgitate whatever the teacher wanted to hear when he was being tested. I allowed that a B grade would suffice in history provided the others were all A's. Fortunately, his first class of the morning was science with Miss Lyon. The door to her classroom was across the hall from mine. She kindly alerted me if he was late which happened when he fell back to sleep after my call. There was a phone in the hallway so I would wake him again with dire predictions of what would happen if he failed to get to class in fifteen minutes.

The whole year was a cliff hanger but somehow he made it. A day was arranged for a field trip for college bound students to tour the Indiana University campus and to meet the Director of Admissions. I asked Steve to come for a briefing about a week ahead of time. Without beating about the bush, I told him that his current appearance would make a poor impression on the Admissions Director with whom I had promised to put in a good word on his behalf. As I anticipated, Steve's antenna went into full alert overdrive. No, he was not about to have a haircut and his rabbit's foot jacket was for good luck. As my request was greeted with intransigence I let the matter go. On the day of our trip, I had to do a double take when Steve boarded the bus. He'd had a complete makeover. Even though he looked a bit surly it was as much as I could do to refrain from hugging him.

While studying to graduate from IU, he held a number of part time jobs to help pay his way. One summer he got employed as a gardener at the Indianapolis Museum of Art. Ambrose and I supplied him with wheels. Unfortunately, Steve has no aptitude for gardening. When asked what assignment he'd been given he said "I'm trying to stop ivy from interfering with myrtle!" He was summarily fired for riding a lawn mower creatively around a large expanse of grass where straight lines were expected.

Once graduated, he landed a job for which he was perfectly suited. A new government program to rescue high school dropouts, and afford them a chance at a better life, had just been started. It was simply called "Seven Thousand and One." That was the number of the bill which launched the program. In Indianapolis, there were three or four offices set up in depressed neighborhoods, and Steve was selected to run the one on the south side.

Here's how the program worked. There were free comic books and flyers that the targeted kids would read with ads that said, "Tired of having no money? Tired of having nothing to do? Phone this number right away." When they phoned, they would be invited to come in to hear all about it. Essentially, there were two prongs to the program. If the person agreed to participate, they would be given a bus pass, clothes money and a job. A number of fast food restaurants and supermarkets etc. had signed on to offer employment. Great importance was placed on always showing up for work on time. To ensure compliance, employers and Seven Thousand and One, kept in constant touch with each other. The second prong was a requirement that the young person would work to complete his or her GED. To facilitate that, Seven Thousand and One employed instructors in the various disciplines. Once the students graduated, Seven Thousand and One would help them find permanent employment.

I was delighted to be on the board and played a part from time to time. For example, I would pretend to be an employer interviewing prospective employees. Following the interview, I would offer constructive criticisms of their behavior and appearance, taking in to account such things as the firmness of a handshake to the way they sat down to ask, or answer questions. Having overcome so many obstacles himself, Steve was skilled at empathizing with those young people. They warmed to him immediately and he proved himself time and again as the consummate motivator.

Unfortunately, it's a rare individual who survives such a difficult childhood unscathed. Steve Wright did not. A deep sense of pessimism, and black humor, is never far below the surface, spelling problems for his intimate relationships. I wasn't surprised when his marriage to Sherry fell apart. She was pretty and pleasant but Steve needed more. He needs a strong woman to be there for him in his dark moods while at the same time appreciating his fine mind and acerbic wit.

He and I saw almost nothing of each other during his marriage to Tressa. How successful that union was, I don't know. It must have had its moments as it produced two sons, Aaron and Andrew. However, it also ended in divorce. I was happy when he married Colleen. She really seemed to understand Steve's inner conflicts and would nurture him through his blackest moods. Best of all, their first offspring was a girl, Meghan. Having already fathered two legitimate sons, as well as two others during his misspent youth, he must have wondered if he would ever father a daughter. In due course Sean Mackenzie (Mac) completed the family.

I wish that I could round out this little essay with the news that they lived happily ever after. They didn't. In 2011, Steve and Colleen lost it with each other. She brought charges claiming that Steve hit her. He was arrested. What really transpired is immaterial. Much of what I've written came flooding back to me when Steve asked me to write a letter to the court in his defense. I did so but not until he assured me that he had not laid a finger on Colleen. I'm convinced that he told me the truth.

# Chapter Fifteen
## *The Oxymoron of Government Intelligence*

Ambrose and I had been together about ten years when he had "the talk." We were staying with his parents in Wiltshire. They had a few acres of land a mile out of the small town of Calne. In the first years when I used to stay with them, their house, Wayside was close to the Bath road. Down the lane, beside Wayside, Frank designed and built a delightful retirement home, for the two of them, called Mile Elm House. We were on a European trip, from Indianapolis, when we stopped by for a couple of nights with them. Dinner over, Frank went off to his room leaving Prue, Ambrose and me chatting in the drawing room. When it was time for bed, Prue bid me good-night and asked Ambrose to stay and help clean up the kitchen. Once I was out of the way, she asked Ambrose whether he would ever get married? He said, "No." He and I loved each other and planned to spend the rest of our lives together. She must have understood the situation for years but, when Ambrose spelt it out, she fell apart. She wanted to know how, as a mother, she had failed him. Later, a badly shaken Ambrose came up to join me in bed. The subject was never broached again and I never had "the talk" with my parents.

We always suspected that, before Frank and Prue married, Frank had had a homosexual experience with Richard Walker, a fellow architectural student. When Ambrose was born, Uncle Richard became his godfather. Once graduated, Richard moved to Nice where he designed villas in the Rivera. With the exception of the Second World War years, he spent his life there. He married in his fifties and outlived his wife by many years. Shortly after Ambrose and I set up housekeeping, on Bywater Street, Uncle Richard came to visit us. Though nothing was said, he clearly sized up our situation. He grew old and frail in a villa overlooking Nice. He'd run out of money so Ambrose paid a check into his bank every month. We regularly visited him until the year before his death, in his late eighties, without ever asking him about youthful indiscretions.

When Pam Bevan had returned to Indianapolis, having given birth to Jessica in England, Jock's mother, Elizabeth, his aunt, Cathy Scott Moncrief, and Pam's mother, Barbara Brook, all came over for a tour of inspection. Unlike the other two, Barbara balked at staying with her daughter. While many people avoid children who are still leaking at either end, Barbara felt that, if babies were unavoidable, at least they should be put into restraints at birth and preferably left there until age twenty five, or possibly older. As Katie, the Bevan's first born, was a sub teen, Barbara stipulated that she would visit on the condition that she stay with us. And so she did.

As she had lived for many years in Knightsbridge, next door to Harrods, we were anxious to give her as favorable an impression as possible of our adopted, and much loved, city. Commendable, as our motives might be, driving into Indianapolis, from the airport, was less than salubrious. From our small, outdated, airport, most people drove into town on West Washington Street. It consisted of miles of seedy sex shops, dilapidated slums and junkyards puncture by the odd power station and abattoir. The alternative, which we took, was to cut up north and drive in on the recently paved 38th Street. It was lined with lots of new construction, strip malls and fast food joints. After a long journey, Barbara was understandably tired. She kept nodding off but, whenever we hit a chuck hole, she'd look out and murmur "mushroom" or "more mushroom." Thinking she might be looking forward to a meal we asked her to elaborate. "Mushroom development, my dear. I doubt that any of these ticky tacky structures were here yesterday and, with any luck, they'll be gone before I leave in a fortnight!"

After a good night's sleep, her mood lightened considerably. She loved the varied architectural influences to be seen in the mansions lining Washington Boulevard and North Meridian Streets. The spacious lawns that flowed from one property to the next, without dividing walls and fences so universally adopted in Britain, particularly impressed her. Dinner at Westerley, as the Clowes's guest, among rare antiques and rooms filled with old master paintings was beyond her wildest expectations of the Midwest. As a lasting souvenir of her visit, she brought us a delightful Lalique vase.

Before departing for London, she promised to join us the following year in Rome. It was to be her first and only visit to Italy. We were in the habit of staying in the Casa Palotti, close to the Ponte Sisto, on via dei Pettinari. It was part of a monastery of Palatine monks built around a quiet courtyard. The rooms were Spartan but kept spotless by subservient nuns who also produced breakfast. Large bathrooms were each shared by a number of rooms. If a crucifix above your headboard, or improbable portraits of a cloying Scandinavian Jesus, is more than you can stomach, the Palotti was not for you. By staying there one was entitled to seats beside the baldachino enclosed altar for the Wednesday papal audience in St. Peters'. (That was before the building of the auditorium which is used nowadays).

Barbara chose to stay in the boutique Hotel Raphaelo behind the Piazza Navona. We met her plane at Leonardo da Vinci airport. As the train to Rome had yet to be built we came in by airport bus. Sweeping around the Coliseum, Barbara remarked, "Good God, my dear, that building's had it!"

The next day, we took her sightseeing. St. Peter's was in the final year of the great council, called together by Pope John XXIII, known as "Vatican II." As he had died in 1963, Pope Paul VI was responsible for the final two years. Bleachers draped in papal purple lined both sides of the central nave, facing each other, to accommodate the princes of the Church. They had gathered together, from the four corners of the earth, for deliberations destined to bring profound changes to traditional Roman Catholicism.

While Barbara's interest in spiritual things, gin excepted, was minimal, she was all in favor of checking out the monuments such as Michelangelo's Pieta. In the south aisle, we came across a group of about fifteen people listening intently to a guide expounding on a Baroque monument to Pope Urban VIII by Gian Lorenzo Bernini. The marble Pope, with hand raised, was looking down towards a woman holding a baby. As the guide explained, she represented charity receiving a papal blessing. "What rot" said Barbara "It's obviously his baby." "Shush" we said, as everybody turned to look at us. "I'll tell you what I need, my dears, and that's a good stiff drink." "Well Barbara," we said, as sotto voce as possible, "we'd better leave because you certainly can't get a drink here." We were standing behind a bleacher. "Are you trying to tell me that all those cardinals and things sit here day in and day out without a drink? I don't believe it." Just then she spotted an overlap of purple drapery, pulled it aside and, believe it or not, there was a wine bar! Needless to say, it was locked up but Barbara had made her point.

Before he died, Pope John XXIII had gotten rid of over three hundred nonsensical saints including St. Christopher, patron of travelers. The nuns operated a little religious shop in the Casa Palotti. When we inquired after St. Christopher they had drawers full of him, in sundry sizes and materials, all at "going out business" prices. We bought a number of small ones to give to Roman Catholic friends in the States.

On the Wednesday morning we collected Barbara, from the Raphaelo, for the papal audience. To mitigate her earlier transgressions, in the basilica, she was demurely dressed in black. She had a black lace shawl arranged around her head, like a mini-Muslim, secured on the side with a large diamante broach. "Do you think the Pope will mistake me for a nun?" she asked. We took our seats, well ahead of time, on a small bleacher just to the right of the baldachino. Barbara sat between Ambrose and me. On my left was a newly ordained American priest on his first visit to Rome. He told me in, an excited voice, how he had celebrated mass at a side altar and how overwhelmed he felt being in such a splendid place built to the glory of God. I asked him if he had seen pictures of the previous basilica. He didn't know that there had been an earlier one. When I told him that the St. Peter's started by the Emperor Constantine in 333 CE, was, in my opinion, far more beautiful, he asked why it had been replaced. The reason, I explained, was that Pope Julius II intended to have Michelangelo design his tomb on such a monumental scale that the old St. Peter's couldn't accommodate it. My naïve neighbor might want to rethink his opinion that this vast edifice was built for God's enjoyment.

Ambrose was chatting up the lady on his right. She was from San Diego, California, on her way home from Moscow where her son had an embassy appointment. Her late husband, she told Ambrose, had taken the surrender of the Italian fleet at the end of World War II. Suddenly, a rotund little man in a white suit, with a mustache and goatee, sat down in front of us. When Ambrose noticed him, the lady said, "Oh yes, that's Colonel Sanders. He's an old friend. We had lunch together yesterday. He's in Rome to open the first Kentucky Fried Chicken in this country and, by the way, he can't stand chicken. He lives mainly on sardines and always travels with a suitcase filled with small cans of them."

All chatting came to an abrupt end in a blaze of almost blinding light and so much noise, from the organ, that the whole building vibrated. The procession entered. Pope Paul was at the tail end, being carried on a litter, flanked by Swiss guards. As I watched them draw near it struck me as odd that, though they were all men, with the exception of the Swiss and Palatine guards, they were in drag. During the proceedings, the

Pope came over to us to ask if we had any special thing that we would like to have blessed. I'd brought the St. Christopher's, carefully wrapped, so that he wouldn't realize that by blessing them he was undoing the good work of his predecessor. How St. Peter sorts all these muddles out at the pearly gates, is anybody's guess.

For a surprising denouement to the papal audience saga, we must fast forward about fifteen years. In the toe of southwestern Indiana, situated on the banks of the Wabash River, is the tiny town of New Harmony. Its curious history might have been lost, but for the ongoing munificence of Jane Blaffer Owen of Houston, Texas. She died in her nineties a full decade into the twenty first century. On a visit to New Harmony, Jane was walking around with us talking about the inhabitants of each house. Approaching a dark green one, she said, "Here lives Henrietta Glassford our expert on protocol." When Ambrose asked for an explanation, Jane replied, "She knows everybody who is anybody and her husband took the surrender of the Italian fleet at the conclusion of World War II" "And did their son have a post in our Moscow embassy?" we asked. "Oh! So you know her?" Jane said. Without further ado we rang the bell and greeted Mrs. Glassford like a long lost friend. Needless to say she didn't know us from two bars of soap. Once we had enlightened her, we celebrated our unlikely re-union with a drink.

Speaking of embassies, brings me to the subject of this chapter; The Oxymoron of Government Intelligence. I applied to the British Consulate, in Chicago, for a new British passport as mine would soon expire. Instead of the customary renewal application form, I received a curt note to say that I was not entitled to a British passport as I was not a British subject. I discovered, to my surprise, that I had been a Ghanaian citizen for about six years! In 1957, the West African country known as the Gold Coast where I was born, gained its independence from the United Kingdom and became Ghana.

With Kwame Nkrumah as first President, their parliament passed a law to the effect that anyone born there during the British occupation, who wished to maintain United Kingdom citizenship, must so inform the Ghanaian government, in writing, within 6 months. Otherwise they would be Ghanaian. As you can imagine, there was no mention of this law in the Hoosier press! In view of the fact that my green card said I was British, I decided that it would be a mistake, on my part, to expect the federal government to be delighted with this new reality. After further consultation with the British consulate, they agreed to grant me a year's extension to give me time to complete a slew of paperwork deemed necessary to change me back into a Brit. That I succeeded is little short of miraculous as almost none of the required documents still existed. In the end, letters from worthy citizens who could testify to the circumstances of various hatches, matches and dispatches were accepted in lieu of the missing certificates and I regained British citizenship.

All my subsequent dealings with government have involved the feds. By 1981, Patric O'Keeffe had retired from Unilever packaging directorship. He was spending a couple of winter months with us. One day he said that he'd like to move permanently to the States. Checking the yellow pages, we discovered that the department for immigration was in Hammond, Indiana, near Chicago. When I phoned explaining what Patric had in mind the lady asked if he had his birth certificate with him. He had. That being so she would send the application form care of us in Indianapolis. Provided he return it completed within ten days, she saw no reason why he shouldn't get his green card before his return to England four weeks hence. Although Patric had always lived in England, he had an Irish passport. He completed and returned the notarized form pronto. Next, we got a call from Hammond. We were to be there by 9 a.m., a few days later, for an x-ray and some other formalities. Before that day was out he had temporary documents and a promise that his green card would be mailed to Indianapolis within two months. The immigration office was as good as its word. Patric flew back to London, got rid of his flat and had his furniture shipped via the St. Lawrence Seaway to Elk Village, Indiana. Once it was cleared through customs, we brought it to Indianapolis in a U-Haul van. No problem, no bribes, no nothing. Patric lived out the rest of his life, nearly twenty years, as a legitimate permanent resident of the United States.

The year before the O'Keeffe hegira, Dad died in England. Before long, a decision was made that Ma would sell the house and move to California to live with Sheila and her husband, George. At the US Embassy in Grosvenor Square, London, she was given forms to be completed which required getting police clearance from every country in which she had resided since age seven. The task took months. Finally, the embassy expected to have her papers ready shortly so she could complete the sale of her house prior to departure. When she showed up, to collect the documents, on the appointed day, they were sorry to inform her that, owing to some remodeling going on in the building her papers were lost. However, they were issuing Mother with a six month visa, by which time they would have replacements, so she could fly back from California for her green card. Yes she would have to fly back to England and no, it was quite out of the question to send it to her in the States.

She was not a happy camper when she arrived in Indianapolis with her tale of woe. "Not to worry" I said. "We'll get you a green card from Hammond. After all, Patric is just a friend, you're my Mother." When I phoned the Hammond office, they as much as accused me of bald face lying. There was no possible way that Mr. O'Keeffe could have been issued with a green card without applying for it, and having it issued, in his own country. Clearly, there was no point in pursuing that avenue.

We had been invited to dinner with Bob and Josie Orr. He was Lieutenant Governor of Indiana. When he heard the story, he said that he would see what he could do. Within days, he called to say that there was no way that Ma could avoid returning to London for her green card.

There was one more ace up my sleeve. Dick Lugar. I'd known him since he was on the Indianapolis school board. By now, he was chairman of the United States Senate foreign relations. Like Bob Orr, he thought he could pull a few strings on Ma's behalf. Even he tried and failed.

Back with Sheila and George in California, my mother heard from the US Embassy in London. The bad news was that her paper work was still not ready. The good news was that she should take the enclosed letter to the Consulate, in San Francisco, where they would issue her with a six month visa extension. By the time that extension had expired, the Grosvenor Square Embassy was confident that Ma could safely return to England, to collect her green card.

When my longsuffering mother poured out her story to the clerk in San Francisco, he told her not to worry. He said that he would deal with the matter. Sure enough, in a couple of weeks, her green card arrived in the mail. No problem, no bribes, no nothing.

Green cards issued in 1957 were good for life. Flying into New York in the late nineteen eighties, the immigration officer had a hard time equating my elderly face with the one on my card. Suggesting that I apply for a new one, he handed me the application form. After filling it out, I left it in my desk. In 1991, I had my billfold, which contained my green card, pick pocketed in Rome. The Consulate in Milan issued me a special visa to enable me to fly home to the States. Arriving at JFK, I was herded into a holding pen, with a number of questionable characters, for a miserable grilling, before being released. Had I not filled out the information on the form in my desk, before losing my green card, I doubt if I could ever have obtained a replacement. When I heard back from the Department of Immigration, in Washington DC, it was to inform me that they could find no record of my being a legitimate resident of the United States.

Senator Dick Lugar, bless him, sprang into action. He sent an efficient lady to see me and to collect whatever relevant data I possessed. I discovered that, after many years without any police record, old files, such as mine, wound up getting buried in Lincoln, Nebraska. Eventually, she ran my dossier to ground and I had a new green card before my next sojourn abroad. However, the law had changed. It was no longer good for life but must be renewed once a decade. That was when I decided to apply again for U.S citizenship.

This time it would be straightforward, because the former requirement, to agree to bear arms, had been removed. In September 1997 I was sworn in as a citizen of the great United States. That day I became the proud processor of a tiny flag, presented to me by a beaming Daughter of the America Revolution. For a brief period, I flew in and out of the country with my treasured American passport. But wait, there's more.

A scary government letter arrived ordering me to appear, at a certain time, on a certain day, at the Indianapolis immigration office for an examination to ascertain whether or not I would be granted citizenship! What kind of a time warp was this? In fact the self same office had examined me previously. Had I flunked the examination, on that occasion, I would not have been granted citizenship. To add insult to injury, the day I had been ordered to appear was a government holiday. The place was locked up. I took the opportunity to write a letter informing them that, not only had I been examined already but if they cared to check the records of September last, they would see that I had been enthusiastically welcomed into our great three- hundred-million family by none other than the revered Judge Dillon.

The Federal Government, in Washington, either didn't bother to check the facts, or didn't believe me. I was summoned for another date. When, after hours of sitting impatiently in the familiar waiting area, as my number came up, I went to the window to show the clerk my certificate of citizenship. After inspecting my treasured document, she said that she would return it momentarily but first she needed to take it to a back office to make a copy. I refused to let it go. I pointed to the lower left corner of the certificate, where was printed, "It is punishable by US law to copy, print or photograph this certificate, without lawful authority." She protested, but I stuck to my guns, saying that I had good reason to mistrust the Department of Justice. With that I departed with the suggestion that they could apprehend me at their convenience. I heard no more.

Chapter Sixteen
*Collecting Silver*


Monica and Dicky Cox, our old landlords from Chelsea came to visit. They brought us a pair of battered old Sheffield candle sticks. Replating reduces the value. We did it anyway, and have treasured them ever since. Monica was to visit us twice more but Dicky developed pancreatic cancer just after they returned to England. He reminded me of the week we had spent together, in Salisbury, while I was a tenant in Paulton's Square. At the time he was directing the Salisbury repertory theatre. I was hired to paint all the scenery for a forthcoming production. I've long forgotten the name of the play, but the principle set consisted of a suburban living room with a view into a hall with stairs going up. The second act, took place in a garden which included a pergola. It was a lot of work for me to accomplish, in one week, on my own. Only after I arrived, did I discover Dicky's hidden agenda. He tried to climb into my bed. When I said that I wasn't available, he politely backed off. That was my first encounter with bisexuality.

Visits from friends and family were interrupted by a call from Alexia Martin, in Long Island. Everett had just committed suicide using a hose pipe attached to the car's exhaust. She had found him in the garage. The timing, she claimed, was particularly thoughtless as he knew that she was suffering with a bad case of the flu! Indianapolis was the one place where she had found peace and happiness so she planned to return as soon as she was well. We found her an apartment to move into because, as she explained, it would be more than she could bear to revisit her old home. Gradually the story emerged. Though Everett was earning a lot more in New York than he had been making in Indianapolis, Alexia found it inadequate to maintain the rented long Island mansion which she was loath to relinquish. The answer was clear. Everett should start his own "moving" company. To that end he began notifying his boss's customers of his intentions. That word of his duplicity soon reached his manager, is hardly surprising, and that he was summarily dismissed was exactly what he deserved and got. After a few job rejections, and a hurried re-writing of his will to ensure that Alexia would inherit nothing other than a fifteen thousand dollar life insurance policy, he settled for the carbon-monoxide exit.

After she had exhausted all her friends with endless doom and gloom, she started a business making uniforms for the staff of nursing homes, catering firms or any other company that dressed its employees alike. Although she did well, she sold out and went to live in the Canary Islands, in search of true happiness. Oddly enough, it eluded her there as well, so it was back to Indianapolis once again. This time she opened a Russian style kitchen-cum-gourmet shop in Broad Ripple called "La Petechka."

Alexia went through two more husbands. One had the temerity to enter the shop after she had ordered him to "take a hike" so she literally shot him in the foot! The other failed to appear at the registry office on the day of their planned nuptials. The previous day, he was doing some mechanical work in the Speedway pit area when he fell into a vehicle, seriously inebriated. Coming to, it was his wedding day but the vehicle, in which he had been sleeping, had arrived in St. Louis. The marriage, though delayed, took place but, like its predecessors, was of short duration. We met him once. They were at a Clowes Hall concert. Alexia introduced him as her "rough diamond." She had brought her swain to the event in the hope of instilling a modicum of "couth" into him. She failed.

Somewhere, or other, Alexia discovered two compassionate gay men with a beautiful country house who listened patiently to the endless reasons why she would soon commit suicide. That Ken Englund and Leonard Paz survived some thirty years of her misery, is more than I can understand. If I'm mistaken, and heaven exists, check them out sitting on pink thrones, on cloud sixty nine!

Though we were still in our thirties, we decided to plan for our own deaths. We were determined to avoid funeral homes. At that age, we figured that a car or plane accident would be our most likely cause of death. Our driving licenses gave permission for the harvesting of all useable spare parts. Unfortunately, that left most of the corpse to be dealt with. As the medical school always needs bodies for dissecting, maybe they'd solve the problem. Not so simple, we discovered. Yes, they'd love to have what's left of our damaged and harvested remains, provided we had died within an hundred miles of Indianapolis. If we crashed in the Alps, it would cripple our miniscule estate to pay for the bodies to be returned. Worst of all, once the medical school had finished mucking about with our rotting remains, they were in duty bound to return them to our heirs. No, we could not be put down the garbage disposal. Other caveats, such as the refusal of the medical school to accept bodies of people who die of a whole litany of communicable diseases convinced us to look further.

Next stop Crown Hill's crematorium. We were shown the oven, the use of which came with two prices, expensive and very expensive, depending on the type of casket. "But we don't want a casket at all" we said. Having done our homework, we knew that, legally, no more than a sack is required. Law or no law, we were told that Crown Hill prided itself on dignified human departures. At that, we made our departures.

Our salvation turned out to be the Cremation Society of Indiana. The bottom line was about a hundred and fifty dollars each. For that they would collect the body, burn it up and return the remains in a tin can to the heirs. Also included was an obituary, with a picture, to be printed in the Indianapolis Star. They would keep the picture and obituary in their office, available for updating periodically. We paid in full, there and then. The money was invested and taxable. In Indiana, it was illegal to throw the cremains away, on the off chance, we were told, that the police needed to check for poison!

We thought that our problems, in that department, were solved. Not so. In 2004 my Mother died in Atlanta, with Sheila and me at her bedside. At the funeral home, they wanted to embalm her. "What for?" we asked. "She's supposed to be cremated right away." Dad being already dead, her three children were her next of kin. They informed us that all of us had to give written permission for her to be cremated and, as Mary was in England, Ma must be embalmed while we awaited her letter. Luckily, George remembered that arrangements for cremation had been made when they lived near Charlotte, North Carolina. A call to the funeral home there produced the necessary permission slips and dear Mama was reduced to ashes before the day was out.

Back home again, in Indiana, I phoned our Cremation Society and discovered, to my distress, that the Georgia and North Carolina laws applied throughout the States. As unmarried gays, Ambrose and I are not next of kin. We each had two sisters. All four had to fill out two permission forms each to grant us cremation rights, depending on whether we died singly or together.

Two years later we moved to Florida where we registered with the Cremation Society of Florida. In this State, I'm happy to report, cremains can be fed to sea fish at no additional cost. Over the years, the price has gone from an hundred and fifty dollars to about six hundred but the stock market has made our original investments worth about fifteen hundred dollars each, with the result that our estates will benefit from our cessation of life.

Mrs. Clowes asked me what to do about a Mrs. Hardy. She had written from Chicago to say that she would like to visit the collection in June. Every year, at the end of May, Westerley was closed for three months while the Duchess and Allen went to their summer homes in Woods Hole, on Cape Cod. A letter explaining this had been sent to Mrs. Hardy, to no avail. She had read about the collection in Connoisseur Magazine where it was printed that it could be visited anytime by appointment. An appointment was what she wanted, and expected. As her letter contained a phone number and as Ambrose and I were going to be in the Windy City the next weekend, I promised to call her.

Mrs. Hardy, it transpired, was from Long Eaton, near Nottingham, in England. She was visiting her daughter, Jane, secretary to the Rockefeller Chapel at the University of Chicago. I explained that all the furniture in Westerley would be covered in dust sheets and the draperies would be down for cleaning. The house re-opened in September. That would be too late as she would be back in England, long before then. As it was only the paintings she wanted to see, I said "OK, give me a call, when you would like to see them, and I'll be happy to oblige."

A week or two later, she phoned to say that she would be arriving by bus so, please could I suggest a hotel by the bus station and how long a walk is it from there to the Clowes collection? She must be very poor, I decided, to be coming by bus. Furthermore she must be totally ignorant of American cities to imagine that anywhere was within walking distance of anywhere else. Worst of all, in 1963, any hotel near the bus station rented bug ridden beds by the hour. Despite her protestations, I insisted that I'd meet her bus and she must stay with us but first, she must tell me what she looked like. "I'm sixty seven, short and stout with straight, short grey hair and I always carry everything in a large carpet bag." I began to wonder if this poverty stricken English woman was a homeless bag lady?

Never, in my wildest dreams did I visualize what a major part she would play in our lives for the next thirty years.

Judging from her fine jewelry, she was no pauper. Over a delightful dinner, chez nous, we discovered that her husband didn't trust planes. She could travel the world, while he stayed home, so long as she did so by ship, train or bus. He had inherited a lace factory in Nottingham. Bored with lace making, he sold the plant in order to pursue his hobby which was collecting antique English silver. This was a subject about which we knew almost nothing. We possessed a fair amount of family silver but almost none of it was even eighteenth century, let alone seventeenth.

In view of our kindness, in inviting her to stay, she had brought us our first treasure in the form of a pair of elegant serving spoons made in 1778 by Hester Bateman. They were the most beautiful spoons we'd ever seen. We were hooked. We too would collect antique English silver.

Muriel Hardy regularly wintered in the US, spending time with her only child in Chicago and exploring different states every year by Greyhound bus. Next year, she would stay with us for a week and give a talk on English silver at the Herron Museum. We became regular hosts, and the Hardys reciprocated. We stayed with them in Long Eaton. Noel Hardy met us at the train station. He wore a tweed cap and rode a bicycle. Having tied our suitcase onto his bike, he pushed it while we walked the mile or so to their run of the mill Victorian row house. I'm confident that neither the kitchen nor the single bathroom had been updated since the house was built.

In a garden shed, Noel had a mammoth roll of tracing paper, given by some pal who was closing a business, years earlier. With pride, he explained that he'd not had to buy toilet paper since the war. He would pull out a length along the work table, cut it into small squares, punch a hole in one corner to string it up to the hanging chain, from the overhead tank and "Voila! How's that for economy?" Never mind the expense of ensuing appointments with a proctologist.

The small rooms were cluttered, not only with the regular furnishings but with a number of safes. They were all over the place disguised, with skirted cushions, as hassocks. Supplied with gloves and a couple of chamois leathers, we were seated at the dining table while Noel kept us busy studying pieces from his priceless collection. He had been a friend of Commander How, whose five portfolio-sized volumes on the history of English spoons is universally considered the definitive work on the subject. Following the Commander's death, his highly respected and greatly feared widow was, arguably, the most knowledgeable person alive on the subject of antique English silver.

How of Edinburgh was a treasure house of priceless silver located in a secluded yard off St. James' Street, London. She had sold Noel most of his collection and would drop by Long Eaton, to visit, whenever she found something which might interest him. He had decided to collect only domestic silver, but he happened to have a communion chalice dated 1627 which he let us have at a bargain price. From that moment on, Ambrose and I became serious collectors, so far as our modest incomes would allow. For the most part we bought from well-respected dealers though, from time to time, we would find an unexpected treasure at an antique show. Apart from the beauty of the pieces, hallmarking of British silver enables one to tell who made it, where and when, sometimes as far back as the fifteenth century. Our earliest spoon was made by James Cluatt, in 1607.

At first we bought anything that we both liked and could afford. Then, an exhibition in 1990, of English women silversmiths, inspired us to see what we could find in the way of silver created by the fairer sex. To be honest, they are a rare breed. Hester Bateman was, by far, the most prolific but we were more interested in earlier and, in many cases, better craftsmen. The only major woman silversmith we failed to collect was Anne Tanqueray. In 2009, we found four beautiful tiny salt cellars by her. The dealer was asking forty five thousand dollars, so even a negotiated price was well out of our league. In the end, our collection included pieces by eighteen women, including at least two pieces of great rarity. One is a Baroque decorated tankard made in 1681 by Dorothy Grant. The only comparable one, by her, is undecorated. It is in the British Museum, London. We also acquired a spoon made by Elizabeth Hazelwood of Norwich, England. It was made in 1697, one of about 30 pieces of silver still known to exist of hers. Almost all her work is exhibited in Norwich Castle Museum. The National Museum of Women in the Arts, in Washington D.C., has a badly worn tobacco box by her. Another item is in the Royal Collection, in Windsor Castle. Apart from those two, plus another spoon in a private collection, I know of no other Hazelwood pieces.

While studying a scholarly book, by Timothy Kent, on English West Country spoon makers from 1550-1750, we were surprised to discover a seventeenth century maker by the name of Ambrose Smith. The pleasure of discovery was somewhat dampened when we read that he had been both dishonest, and rather stupid. In 1631, word had reached Goldsmith's Hall, in London, that a number of West Country silversmiths were making and selling underweight silver (Sterling, by law, is 92.5% pure silver). By adding more than 7.5 % base metal, dishonest silversmiths stood to make more money unless they were caught. Wardens swooped down from London with a view to catching, and prosecuting, makers of underweight silver. As the dress of London wardens differed greatly from that of country yokels, most of the guilty silversmiths hid their stock and claimed to have nothing to sell. Ambrose Smith, whose silver contained almost double the legal maximum of base metal, happily sold spoons to inspectors. Found guilty, he was heavily fined and his stock was destroyed. He must have been dumb as an ox for he was caught in the same way seven years later. There was an illustration of a sterling spoon, by him, in Kent's book so we contacted John Bourdon-Smith, the undisputed leading dealer for antique English spoons. Spoons by Ambrose Smith were as rare as hen's teeth, they informed us, but they would do their best to find one.

Every year or two, we would check with Bourdon-Smith and, no they had not forgotten about us, they were still diligently looking. A phone call, from Brad Luther informed us that Robert Lloyd, a New York dealer, was advertising a spoon by Ambrose Smith. We sent for, and received, detailed pictures and a description, of the spoon, from Lloyd. It was dated, he estimated, about 1650. It had a small, almost invisible, repair. After exchanging e-mails, I asked him to call me to discuss a possible sale. When he gave me the price, I exploded. "Let me tell you something, Mr. Lloyd," I said, "we recently acquired a similar West Country spoon from John Bourdon-Smith, who as you know, is as expensive as they come. What's more, that spoon is twenty years older than yours and bears the mark of the Marquess of Breadlebane's collection, has never been repaired and was a full thousand dollars less than what you are asking for your damaged one." "Well," he replied. "Let me tell you something. I've got a fax in front of me from Bourdon-Smith offering to buy my spoon, so you can take it or leave it." Of course we bought it knowing full well why Bourdon-Smith was after it. However, I wrote a letter to Mr. Bourdon-Smith, in London, enclosing all the photographs. I told him that we'd found it in New York and that it might be a forgery as the mark differed slightly from the one in Kent's book. In any case, as it was slightly damaged, we still hoped that he would eventually find us a perfect one. He kindly replied to my letter saying that I had as fine a spoon by Ambrose Smith as exists. He added that he would date it a decade earlier at about 1640.

That's enough said about collecting. We called it quits in 2010, giving the bulk of our collection to the Indianapolis

Museum of Art where it's beautifully displayed and much appreciated.

Noel and Muriel had a house keeper named Lilley. She did everything and more. Not until Noel died, did Muriel discover the real reason that she had to travel by ship. It was to extend her travel time to ensure that she wouldn't return unexpectedly and catch them inflagrante. Dear, dear, men were deceivers ever.

Their daughter Jane was a sweetheart. Like her mother, she didn't drive a car but Ken Drilling did. He lived alone, with his piano, in the same building, always willing to chauffeur here or there. Just as well, in view of what happened when Muriel came to stay with us just prior to her departure, by ship, for home. She went up early to bed while we were watching the train, on TV, transporting President Eisenhower's body back to Abilene, Kansas. On hearing a crash, we rushed upstairs to find Muriel collapsed in the bathroom. We called Reg Bruce, our doctor, who sent an ambulance and met us at Methodist Hospital. Her alimentary canal was blocked. A tube was inserted down her throat to pump her out. The job took ten days and left her too weak to stand. As her ship had long since sailed, she was told that she should stay with us for the next six weeks to regain her strength. Ken fetched, and carried, Jane to O'Hare every weekend so that she could fly in to Indianapolis to check on her Mother's progress. Noel Hardy sent us a beautiful snuff box in gratitude.

The "incident," as it came to be known, cemented our friendship with Jane and Ken and led to their getting married. Sadly, it was only a couple of years later that Jane's cancerous bladder had to be removed. She handled the loss with commendable courage and grace. Oblivious to the fate in store for her, Ken took her to England, to visit her parents. She died in Long Eaton.

Ambrose and I drove to meet the plane bringing Ken and Muriel back without her. Fortunately, we managed to get a key to their condo, ahead of time, so we were at least able to dispose of the equipment which she had needed for her miserable disability. Muriel handled her terrible loss better than Ken. As a practicing psychologist, his job involved dealing with his patients' mental anguish. It seemed to rub salt into his own wounds. After he retired, he moved to Indianapolis to be near us and in the hope of finally shaking off the malaise that possessed him. As the years have gone by, he has become an almost total recluse. He lives alone in his house listening to classical music or playing the piano. A sad story with a sadder ending.

Chapter Seventeen
*Times A-Changing*

Some six years into my eight year teaching career, at Harry E. Wood High School, I was head hunted for a part time evening job. Indiana University and Purdue were engaged in wedding plans but not yet married. There were a few old buildings in the downtown area, plus another on 38th Street, constituting IU's Indianapolis extension. All degree seeking students were required to take a three hour course in theater, music or art appreciation. Allene Doddoli, the gifted wife of Adolfo, who taught three-dimensioned arts at Herron, gave a course in art appreciation in an old building off Delaware Street.

That fall I began a three year stint as the second art appreciation teacher at the IU extension. Thanks to Allene, I learned the drill. "The Story of Art," by E. H. Gombrich, was the text. We shared a walk-in closet, of an office, which contained a small slide collection. Entrusted with a key for the freight elevator, we would transport the equipment, on a cart, to the floor where our classroom was located. Unlike many of the teachers, I required an original seven to ten page paper from each student. Among the topics I would assign was to trace the architectural ancestry of buildings in Indianapolis. Term papers, I discovered, were anathema to most students. I have always felt that it is important for an educated mind to be able to express ideas clearly and succinctly. For better or worse, all students who took my courses could expect to write term papers, even though correcting them required extra work from me. When I suspected plagiarism, the simplest way to nail culprits was to zero in on obscure terms which had been used and ask him, or her, to elucidate. The more time consuming way was to find the book or books that had been plagiarized. Either way, I made sure that the word got out that Ian Fraser did not tolerate cheating.

Both higher education and art, in Indianapolis, were at a crossroad in the mid-sixties. A large tract of land on the near west side of downtown was to be cleared of its population of poor, mainly black, people to make way for a new university campus. It was to be called Indiana University Purdue University Indianapolis. Today IUPUI is close to rivaling, in size, the main campuses in Bloomington and West Lafayette. The unwieldy name has spawned such abbreviations as "Ooee-Pooee" and "Oopee-Poopee."

Until the nineteen sixties, Herron School of Art students, seeking a degree, did so through Butler University. With the establishment of IUPUI, Herron was to change that affiliation through a painful and, at times, acrimonious process. Since 1902, The John Herron Museum of Art and the Art School had been joined at the hip. Never expecting a divorce, they shared, among other things, a library. Another complication was the nature of the school's curriculum.

Herron is the only professional art school in Indiana. Professional art schools differ from regular university art schools, or art departments, with regard to the distribution of course requirements. To major, for example, in painting requires that the professional art school student devote a large proportion of his courses to painting. By contrast, in most art schools one is only required to take a certain number of course hours of painting. Let's say that you need a hundred and thirty hours of undergraduate courses to graduate, and that all students need some science, religion and a foreign language. The professional art school student has to look at his graduation requirements from the professional standpoint. Every science, English or humanities credit that is required of all graduating students automatically increases the number of art courses required for both his major and minor. The bottom line meant that, by becoming part of Indiana University, it would take almost as long to graduate in art as to become a medical doctor. In the end, some accommodation has been reached to mitigate the burden on art students. Even so, it's virtually impossible to get a Herron degree in less than five years.

Another stumbling block was the proximity of the art school buildings to the museum. All the movers and shakers were in agreement that something must be done about the art museum. It was not only bursting at the seams, but until a larger more secure and climate controlled building was built no major gifts were likely to be forthcoming. Three alternative plans were up for consideration.

The first called for incorporating the existing building in to a large complex. To make that possible, two or three blocks of Talbott Street would be closed off and a few old houses torn down. That plan preserved the city's heritage and kept the museum easily accessible to the population of the inner city, an important consideration.

From the point of view of accessibility, plan two was the best. It called for sacrificing the central block of War Memorial Plaza between North and Michigan Streets. Mr. Paul Rauch was its chief advocate. He wanted to have the new museum built in the style of a Greek temple. Had his plan born fruit, surely the Hoosier capital would have been the butt of much unsolicited architectural scorn.

Plan three was to build a new museum within the planned IUPUI campus known, at that time, as Foggy Bottom. It also had the merit of proximity to downtown. Furthermore, if plans for the Herron school of Art to move onto the campus were realized, the school and museum would be reunited.

The question of where to locate the new art museum hit a snag when, at seventy three, Mr. Josiah Kirby Lilly II died intestate. The year was 1966. The Landon house, which he and his late wife Ruth had bought, was in the township of

Woodstock. Over the years, he had acquired all but one of the homes in the township, demolished them and erected gates, on the right of way, to keep the public out. Only Lilly could do such a thing and get away with it. Facing crippling inheritance tax, the children, J.K. III and Ruth, offered the fifty two acre estate to the city to as the home for the new museum of art.

The Philistinian mayor of Indianapolis, Mr. Barton, balked. The Lilly estate was west of Crown Hill cemetery at 38th Street and Michigan Road. Whatever site was chosen for the Museum, it must be in, or very close to, the downtown. At a forthcoming meeting in City Hall, Mr. Barton was all set to turn the offer down. He hadn't reckoned with the aging, but still formidable, Duchess. Mrs. Clowes invited the mayor to tea. She pulled out all the stops. With a map showing the development of Indianapolis, she was able to demonstrate that the center of population had shifted north of 38th Street, making the Oldfields estate about as central a site as could be hoped for. With large shopping centers springing up the busses, which connected them to downtown, could easily service the Lilly estate without much of a detour. Furthermore, the Oldfields grounds had been landscaped by the Olmstead firm who had done Central Park in New York. It was a gift too valuable to be turned down. Another cup of Earl Grey, drunk from eggshell porcelain, and Mr. Barton had changed his position. In the end, Indianapolis acquired as fine a site as any museum in the world. Thank you, Edith Clowes.

She deserves another "Thank you," for a painting which she gave to Harry E. Wood High School. When I told her about Dick Emery, and how much he was contributing to helping the disadvantaged, she offered a large landscape oil painting by Thomas Barker of Bath, as a gift to the school. Barker, who lived from 1769-1847, was a follower of Thomas Gainsborough. A handsome showcase was custom built to display the painting in Wood's front hall. For the unveiling ceremony, Mrs. Clowes and Allen rolled up in her chauffeur driven Austin Princess. She alighted in a silver mink to be greeted by Mr. Emery and a sea of gob-smacked students. Sadly, that was her last hurrah. She had already been through major surgery for colon cancer. By then it had spread to her liver and was deemed inoperable.

In early 1967, Mrs. Clowes had taken to her bed with round the clock nursing service. Allen almost never left the house. He spent most of every day at her bedside. I dropped by daily, after school, to read to her. Sometimes I'd get through a chapter or two but, as often as not, the pain drugs would kick in and she'd fall asleep. She lingered on into May becoming weaker and more confused with every passing day. Whenever she woke she called for Allen.

One evening friends prevailed upon Allen to go to a party. He went, drank too much and failed to stop at the sign where the minor road joined 421. He hit a car being driven by a young man with three passengers. At least one died, in the accident, and the rest were seriously injured. Allen almost died. A frantic call at 1:00 a.m. sent us hurrying to Wishard Hospital where we found him unconscious, on a gurney. Saving his life necessitated major surgery including the removal of a ruptured spleen. That he wasn't already on the operating table is due to the fact that no family member could be located to give permission. With his mother nigh unto death, they had tried to contact his brother George, without success. He was sailing in the Atlantic without radio or phone. Fortunately, the hospital director knew Allen and gave the necessary go ahead for the operation. It was three days before he regained consciousness. In the meantime Mrs. Clowes died and was cremated. It was another six weeks before Allen was well enough to attend a memorial service at Trinity Church. Even then, he was confined to a wheelchair. The suit brought by the victims, of the terrible accident, was settled out of court and never mentioned again. From that time on, Allen, who had already had bouts of depression knew nothing but unhappiness.

Well before her death, Mrs. Clowes made me promise to look after Allen once she had gone. If we failed it was not for lack of trying. At the same time, she also talked about the future of the collection. Her hope was for it to remain in the house. She fancied it as a mini Midwestern Frick Museum and wanted to know my opinion. Frankly, I thought it was a terrible idea from almost every point of view but most of the reasons I kept to myself. What I said was, because Westerley had been built as a house, rather than as a museum, sooner or later it might well suffer a catastrophic fire. On the other hand, the cost of making the existing structure truly fireproof would be prohibitive. In all likelihood, it would necessitate its total demolition and rebuilding. Of paramount importance, we both agreed, was the safety and preservation of the paintings. She had always loved the Isabella Stewart Gardner Museum, in Boston, and especially the idea of a courtyard with flowers. The Duchess was an excellent gardener as anybody who ever visited Westerley, in Indianapolis, or Easterley, on Cape Cod would testify. Work had already started on the Krannert pavilion. It was to be the first part of a new Indianapolis Museum of Art, on the grounds of Oldfields. If Allen and George agreed with me, that the paintings could not be safely left in situ, then she would not bind them to her wishes. In any case, she wanted me to remain as curator, of the collection, and to write a catalogue *raisonnée*.

Growing up as a member of the establishment, and of all the WASP clubs, and with a father and brother who sensed his obvious effeminacy, poor Allen Clowes never faced his own sexuality. After World War II, he spent a few years on Wall Street. If he ever had a homosexual encounter it probably would have been then. From New York, he returned to Indianapolis to live with his parents. His father died in 1958 so, from then on, he lived with his mother. Many years of dating Marjorie Flickinger almost lead to marriage, but he backed out

213

at the eleventh hour. That debacle caused Marjorie a mental breakdown and turned her parents against him.

How he met Françoise Hageneau, a French microbiologist who lived and worked in Paris, I don't know. They dated off and on for a few years. During a visit to Indianapolis, she extended an invitation to Ambrose and me to have dinner with her next time we were in Paris. We did so. She lived on Avenue Foch in half of a lovely mansion with her lesbian lover. I think Allen had suspected as much.

A much vaunted rumor was that Jack Von was Allen's boyfriend. Neither Ambrose nor I believed it. What is true is that he had first used Jack's services to do some interior decorating at Westerley. He then bought an Italianate mansion on Delaware Street in about the fourteen hundred block and bank-rolled a high end antique shop and gallery for Jack to run. The whole thing ended three or four years later when Jack Von died of AIDS.

At the time of the car accident, Allen's usual date was Leila Holmes from Macon, Georgia. She worked at the IU Medical Center and wrote a weekly medical column in the Indianapolis Star. Her office was a short walk from Wishard Hospital. She was at Allen's bedside when he awoke from his surgery, and visited him faithfully, every day, until she went on vacation with Jo Jameson, bound for Paris and London, during the summer of 1967. I had been in Europe since about a week after the accident, in May. When I met up with the ladies in Paris, I discovered that Leila and Allen were to be married in Macon, that October. She was probably in her middle forties and he was in his early fifties. When news of the engagement got out, the consensus was that she was a gold digger. George Clowes got Allen to sign a prenuptial that would limit her inheritance to a million dollars if things were to go awry. Leila is still a friend of ours and I must say, here and now, that she is not, nor ever was a gold digger. There's no denying that she was naïve.

I'm certain that she had no conception of what she was getting into.

Ambrose and I gave a party, at our house, for about forty of Allen and Leila's friends to celebrate their engagement. Unbeknownst to the guests of honor, everybody else was asked to dress as a work of art. Some of the costumes set a benchmark for future parties. Emma Lou Thornbrough, as the Empress Theodora, looked for all the world as if she had stepped straight out of the Byzantine mosaic in St. Vitale, Ravenna. Jock Bevan had made up her face to closely resemble tesserae. Fortunately, a photograph has preserved her image to this day. Jock turned Pam into a classical Picasso and, being tall and bearded, he easily transformed himself into El Greco. At about six foot tall, Jim Rogers made an unconvincing Toulouse Lautrec self portrait though Mary was recognizable as Jane Avril, one of Lautrec's muses. Sister Sheila made a more than passable Zurbaran monk while Ambrose and I turned up as a couple of paintings by Jackson Pollock. Perhaps the cleverest short cut was Nancy Woollen's outfit. It consisted of a black dress and jet jewelry. She claimed to be a painting by Bridget Riley called "Black on black!" The fun and games, of the evening, was briefly interrupted by a freak accident. Martha Slaymaker, an artist herself, was roaming all over the house looking at our pictures. In the middle of the upstairs sitting room was a glass shaded ceiling light which chose the second that she walked under it to shatter. It propelled a shard through her costume wig into her scalp. Her scream brought several of us running. There was a bathroom next door to the sitting room which was just as well because the wig couldn't absorb any more blood. Once removed, the cut on the top of her head was clean. A Band-Aid covered the wound. However, spending the rest of the evening wigless made the identity of her impersonation hard to deduce.

A few days later, we all headed to Georgia for Leila's family to entertain us with traditional southern hospitality for a couple of days before she married Allen. After a white wedding in Macon, and a brief honeymoon at Sea Island, they returned to a Westerley nightmare. Fortunately, Mrs. Clowes' longtime faithful personal maid, Irené, and most of the other help had stayed on. Apart from the staff, Leila was on her own with a rapidly deteriorating Allen. All day long, he would silently follow her about like a lost puppy.

Prior to Mrs. Clowes' final illness, we had a tradition that she, and Allen, regularly came to dinner with us on Sundays as their help were off duty that night. Back from their honeymoon, Leila was delighted to continue the tradition. However, every Sunday afternoon, Allen got Leila to phone, saying that he wasn't feeling well enough to come over. One day, at her wit's end, she called and agreed that next Sunday she would bring him over whether he was feeling sick or not. They showed up at our house but he looked utterly forlorn and was totally silent. When offered a drink or something to eat he just stared. Finally, I said, "Allen, please tell us what's the matter?" He still said nothing but both eyes turned into uncontrollable taps. That was the end of Sunday dinners and the start of Allen recluse.

Somehow Leila survived the winter alone with Allen, in Westerley. Hoping that a change of air would help the malaise, they went to Woods Hole in the spring. There, Allen had his own delightful house, Whitehill, across the road from Easterley which had been inherited by George and Peggy. One look at his brother and George sent for the well-known Boston psychiatrist, Harry Kozol. He later became a household name during the case of Patti Hearst and the Simbionese Liberation Army. Within days Dr. Kozol was ready to put his plan into action. First off, the six month marriage must be terminated with an agreement that Allen would pay Leila off at the rate of a hundred thousand dollars a year for ten years. Armed with her marching orders, Leila returned to Indianapolis and moved out of the Golden Hill house into an apartment next to Jo

Jameson. At Allen's expense, Dr. and Mrs. Kozol took their patient off for a long luxurious Mediterranean cruise. On return, He remained with the Kozols, in Boston, for several months.

I received a call from Clarence who, at nearly ninety, was still the Clowes' most trusted servant. He said that the Kozols had moved into Westerley bringing Allen with them but nobody was supposed to know. From then on, I kept in touch with George in case there was any change, but for the time being nobody was allowed to have any contact with Allen. After some moths of this stalemate we hatched a plan. I phoned Westerley and asked to speak to Mrs. Kozol. Explaining who I was, I expressed gratitude for all the help they were giving to Allen, and by way of appreciation, we'd be honored if they would come to dinner with us. They came as bidden, and before the evening was out, we concluded that they were an unsavory couple. Once they were gone, I phoned George with our assessment. He wasted no time in firing them. Before they left, they had talked Allen out of his valuable collection of oil paintings by the Boston Impressionist Arthur C. Goodwin.

George asked us to move into Westerley with Allen, with the promise that we would never want for money and that, if we found it impossible to live under the same roof, they would build us a house in the garden. We flatly refused any financial reward, but agreed to move in at least temporarily. Upstairs a hallway runs the length of the house with Allen's room at one end and his mother's at the other. The first thing we discovered, when we moved into her room, was that he got very upset if we closed the door. He liked to look through to that room from his bed. All day he would sit, like a Buddha, on the library sofa, reading whatever was at hand awaiting our return from work. If I had nothing to do when school let out at 3:30 p.m., I would be back at four, which was Allen's tea time. Often I was delayed attending a meeting or for some other reason, only to arrive back to find him very agitated. Ambrose always returned, as expected, around six. He would clean up and join us for a drink in the library before dinner at seven. As well as a bedroom and bath, we had our own upstairs sitting room but Allen always wanted us to be in the library with him. We regularly swept by our house, on Delaware Street, to check that everything was OK and to collect the mail.

After a few weeks, Allen seemed better. We suggested inviting Percy and Hinda Simmons, mutual friends who collected old master drawings, to dinner. He agreed, but as the day approached he became increasingly nervous. In the end, he couldn't face it and had dinner alone in his room while we dined downstairs. That was the only time we invited anybody into the house. To keep Allen on an even keel, we had to be with him for dinner every day. Some two months after moving into his home, we felt that we had done all we could. The time had come for us to move out and get on with our lives. We broached the subject at dinner, and rather to our surprise, Allen agreed. We informed George of our decision, returned to our house while promising to continue monitoring the situation.

We need not have worried. No sooner were we out than Betty Roberts moved in. Allen's office was at Washington Boulevard and 38th Street and, since his longtime bookkeeper Mrs. Thompson had retired a couple of years earlier, Betty Roberts had replaced her. Every April the board of the Clowes Fund met in Indianapolis to decide on which causes to support, and to what extent, with the bookkeeper in attendance. At dinner, after one such meeting, Peggy Clowes, George's wife, summed Betty up in one word—"Grabby." Once installed, she got rid of all the household help, one by one, and employed others. Next, she announced that she and Allen would be getting married! When news of the forthcoming nuptials reached George's ears, he sprang into action. Wedding plans were permanently tabled.

With the new art museum getting set to open, plans were being drawn up to add a wing to be known as the Clowes Pavilion. Kurt Pantzer had amassed a major collection of works by, and related to, the English artist William Turner, including about forty of his watercolors. It was agreed that the first floor of the Clowes Pavilion should house the Clowes collection. Three galleries, on the second floor, would contain the Pantzer collection, leaving three galleries for changing exhibitions. The lower level was for a lecture hall, classrooms and offices. Before discussing the fulfilling of these dreams, we must back track a couple of years, to 1968.

Chapter Eighteen
*House Plans*

Mrs. Clowes had left each of us ten thousand dollars in her will. Thanks to her bequest, we were totally in the black for the first time in our lives. We paid off our mortgage and paid cash for a new Chevy so that we could give the old Valiant to Steve Wright.

When opportunity knocks we've always believed that, if you're interested, you'd better not procrastinate. Ruby Williams, our neighbor, was ready to sell her house. We saw potential, and bought it. Being a corner house immediately to our north, it faced 37th Street with its two-car garage to the west of it. The rear wall of her garage helped enclose our delightful back garden. By putting a door in that wall, we shortened the distance to our kitchen door, compared with the distance from our own garage. Our house, like Ruby's, was set sideways on the lot. Ours faced south. The driveway, from Delaware Street, ran south of the house to the garage, which was to the very back of our lot.

Ambrose, forever an architect wannabe, set about a series of alterations which transformed out typical 1930 brick, four-bedroom, one and one half bath into a true Shangri La. He stopped the driveway at the west end of the house with a solid six-foot fence. That allowed for four or five cars to park on the driveway. Beyond the fence, we tore up the asphalt to enlarge our walled back garden. The garage, we turned into a delightful pavilion with a cathedral ceiling and an Italian tiled floor. The garage doors were replaced with brick pilasters and four French doors of small leaded glass panes. A twenty-four foot long, built-in, banquette against the back wall served double duty for storage and as comfortable seating to enjoy a view of the garden. It was to prove a remarkably versatile addition for meetings, parties, classes and dancing. When the dancer, Merce Cunningham, performed in Indianapolis, we had a catered sit down dinner for twenty in our pavilion. Aaron Rosand, the violinist, always used it as his practice studio whenever he was concertizing in Indianapolis.

The front door of our house opened into a pleasant hall with large doorways leading into the dining room, to the left, and into the drawing room, to the right. The east wall of the drawing room had sliding doors out to a traditional porch facing Delaware Street which we demolished and replaced with a two-story glass conservatory. It completely enclosed the Delaware Street end of the house. Below the conservatory floor, we dug out flower beds, and a fountain pool, to a depth of four feet. Above the drawing room were two guest bedrooms with windows looking into the conservatory. We removed one window and replaced it with a door onto a balcony running the length of the conservatory. With the skilled help of our friend Ann Ryder, the conservatory became a tropical paradise.

Forgive me for digressing again but, I must tell you about Ann. At eighteen, she had suffered a serious breakdown in her relationship with both parents, especially her father. Finding a gardening job at the Indianapolis Museum of Art, she met our friend, Mary Meek, a long time docent. When Mary brought Ann to visit us, she decided that we were the fathers she'd longed for. Though we had a pretty garden, it was more by luck than knowledge. Ann would drop by, in her bib overalls, several times a week with plants for us. Before long, she was one of the family house-sitting for us while we were in Europe.

At the Indianapolis Museum of Art, Ann Ryder had been befriended by Mrs. Bowman Elder. She gave the Museum its greenhouses along with her collection of orchids. Auntie Mad, as Madeline Elder was known, spent long hours working alongside Ann, teaching her how to transplant, and propagate, orchids.

Ann arrived at our house looking depressed. She told us that, having saved enough money for the fare, she had taken a bus to Longwood Gardens, Pennsylvania, to apply for an internship. She had been turned down, flat. Yes, she knew that Mrs. Elder had been president of the Garden Club of America and yes, she realized that a note from her would have secured a Longwood Gardens internship but no, she was not about to become beholden to anybody, SO! "So you blew it, Ann?" We tried to point out the value of life's connections, but Ann's pride stood in the way of her asking for help. A few weeks later, she came over, brandishing a letter and beaming with delight. She had heard back from Kew Gardens, in London! Off she went, for a six month internship and to stay with Yanie LeBas and Ann Wells. Once she returned from that world famous botanical garden, she was welcomed, with open arms, at Longwood. Finally, with a Purdue University horticultural degree, the world became Ann's oyster.

A bedroom, at the west end of our house, overlooked a formal walled garden. We turned it into a sitting and TV room. Then we cut a door through an exterior wall onto a flat roof on which we built a smaller conservatory. There we cultivated a prolific night-blooming Cereus. The master bedroom was large enough to carve out a second full bathroom. We removed the large dining room window and replaced it with a bay one. Finally, we doubled the size of the kitchen by incorporating the breakfast room into it. Now we were both able to work at the same time without bumping into one another.

One block west and eleven blocks north of us we bought the only vacant lot in the fifty seven hundred block of North Pennsylvania Street. We paid fifteen thousand dollars for it. The dimensions were perfect to accommodate the corner house which we had bought. Better still, it was a red-tiled brick Dutch Colonial, similar to others in the new neighborhood. Best of all, we stood to make a profit because, as a result of 'white flight', we could expect to sell it, in the new location, for twice what we had paid. The estimated cost of the relocation was thirty thousand dollars. Here's the breakdown. First we needed to prepare the future site with a driveway, foundation, and basement—estimate: ten thousand dollars. Next, there were some overhead utility wires that needed to be moved. They hung too low over the proposed route—estimate: five thousand dollars. Finally, the moving company would jack up, move and reset the house on the Pennsylvania Street site for fifteen thousand dollars. A slam dunk? Not quite.

Twelve feet into our new lot, on the south side, ran a hedge in front of which the neighbors had planted flowers. We talked to them and were assured that it wouldn't be a problem. They knew that they had been enjoying land that wasn't theirs and fully understood that the strip would, of necessity, become a driveway. What they didn't divulge was that they had just sold their house to a lawyer. He took us to court. Indiana had a quirky law whereby uncontested squatting, lasting seven years or more, gave the squatter certain rights. An out of court settlement split the contested strip between us and, in doing so, made the reduced lot useless for our plan. We sold the lot to an architect who built a charming home for his own family. Then we sold 3780 North Delaware Street to Charlie and Anita Giddings. They built a neat garage attached to the side of their house. Our initial disappointment was short lived. Charlie and Anita became treasured neighbors.

## Chapter Nineteen
### *Catalogue Research*

Now let us return to the fulfillment of the Clowes' family wishes for their art collection. While the Clowes Pavilion was under construction, I was working on the catalogue. Were I to elaborate on all the research involved in pursuit of accurate attributions, with regard to dating and authorship, this book would probably double in length. In addition, I suspect it would only be of interest to a handful of art historians. However, in the course of writing these memoirs, I will talk about a some of the Clowes paintings as they fit into the ongoing story. At this time, I plan to discuss a few pictures with problems that had to be solved if the catalogue was to be credible.

There was a, badly surface-abraded, profile portrait of a young man on a sixteen-sided, but roughly circular, wooden panel. In the early 1940s, when Dr. Clowes had acquired it, all the leading quattrocento art scholars agreed that it was by Paolo Uccello, ca. 1397-1485. Modern science thwarted any simple catalogue entry, when it appeared to be painted on a panel of solid mahogany which first reached Italy in the seventeenth century! Presumably we were now looking at a forgery? Despite the evidence, a hunch told me otherwise. When forgers create a fake, they have to accomplish two things. First, it must look convincingly like the work of the artist they are emulating, and second, it must appeal to a modern buyer. For this second reason, forgeries that go undetected for awhile eventually reveal telling characteristics of the prevalent taste of the period of execution. In this case, the abraded surface of the face along with obvious in-painting in the hair suggested to me that we had an original Uccello. An x-ray revealed the reprieve we had hoped for. The painting was executed on a rectangular fifteenth century Florentine poplar panel, in tempera paint. However, it was riddled with worm holes. Evidently, an early restorer, probably in the nineteenth century, had planed off the back till it was little more than an eighth of an inch thick. In doing so, he had abraded the surface paint. Then he had carefully inserted the fragile panel into a rectangular well which had been carved out of the mahogany hexadecagon. Finally, after skillfully filling in the cracks, he continued the plain black background over the rest of the panel. You might well ask why he went to such lengths and, to be honest, one can only guess at the answer. My thought is that a collector had another Renaissance profile portrait on a circular panel, facing the other way, and wanted a balanced pair for decorative reasons.

A more contentious attribution concerns a painting of a sleeping cupid. It had been discovered in an Irish convent over-painted as a Christ child. About 1945 it arrived in New York where the over-painting was cleaned off and, with clumsy in-painting, restored to its original subject matter. At that time, as it was about to enter the Clowes collection, it came to the attention of Walter Friedlaender, the leading authority on Caravaggio. He was well aware of a second version of the painting that hangs in the Pitti Palace in Florence. That one is documented as an original Caravaggio, painted in 1608, in Malta, for Fra Francesco dell'Antella, grand master of the Knights of Malta. Nevertheless, Professor Friendlaender was persuaded that Caravaggio had painted both pictures at about the same time. The matter might have rested there had we not loaned the Clowes canvas to an exhibition held in Detroit in 1965. At that time, Alfred Moir, who wrote that catalogue, was the noted Caravaggio expert. In his opinion, the Indianapolis painting was by Giovanni Caracciolo, a Neopolitan follower of Caravaggio. He cited a clumsily painted left foot to support his attribution. The time had come for an in-depth study of our painting. X-rays gave us reason to hope that ours was by

Caravaggio and that it was the earlier of the two versions. Cupid's left wing is folded under the sleeping boy. The *pentimenti* revealed that the artist had had several changes of mind in his attempt to make it appear natural. The same was true of the boy's head. More telling still, under the background in the upper left is a sketched-in head which shows all the characteristics of Caravaggio's initial brushstrokes. Next, David Miller, the chief paintings conservator, cleaned off all the in-painting, that had been done by previous restorers, and lo and behold, a beautifully painted, if somewhat abraded, left foot emerged. All that good news was sufficient to re-attribute the painting to Caravaggio. Several years later, I found out that the Clowes picture predates the one in Florence by about fourteen years. An art history Ph.D. candidate, who had been doing research at the Pitti came to the Indianapolis Museum of Art as an intern. One look at our canvas and lights went off in her head. Our painting is smooth and thinly painted in the manner of all Caravaggio's early works done when he was in Rome. At that time, he was painting homoerotic boys to satisfy the taste of his his patron, the catamite Cardinal del Monte. The most renowned painting which he did, for that man of God, is today in the Metropolitan Museum of Art, in New York City. The subject is four pretty boy musicians. It is dated about 1595. By 1608, which is the date of the Pitti *Sleeping Cupid,* Caravaggio was painting in a thick *impasto,* a very different technique from his early days. As if any further proof were needed, a madrigal written in the 1590s refers to a painting of a sleeping Cupid by Caravaggio.

The last word has yet to be written on a number of the Clowes old masters. One such is a panel painting long attributed to Hieronymus Bosch, ca. 1450-1516. The subject is *The Temptation of St. Anthony.* A larger version of the Clowes painting constitutes the central panel of a triptych in Lisbon, Portugal. As there are four other sixteenth century paintings, of the same composition, known to exit, I was not prepared to accept ours as by Bosch. In fact, I catalogued it as *School of Hieronymus Bosch.* Had I known in 1970 what I know now, it should be catalogued as *After Hieronymus Bosch.* Thanks to modern technology, we now know a great deal more about that painting than any study of the surface can reveal. The science of dendrochronology reveals that the wood panel is oak from near Antwerp, Belgium. It also tells us that the tree was cut down in 1520, some four years after Bosch died. An x-ray shows that there is a man's portrait under the *Temptation of St. Anthony.* He is wearing a small beret of a type that was an Antwerp fashion in the 1520s. In his hands he holds a white card. Using a technique known as "infrared reflectography," this x-ray camera can back away from the painted card to photograph what's written on it. Apart from the word "Antwerpen," which was written twice, and a monogram of "MN," nobody at the Indianapolis Museum of Art could translate the words.

I was put in touch with a specialist in medieval languages at the British Museum. What we discovered is that it is written in fifteenth to sixteenth century Swiss-German. It doesn't say much except to name, and praise, the sitter "Hieronymus Sulzer." Hopefully, a future art historian will solve the problem of Herr Sulzer and technology will enable us to separate the two paintings, while damaging neither. Rather than leave you in limbo, I'll guess at an explanation. Hieronymus Sulzer was probably a Swiss businessman in the importing of goods to sell in Switzerland. Antwerp, being Europe's biggest *entrepot,* in the sixteenth century, Sulzer would have reason to travel there from time to time. While there, he sat for a painter, whose initials were "MN," to have his portrait done. The artist would bring the picture to completion in time for Sulzer's next visit from Switzerland. What happened next is anybody's guess. Perhaps it was an unsatisfactory likeness and, Sulzer refused to accept or pay for it. Or perhaps bandits attacked, and killed, the merchant, and he died en route to wherever. We may never have all the answers.

I realize that researching works of art, while it fascinates me, can be one big yawn for many people. Because it has been such an important part of my life, I will be returning to the subject but, hopefully, in easily digestible bite-sized portions.

# Chapter Twenty
## Blessings?

A Blessing? No gay, or straight male contributor to the cultural life of Indianapolis during the third quarter of the twentieth century, didn't know Alberta Blessing. She was the quintessential fag hag, and the source of all gossip, whether true or false. Her source of income was cutting all our hair. She plied her trade in a street level apartment at Alabama and 14th Streets. In fact, she had two apartments, across the hall from one another. She lived, and entertained, in the larger one and cut hair in the smaller. She was always in her middle sixties, had straight white hair, worn in a chignon and, when working, would wear duck-like space shoes. Her gravelly voice, and laughter, betrayed a lifetime of smoking. The sign on her door simply read "A blessing?" which is also the way she signed everything, including checks. Her friends and customers were one and the same. They included such luminaries as Izler Solomon, the symphony conductor, Mr. Richard Wood, Lilly's CEO, and every metrosexual worthy in the city.

Alberta's library of pornography would have given the Kinsey Institute a run for its money. A coffee table creaked under the weight of all the standard fare, from Blueboy through Freshmen to Playgirl. Elsewhere, she had hordes of publications from the four corners of the earth, all guaranteed to slake the curiosity of the curious and titillate anybody whose sexual interests were kinky, or thoroughly bizarre. Where she came by her more *outré* publications is anybody's guess. In view of the possibility that they might have Arabic, or Chinese, texts scholarly linguists had a unique opportunity to add to their vocabulary.

Her salon was strictly limited to haircuts and news of the day – not necessarily in that order. She neither washed nor dyed hair, and customers were expected to take care of their own finger and toenails. As the price, which included coffee or a drink, was perennially five dollars, nobody complained about the limited offerings. Ambrose remained a faithful client till illness put her into the "turf business," but I only lasted a couple of years. At my final appointment, she got so involved in recounting a story that she cut one side of my head twice while forgetting the other.

Socially she was everywhere. During Clowes Hall intermissions, if you spotted a scrum of men, in all likelihood you'd find Alberta where the ball should be. One curious story comes to mind. It was a Memorial Day weekend. She had invited us to a party. Ambrose pulled out a Ouija board. It being our first exposure to one, somebody told us what to do and suggested we ask it who was going to win the five hundred. The race was to be run the next day. I don't remember the name that came up. Let's say it was "Kevin." Alberta produced the sports section of the paper to check, but there was no driver with that name. On race day we were working in our garden listening to the radio. Excitement was rising during the final laps as three cars were making the outcome too close to call. If my memory serves me right, it was an Italian, maybe Mario Andretti, who won that year. At any rate, as soon as the race was over, the commentators were analyzing the outcome, when one said, "And it's another great win for Kevin!" It transpired that he was the driver's longtime mechanic.

Dad retired in 1969 and celebrated by bringing Ma over for an extended visit. Ambrose and I picked them up at New York's Kennedy airport and drove up to Scarsdale to stay with Freddie Thomas. He had been working for an English antique importer, in Manhattan, since Banner-Whitehill had gone into receivership. Tired as the parents were, we all stayed up to watch "One giant step for man," as Neil Armstrong landed on the moon. From New York we drove to Pittsburgh to visit our friends Sid and Dorothy Kweller. Today, still spry, in their middle nineties, they are among our special treasures. The unusual circumstances of our initial meeting bears repeating.

For several years, beginning in the late 1950s, Patric O'Keeffe was in the habit of spending Christmas in Malaga. He always stayed at a tiny hotel called The Emperatrice, which was run by an old soak, Bob McDonald. Patric heard American accents, in the bar, and introduced himself. When Dorothy mentioned that she'd been born in Indiana, Patric screamed delightedly "You're a Hoosier!" Further conversation elicited the information that Sid had spent time in a small place called Lebanon, Kentucky. As luck would have it, we had taken Patric there on vacation. The Kwellers hadn't been in Indianapolis for decades but, with Patric's encouragement, they visited us sight unseen. It's been a devoted relationship ever since. Among their myriad talents, she was a long time librarian, and he is an extraordinarily gifted artist with an enviable sense of kindly humor. A couple of nights with them, in Pittsburgh, and we drove to Indianapolis where my parents already had several friends.

Never one to sit idle when she could be doing handiwork, Ma went shopping in Ayres, Indiana's largest department store. Having spent most of her life speaking English, she assumed that Hoosiers do the same, albeit with a different accent. She was about to be disillusioned. After explaining to her that, with nine floors of merchandise, she might save time finding the things she wanted by inquiring at the information kiosk, in the middle of the first floor. Knowing that I also spoke English, and trusting that I knew what I was talking about, she took the escalator up one floor, only to discover to her dismay that she was now on floor two. Returning to what she persisted in calling the "ground floor," she soon located the information lady and asked for "haberdashery." Never having heard of haberdashery, the kind lady asked Ma what items she wanted

231

to purchase. "I'm looking for cotton," Ma replied. At the pharmacy department, where she was directed, the sales person showed her such things as "wadding," "balls," and "q-tips." Dismissing all of them, she explained that she was seeking a "reel" of cotton. The perplexed assistant asked her what one does with a reel of cotton. Thinking that she must be dealing with a simpleton, Mother patiently explained that, with a needle in one hand, you lick the end of the cotton to stiffen it. After carefully sliding it through the needle's eye, and after you've cut off a length of the cotton, with scissors, you use it to sew things. Her careful explanation had done the trick. What Mother needed was a spool of thread, which she would find on the sixth floor, in "notions."

Ma's first encounter with the language barrier reminded me of Sheila's early experience as a nurse in Chicago's Billings Hospital. While a seriously ill patient was out of his room, Sheila was straightening things up when the matron looked in and asked what had become of the patient? "Oh," said Sheila, "he just went on the trolley to the theatre." My poor sister got a tongue lashing for making a joke when the wretched man was in such a parlous state. She soon learned that the correct answer to the matron's query should have been "They've just taken him on a gurney to the operating room." I believe it was Oscar Wilde who said that the United States and Britain are separated by a common language!

Stan and Eva Chipper had a Scandinavian styled house on a lake near Terre Haute, Indiana. The day we visited them, Stan was out of sorts because they were in the middle of an extended visit from his dreaded mother-in-law, Mrs. Federman. All three of them had escaped to England, from Czechoslovakia, when the Nazis had moved in. While Stan and Eva immigrated to the States, Mrs. Federman remained in the United Kingdom. She was in the habit of complaining about almost everything in a singularly whiny voice. Ma made the mistake of telling her that we had driven to meet their plane in

New York. That was enough to elicit a grumble that Stan would never do that for her. No, no, he was much too lazy. He made her fly all the way to Chicago. This brought Stan into the conversation. "It would have been a fine state of affairs," he said, "if he had driven to New York. Two three hundred and fifty mile round trips to O'Hare, was bad enough!" After bringing his mother-in-law and her luggage back to Terre Haute, she realized when the key didn't fit that it wasn't her bag!

In a pathetic attempt to help lower Stan's blood pressure, I offered to entertain the old lady with a tour of the Indianapolis Museum of Art, and to give her lunch. He gratefully accepted. I did my best to listen politely to her litany of gripes while we drove to the museum. We were parked in the IMA garage, ready to alight, but she was busy complaining that there was no chutney to be had in all of Terre Haute. When I gave her a look of disbelief, she assured me that was the case. Every day, she had her daughter Eva drive her all over town on a quest for chutney. They had come up empty-handed everywhere. By now, I was out of the car holding the passenger door open for Mrs. Federman. I assured her that, after visiting the museum and having lunch, we'd sweep by Atlas Supermarket to satisfy her desire for chutney. "No," she said, staying put in the car. "If you're sure they've got some, we should go now in case they sell out!" I was beginning to sympathize with Stan. Shutting the car door as gently as the circumstances allowed, we departed the museum for Atlas. Few stores carried a larger selection of chutneys than that unique supermarket, so it was with confident pride that I steered her to the appropriate aisle. With a beady eye she slowly scanned the shelves before turning to me, with an infuriatingly complacent look, as she whined, "So you see I was right, there's no 'Green Label.'"

Sheila was nursing in the San Francisco Bay area, so we drove west to meet up with her, visiting friends and sightseeing en route. The vast stretch of salt desert, west of Salt

Lake City, called for a closer look, so we stopped the car. All was silence, with nothing but pristine salt flats in every direction, until Mother stepped out onto still wet chewing gum! Like winning the lottery, the chances of such an encounter must be one in umpteen million, unless you're my mother. At a Nevada border town, we stopped for a cup of coffee. It was the first time that we had come across one-armed bandit fruit machines. Ma, the last of the great spenders, risked a nickel. That investment, I'm happy to report, paid for all our refreshments and more. All in all, it was a great trip, one that enabled us to experience many of the varied wonders of nature to be enjoyed in these United States.

The author with Hogarth's
portrait of Simon Lord Lovat.

The headmaster's office and
house, Munro College, Jamaica.
Water color by the author
aged 13.

Newbattle Abbey.

Opening day of Achimota College,
Ghana 1927. From left, Dr.
Aggrey on lower step, Sir Gordon
Guggisberg (in plumed hat)
and Alec Fraser.

Newbattle Abbey. The library.

Mary and Ian Rutherford 1947.

Yvonne Gilan 1947.

The author modelling circa 1954.

The author at Newbattle
Abbey aged 18.

Jo Jarrett (Pussy) on phone.
Jo Scott (Pixie) smoking 1956.

Tessie O'Shea and Pat Meaney at
Tessie's home in Blackpool 1950.

The "Ian Fraser" shop 1955.
Coffee table and side chair
designed by the author.

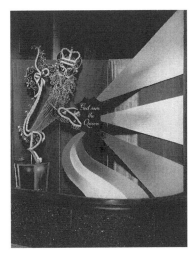

Window display for Coronation
of Queen Elizabeth II.

Ambrose (left) and Ian (right) as
ushers at Barbara Colden's
wedding 1953.

Chair designed by
Ian Fraser 1954.

25 Bywater Street, Chelsea,
London. First home for
Ambrose and Ian.

Pat Meaney in the Lido,
Champs Elysées, Paris.

Left to right, Sheila, Ian, Sandy, Phil, Oliver Robinson and Mary. The author's family circa 1962.

Left to right, Ian Fraser, Penelope Sampson and Barbara Brook.

Barbara Brook.

The author as a salesman at Banner Whitehill circa 1960.

The Regendanz's London home.

Ambrose 1958.

The author's grandparents, Alec
and Bea Fraser in 1956.

Sheila.

Left to right, Bernice McLane,
Prudence Douglass and
Marguerite Mitchell 1956.

Ambrose with Sid and Dorothy
Kweller in Pittsburg circa 1995.

Patric O'Keeffe circa 1975.

Quentin Crisp and the author
in Runnymede.

Monica Merlin.

Ambrose and Raymond Leppard
in the maestro's home,
Indianapolis.

Kerry Ferguson and Brad Luther
in the Block 2004.

Helen Pilgrim-Minor

Annette Kaufman and Keith
Jameson in Santa Fe circa 2009.

Ambrose with Herb Budden
in Runnymede.

Left to right, Dick Emery, Allen
Clowes, Edith Clowes and Ian
Fraser. Barker of Bath painting
being presented to Wood
High School

Bernice Fraction.

Emma Lou Thornbrough
as the Empress Theodora.

Leila Holmes and Allen Clowes.

Cecil Gould.

Sandy and Phil Fraser dressed
for tea with Queen Elizabeth II.

Sheila, Ian and Mary circa 2007.

Phil Fraser with Ryan Messer
2001.

Muriel Hardy.

Ambrose and Ryan 2003.

Left to right, Jock, Ambrose,
Pam and Ian at Bonnet House,
Fort Lauderdale 2006.

Ambrose sailing at Longboat
Key 1986.

Ambrose 1992.

The author 1992.

An Ionic moment!

Steve Wright graduates.

Ambrose turns 70.

Left to right, Bill Grimes, Ian Fraser, Ed Kelley, Mary Lou and Bret Waller, IMA Director 1995

Ambrose becomes a citizen.

Ambrose as Eve and Ian as Adam.

**Left to right, Thor, Miranda and Ian Cutler.**

**Phil Fraser.**

**Left to right, Ryan, Ambrose and Ian.**

## Chapter Twenty One
### *Wonderful Friendships*

1970 was to be Dick Emery's last year as principal of Wood High School. He was replaced by Tom Jett, the assistant principal. As many of us feared, he turned out to be your typical play-by-the-rules educational Jack-in-office. Consequently, after a year, several of us teachers asked for, and received, transfers. In my case, it was back to Shortridge, but this time, to teach in the high school. The flourishing art department was headed by Sheldon Kantor, a gifted teacher of both ceramics and photography. His father-in-law Roy Aberson, was the school's head coach. Though I missed the students at Wood, I quickly bonded with several teachers. Some remain among our closest friends.

Richard Cohen and Carolyn Fay who were friends from Wood had, like me, transferred to Shortridge. Cynthia Snowden was a counselor as well as an English teacher. She was a country girl from Parke County, which is noted for its many covered bridges. Her lunchbox was always replete with organic surprises. As an avid reader, she was never at a loss for interesting lunchtime conversation. Nathan and David, her sons from a previous marriage, were Shortridge students. Herb Budden also taught English. Bonnie, his wife, taught small children within the Indianapolis school system. Whenever possible, I would join Cynthia, Carolyn and Herb for lunch. Of all our wonderful friends, none has a better sense of the ridiculous than Herb. His infectious laugh can escalate to the point that he is in danger of falling off the chair. A few minutes of his company is all it takes to bring sunshine into the gloomiest day.

As luck would have it, he and Bonnie had bought an historic yellow clapboard cottage, on 32nd Street, within easy walking distance of our house. In fact, all of us friends lived on the north side of town, fairly close to one another. As a loose-knit group of friends, we frequently got together, at some watering hole, for drinks and dinner after school on Fridays. Parties in each other's houses were commonplace. From time to time we would take weekend trips to Cincinnati, Columbus or Chicago. Wherever we went, we could rely on Cynthia to make sure that everybody paid their fair share to the nearest penny! The halcyon days of spending time, simply enjoying one another's company, were doomed with the advent of the Internet, but in those comparatively primitive days, we had little notion of what lay just around the corner.

What lay just around the corner for Cynthia is that she would marry Jim Rogers. By day, he edited text books. His knowledge of music enabled him to present regular concerts on the Norbert Neuss classical music FM station. We had known him for years. His first wife had been Mary Forman, who he met in company with Ambrose and me at a Paul Spheeris party. For both Cynthia and Jim-Jams, it was a third marriage and I'm happy to report that the third time was a winner. They are now well into a fourth decade together. During his marriage to Mary, she would complain when he played what she called "Po-music." Jimmy, who is American, never understood what his British wife was talking about. "Po," to the Brits of our primordial era, was the standard abbreviation for "chamber pot," which to Mary's mind was as unsavory as chamber music!

Ground was broken in 1968 near Batavia, Illinois, for Fermilab. Its purpose was to accelerate atoms almost to the speed of light before smashing them together in the hope that the resulting particles would turn out to be the one universal building block. The lab required for this cutting edge experiment was so large that a small town had to be

236

demolished in order to build it. Brilliant physicists were employed to design the experiments and to analyze the results. One of these was a young Bavarian Ph.D., Klaus Pretzl. Sight unseen, we knew we'd like him because his wife Geli (Angelica), was the younger daughter of Irmi Werth. Irmi was the middle daughter of my almost mother, Elsa Regendanz. We were not disappointed.

Always making light of his erudition, he could draw one's attention to profound truths with good humor and incisive wit. During their years outside Chicago, we were to spend many happy holidays together. After he was enticed to Switzerland, where an even larger accelerator known as CERN was being built, we vacationed with them there.

Klaus smoked cigars. In a futile attempt to quit smoking, Ambrose had switched from cigarettes to Muriel cigars. They were small cigars built in to plastic holders. On a weekend visit to the Pretzl's, Klaus warned Ambrose that Muriels were the worst thing you could smoke because they contained asbestos. When we returned home, I suggested that Ambrose check the matter out. He did not. He continued to smoke Muriels exclusively. That Thanksgiving, the Pretzls joined us in Indianapolis. After dinner, Klaus and Ambrose lit up, and Klaus said, "I'm so happy to see that you no longer smoke Muriels." I couldn't believe my eyes. Ambrose was nonchalantly puffing away on a conventional cigar! I held my peace.

Freddie Thomas had bought the Old Village Inn in Ogunquit, Maine. He invited us there for Christmas. I was packing Ambrose's suitcase with everything he had put out for the trip, when I noticed there were no cigars. I found him in the kitchen and asked how many packs he planned to take? "None," he said, "I'm not going to smoke anymore." And he didn't. He quit cold turkey. Though he suffered no detectable mood swings, he gained about twenty pounds in fairly short order.

Right after Klaus and Geli returned to Europe, the Marinellis arrived from Florence, Italy. Enrico, on graduating from Harvard, had been head hunted to work for Lilly. With a plant in Prato, near Florence, Lilly hoped to greatly expand the Italian share of the pharmaceutical market and Enrico Marinelli was the man to make it happen. Along with Gloria and two toddlers in tow, they arrived in Indianapolis for a two-year stint in the States. We became friends and discovered that we shared many interests.

Lorraine Price was selling her house in Golden Hill. It had been built many years earlier by the Woolens in imitation of a small sixteenth century Florentine palazzo. They had filled it with genuine Renaissance antiques. Mr. Mulholland, the new owner, had no use for old stuff, so the Marinellis seized on the chance of a lifetime, bought the lot for peanuts and shipped it all back to Florence from where it had originated half a millennium earlier. A few choice pieces they kept for their Florentine apartment. The rest they sold for considerable profit.

That choice apartment is the top two floors of the building catty-cornered to Orsanmichele, at the intersection of Via Dei Cimatori and Via de Calzaioli. Among their art treasures they own the original modello, which Paul Manship created for his monumental golden Prometheus on the plaza of the Rockefeller Center in New York City.

Enrico's father owns the family business on Via de Fossi, selling Renaissance sculptures and reproductions. He owns a number of priceless original plaster casts, including those of the so-called "Doors of Paradise," designed by Ghiberti for the cathedral baptistery. Following the Arno flooding in 1966, it was decided that the original doors, once restored, should be kept henceforth in the Museo del Duomo. Marinelli released the original plasters in order to cast two pairs of bronze doors. Both pairs were paid for by the Japanese. They kept one pair, to be exhibited in the Tokyo Museum of Western Art, while the other replaced the original on the east front of the Florence baptistery.

Another plaster in the Marinelli collection is by Giovanni Bologna of Mercury, messenger of the gods. A cast of it graces the entrance lobby of the National Gallery in Washington, D.C. The sculpture is about five feet high. Marinelli decided to cast a bronze three times the original size as an eye-catching centerpiece for his showroom. He never expected to sell it. At the entrance to his gallery, the old gentleman has always kept a book which customers are asked to sign. Within days of the fifteen foot Mercury's installation, a weird looking young man—as Marinelli described him—walked in, paid cash for the sculpture, and arranged to have it shipped to California. The next day, another weirdo walked in and asked to buy the previous day's sign-in page. It was only then that he found out who Michael Jackson was. The statue was installed at Neverland.

The Wellivers were Florentine wannabes. Janet Welliver was old Indianapolis money. They had owned an evening paper called The Indianapolis News. Holliday Park was named for them. Carol Holliday who had had difficulty touching me after I had kissed a black cheek, was her sister-in-law. They could hardly have been less alike. Few people I've known exuded more genuine charm than Janet. She faded away in her mid 90s, at Marquette Manor. Her husband Warman was a Renaissance man. If anybody knew more about the Medicis it would have to be the family itself. Having written extensively on their banking system, he turned his sights onto their art collecting and patronage. As a self-taught scholar, he brought a refreshingly original viewpoint to Botticelli masterpieces about which we erroneously believed that everything that there was to say had already been said. He wrote fluently in both Italian and English. When he died of breast cancer, I had his collected papers leather bound and put into a special container before gifting them to the Indianapolis Museum of Art library.

The Welliver's Indianapolis home was between Meridian and Pennsylvania Streets near the middle of the block on the north side of 48th Street. They had a daughter, Lucy, and a son, Charlie. Charlie was autistic and tended to have short lived interests. Whatever they happened to be, his parents spared no effort to encourage them. He had just developed a fascination with African talking drums, and was exploring their potential, when we were visiting with my Dad who had experienced them in northern Ghana. Charlie and Dad had a great time while we visited with Janet and Warman. I remember a concert in their drawing room. On that occasion, the musicians consisted entirely of the Indianapolis Symphony Orchestra's brass section. Ambrose and I sat as far away as possible, but it was still painfully loud.

Being that certain kind of scholar, Warman took nothing at face value. That is one thing, when you insist on studying the Bible in the original Greek, but quite another, when you apply it to everyday life. Charlie expressed an interest in learning to play billiards. Warman did his homework. Though nothing was too good for his son, he pinched pennies wherever possible. There was sufficient space for a full sized pool table in Charlie's room. However, it wouldn't go up the stairs. One manufacturer made a table in three sections, to be bolted together later. It would go up the stairs. The problem was that, once assembled, the two horizontal cracks might affect the roll of the ball. Careful measurement seemed to offer the solution. The window in Charlie's room was large enough to admit a full sized billiard table endwise. To save money, Warman rented a forklift. He was spotted heading south on Meridian Street driving the vehicle with the billiard table aloft. The one thing he had failed to consider was the flower bed below Charlie's room. Before reaching the optimum spot, the front wheels had sunk down to the axle. It was immediately apparent that access through Charlie's window was out. Next, Warman rented a tow truck to retrieve the forklift. By then, threatening skies had turned to rain, so there was no time to lose. The master bedroom window, though it was the same overall size as Charlie's, was in the form of three sash and casement windows with dividers for the counterweights. Under the circumstances, there was nothing to be done but to wreak the triple window. Penny pinching Warman spent plenty of them to fix that mess. The billiard table came to rest in Janet and his bedroom. As it was too large to go through the door, it became an unusable fixture in their bedroom as much of the floor was occupied by a king sized bed. The problem was moot, because Charlie had lost interest in billiards.

In some ways, Janet was equally eccentric. Their daughter Lucy was married to a university professor in Athens, Georgia. On the back stoop Janet kept a saucepan, used exclusively to boil up a historically sanctioned brew of borage, and other medieval herbs, to cleanse the putrid kitchen air. She excitedly informed us that the temporarily abandoned saucepan had grown a perfectly beautiful mold. We listened to her enthusiastic description with as much feigned interest as we could muster. Hating the idea that Lucy was missing out on such a rare treat, she set about rectifying the matter. She emptied a box of Droest chocolates, as it was the correct diameter. After lining the box with damp cotton, she must have spent an inordinate amount of time transferring the mold, undamaged, to its new home. Circular and slightly domed boxes resist conventional wrapping, but the ever resourceful Janet was up to the challenge. She remembered that Warman had been given a box of fine cigars. Finding it in his study, she dumped the contents. Janet had legs of differing lengths, but there was nothing wrong with her eye. The chocolate box was a perfect fit so, in a jiffy, the treasured mold was on its way to Georgia. History doesn't relate what either Lucy or Tim had to say when the package's contents saw the light of day. Lucy, with years of experience, probably smiled indulgently as she dropped it in the garbage. Tim may have worried that, one day, his wife might wind up as kooky as her mother.

Warman decided to take classes in portrait painting. He found a teacher in New York City and signed up for private lessons. When I discovered that he commuted by train, a journey which involved over forty hours of weekly travel, I posed the obvious question. His surprising response was that he found mindless Muzak so offensive that he was prepared to go to any length to avoid being subjected to it. In airports, it's inescapable.

His classes behind him, finding no willing models, he settled for the dog. Certain human sounds caused the dog to prick up one ear. That was the canine expression which our fledgling artist wished to capture. Unfortunately, as soon as the raised ear had noted the source of the sound, it flopped back into its customary position. I visited Warman in the bedroom which was serving double duty as a studio. The docile dog was posed on the billiard table, clearly bored stiff, with both ears flopped. In a futile attempt to gain, and hold, the pose he was after, Warman used a clothes peg to clip both of his pet's ears into an upright position. Not surprisingly, Fido took a dim view of this perceived humiliation. He quickly scratched it off. With me to help, our dauntless *limner* had another idea. I was to hold the ear aloft while he painted. It soon became clear that the dog was not going to cooperate, as the proximity of my hand to his face was an invitation to have it licked! Like father, like son. A future in portraiture was soon in the past.

As well as a house on 48th Street, the Wellivers had one overlooking Florence. It is in San Domenico, half way up the hill to Fiesole. The house is ancient, small and charming with a spectacular view of the Duomo, San Lorenzo and the Arno. Most people, with comparable homes would divide their time between the two, spending certain months each year in Italy. The Welivers of course, were never like most people. One time they stayed in San Domenico for seven years. I would visit them, most years, to let them know that all was well in Indianapolis and to learn things about Florence, from Warman, that would fall well below tourist radar. Those were the years that Warman was researching the Medici dynasty.

Next door, in San Domenico, lived Fernanda Bramanti. Her late husband had been an artist. She was head of the Dutch Institute in Florence. For years after the Wellivers had left, Ambrose and I remained friends with Fernanda. Sometimes, her son Donato would come on an expedition with us. I recall an occasion when, after drinks at her house, we drove to a restaurant. She had reserved a table for four. Once seated, I asked whether she had expected Donato to be with us. "Oh! No," she said, "I always book an extra place so that you have someplace to put coats and handbags." Good lesson learned.

# Chapter Twenty Two
## *Problems of Attribution*

The spring following Betty Roberts' take over of Westerley, she took Allen to Woods Hole where his mental condition continued to deteriorate. In fact, between Cape Cod and the psychiatric wing of Methodist Hospital, Allen was out of his home for about five months. When he finally returned, the Clowes Collection was gone. The Krannert Pavilion, of the new Indianapolis Museum of Art, had opened and work was well under way on the Clowes Pavilion. With Allen out of the house, Carl Weinhardt, the museum director, and I prepared all the art for moving and completed the necessary paperwork.

The physical move took place one night as a closely guarded secret. A section of the museum's storage area had been set aside for the collection. David Miller, the chief paintings conservator, had cleared his schedule, for the next few months, in order to carefully examine each piece, and to clean or conserve it, as required.

For my part, I had been working on entries for the anticipated catalogue since the death of Mrs. Clowes, four years earlier. You must forgive me for spending some time discussing art scholarship and connoisseurship with special reference to the subject prior to World War II. It is estimated, for example, that of the less than six hundred original oil paintings in the world by Rembrandt, in excess of ten thousand entered the United States, through the port of New York, in the years between the two world wars! Oddly enough, almost none of them was a forgery. They were misattributions. There were scores, if not hundreds, of exceptionally gifted Dutch seventeenth century painters. However, few modern collectors, or even dealers, could identify more than a handful. One reason was that the standard treatment for grimy old paintings was to slap on another coat of varnish. This had the effect of obscuring the, already dim, subject matter still further. If the overall appearance resembled a well polished old brown shoe, it was probably by Rembrandt. Of the seven Rembrandts in Indiana, in 1973, none remained unquestioned a few years later. At last, the dust seems to have settled. Now, there are two, one of which has had a lot of later in-painting.

In the early 1970s, five Rembrandt experts formed a corpus in Amsterdam to settle, once and for all, the question of which paintings are, and which paintings are not, by the master. Their intentions were good but their methods were flawed. They lacked modern technology. Today we still cannot guarantee that a picture is by Rembrandt, but we can easily prove that he could not have painted it. The five men traveled the globe in pairs studying every purported Rembrandt.

The seven Indiana wannabes were in the Indianapolis Museum of Art conservation lab. Dr. Levie, director of the Rijksmuseum, was chair of the corpus. He and Dr. Bruyn came to Indianapolis. A few years earlier, the IMA had acquired a Rembrandt portrait of his wife Saskia. It was neither. The three Rembrandts in the Herrington collection were all misattributed. A portrait of a man in Earl Townsend's collection was genuine, though somewhat altered and in-painted by later hands. The remaining two were in the Clowes Collection. One was of an old man with a tall fur-edged red cap. Not by Rembrandt, they said. "Well," said I, "don't you think it's a study for the Rembrandt portrait of an old man seated with a staff in his hand, in the Dahlem Berlin museum?" They agreed that the Clowes picture was indeed a study for the Berlin one. The problem was that the Berlin painting wasn't by Rembrandt either. In all likelihood, they were both painted by Aert de Gelder, a late pupil of Rembrandt's.

We discussed the self-portrait. It is, without a doubt, a portrait of Rembrandt at the age of twenty two or twenty three. On this picture, they were withholding judgment because they still needed to study two other versions of the same picture, one in New York and the other in Switzerland. As I was to be in Amsterdam a few months later, we would dine together and they would let me know, at that time, what conclusion they had reached. In the event, Levie was out of town, but I had dinner with Dr. Bruyn. The New York picture was crap. The Swiss painting was lovely and slightly larger than the Clowes one. In their opinion, the best version was in Indianapolis, but all three were copies of a lost original. I was very distressed because my own connoisseurship told me that the Clowes painting was indeed genuine.

Many people think that a genuine signature makes a picture genuine. Unfortunately, t'aint necessarily so. In Rembrandt's case, he had many pupils, and if he was totally satisfied with their work, he would sign it. Often it's fairly easy to tell the difference between an original work of art and a copy. An x-ray of the Clowes Rembrandt self-portrait reveals that the artist changed the composition several times, especially with regard to the outline of his cap. Such under-drawings are known as *pentimenti* and are a sure sign of an original composition.

We sent x-rays, and infrared photos, to the corpus in Amsterdam in the expectation that the picture would be exonerated. When volume one, of the six planned, arrived, I couldn't believe their convoluted opinion. Under normal circumstances, *pentimenti* would argue for an original work, they said, but in this case, a certain hesitancy and weakness around the corners of the mouth forced the corpus to conclude that the painting in Switzerland was an original Rembrandt self-portrait. I was outraged, but not for long.

Dr. Christopher Brown, who at that time was keeper of the Dutch paintings at the National Gallery, London, and a noted Rembrandt scholar, came to visit us expressly to study our painting. He was convinced of its authenticity. I needed an authority of his stature as some of my trusted colleagues were abandoning ship. My most serious antagonist was Tony Janson, who was chief curator at the IMA. In his opinion, we had an original painting by Jan Lievens. As young painters, Lievens and Rembrandt had shared a studio in Leiden. During those years, their colors and techniques were very similar. However, Lievens always had a slightly softer, or less assured, touch. Also, unlike Rembrandt, he never used the butt of his paintbrush to put squiggles into details like hair and beard. In my opinion, an even more telling argument is the lighting. Self-portraits, of necessity, are created by the artist looking in a mirror. This turns everything back to front. If one really wants to see what the artist looked like, you need to look at the painting's reflection in another mirror. Rembrandt has left us more than fifty self-portraits. Being right handed, he needed to have the window on his left. Under the circumstances, I argued, the only way the Clowes picture could have been painted by Lievens would be for the two artists to have swapped places in the studio. It was vital to get Janson on my side, as we had agreed to cooperate on a museum catalogue.

The painting in Switzerland was in a bank vault as security for a loan. It belonged to a Swedish collector. From the bank's standpoint, whether or not the hocked object was by Rembrandt was of considerable monetary importance. In the late 1980s, I heard from Christopher Brown. He informed me that the Swede's painting had been bought by a Japanese monastery in Atami, known as MOA. As part of a planned Rembrandt exhibition in Tokyo, he would like to borrow both pictures to be hung side by side. I was delighted and flew to Japan with the Clowes painting only to discover that MOA had decided against loaning their picture. On Chris Brown's suggestion, I took a train to Atami where I met with the MOA curator. True to Japanese custom, he entertained me with a tour of the remarkable hilltop museum, including the "Rembrandt self-portrait," followed by tea. I sympathized with

MOA's refusal to loan their treasure for a lengthy exhibition so soon after its acquisition. On the other hand, here was a unique opportunity to study the two panels side by side so that x-rays and photographs could be taken. With that in mind, Toshiharu Nakamuro, curator of the National Museum of Western Art, in Tokyo, offered to transport the MOA painting under tight security, for one day only, to the Tokyo conservation lab. It was not to be. Whatever MOA had paid for their painting, it was obviously too much to be told that it was a copy.

Sooner or later, truth will out. In this case we waited until 1992 with the publication of two articles in the April and May issues of Art and Antiques, written by Michel Van Rijn, a well known, unscrupulously dishonest, Amsterdam art dealer. For readers interested in art chicanery, I recommend these articles. They can be found under the overall title of "Rembrandt's Castle." For our purposes, we'll cut to the chase. Van Rijn had been selling art to the Japanese for some years when he discovered that MOA was in the market for a Rembrandt. With the first volume of the, anxiously awaited, definitive Rembrandt catalogue in the works, it became urgent to sell off doubtful works before publication. Both the Swedish collector and the Swiss bank, where the picture was being held, would have known that the corpus planned to publish it as a copy. When Van Rijn offered to sell it to the Japanese, as an original, both bank and collector jumped at the opportunity. The dealer underestimated his clients. They showed up, in Amsterdam, to study the picture and to get a written scholarly opinion from Dr. Levie. As we know, Dr. Levie believed that the picture in question was a copy, and in view of the supporting evidence, which we had sent from Indianapolis, that the Clowes painting was an original. Incomprehensible as it may seem, all it took was a twenty five thousand dollar bribe, from Van Rijn, for a dishonest written opinion which ultimately cost Dr. Levie his job and ruined his reputation. By now, no serious scholar doubts the authenticity of the Clowes self-portrait.

Of all early self portraits by Rembrandt, the one with the most unassailable provenance is in the Art Gallery of Liverpool, England. That one was actually bought from the artist himself in 1628 by Robert Kerr, Earl of Ancrum, (ancestor of Lord Lothian) while on a diplomatic and buying spree for King Charles I. Through the science of dendrochronology we now know that the wooden panels used for both paintings came from the same tree. A few years ago, there was a major exhibition, in Europe, devoted to Rembrandt self-portraits. Not only did it include the Indianapolis picture, but, the catalogue entry carried a new appraisal by the Rembrandt corpus. They accepted it as genuine.

Thanks to Dr. Bruyn, of the Rembrandt project, we became friends with Dr. Willem Russell and his family. They had two adjoining houses on Beethoven Straat in Amsterdam. The Russells and their five children lived and entertained in one of them. The other contained the overflow of their extensive collection of paintings, antique furniture, and *objets d'art.* Originally of English extraction, they were fifth or sixth generation Dutch. Dr. Russell was the senator for Amsterdam in the Dutch parliament. His wife had inherited a chain of department stores including at least one on Fifth Avenue, New York City. Among other treasures, they had an outstanding collection of old master paintings, mostly, but not exclusively Dutch and Flemish. Their taste ran to small jewel-like examples of Golden Age painters. At the time we first met them, the National Gallery, in London, was mounting an exhibition entirely drawn from their collection. Apart from their treasures, one would never have guessed that they were so wealthy. Neither house appeared to be anything but typically bourgeois Dutch, at least from the outside. Whenever we dined with them, Mrs. Russell did the cooking and the children waited table.

Dr. Russell said he had a painting which he would be glad to give to our museum if we just paid the fifteen thousand dollar shipping and crating costs. He had managed to get the enormous canvas into their storage house, where it lay on its side in the hall. Astonished that he'd bought something far too large for his home, he promptly explained. A Roman Catholic Church, in Amsterdam, had a few paintings and altarpieces to sell. The picture Willem particularly wanted was by Ribera, a Spanish seventeenth century master who painted in Naples. However, the church was offering all or nothing, hence the huge canvas we were looking at. We jumped at his generous offer. The altarpiece was painted by Erasmus Quellinus. He became official painter, to the city of Antwerp, after the death of Rubens. The subject is of St. Francis Xavier praying before a vision of the Virgin Mary, Jesus and several cherubs. The painting of St. Francis' surplice, is unsurpassed in Baroque painting. Not only is the Indianapolis Museum of Art fortunate to possess this major altarpiece, but it is a rare example of a seventeenth century work that is fully documented. It contains the coat of arms of the Catholic Dutch widow who commissioned it from Quellinus, in 1671. The family was Roman Catholic. Holland, at the time, was almost entirely Protestant, so the good lady had to look to Flanders to find a suitable artist. The altarpiece had been in the same church, in Amsterdam, until Dr. Russell bought it.

Quite a number of paintings in the Clowes collection were, in my opinion, wrongly attributed, or not recognized as having been done by any known artist. A case in point, concerns a circular panel, known as a "tondo," which Mrs. Clowes had bought in about 1960. We had loaned it for an exhibition as a "Fifteenth century Tuscan tondo." The black and white illustration in the catalogue labeled it that way. Shortly thereafter, an article appeared in one of the scholarly art journals written by a Dr. Fahy. He attributed our painting, of the Holy Family with St. John the Baptist and an angel, to the Master of the Naumburg Madonna. For non art historians, this calls for an explanation.

Many old paintings are by unknown artists. Art historians often choose to study such pictures in the hope of finding others by the same artist. Occasionally they strike gold when they find one with either a signature, or a paper trail, that leads to a named painter. In the meantime, the investigating scholar invents a name based on the original painting he's studying. Considering this case, a picture of a Madonna and Child had been given to the Fogg Museum, at Harvard University, by people called Naumburg. Dr. Fahy was assembling a body of work that, in his opinion, was by the same hand.

In order to write as accurate a catalogue as possible, I visited Boston to study the Naumburg picture. It only took a moment to see that the Fogg and Clowes works are by different artists. Both are painted, in tempera, on wood panels but there the resemblance ends. In five hundred year old paintings, one can usually see through the layer of surface paint to the preparatory layer. The gesso of the Indianapolis tondo was first painted pea green, a color favored around Siena. The Naumburg panel was underpainted with a burnt ochre. In fact the colors used throughout were so different that there is no possibility that they could have been done by the same person. Fahy had only seen a black and white photograph of the tondo. Had he ever seen the painting, I'm confident that he would not have goofed.

While East, I took the opportunity to spend some time at the Metropolitan Museum of Art, in New York. I happened upon a heavily restored tondo by Sebastiano Mainardi, ca. 1460-1513. The more I looked beyond the superficial improvements, which sundry restorers had imposed upon it, the more certain I became that Mainardi painted the Clowes picture. He had spent most of his life working in his hometown of San Gimignano which is best known for its many tall towers.

In Italy that summer, I went to Montepulciano to study a Madonna and Child by Mainardi. It belongs in their small museum but, on arrival, I discovered that it had been sent to

Siena for conservation. Next stop the Siena Pinocoteca, where I was directed to the curatorial offices. I met with an elderly scholar who, I quickly realized, knew exactly what he was talking about. When I showed him a photograph of our painting he immediately identified it as a work by Mainardi with the exception of a small landscape, in the distance, behind the shed holding the Holy Family. Though it is impossible to detect in a photograph, I knew that he was spot on, because, while the rest of the painting is in tempera, the glimpse of landscape is in oil, a medium unknown to Mainardi.

As to the Montepulciano painting, Donato Martinelli, the local restorer, had it in his studio. I found him, and it, on the top floor of a nearby building. He turned out to be a delightful young man whose services we would need within a year. First, however, we studied the painting I'd come to see. It showed all the Mainardi characteristics I had anticipated.

I noticed that he was painting a large silk flag and asked about it. The ancient city of Siena is divided into seventeen *contrada* or parishes. Each one has a name like "Goose," or "Elephant and Castle." Twice a year the contrada compete in a crazy downtown horse race. The inhabitants of each contrada have their own flag and distinctive costumes. Martinelli's grandfather had modernized all the costumes and Donato continued the family tradition by hand painting all the most important flags. He was currently under contract to complete a full set of seventeen for the Siena city hall.

Back in Indianapolis the Clowes Pavilion was nearing completion. The galleries were arranged around a courtyard, as a nod to the Isabella Stewart Gardener museum, in Boston, much admired by Mrs. Clowes. Carl Weinhardt was concerned that the courtyard needed color. It looked gray and bleak. How about a set of Sienese flags? It took Martinelli nearly three years to complete all seventeen but, once they were done, they hung from the upper cloister, over the courtyard, for the next thirty years.

Allen Clowes finally returned home alone. Betty Roberts continued to deal with his mail and manage the help, but from then on, he lived as a recluse for ten years. Not only did he never go out, he didn't want to have anybody visit him, including me. He would talk to me whenever I phoned and often agreed to let me drop in for a chat. However, after the phone call he would have one of the servants call me back to say that Mr. Clowes was sick and would be unable to see me after all. I did visit him, once or twice a year, by not answering the phone and just pushing in once the door was answered. Oddly enough, when I did barge in like that, Allen seemed to be glad to see me. So strange.

Chapter Twenty Three
*The Art Scene*


The Indianapolis Museum of Art opened its doors in 1970 with a number of special exhibitions, most notably a diverse loan of treasures from the Metropolitan Museum of Art. A smaller exhibition was devoted to the paintings of Milton Avery, drawn from the collection of Louis and Annette Kaufman, of Los Angeles. As part of the opening celebrations, the Kaufmans performed a lovely recital, before a select audience, in the member's room.

Louis Kaufman is, arguably, the world's most recorded violinist, having done, among other things, the sound tracks of over five hundred movies. Annette is a distinguished pianist. Although the Clowes Pavilion had not yet opened, the paintings were already installed. After the concert, Carl Weinhardt asked me to show the Kaufmans around the collection. That was the start of a friendship that lasted, with Louis, until his death in 1994, and still continues with Annette. From the opening of the IMA, for almost thirty years, I had a wonderfully rewarding part time job as curator of the Clowes Collection.

Unlike the other curators, my office was in the Clowes Pavilion, and best of all, I didn't have to attend curators' meetings. Most of my responsibilities were behind the scenes. At first I was consumed with completing the catalogue, which was printed in 1972. In truth, there was so much research to be done that it is still ongoing. Some of the more intriguing problems became the subject of papers presented at College Art Association conventions.

Once the catalogue was out, letters started coming in. Some corrected errors or added information about some hitherto unknown related work. Others wanted detailed photographs. One scholar was doing research on haloes found in Italian Primitive paintings. He needed photographs, taken under a raking light, to accentuate indentations into the gesso. Artists, of the period, made little metal tools to stamp halo rays. As fourteenth and fifteenth century painters almost never signed their work, halo study is one tool used to identify the artist. Still other letters requested loans, from the Clowes Collection, for special exhibitions.

Loaning, and borrowing, works of art have long been standard practice in the museum world. There are several reasons to loan treasures to other institutions. One is a matter of reciprocity. A major museum is organizing an exhibition and wants to borrow one or more works that will fill in certain gaps in their own holdings. By loaning the requested works, one puts the borrower in one's debt for requests to borrow unspecified works at a later date. Sometimes, by lending a minor work, to a major exhibition, it acquires an unexpected luster.

John Constable, was one of the two most distinguished nineteenth century English landscape painters. The other was William Mallord Turner. Unlike the latter, recognition of Constable's extraordinary gifts came late in life. At his death, in 1837, Parliament was embarrassed to discover that there were none of his paintings in the National Gallery, in London. To rectify the matter, they bought a masterpiece from his estate known as, "The Cornfield."

Constable's major works were all painted in his studio. Unlike others of his generation, he was one of the first artists to do small oil studies sitting, or standing, at an easel outdoors. Many purported Constable oil sketches have turned out to be of questionable authenticity. One such is in the Clowes Collection. I believed it to be the oil study for the National Gallery painting, executed about 1826, but at least two scholars had dated it about 1880 and attributed it to the artist W.W. Warren.

A young Midwestern art historian, who was curating a small New York exhibition of nineteenth century English landscapes, came to look at both of our hopeful Constables. The second one is a finished painting of Harnham Bridge, Salisbury, of about 1821. Dr. Mark Roskill had attributed that one to John Dunthorne. Consequently, both pictures had controversial attributions. The curator, for the New York exhibition, agreed with me that they are autograph works by Constable. That being so I loaned both canvasses, because they would be published as such. The gamble paid off.

In 1976 London's Royal Academy organized a major Constable retrospective exhibition to celebrate the bicentennial of the painter's birth. They happily paid for me to fly over with our "Cornfield" sketch. It was hung next to the National Gallery's great painting. That exhibition also helped to confirm the attribution to John Constable of our "Harnham Bridge." Evidently ours is one of a pair. The other one, which is identical in size to ours, was included in the London exhibition. It is the same view, looking across the river, but from the other side of the bridge. The Clowes picture has the bridge on the left with the spire of Salisbury Cathedral on the right. The painting in the show has the bridge on the right with the cathedral eclipsed by trees. This story illustrates another important reason for loaning works to exhibitions, especially if the exhibition is devoted to a single artist.

We come now to the three main avenues, used by art historians, to reach an opinion concerning the authorship of any work of art. The first is connoisseurship. This, for most of us, requires many years of looking long and carefully at related works. An analogy would be handwriting. Everybody has distinctive handwriting. A writer can instantly tell whether a written note is his, or not. The same is true of an artist's technique. Differences are often obvious between the works of modern masters. When it comes to old masters, connoisseurs look for tiny clues.

Bernard Berenson was a leading connoisseur of fourteenth and fifteenth century Italian painting, during the first half of the twentieth century. Having an almost photographic memory, he could look at a painting and immediately recall other works by the same hand. His lasting contribution was to create lists of paintings by almost all the artists who were active during the Proto and Early Renaissance. Even today, his opinions are frequently consulted and found to be correct.

The second avenue is scholarship, the core of which is provenance, or the history of the work under consideration. An analogy, in this case, would be researching of a name in your family tree, to see if an ancestor came over on the Mayflower. Scholarship, while both invaluable and fascinating, can also be misleading. Take for example Mona Lisa, perhaps the world's most famous painting. Scholarship tells us that Leonardo da Vinci painted this portrait of Lisa Gherardini, in Florence, from 1503 to 1504. There is a wealth of contemporary documentation to justify that assumption. There is also evidence that he never finished the commission, and that he took it with him to France in 1516. Under the King's patronage, he lived there, for the last three years of his life, in a small château near Amboise. In his will, he left the painting to Jacopo dei Caprotti, known as Salai, believed to have been da Vinci's lover. Salai survived Leonardo by five years. At his death, the picture was bought by King Francis I of France. This accounts for why it hangs in the Louvre Museum, in Paris. As all these facts are verifiable, we should be able to say, unequivocally, that the painting, barely visible through bulletproof glass, in the Louvre's *galerie des états*, described as "La Giaconda", by Leonardo da Vinci 1450-1519, is exactly what the label says it is. But wait, there's more.

How do we know that the painting that Leonardo began in 1503 to 1504 is the same one he took to France? It would be another four hundred years before photography was invented.

For evidence, we are dependent on written accounts. As there happen to be several other contemporary versions of the painting, who's to say for certain that there's never been a changeling along the way? In August of 1911, the Louvre's painting was stolen. How do we know that the picture, recovered two years later, is the same one? The honest answer? We don't. If the great artist were to reappear, I doubt that he could identify which, if any, of the extant versions of Mona Lisa he painted. For one thing, after five hundred years, colors change and fade. Add to that, various attacks by deranged people with acid, paint and a veritable arsenal of missiles, followed by many attempts at conservation of the paint surface, and stabilization of the splitting panel, and change is inevitable.

To ascertain whether, or not, the Paris painting is by Leonardo, we must turn to science and connoisseurship. Microscopic samples of paint, compared with samples from other works by the same artist, show that the pigments are consistent with the palate he used and date from the early sixteenth century. Dendrochronology can determine, within a few years, when the tree, from which the panel has been sliced, was cut down, and even where the tree was grown. While there is, so far, no scientific experiment to prove who painted the Louvre picture, we now know that it was painted, on a panel of Tuscan poplar, around the turn of the sixteenth century by an artist who used the same pigments as Leonardo da Vinci. With everything pointing toward the authenticity of the work, we turn finally to connoisseurship.

Leonardo was known for his *sfumato,* a rather misty or smoky effect, such as one notices at dawn, or twilight. Most da Vinci experts agree that the Louvre painting exhibits all the hallmarks of Leonardo so, for now, that seems to settle the matter. While I plan to discuss a few of the more interesting problem pictures in the Clowes Collection, let us now return to the ongoing adventure of life.

I doubt if it's possible to pinpoint a particular year when the sleeping beauty so often unkindly referred to as "Indian-no-place," woke up. Nonetheless, by the time the Indianapolis Museum of Art opened in 1970, the city was coming to life. The near west side of downtown was rapidly emerging as the IUPUI campus. Among the state-of-the-art facilities was a natatorium which was to become an incubator for Olympic swimmers and divers. The city was becoming a hub as it was being absorbed into the interstate system of roads. The long neglected Massachusetts Avenue was springing to life with the opening of new art galleries, clubs and restaurants.

On Friday evenings, hundreds of pedestrians could be seen, wine glass in hand, strolling from one art opening to the next. As pioneers, Bob Pace and Dana Reich deserve credit for bringing a sense of excitement to contemporary art galleries. When the ancient and reclusive Miss Florence Butler died in her near-north side overgrown house, the nearby church planned to demolish it for a parking lot. Bob and Dana scraped together seven thousand dollars to save the place. Today it is revered as the Morris-Butler museum but, in the early to middle sixties, it was being used as a gallery known for spectacular openings. As the coal-fired furnace had the disagreeable habit of belching black soot, the house was repainted for every exhibition.

There are three spacious floors, plus a tower, above the basement. All of it was gallery space. While the exhibits have faded from memory, the opening parties have not. Every room had a rudimentary drinks bar, plus a table, dining or cocktail, groaning with edibles. On arrival, the first person you were likely to see was the artist Joanie Johnson. Being too large to manage the stairs, she was easily recognizable plopped on the floor within reach of sustenance. As she never moved, friends roaming the galleries would arrange to meet later "by Joanie!"

On one occasion, Jane Collins appeared with a train that must have been, at least, a hundred feet long. Her progress around the house, could be monitored by all, as the train shifted to follow its owner. By the time she reached the tower, sections of the unraveled bolt of fabric snaked its way throughout the galleries. Everybody kept an eye on the satin river to avoid standing on it. At some point, Jane must have moved swiftly because part of the train suddenly mounted a cocktail table sending plates of refreshments and ashtrays flying. The large eccentric, to whom it was attached, was an interior decorator noted for her novel touches. When she was the chosen decorator for a bathroom in the Decorators' Show House, she ensured that nobody would sully her masterpiece by putting goldfish in all three fittings!

The high rises of Riley Towers, had been an early attempt to attract people to live downtown. There were many more planned but the lukewarm reception which the first four received, put that idea on hold. The remaining bulldozed acreage lay fallow for years. Bob and Sandra Borns, who had developed Pickwick Farms and Pickwick Place, two residential apartment complexes on the north side of town, bought that parcel of downtown land. They transformed the eyesore into pleasant, modestly priced townhouses. The entire complex sold out in one day.

With that success under their belts, Bob and Sandra turned much of the abandoned Union Railroad Station into a festival marketplace. It was such a novel idea, at the time, that Ambrose and I were recruited to attend all kinds of meetings and dinners to show a brief movie and answer questions in the hopes of attracting visitors from all quarters of the city. Though the opening was a phenomenal success, it quickly faltered and closed within two or three years. The idea might have worked had Circle Center been built.

Circle Center was one huge bomb site, still waiting to have the underground parking completed. Work on that major project had been delayed for years for various reasons. Historic Landmarks Foundation was determined to incorporate as many historic facades, as possible, into the new shopping center. With that in mind, a number of buildings on Washington Street, and throughout the warehouse district, had their street facades carefully removed and put in storage before demolition began. The original grand concept, which included part of the southwest segment of the circle, was revised, and modified, a number of times before construction started on the reduced mall. It was 1995, before the Circle Center mall, as we know it today, was opened to general approbation. So began a period of residential boom in downtown Indianapolis

In 1968, the ten year sojourn of the Bevan's came to a halt. You may remember that Jock's sister Helen Bevan had spent four of these years with them in Indianapolis as head teacher at St. Richard's School? Once back in the UK, she got involved in prison outreach, where she met and ultimately married John Armstrong. He was about to be released after serving time for having killed his child. From the point of view of her several maiden aunts, the marriage, and consummation thereof, put her permanently beyond the pale.

Jock and Helen's mother, Elizabeth, was one of five Scott-Moncrief daughters. Her parents had had no sons. Elizabeth was the only child to reproduce. Jock, his brother Robin, and Helen were her three offspring. In the small fishing village of Elie, in Fifeshire north of Edinburgh, stands a Grade A listed sixteenth century keep with a fair-sized seventeenth century addition. Known as "The Castle," it had been a property of the Scott-Moncriefs for generations. Recently, it had been the domain of the female side of the family. At the time, it was jointly owned by three unmarried aunts who had intended to leave it to Helen. Her marriage to a felon, changed all that.

Robin, and Sue Bevan, had settled in New Zealand where he had his medical practice and they were raising a family. From their standpoint, a return to Scotland was out of the question. Jock's favorite, Aunt Cathy, with whom he'd lived as a bachelor in London, flew into Indianapolis to discuss the matter.

As a boy, Jock had enjoyed many holidays at the castle. It sits right on the Firth of Forth as it transitions into the North Sea. For Jock, who loved sailing, it was a veritable Shangri La. Now it was his for the asking. Of course he wanted it, and of course there were strings attached. If Jock was to have it, the ground floor would be converted into a flat for Aunt Isobel Scott- Moncrief to live out her days. She died there at the age of 103. The rest of the place would be Jock's, but only if he made it his home. The decision was hard to make. Not only had they found Indianapolis very much to their liking, but Jock was becoming well known as an outstanding visualizer and was making a good living for the family. As he was in his middle forties, the prospect of starting over in Scotland was daunting. Pam, who had never lived there was less than enthusiastic at the prospect, but in the end, she agreed to move.

They sold their house and Pam took the children to Elie so that she could supervise the alterations required to create Isobel's separate flat. Meanwhile, Jock rented an efficiency in Broad Ripple. He had a number of commissions to complete, so he commuted between Scotland and Indianapolis for the next two years.

Once the Bevans were all ensconced in The Castle, Ambrose and I paid them a visit. Pam had been having a difficult time adjusting. From her point of view, the worst thing was the cold. With four-foot thick stone walls, even the summer heat failed to penetrate. Fifty five degrees Fahrenheit was about was warm as it ever got. Many rooms had fireplaces but, for the most part, all the heat went up the icy chimneys. She had installed a number of electrical units which were supposed to help. What they did, was to dry the air to the point that much of the antique furniture, and Jacobean linen-fold paneling, began to warp and split. One night, Jock and Pam awoke with a start. It sounded like gunfire downstairs. In his pajamas, and armed with a cricket bat, Jock ran down to discover that it was paneling splitting. By the time the heating elements had finished their destruction, the top of the eighteenth century mahogany sideboard, in the dining room, had curled up like a canoe. It remains horribly disfigured to this day.

When we arrived, we mentioned that we wouldn't be averse to a hot bath. Aunt Isobel had installed a bathroom in her flat to supplement the only other bathroom in the house. There were two rooms off an upstairs hallway. One contained an antique flush toilet, the other, an enormous bathtub and hand basin. They each sported a single tap...cold. A hot, or at any rate, warm bath would be possible. We should take the rope that was coiled up on the bathroom floor and let it out of the window. Two floors lower down was the window into the laundry room. That room had a small gas heater that heated water as it passed through it. The tap could be connected to a garden hose. Having attached the rope to the other end of the hose, we were able to haul it up to the bathroom. Sure enough, we soon had a steady trickle of warm water! By a stroke of good fortune, shortly after that memorably chilly visit, a long lost aunt of Pam's expired in Suava, the capital of Fiji, leaving her niece just enough money to install six bathrooms.

# Chapter Twenty Four
## *IUPUI and "At Home with the Masters"*

Shortly after the opening of the Clowes Pavilion at the Indianapolis Museum of Art, in 1972, I received a letter from the Herron School of Art. Ambrose had forwarded it to Europe, where I was doing research. I had been recommended for full-time art history teaching. It was tenure-track and mine for the asking. I was thrilled and not a little surprised as I only had a Master's degree from Indiana University. Generally, art history teachers needed a Ph.D. though they were often appointed before completing their dissertations. In my case, the board was sufficiently impressed with my work on the Clowes Collection catalogue, to offer me a contract without any further degrees. My long-term future, with the university, would be judged on my performance.

As soon as I had written a letter of acceptance, I phoned Sheldon Kantor to let him know that I would not be teaching at Shortridge, any longer. Once as he stopped banging his head against the wall, I told him why. He readily admitted that if he'd received my offer, he'd do the same. I had been with the Indianapolis Public Schools for eleven years.

Dr. Sam Roberson, a Yale Ph.D., had been recruited to head up the art history program and to design, and implement, an undergraduate degree program. As the second fulltime teacher, I was assigned to work closely under Sam to help bring that project to fruition.

Dr. Roberson taught courses in American eighteenth and nineteenth century art and architecture, and European Baroque. I was to teach Romanesque and Gothic and Renaissance art, both Northern and Italian. We would each teach one section of Introduction to Art History, a two semester requirement of all art students. Mel Meehan, who had married Tom Solley and lived in Bloomington, gave a course in modern art. Cathy Mino, wife of the Indianapolis Museum of Art oriental curator, taught Chinese and Japanese art. Martin Krause taught history of print making and Carol Ward offered a course on crafts. Allene Doddoli, who was one of the art appreciation part-time teachers on the main campus, added a string to her bow by teaching a practical course on historical painting techniques. Considering that we had only two full time teachers, we had a reasonably broad offering of courses. We soon added Ted Celenko, of the Eiteljorg collection, to teach African art.

Dr. Nagy, a humanities professor on the main campus, was to meet regularly with Sam and me to give us advice and encouragement as we developed not only the nuts and bolts of the art history degree program but, also, a thoroughly well-reasoned justification for it. With the latter in mind, I designed a questionnaire, to be given to students in various disciplines, to gauge interest in such a program.

It wasn't long before I noticed a pattern emerging of Sam canceling, or failing to turn up at planned meetings. When he did appear, he had been too busy, to do whatever assignment he'd undertaken, to move things forward. Only when we roomed together, at the College Art Association Annual Convention in New York City, did I get a hint of all the trouble I had in store for me. There were so many interesting symposia to attend, and papers being presented, that I barely had time to grab a bite to eat. Sam and I had a falling out when he discovered that I was not interested in getting drunk and still less in finding a girl to lay. Somehow, we managed to teach in the same institution for more than twenty years with each Dean sweeping the ever-mounting problems under the rug. Though he joined Alcoholics Anonymous, and successfully dried out, his personal life remained in turmoil. As a tenured professor, he skated by with minimal committee work and poorly prepared classes.

Dean Weber appointed me chair of the art history program. With his help, I completed the work to apply for the degree in art history. A conference call was arranged for all eight campuses to discuss and vote on the proposal. Only Bloomington balked, so the motion passed to my great joy and relief. The major objections were an inadequate reference library, only two full time professors and no money to rectify either. Bloomington had a fine library, plus a well organized overnight interlibrary loan system. That answered the first objection. A third full time faculty member, however, was essential.

Mel's husband had dumped her in favor of one of his typists at the Indiana University Museum of Art. Armed with a tough lawyer, she took him to the cleaners and wound up with a Fifth Avenue penthouse across the street from the Metropolitan Museum of Art, in New York, as part of her settlement. Under the circumstances, I certainly understood her decision to move permanently to the Big Apple. Rather than leave us in the lurch however, she commuted by air, twice weekly, for one more semester to teach her course in modern art. She even returned her salary to help needy students.

Mel's father had just stepped down as president of Hunter College in order to care for her mother, who was fighting cancer. The faculty had a luncheon planned, at a New York restaurant, to honor him in his retirement. As the lunch was winding down, he excused himself to go downstairs, where there was a telephone, to let his wife know what time he expected to be home. He never made it. Dr. Meehan was found unconscious, by the telephone, in a pool of blood, his ear almost severed by a blow from an unknown assailant. He never regained consciousness, but survived in a vegetative state for seven more years. As he had expected to care for his ailing wife until she died, that vicious attack led to her devoting all her time to nursing him.

During her marriage to Tom Solley, Mel had grown very close to the children, from his first marriage. Now his son was dying of AIDS. Tom had an opportunity to make amends for his despicable behavior, leading up to the divorce, by showing compassion for the boy as he faced death. Far from it. His homophobia stood in the way of his building a relationship to his son. Mercifully, Mel took care of him till he died.

After a couple more ill-advised marriages, she met a guy who delighted us all. Jack's business was mainly posters, which was a perfect fit for Mel whose business was, and still is, war posters. Indeed, it would be no exaggeration to say that if you are interested in collecting in that field, Mel Meehan is the number one go-to person. Jack had a shop in lower Manhattan which was run by Louis Bixenman who, along with his partner Sterling Zinzmeyer became special friends to Ambrose and me.

Jack also had a *pied à terre* on the Left Bank in Paris. He kindly loaned it to us, one summer, when I had one of my French summer schools. Not to be outdone, Mel gave us the use of her penthouse while she was out of the country. As the place is filled with rare antiques and fine works of art, every time we've stayed there, I have had to pinch myself to ensure that I'm still alive.

Strange to say, some ten years after his arrival on the scene, Jack Banning moved out, explaining that he'd come to the realization that he's mentally a lesbian and must go forward with a sex change to accomplish his goal! When that happened, we began to wonder if Mel was ever destined to meet Mr. Right. Believe it or not, she did. She had been friends with Dick Oldenburg and his wife. Dick was director of New York's Museum of Modern Art. Sometime after his wife died, Mel and Dick married while agreeing to keep their own apartments. Good luck to you both!

With no funding for the obligatory full time contemporary art historian, we were all set to follow many other degree approved programs which automatically expired when they were not implemented within five years. After consulting with the dean, I put a thoroughly devious plan into action. I cancelled all seven sections of art appreciation, to free up a salary for Dr. Annemarie Springer to fill the vital gap in our art history program. As anticipated, I was castigated from left and right. The part time teachers were naturally upset to lose the extra pin money that they counted on, quite apart from the fact that they enjoyed teaching that course. From Herron's point of view, it was a non-issue because credit for art appreciation didn't apply to any art degree. While the art school paid all the salaries for art appreciation teachers, it received nothing in return. For every undergraduate in the university, with the exception of art students, a three hour course in music appreciation, theater appreciation, or art appreciation was a requirement. If less than ten students enrolled, then that section was cancelled.

For some reason, art appreciation was by far the most popular student choice with the result that, as often as not, it was the only available option. No sooner had I pulled the plug on all sections than I started getting calls from the various schools demanding their reinstatement. My reply was this. "We'd love to oblige but, unfortunately, we have no money to pay the teachers as all our meager funds are earmarked for the art history degree program. However, if liberal arts (or whatever school it happened to be) will pay the instructor's salary, as you do for every other course, we will be happy to recommend several well-qualified teachers." The ruse worked, and following a one semester hiatus, an increased number of art appreciation sections were offered without Herron footing the bill. As part time teachers were shamefully underpaid, it didn't amount to very much, but I was so pleased with my cunning that I felt fully prepared to manipulate Wall Street to my advantage!

The IUPUI Herron School of Art has long enjoyed a reputation as one of the finest in the nation. Today, it justifiably takes pride in its art history degree program, with six fulltime professors. Few things in life give me more pleasure than hearing success stories from old students who graduated in art history once we made it an option. So often, I found that if you open the door just a chink, there's a young person ready to push it all the way and rush into the sunlight. Whenever that happens I'm on cloud nine. All in all, my life as a professor of art history was satisfying beyond my wildest dreams.

Though Herron occupied most of my daily time, I remained curator of the Clowes Collection. Once the Indianapolis Museum of Art opened, I began giving a series of monthly talks. For the first year, I had a small dedicated group of aficionados who followed me around the galleries with notebooks and folding stools in hand. Like most museum guides, I'd stop in front of a work which I planned to discuss. The dozen or so patrons would sit on their stools breathlessly awaiting longed-for enlightenment. At the conclusion of the designated hour, we might have discussed about ten pictures.

By the following year, a well trained group of volunteer docents rendered my approach redundant. That year, I gave a series of talks in the Members' Room, overlooking the lake, on the third floor. Each lecture was devoted to a specific artistic technique such as lithography or bronze casting. By the third year, with the Clowes Pavilion complete, I began a series which lasted some twenty five years called "At Home with the Masters."

The DeBoest lecture hall, with bench seating, held nearly two hundred people. The talks were from 8-9 p.m. monthly, on a Thursday, eight months of the year. Usually, I chose a single artist as my subject. Let's say it was to be Vincent Van Gogh. I would read several biographies before taking books to the slide room marked up with the pages that required a slide.

For my talks, I used two projectors. The projectionist would turn them on when I gave him the signal to do so, following my introductory remarks. From then on, I would sit at the side of the stage changing them with remotes. Rather than give a chronological illustrated biography, of the artist's life, I always tried to put it in context. It was a hardscrabble life in Groot-Zundent, the Dutch village where Van Gogh was born and where his father was the Calvinist minister. Five years earlier his mother had given birth to a boy who died. They had buried him under a tombstone at the church entrance. His name was also Vincent Van Gogh. For sixteen years the future artist walked past the Vincent Van Gogh grave, every time he entered the church. In an effort to bring the subject of my talk to life, for the audience, I would have slides made of the village, the church, and details of the door and tombstone. Hopefully, in the hour at my disposal I would succeed in presenting a fleshed-out artist whose oeuvre could be seen, and understood, in terms of the changing circumstances of his turbulent life.

I have been blessed with a gift for recalling details, and dates, when I lecture. In a classroom setting, I use notes because I want to make certain that I impart all the information that I consider important for the students to know. As I prepared for museum lectures, I would make notes from each of the various books that I read. Then I would take those sheets of notes and write out the story as I planned to tell it. I would learn what I'd written, by heart, and then arrange the hundred or so slides to illustrate the story. Before lecturing, Ambrose would give me dinner, in silence, so that I could use the time for a final rehearsal in my head. On arrival at the hall, Ambrose would glad-hand the arriving audience, while I would seclude myself backstage to keep my mind focused. I always dressed in black tie. A wine and refreshments party followed the lecture. It was held above the auditorium, in the Clowes courtyard.

Over the years, At Home with the Masters became increasingly popular. Against fire regulations, stacks of chairs would be carried in to accommodate people in the aisles after everybody had been persuaded to squeeze closer to each other on the benches. On one occasion several hundred people had to be turned away because in those days there wasn't a larger theater available.

For the most part, my audience consisted of museum members. They tended to be white with a fair amount of disposable income. Among the few minorities was a tall black lady, invariably dressed in a colorful poncho over black slacks. As she attended regularly, we got to know her at the post-lecture receptions. Her name was Helen Pilgrim-Minor, a high school teacher of French. A beaky nose suggested some Native American ancestry. We received an invitation to her farewell party at Riley Towers. She was taking early retirement and heading to Zaire (today the Democratic Republic of Congo) for a two year stint, to write for some Christian periodical. She was a good writer and we kept in touch.

Because she had given up her Indianapolis flat, we invited her to stay with us for awhile following her return from Africa. As we were going to Europe, she house sat for us while we were away. She told us that she particularly appreciated the fact that we never pried into her private affairs. I answered that we had been given wise advice by Barbara Brook. "Never ask anybody anything. If they want you to know, they'll volunteer the information. If they don't, they'll lie."

Having experienced life in Zaire, she was determined to see as much of the planet as possible. To this day, she's probably the only black woman who's been to both poles. When she went to the North Pole, she had to stay in an Inuit community, in the far north of Canada, for about three weeks, waiting for a break in the weather before she could fly to the pole. She occupied herself volunteering in the school. On the bulletin board were pictures of the changing seasonal appearance of deciduous trees. The children wondered what would happen if you were under a tree in the fall. Could the blow from a leaf kill you?

Just after Chernobyl, Helen was booked on a Russian freighter sailing west from Gdansk. It was a large vessel, with accommodations for about twelve passengers. Owing to the nuclear disaster, all the passengers, except Helen, had cancelled. That trip lasted nearly six months. She spent much of the time on the bridge with the captain, the only person on board who spoke any English, or French. If it was a nice day, he'd enquire whether she would like a swim, before phoning the engine room to tell some sailor to fill the pool, "For our guest." At every port she was free to come and go as she wished. In Auckland, New Zealand, where they spent several days, there was a tourist center offering local people to host you, in their homes, and to show you the sights. When Helen told the captain about the nice people she'd met that way, he told her to invite them onboard for a party!

She was an excellent photographer, and gave illustrated talks for her friends and church, whenever she returned to Indianapolis from one of these adventures. When she took the Trans-Siberian railroad all the way to Vladivostok she traveled, as she often did, with no luggage. Her poncho had two large pockets. She also had a shoulder bag. With disposable paperbacks to read, a change of underwear to rinse out daily, and a few things like a toothbrush and some essential pills, along with her camera and travel documents, she was hot to trot. After a few years of crisscrossing the globe, Helen settled in Paris. She found a working woman, with a room to rent, just outside the périphérique, and dropped anchor.

Among the young people employed to install museum exhibits at the Indianapolis Museum of Art, were Jane and Henry Eckert. The pay was rotten and the work hard so they soon quit with a plan to open an art gallery. As most of the Indianapolis galleries sold the work of local living artists, they filled a missing niche. They sold Hoosier old masters. To get things off to a good start, they were instrumental in having a glossy coffee table book published in nice time for Christmas. In short order, a William Forsyth painting that Ambrose and I had bought for a hundred dollars would be worth a couple of thousand. The Eckerts were on to a good thing.

It wasn't long, however, before the supply of such paintings ran dry. Henry was up to the challenge. He found a competent artist, in the southern part of the State, who could turn out remarkably convincing T.C. Steeles and W. Forsyths to order. Soon there was a steady supply of new old masters for sale in the Eckert gallery. Several buyers began to get suspicious. One by one, they brought their fakes to the Indianapolis Museum of Art, for inspection. Martin Radeki, the chief conservator, easily detected the fraudulent works and kept them, as evidence, as the case was building.

With Marty's fortieth birthday approaching, the conservation department cooked up a special surprise. Linda Wittkowski, a paintings conservator, painted a fake T.C. Steele. Once the paint had dried, using transparent color that fluoresces under ultraviolet light, but is otherwise invisible, she wrote all over the painting "Happy Birthday, Marty!" Next they hired a stripper who, dressed in a fur coat, showed up with the painting claiming to have purchased it, as a Steele, from Eckert galleries. Marty examined the work with care, and declared that it looked suspicious, but to make sure, they should take it into the darkroom to study it under ultraviolet light. In the mistaken belief that the room was empty, Marty led the lady into the room, turned out the lights as he switched on the ultraviolet. While he was holding the painting, under the ultraviolet, awaiting results, the stripper stripped and we all slipped out of our hiding places. As soon as the words fluoresced, lights and music filled the room and an acutely embarrassed chief conservator found himself involved in wild gyrations with a nude of whom his wife would not have approved! Marty's birthday surprise was a bright moment in the midst of this dismal saga.

A sudden police raid, into the Eckert Gallery, yielded the rest of the necessary evidence to prosecute Henry Eckert. Although he was guilty, he got away with a small fine coupled with restitution to his customers because, under Indiana law, forgery was limited to signatures on checks or other financial documents. Hoosiers being quick to forgive and forget, the Eckerts have gone on to make a fortune in the art business.

Having lived in England, I was asked my opinion about an itinerary that was being considered for a museum members' trip to the old country. One glance and I spotted problems. There were too many changes of hotel. People love to be in London especially in the evening, for theaters, clubs and restaurants. After two nights there, the plan was to go to Brighton for one night and then on to Salisbury and Stonehenge. What, I asked, would our members do in Brighton that evening, after the hour spent visiting the Pavilion? Brighton being one hour south of London by coach, why not return to the city before dinner? The drive from London to Salisbury is marginally shorter, and faster, than it is from Brighton. Furthermore, fewer hotel changes means less packing and unpacking.

By the time I had finished making suggestions, I was asked to conduct the tour. I gladly agreed to do so. As a bonus, I arranged for a number of friends and family to entertain all thirty five of us! For a great overseas experience, there's nothing to compare to being entertained in private homes. The entire trip was a resounding success. From then on, I conducted at least one, and often two, European tours for the IMA every year.

During that first tour, Yanie Le Bas and Ann Wells gave a party for us at their house in London. Yanie's brother, Philip, (who had first introduced Ambrose to me), was there. At the time of his college graduation, he had painted two large paintings, one of which Ambrose had bought. The subject was of an operation, in progress, in a hospital. It was dominated by large red oxygen tubes. Painted over sixty years ago, it remains an arresting composition. The other picture was of three street musicians. I remembered it well, and regretted not having bought it. Seeing Philip at the party, I asked him about it. "Oh yes," he said, "I sold it, at about the same time as Ambrose bought The Operation, to a guy who lives somewhere in the west of England."

The following day was our trip to Brighton. Driving down on the coach, I gave everybody a potted history of the town and of the astonishing Indian-Gothic architecture of the Pavilion. As they would be touring the building independently, I asked them all to look out for a small painting by Rex Whistler, that should be hanging in the Prince Regent's bedroom. Under the title of The Prince Regent Discovers the Spirit of Brighton, it depicts a rotund, lecherous prince, naked but he for the noble order of the garter mounting a supine *grande horizontale*. It was not there. On inquiry, I was told that it had been moved to the Brighton Art Gallery. With half an hour to spare before the coach left for London, I hurried over to the gallery. Imagine my surprise, when I reached the Rex Whistler, to find it hanging next to The Street Musicians by Philip Le Bas! No doubt, everybody experiences coincidences from time to time, but I seem to have had more than my fair share of them.

## Chapter Twenty Five
*Summer School in Europe and IMA Tours*


You may recall that we had bought the house to the north of ours, with a view to moving it? Now, our neighbors to the south planned to move. They were a charming old couple who had lived in the house since its construction in the nineteen thirties. It was very similar to ours and, like ours, was turned sideways on the lot facing south. When we had first moved in, Mrs. Fitzpatrick had come over to welcome us into the neighborhood and to invite us to join them at the Methodist Church for service on Sunday. When we politely declined with the explanation that we were atheists, she said, "Oh dear. In that case you'll probably want to join Trinity Episcopal Church at 33rd and Meridian?" We sometimes wondered if she was privy to information denied us. At any rate, we agreed to a price and briefly found ourselves proud owners of three contiguous houses.

The Fitzpatrick house had been well maintained though it needed painting throughout. When my parents learned the news, Ma foolishly wrote to say that they were sorry not to be with us as to help with the decorating. She quickly learned that you should be very careful what you wish for, we sent them air tickets by return post! They arrived from England with a suitcase full of painting gear and set to work the next day. Dad slapped paint everywhere. Ma cleaned up the mess. The final result was acceptable and we rented the place to four young men. What a mistake! They were jazz musicians with boom boxes that resonated a block away. Fortunately they hadn't signed a lease so we parted company in a month.

We were wondering whether or not we were cut out to be landlords, when we got a call from Sheldon Kantor, head of the art department, at Shortridge. He and Lisa had had enough of their little house on College Avenue, and wondered if we would consider selling the Fitzpatrick house to them? We did. They proved to be wonderful neighbors. We took great pride in our garden but, ere long, we realized that Sheldon was an incomparably better gardener than either of us. He was forever giving us starts of this and that, to keep us up to par. Our faithful housekeeper, Alberta Spaulding, was soon employed by them as well.

Lisa worked at Blue Cross Blue Shield while they both worked at trying to start a family. Failure in that department, elicited the diagnosis that an earlier illness had damaged Lisa's fallopian tubes triggering several painful operations, all of them useless. Her office being downtown, Ambrose dropped her off every day on his way to Mallory's. The arrangement worked well. Lisa was only one, of a number of our friends, who was temperamentally incapable of learning to drive a car. Sheldon had become interested in art history. He started taking classes at Herron, even though he already had earned a master's at Indiana State University, in Terre Haute.

Teaching and scheduling the art history and art appreciation courses for IUPUI, were my principal responsibilities. At the same time, faculty members were expected to volunteer to sit on two, or three, of countless university committees for a limited time, before moving on to others. Most of the committees were fairly perfunctory, and offered little of interest to me. Early on, however, Dr. Miriam Langsam, sometime Associate Dean of Liberal Arts, asked me to sit on the Honors Council. We turned out to be made for each other and, for a number of years, Miriam directed the honors program and I was her chairman. She encouraged me to design, and implement, an honors course for overseas study in art history.

Dr. Peter Sehlinger headed up the overseas studies programs, on the main campus of Indiana University,

Bloomington. He was unstinting in his help and encouragement. Before long, H495, "Summer School in Europe," was approved as a six credit hour, variable title honors course, and I was to teach it. Once a student had taken one of these courses, he or she could apply to do an in-depth individual project, usually in the form of a minor thesis, based on the European experience, for a further three credit hours of honors credit. As I planned to offer peripatetic courses, alternating between France and Italy, it would be possible for students to accumulate a maximum eighteen hours of honors credit, if they were to participate in both summer schools. Aware that each course would require considerable preparation on my part, I resolved to offer courses on alternate years starting with France in 1979.

The main thrust of the French course was Romanesque and Gothic architecture, sculpture and stained glass. The first two weeks were to be based in Paris, followed by four weeks visiting major monuments throughout France. We would rent minibuses to cover over fifteen hundred miles. The year before each European summer school, I would advertise an open meeting for interested students. After outlining plans and expectations and answering student questions, I would distribute a questionnaire. All students, seriously interested in participating, would fill it out with the assurance that I would contact each of them during the next two weeks. They were asked to list the art history courses they had taken, and their overall GPA. With faculty access to records, it was easy to eliminate the "C" student, who claimed honors status.

The minimum requirement, for students to participate in France, was to have taken both sections of introduction to art history plus Romanesque and Gothic. Though all students were expected to maintain a 3.3, or above, GPA, I sometimes made exceptions for those with lower grades provided that they had earned A's in all art history courses. Having given a ballpark estimate of the costs involved, the form asked if the applicant would have the necessary funds. When I spotted a really promising but, impecunious student, I usually managed to find some grant money, coupled with work-study, to enable him or her to participate. I was allowed to have one work-study student who could be paid ahead of time.

Once the dozen or so students were selected, they were expected to give up every Sunday evening throughout the spring semester to come to our house for meetings, conversational French and dinner. Nellie Perez, a French teacher, born and brought up in France, had escaped to the United States about 1940. We hired her to teach us the basic essentials of conversational French. Tout le monde loved Nellie. Her conversation would have been music to Miss Manners' ears. Unfortunately, the French youth of today have long since abandoned the flowery speech of their grandparents. While Nellie was teaching everybody to say "Pourriez-vous m'indiquer la direction du Louvre?" Or "Bonjour monsieur, comment allez vous aujourd'hui?" what they really needed to learn was "Où est le Louvre?" and "Ciao!" Never mind. The important thing was that our students became familiar, not only with the sound of the language, but also with each other. I felt that, in view of the fact that we were all going to be living together in very close and often uncomfortable quarters, for six weeks, we should know as much as possible about each other well ahead of time.

Every Sunday the students would arrive at 5:00 p.m. Each week four students brought dinner on a rotating basis. One brought hors d'oeuvres another, the main dish. A third student brought vegetables or salad, the fourth dessert. Ambrose and I did all the drinks, china and silverware. That arrangement meant that each student would make a contribution roughly every three weeks and should only have to produce the entrée once. An hour of French conversation would be followed by a break for dinner. Later, there would be various activities before we broke up.

279

Sometimes, we might watch a movie about France, borrowed from the public library. More often, I had books and maps as a basis for discussion of all the things we planned to accomplish in France. All the students were encouraged to read as much as possible about the country, and French culture, to prepare for summer school. I also drew up two lists of topics. Each student would choose one from each list. As the main thrust of the program was Romanesque and Gothic, one list was devoted to the most important monuments to be visited. For example, a student might choose the basilica of St. Denis. It dates from the earliest Gothic period, though it sits over a much earlier church. With, or without, my help, that student would prepare to lecture the rest of the students on the day that we would visit St. Denis. Meanwhile, the others would be expected to know enough about the subject, to ask good questions. In this way, many of our field trips were thoroughly interactive. Some grading was based on intelligent participation. The other list was more general. It might include subjects as diverse as "The Romans in France," "The Albigensian Heresy" or "The Sun King." By the end of spring semester everybody was as prepared as possible to meet me in Paris.

A year earlier than that first French summer school, Ambrose's mother, Prudence, flew over for an extended visit. Frank, his father, had been in failing health for several years so, coming to see us only became possible after he died. While visiting an automobile show, Prue and I were both taken with the smallest car imaginable. It was a Fiat X19, hardtop convertible, for two people. The engine was fitted sideways across the car immediately behind the seats. That allowed for the car to have two trunks, a small one at the rear, just behind the engine, and a larger one at the front. The latter, also had a place to snap in the convertible roof. The list price was less than eight thousand dollars, so we went off to talk turkey at the Fiat dealership.

My plan, for the following summer, was to begin by taking about forty five Indianapolis Museum of Art members to France for a two week trip. Among the participants were Mary Jo and Jack Showley and Jean Buzan who was to remain on as a summer school student. At the conclusion of the IMA tour, the three of them planned to remain in Europe and fly with me to Rome for a few days. The Showleys were to return to Indianapolis from Rome, but Jean agreed to remain with me, for a further three weeks, to scout out an IMA Sicilian tour for the following year.

I had arranged to take delivery of the Fiat from the factory in Rome. At that time, no X19s had been released for home consumption, so my car was all set to be a gob-smacking novelty in Italy. Because it was ultimately destined for the States, it was built to comply with American standards. For example, it was calibrated in miles, and gallons, rather than kilometers, and liters. By that time, this country had gone lead-free. Europe had not. To ensure compliance, new cars were built with an entrance to the gas tank that was too narrow to admit the old leaded hose pipes. As leaded gas ruins the catalytic converter, the factory in Rome would give me a spare one to be installed in Indianapolis.

On the day that the Showleys left Rome, Jean and I took a taxi to the Fiat factory to get the car. Leaving the works, we noticed that we were running on empty, so we pulled into the first gas station. Now all Italians are crazy about cars, so whenever an unknown model of an Italian car appears it is totally surrounded in a nanosecond. Whoever won the battle to fill it up was in for a shock. The nozzle wouldn't go in, so the poor man got doused in fuel! Leaving the new car where it was with Jean Buzan to guard it, I headed for a nearby hardware store to buy a funnel. It was now possible to fill the tank, albeit very slowly. Any attempt to speed the process, guaranteed a splashed face. Self service didn't exist in Europe, and my Italian was too limited to alert attendants to the hazard ahead, so for over nine thousand miles we drove from one crisis to the next.

Jean and I spent the next two weeks planning an IMA Sicily tour. Oddly enough, the most important consideration for museum members is toilet facilities. The number of participants varied, but sometimes we had as many as fifty five. Women usually outnumbered men two to one. Though we always hired coaches with a rest room, it was only to be used for an emergency. Consequently, pit stops were planned to be within two hours of each other. In much of Europe, including Italy south of Naples, salubrious facilities are few and far between. For men, that's not much of a problem. Necessity being the mother of invention, most men can find satisfaction behind a tree at the roadside. Sadly, women find the great outdoors totally unacceptable, for that purpose and, as we always aim (no pun intended) to please, Jean and I devoted a major part of our trip in pursuit of adequate facilities. If you think that filling stations often boast clean restrooms, you'd be right. The problem is that in most cases they are designed for single occupancy. Now, if you've got about forty women, all ready to divest themselves of their breakfast coffee, and they average three minutes each, not only will the entire operation take two hours, but the lady who went in first may well be ready for a return visit. Bus drivers like to suggest filling stations, because parking is no problem, and they can smoke and sleep while the ladies rotate through the rest room.

If any sightseeing is to be accomplished during the day, filling stations must be just that. In the event that a two hour bus ride brings everybody a prearranged lunch, or a site to be visited, all is usually OK. Our challenge was to find places for the several days when three, or more, hours of travel were needed to reach a destination. Diverting into a nearby town doesn't work. Many streets are too narrow for buses and there is seldom parking available. Nowadays, a network of superhighways, with strategically placed oases, generally solves the problem. Forty years ago it was a very different story.

Two occasions spring to mind. One was in Greece. The year before taking an IMA trip there, Ambrose and I were joined by Emma Lou and Gayle Thornbrough to help plan the itinerary. No facilities, worthy of the name, were to be found in the central Peloponnese. From Epidauros to Marathon, some three hours away, there was nothing. When I took the IMA trip, I warned everybody to go easy on coffee, at breakfast, and to brace themselves for communion with nature at lunchtime. As luck would have it, not only was it perfect weather but, back home in Indiana it was 500 mile race day.

Linda Huddleston, head of IMA membership, was with us, along with a Greek lady from the travel company. Marathon today, consists entirely of the archeological site dominated by a wonderfully preserved theater. The bus stopped right at the theater stage. In front of it was a labyrinth of ruins for men to explore. Meanwhile we directed women up to the top of the theater where they would find ample space away from prying male eyes. As soon as everybody was out of sight, the Greek tourist lady, Linda and I sprang into action. While I spread black and white checkered cloths, napkins and paper plates, etc. along the low wall separating the front row of seats from the orchestra, the other two brought out a spectacular picnic. By the time the first of our people hove into view, all was ready. The inconvenient conveniences were quickly forgiven and forgotten.

The other occasion, which was thoroughly unpleasant for the ladies, occurred in India. We had just been in Varanasi and needed to get to Patna, for a flight to Calcutta, due to depart at noon. We were scheduled to make the sixty mile journey by train. Unfortunately, riots and gunfire, in anticipation of imminent local elections, had erupted in Varanasi, causing us all to be confined to the hotel grounds for most of the previous day. Colonel Ramaswamy, our Indian escort, told me that, because of a threatened train attack, we would hire a bus. We would breakfast at 3:30 a.m. and set off at four. Whining that buses, back home, covered sixty miles in an hour got me nowhere. If we were to make a noon flight out of Patna, he said, we must depart Varanasi no later than 4:00 a.m. The bus turned out to be a thoroughgoing rattletrap, devoid of all creature comforts, including heat. Being January, it was cold. The bus windows all kept rattling open. We set off at the appointed time with a bus driver and his mate. The latter stood on a running board from which he alighted, every whipstitch, to gently persuade sacred cows to allow us through. Within two hours, the cold had penetrated all our bladders. I alerted the colonel that a rest stop was urgent. Anything remotely akin to functioning plumbing, on Indian country roads, is non-existent. We stopped at the ruins of a burnt-out house, illuminated by our headlights. While we men peed into the ditch, on one side of the bus, a petrified group of Indianapolis dowagers picked their way into the overgrown ruin, barely illuminated by a waning moon, accompanied by a shouted warning, from Ramaswamy, to "Watch out for snakes!"

Why we needed eight hours, to travel sixty miles, soon became apparent. The bus came to a standstill among a critical mass of animals and people. A number of the latter were cooking over makeshift stoves. To our left was a dried up river bed, roughly a mile wide, and ahead was a single lane covered bridge, over it. Traffic, some of it in the form of single-legged pedestrians, swarmed over, for several hours, from the other direction before it was our turn. We were in time for the plane with less than an hour to spare.

While on the subject of India, I must tell you about a discussion I had with Colonel Ramaswami's Brahmin wife Malathi. We had visited Mathura in Uttar Pradesh, the Bethlehem of India and birthplace of Lord Krishna. During our days together, Malathi had regaled us with a number of Hindu myths, in many cases, paralleling Christian ones. Even the names, Krishna, and Christ, are derived from the Sanscrit word for God. Like several of Jesus' predecessors, Krishna was immaculately conceived as the middle one of a trinity of gods. The biggest difference between the two is that Krishna was a big time, unapologetic womanizer. He also predates Jesus by more than three thousand years. When I mentioned many similarities to Malathi, she said, "Why are you surprised? Surely you know that Jesus lived in India for about sixty five years?" To be perfectly frank, this was the first time that I'd heard it and, I dare say, this may be news to some of my readers? When she asked me where Jesus had been between the ages of twelve and thirty, I had to admit that no record of those years has been found. The reason the New Testament is silent on the subject, she said, is because he was becoming a holy man, in India. When I looked somewhat skeptical, she patiently explained that he studied the breathing exercises which induce a state of suspended animation, and which enabled him to survive crucifixion. "You mean to say that Jesus didn't die on the cross?" I asked. "Certainly not. He came straight back to India with his first wife. Christians call her Mary Magdalene," she continued with that tone of certainty which is the hallmark of faithful believers. "Well," I said, "he couldn't have come straight back here, because he visited America, for a few weeks, first." What in the world was I talking about? No, she'd never heard of Joseph Smith, the Angel Maroni, golden tablets, or Latter Day Saints. It was fun providing Malathi with a footnote to her own improbable biography of the boy from Nazareth.

According to Hindus, Jesus, who was one of their holy men, took an Indian wife and died when he was about eighty. His twin brother, Thomas, also known as "Doubting Thomas," had founded Christian churches in Goa, south of Bombay. As an afterthought, it's worth noting that though Lord Krishna was not a twin, Romulus, born about 700 BCE., was, and their mother, a Vestal Virgin, was impregnated by the god Mars.

Please forgive me for yet another digression from my exploratory tour of Sicily with Jean Buzan?

Owing to the unusual alignment of the Fiat X19s engine, it needed a special cooling system. Sometime after the engine was switched off, it came into play and went on for ten or fifteen minutes depending on how long we had been driving. About six o'clock, one evening, Jean and I drove up to the Villa Athena Hotel, in Agrigento. We parked beside the kitchen. Before we were out of the car, half of the hotel staff was watching us, through the windows, with undisguised fascination. Jaws visibly dropped open, as we took luggage out of both ends. No sooner had we checked into the hotel, than a frantic member of staff rushed in. His eyes were popping out like chapel hat pegs, as he gasped that the engine, of my car, had started of its own accord! Mama mia, pensa fa tutte!

It was in Agrigento that we noticed half the cars in the parking lot had the driver's window broken out. Every victim had the same story. To visit the main sites in Sicily nearly everybody arrives at Palermo or Messina. If you take the short ferry ride from Villa San Giovanni on the mainland, to Messina as we did, you drive the circuit of sites clockwise to Palermo followed by an overnight ferry to Naples. All the hotel guests who were traveling anti-clockwise were the ones with broken windows. They had been victimized in downtown Palermo where traffic crawls, at best. As certain numbers are assigned to the license plates of rental cars, the criminals know exactly what to look for. They travel in pairs on Vespa motorbikes. The driver cuts in front of the victim's car forcing him to stop while the other guy jumps off, pick in hand, to smash in the window and demand all billfolds, money and jewelry. Not one of the hotel guests, who had been in Palermo, had escaped unscathed. All the rest of us were heading there in fear and trepidation.

Jean and I were lucky. We had booked rooms at the Villa Igea, just west of downtown Palermo, with a secure parking lot behind high walls. We reached our hotel in safety and parked the car till we were ready to leave, three days later. To sight-see in the city, we took the bus. On one of the days, after lunching downtown, we were ready to return to the hotel without taking into consideration protracted Sicilian siestas. The buses had stopped and the entire bustling city was silently shuttered, so we decided to walk. While traversing a slum area between downtown and the hotel, we heard footsteps gaining on us. Sensing trouble, without looking behind us, we decided on a plan. We continued walking until the approaching footsteps were close. Suddenly, we walked straight across the empty street to continue our walk on that side. Having evaded our followers, they continued walking and, we could see them from behind and surmised that they were a couple of young men up to no good. They picked up speed and, when they were well ahead of us, crossed the street to our side and shot down a narrow alley. Now we were really scared as there was nobody to be seen in any direction. Rather than cross that alley, we went back to our original side of the street, walking as fast as we could. Fortunately, the hotel was, by then, very close. We reached it safely, but shaken. I must have led a charmed life because, that's the closest I've ever come to a mugging.

During the IMA trip the next year, I'm happy to report that none of our members was robbed or molested. At the same time, I'd be less than truthful if I said that it went off without incident. Accepted wisdom has it that there's a rotten apple in every basket of them. On that tour, we had an eccentric Russian lady.

No doubt, some things that Tamara said were true but, separating fact from fiction proved too much for most of us. That she had been a Bolshoi dancer is fact. She had bolted from the company, when they were on tour in Paris, to join Ernest Jacques, an American civil servant she'd met in Moscow. The US government shipped them stateside and gave him a post at Fort Benjamin Harrison, in Indianapolis. She claimed to have a sister in Kiev who would be starving, were it not for Tamara sending monthly checks. In view of the fact that the Iron Curtain was still in place, we doubted that such transactions were possible. Be that as it may, one day she planned to remain at the Villa Igea to phone the sister, while we took a trip to Monreale. On our return, she claimed to have had a long talk to her in Kiev, and we were all subjected to a litany of the miserable woman's cruel deprivations. Unlike other members of the group, I believed that she had called Kiev and soon found myself on the hook for a fifty dollar bet.

Next morning, as we were checking out of the hotel, Tamara and I were settling our accounts at the same time. She was protesting about an item on her bill and called on me to arbitrate. It was for a bottle of wine which four of us had had for dinner. In fact, Tamara was right. Another lady had ordered the bottle which had been charged to Mrs. Jacques. That matter being satisfactorily settled, she claimed to owe the hotel nothing. "Oh yes, you do!" said Jane Meyers, who was also at the counter. "What about your Russian phone bill?" Claiming to have paid for it, the previous day, Tamara departed, but Jane pursued the matter, and I wound up fifty dollars the poorer.

While enjoying a few minutes downtime in my hotel room, the phone rang. It was Tamara. She needed me in the gift shop right away. She had found a tie to buy for Ernest. Before doing so, she needed to know if I thought it looked too old for him. Not amused at having been summoned for such an inconsequential enquiry, I said, "Well, tell me Tamara, how old is Ernest?" "What terrible question," she replied, "you never ask person age." "In that case," I said, "I won't be able to help you decide whether, or not, that tie is age appropriate." However, anxious to keep problems to a minimum, I added that I would be delighted to be given such a tie and therefore, I felt confident that Ernest would be equally pleased. I had every reason to choose my words with care following what had happened in Taormina.

We had been staying at the San Domenico, an old monastery which has been converted into a five-star hotel. Our friends Mary Jo, and Jack Showley, had brought Ivy with them. She was eleven, sharing a room with Tamara, to spare each of them the cost of a single supplement. Ivy was a model child but, from day one, Tamara referred to her as "Poison Ivy."

Jack and Mary Jo had waited some time, at the dinner table for their daughter to join them. Jack became impatient and went in search of her. Reaching her room he heard crying. Tamara had locked Ivy in the room, during the afternoon, and not returned. Jack Showley is a big man with a short fuse. He exploded, flinging his entire two hundred and eighty pound bulk with such force, at the antique door, that it shattered!

As tour leader, I was summoned to the manager's office to offer an explanation and establish responsibility. He appeared to be a good family man and, as everybody knows, a good Italian family man loves his children with unsurpassed devotion. Somehow I managed to convince the manager that Dr. Showley might be American but he shared with Italian fathers a single minded love for his child who needed immediate help. The hotel never charged us for the damage but, there was plenty of walking carefully, on egg shells, from then on.

While on the subject of Sicilian adventures, I recall a couple of Mafia related ones, from later trips, which I'll take the liberty of sharing with you now, before returning to the mainland with Jean Buzan, for our first French summer school.

Fast forward some fifteen years to 1995. By that time we had embraced Susie Orso, a partner in an unusual travel agency called Special Tours. Each of her employees brought specialized knowledge of one or two countries. In Susie's case she was English but married to a Florentine banker with a wide circle of influential friends. Among the tours which she arranged, and couriered, for the Indianapolis Museum of Art, was one to Sicily.

Susie counted the Prince and Princess Borghese, of the ancient and illustrious Roman family, among her friends. In search of a more productive life, they moved to Sicily to grow citrus fruit, organically, for sale and distribution on the mainland. During our tour, the Borgheses invited us to lunch, at their estate outside Catania, and to see their renowned cactus garden. They were still reeling from recent Mafia reprisals. Like all business people, the Borgheses were obliged to regularly pay Cosa Nostra protection money. The Prince had advertised for a manager to oversee the citrus groves. The man they hired soon proved incompetent so he was fired. What they didn't know was that he was a Mafia plant. Presumably, the Borgheses were suspected of making more money than they claimed so, a spy had been sent to check the books, with a view to finding out how much more could be demanded of them. At any rate, they received a phone call threatening reprisals unless they rehired the overseer. Of course they refused. What happened next, sounds like science fiction.

After dinner one evening, the entire Borghese household, servants and all, fell into a stupor. By the time they came to, the place had been ransacked. All the Renaissance and Baroque heirloom family furniture had gone. The library was a shambles. The floor to ceiling bookcases had been stolen, the books strewn everywhere. Not surprisingly, the Sicilian police failed to trace a single piece of the heist.

Shortly thereafter, Susie took a British group on a Sicilian tour. They started in Syracuse, home of Archimedes, who is best remembered for streaking the town in the middle of the third century BCE. On her advice, most of the people left money and valuables in their room safes. Next day, at a souvenir shop, several of her group discovered that their large denomination bank notes were forgeries. As they had all changed their English money at the same airport exchange office, it seemed obvious where to place the blame. The immediate solution was for Susie to loan them money. Nicki, her banker husband, always made sure that she had plenty of cash on hand before setting off with tour groups. You guessed it. Her hundred thousand lire bills were from the same run of fakes as the ones which the Brits had. Until then, I had often made use of my room safe in the naïve belief that it could only be opened by my own code number. Of course, every cleaning person has a number that opens all the room safes, so they can be cleaned out and left open for the next hotel guest. Now, if you're still with me, following all these digressions, and transgressions, let us return to the summer of 1979.

Back in Rome, from Sicily, Jean and I went our separate ways. She headed to Paris in pursuit of some distant ancestors. Ambrose flew into Rome to join me for two weeks. If I had to choose one city, in which to spend a lifetime, it would be Rome. Within the Aurelian Walls, I must have walked almost every street, yet there's always some new archeological find to be explored. Consequently, I never pass up an opportunity to spend time there. Discovering Roman remains, that illustrate the metamorphosis from Paganism into early Christianity is, for me, endlessly rewarding. Add to that, good food and abiding love, and you have my all time favorite recipe for a fascinating life. Ambrose and I spent ten days seeking out such treasures before heading north, through the Alps to Paris. As he boarded a plane back to Indianapolis, I greeted the students arriving for our first summer school in France.

Jean Buzan had gone out to Charles de Gaulle airport, to help everyone get loaded into the correct city bus. I had arranged for us all to stay, for the first two weeks, at the United States Foundation building, in the Cité Universitaire, just within the *périphérique* on the south side of Paris. The Cité Universitaire consists of a large acreage of dormitories, to house students from many countries. Each building was erected by the relevant country so the whole estate is a veritable hodgepodge of architectural styles, some delightful and inviting, others merely dull or, as in the case of ours, almost brutal. Off the entrance hall were communal rooms for dining and relaxing. Beyond were two wings, to the left for men, to the right for women. The ceilings were high. We were all assigned third floor rooms. In the United States we call that the fourth floor. There were no elevators.

No sooner had I reached my room than Mr. Frazier, the manager, paged me. Only Jean Buzan had managed to carry her own luggage. The other five women needed help and as no male students were allowed into the women's wing, it was my responsibility. I was aghast at the sight that greeted me in the lobby of the women's staircase. There may have been one or two outsized suitcases, but it was mostly trunks. As one who only travels with a small carry-on bag, I was flabbergasted. By the time I'd lugged the final load up four flights, I wondered if I might be invalided back stateside before summer school had even started. Collapsing on my lumpy mattress, I vowed never to allow such a thing to happen again. Thenceforth, every group of summer school students was issued with a non-negotiable packing list. At our final Indianapolis meeting, I would bring in my fully packed case, unpack it to demonstrate that it not only contained everything on the list but, as I was the teacher, mine also contained all the pertinent paperwork, maps and guidebooks.

Once we left Paris, we would be traveling in two rental cars plus my tiny Fiat. There was no possibility that even one of those monster trunks could accompany us. Mr. Frazier found a secure basement room for all the luggage. There it could remain during our four-week tour. I visited a supermarket and conned the manager out of a number of plastic sacks. Each student got four of them in lieu of luggage. Even then, traveling was a tight squeeze.

The first morning of summer school, we took the Metro to the Ile de la Cité. As you emerge into daylight, the west front of Notre Dame Cathedral is right in front of you. One by one, the students came out, gasped, and looked in awe at the world famous façade. It had recently been cleaned and never looked lovelier. Even without cleaning, its sublime proportions are, in my opinion, barely surpassed by Agra's Taj Mahal. As my students stood there absorbing the beauty before them, my mind shot back six weeks to my arrival, from Indianapolis, with all the IMA contingent. The first day with them, we had a luxury coach to tour the major city sites. The first stop had been in front of Notre Dame. On the bus I had done my best to prepare them for the treat in store but, it seemed their main interest, on alighting, was either where to shop or whether, or not, they had to pay for their own lunch today! The contrast was so stark that, from that moment on, I was always happier sharing a baguette and a bit of cheese, sitting on a rock with the students, than eating foie gras in a three-star restaurant with the IMA's well-heeled patrons. Not that I didn't enjoy all the tours I conducted. I most certainly did. At the same time, enabling young people to have experiences, which so often exceeded their wildest dreams, I've always found profoundly satisfying.

There used to be an old family run restaurant, in Paris, called André. It had those old-fashioned paper menus, scribbled in purple ink. I made a point of treating each student to dinner there. We would drive in my car. Being tiny, parking was easy even though the restaurant happened to be just off the Champs Elysées. After dinner, we'd tour around town enjoying all the fountains and floodlighting. It was a rare night that we weren't stopped by the police, to question the car's lighting. All cars in France had small, so-called, running lights. By Law, they should be on at night. Headlights, on the other hand, even dipped, are illegal in Paris. Fiat X-19s, made for the US market, didn't have running lights, so I was between a rock and a hard place. Every time I was stopped, the cop would check all my controls until he was satisfied that my compliance with the law was impossible. As he let me go, I would leave him scratching his uncomprehending head.

Our first field trip out of Paris was to Laon, some eighty miles east. I was to lead the way with one student, the others following in the two rental cars. At some point, out in the country, they decided to speed things up by overtaking me. As they did so, I was mooned by all except the drivers! Whatever, pray tell, happened to respect for professorial gray hair?

Laon has, arguably, the finest of all early Gothic cathedrals, even though it's almost devoid of stained glass. Aided by a modest *pourboire*, I persuaded a verger to unlock a door and take us on a tour of the tribunes. For safety's sake, they are closed to the public. We followed him up a torturous spiral staircase in one of the west towers. Once at tribune level, he lead us to a spacious area in the north transept. There we stopped to hear his own version of the building's history, since its inception ca. 1160, while I struggled to politely translate whatever he said into English. Suddenly, I stopped in midsentence, as I spotted Brad Luther, through a window, climbing about on flying buttresses. Nor was I alone. The verger's entire audience had seen Brad, and was enjoying his antics rather more than the talk to which they were being subjected. As luck would have it, the man had his back to the window and must have thought that the air of collective merriment was being brought on as a result of his own scintillating personality. Aware that there would be hell to pay, if he spotted Brad, I did my best to keep him talking as we made our way back down. Even then my troubles were not over as Brad was still up there as the verger was producing a large key to lock the door. Mumbling something about a diligent student, who must have been left behind taking notes, I shot back up the stairs to meet the miscreant happily running down. The nice verger was none the wiser. He was so impressed, with the students, that he gave me his name and address, which was close by, and told me that whenever I brought other groups I could get the key from his house. On several subsequent trips, I did just that.

With several cars, in the days before GPS, you might wonder how we avoided getting lost? In France, where the subject was Romanesque and Gothic, the problem was minimal. The monuments we were headed for, were usually cathedrals, generally soaring above the rest of the city, and often visible from miles away. If we got separated, everybody knew to follow *centre ville* signs, find somewhere to park, and meet at the cathedral's west front. If we were bound for a monastery, that was a no-brainer. They are almost invariably out in the country, by themselves.

From a practical point of view, the work-study student handled the "common purse." When we were running out of money, we'd all chip in the same amount, to be used for all the things that everybody did together, such as daily lunch picnics, entrance tickets, and gas.

Only in Paris did we have accommodations booked. As we traveled, everybody knew what town was to be our destination for the night. French towns are fairly predictable. Most have a railroad station close to the downtown area with a parking lot in front of it. Around the station are usually several dirt-cheap, if a trifle tawdry, hotels. From my red Michelin guide, I would select one and say that I planned to stay there, and would meet everyone in the lobby, once they had found themselves rooms for the night. The game became quite competitive with all the students vying for the best bargain. So far as I remember, the prize goes to Poitiers, where the guys found a five-bedded room for three dollars each. It was certainly in Poitiers, when I was sitting at a table, in front of the hotel, enjoying a well-earned aperitif with some of the students, when Hugh Haynes screamed, "Look!" We all looked, just in time to see a woman jump out of an upstairs window, half-dressed. Her fall was broken by an awning, over some café tables, deflecting her into the gutter. Almost immediately she was surrounded by people and, within minutes, an ambulance arrived. What became of the poor lady, and what precipitated the jump remains a mystery, but the scene is embedded in my memory as if it happened yesterday.

Throughout summer school, the students kept journal notebooks, checked weekly by me, as a grading component. Patricia Bennett kept excellent notes. Every now and then I would see an activity mysteriously marked "PP." On enquiry I found that it was the abbreviation for "Pampering Patty!"

It was a student's birthday, so a party seemed in order. In the market were some tiny melons from which the seeds were carefully extracted and replaced with port, to marinate all day. During the ensuing bibulous affair, the students presented me with a wrapped gift. I certainly had neither expected nor deserved anything, but before touching it, I said, "This is absurd, but I know what it is." It was a small reproduction of one of the capitals in Autun cathedral depicting the three wise men asleep. For the life of me, I couldn't tell you how I knew. It was just one of those curious things that make life so delightfully unpredictable.

By the end of summer school, the students had written a song to the tune of "Old Macdonald Had a Farm" with innumerable verses aimed at roasting me. The refrain had something to do with flying buttresses with, "Here a butt, there a butt, everywhere a butt butt!" sung for my benefit, in the unlikely event that I had forgotten the 'mooning' incident. That was the first of many wonderfully rewarding European summer schools. Not until I returned to Herron, did I hear of a mishap. The students had flown home without me as I needed to make arrangements, in Rotterdam, Holland, to have the car shipped to New York. They flew into Chicago where two or three of them were being met. The rest rented a van to drive the hundred and eighty miles back to Indianapolis. Hugh was driving when they hit a deer. They were all shaken by the accident. Fortunately, no one was seriously hurt, though the van sustained considerable damage.

A more scary series of mishaps occurred during a later French summer school. We were concluding our time in Paris with a free day. Madeline Yurtseven was planning to spend it with her husband and three-year old son. They had stopped in Paris, en route back to Indianapolis from Istanbul, where they had been visiting his parents. The rest of us had been invited to spend the day with Edmé and Fanny Nérot, friends who had a family home in the village of Bourron-Marlotte, in the forest of Fontainebleau. On returning to Paris, in the evening, the following story emerged.

That morning, the Yurtsevens were in a crowded Metro train, getting jostled by some women. Madeline was concerned with protecting her child. No sooner had the women left the train, than she realized that they'd made off with her bag. The three of them jumped off at the next station, Roosevelt, where there are major banks. Once they'd taken stock of their losses, they entered one to cancel the stolen travelers' checks and apply for replacements. Their timing could hardly have been worse. They were standing in line, when armed gunmen stormed in and ordered everyone to hit the ground. When Madeline did so, she smashed her glasses. She had very poor eyesight and no second pair in France. Her husband, an engineering professor at IUPUI, was a tower of strength in trying to figure out what to do next. So far as I recall, they did sort out their travelers checks, though they may have done so at another bank. They went to the American Embassy to report their stolen passports. On arrival, there were so many people in the same predicament that the Embassy could only deal with those whose flights home were scheduled during the next twenty four hours. Madeline was given a form, and an appointment, for two days later. The only bright spot, in this otherwise dismal tale, is that Ambrose was due to join us, from Indianapolis, in a few days bringing replacement glasses which were entrusted to him by Madeline's husband.

# Chapter Twenty Six
## *The Rev. A.G. Fraser International Travel Fund*

The second of my European summer schools was to Italy. Two or three days before it concluded, we were in Florence when I received a call from my mother. Dad had suffered a massive stroke, following eighteen holes of golf. After a hurried consultation with the students, and a visit to a travel agent, I changed my flight. We had all planned to fly home together from Rome but, in the event, I saw the students off before taking a flight to London to visit my parents.

Dad was paralyzed on one side, but he could talk. He asked me if I'd heard of the Hemlock Society, a self-help organization for committing suicide. I had heard of it and asked him if he belonged. He did not, but wished he did. All he wanted now, was to die as quickly as possible. Please would I go to see his doctor to find out what could be done to speed his end. He was in a large ward, of a nursing home, not far from Chaldon, Surrey, where he and Ma lived. First, I went to see her, told her about Dad's wishes, and asked whether she was ready to let him go. Hearing what Dad wanted, she gave me permission to talk to the doctor, who's improbable name was Dr. Honeybun.

Knowing very little about medicine, I was interested in the doctor's advice. As I suspected, he could neither inject Dad with a fatal dose, nor could he hand the old man a potion, to drink, while he looked the other way. Dad, he said, should force himself to walk up and down, with a walker, in the hopes of bringing on a fatal stroke. He warned that, if Dad took to his bed to await the inevitable, it might take years. That prospect really struck home. We all remembered my great Aunt Mag's husband, Uncle Joe. By the time he had a debilitating stroke, he was both blind and stone deaf. The wretched bed-ridden man, who longed for death, survived for several years. Dad lucked out. He died about six weeks after his stroke.

My Father was the first born of his parent's five children. At seventy nine, he was the youngest into the turf business. All five died, not only in the order of birth, but each survived to a greater age than the deceased siblings. Auntie Jean, the youngest, phoned me from Stirling, Scotland, in 2010. She said that she was about to go upstairs to bed aided by her daughter, Penelope, and son James in order to die. Two days later, an email from James informed me that she had died peacefully at ninety four. I had expected at least one of them to pass the century mark. Grandfather had died at eighty eight, despite almost fatal bouts of sleeping sickness and malaria, not to mention the motorbike accident in his eighties. Granny had also suffered from tropical diseases. She nearly joined the feathered choir before she turned thirty, during an outbreak of blackwater fever, in Uganda, yet she only missed her centenary by fifteen months.

Dad earned his early death. Almost all his life he had been a chain smoker. He did nothing about his cholesterol, even after a blood clot in his leg followed, within a year, by another in his left eye. There's a lot to be said for going out of this world with your boots on, and my father did his best to do just that.

I did not return to England when he died. I was in the midst of fall semester at Herron. Instead, I returned at Christmas to be with Mama and help sort out his things. Among the books, in his office, were two or three on human sexuality with dog-eared corners to mark sections on homosexuality. Ma encouraged me to help myself to whatever I wanted. I brought back his desk chair, a handsome Georgian antique. He also had a signed photograph of Rabindranath Tagore, the Bengali poet and humanist, who had been a family friend. I gave it to our friend, K.P. Singh.

When the Herron students heard of Dad's death, they started a fund in his memory. They called it the Rev. A.G. Fraser

International Travel Fund. The object was to raise money to help finance able, but impecunious, students so they could participate in European summer schools. We are all familiar with the problem of memorial gifts. They are one-time offerings. The initial outpouring was generous beyond all expectations. We were soon in a position to help students in a meaningful way. To supplement the fund, we had a number of special events each year. Usually they took the form of a cocktail party held in some art lover's mansion. Many were elegant, glittering affairs, but there is a limit to the number of times you can expect to feed at the same trough. The school's development officer did an excellent job of writing letters to previous donors, in an attempt to persuade them to make an annual gift. During summer school, I would supply each bursary-receiving student with the names and addresses of contributors, so that they could write appreciative post cards.

On retirement from the Ball Corporation in Muncie, Indiana, Bob Mohlman, and his wife, Ina, had moved to Indianapolis to become major supporters of the arts. They went on most of my overseas trips. It was customary for these trips to end with a farewell dinner, affording everybody the opportunity to reward the courier, and coach driver, with substantial tips. At these dinners there would be a number of impromptu speeches and toasts. Bob always gave the Fraser Fund a pitch. He would say, "I know that we all recognize that, without Ian, we would not be here tonight, and would like to do something to thank him." He would let everybody know that he had the name and address of the fund so that contributions could be made. As a result of his encouragement, fresh names were added to the list of donors with each overseas trip.

Bob and Ina became close personal friends. Sadly, Bob suffered a series of strokes, and eventually died. Ina, now frail, but about to enter her tenth decade, has courageously carried on where Bob left off. With a view to ensuring that the fund would be there in perpetuity, she joined the committee to help create an endowment. Thanks to her determination, and generosity, and that of a number of others, under the chairmanship of Brad Luther, of the Laon Cathedral flying buttress escapade, the endowment goal was surpassed when both the Clowes Fund and the Allen Whitehill Clowes Fund made substantial gifts.

Today, the Rev. A.G. Fraser International Travel Fund awards up to seven two thousand dollar scholarships annually. Until my retirement in 1996, I was the only teacher to conduct overseas courses but, since then, it has blossomed. Now there are courses offered in China, England, Ireland, Germany, and the Benelux countries, in addition to France and Italy.

Ina Mohlman was Swiss born and bred, then shipped for university studies, to Chicago, where she met, and married, Bob. Back in Switzerland, her father had gradually acquired a magnificent antique Meissen dinner service. The pattern, known as *Blumen und Insekten*, is one of the most detailed ever done. No two dishes are alike. At some point, after World War II, he shipped the whole lot, in crates as a gift, to Bob and Ina. Unfortunately, by the time the Mohlmans reached New York City, to clear it through customs, all the crates containing the serving pieces, as well as cups and saucers, had disappeared. The loss still left a dinner service of about sixty pieces dating from about 1850. Over our protestations, Ina gave us the lot! I realize that, though it is museum quality, no museum wants more than one place setting. On the other hand, both Peter and David, the Mohlman offspring, are married with children of their own, but Ina insisted that her family have no interest in fine porcelain so that was the end of the matter.

Bill Grimes, a sculpture major, turned out to be one of my best art history students. His papers were excellent and, if he didn't score a hundred on every test, he came very close to it. Always involved in the Army Reserve, he was somewhat older than most of the students. A tough childhood, with no father to guide him, had taught him self-reliance while, at the same time, leaving him both defensive and in need of approbation. This attitude sat poorly with many of my students, but my own childhood enabled me to empathize with Bill. Though very different from each other, we formed a strong bond and, before long, he started calling me "Dad."

During the first French summer school, Bill was one of the students. Nearly everybody was short of money and had forgotten to bring various necessities. After making a list of what was needed, he ran to an Army PX and returned, like a pack mule, with everything. Bill is one of those rare individuals who, just about the time you feel like killing him, does something wonderful.

As the art history program developed, in order to offer a wider range of courses, we amalgamated all three sections of H101 and H102, Introduction to Art History, into one. This involved between a hundred and a hundred and twenty students at a time, to be taught by me. Bill Grimes became my right arm. He not only ran the projectors, he did review classes, supervised and graded tests. I couldn't have managed without him. He was unfailingly there whenever I needed anything.

For a number of years Bill was married to Julie, a Mexican nurse, with whom he fathered his only child, Cramer. Eventually, that marriage fell apart. He's been married to Ginger, a divorcee with grown children of her own, for many years. Though Bill retired from Herron when I did, he stuck with the army, wound up in Houston, Texas, and finally took full retirement in 2013.

Dr. Annmarie Springer, our Modern and Contemporary Art professor, retired after two or three years with us. She was a good and popular teacher who would be hard to replace. That year, the College Art Association annual convention was in San Francisco. It is the number one venue for recruiting and hiring teachers. Most of the job seekers are recent Ph.D. graduates or, "all but dissertation." I interviewed a number of such people, any one of whom would have been more than qualified for the

IUPUI position. Suddenly, I found myself interviewing a soft-spoken bald man of forty two. His thesis had been on the influence of the Baha'i Faith on the art of Mark Tobey, an esoteric subject to be sure, but hardly cutting edge. On the other hand, I found his story compelling.

While he had been completing his art history Ph.D. in Texas, his wife Dee had gone with their two daughters to Bhutan, to take a job as a nurse. While they were there, a small boy in a coma was brought into the hospital, near death from malnutrition and TB. Dee Kelley nursed him back to health. Soon Phurba, who was between the two girls in age, was adopted by Ed and Dee. Having successfully defended his dissertation, Dr. Edward Kelley joined his family in Bhutan. Thanks to the King's brother, he was employed documenting Bhutanese art, and culture, and teaching English. They were the only Americans living long-time in Bhutan. After five years, they returned stateside to give the children an appropriate education.

Happily, the search and screen committee agreed with me and hired Dr. Kelley as our new modern art history professor. Everyone was pleased with him. Above all he was a first-rate teacher who seemed to instinctively understand what a student's problem might be and then, effectively, set about solving it. He designed a summer school course, aimed at senior fine arts majors, to help them market themselves following graduation. The last few days of the course were to be spent in New York City, attending gallery openings and meeting owners and collectors. The last night in the city, he hailed a taxi and piled in with three students, to return to their hotel. A car, running a red light, crashed into the taxi so violently that Ed was ejected into the street. The students, who were unharmed if badly shaken, found him lying knocked out. Once he regained consciousness, with no bones broken, he decided not to go to hospital. Instead, he returned to

Indianapolis the next day with all the students and a splitting headache.

The fall semester began. Ed seemed to be coping OK, in spite of ongoing headaches. However, about three weeks in, he came to me in tears to say that he'd just taught his last class. All weekend, he had been preparing a lecture on Jackson Pollock, an artist whose work he knew well, only to discover that he hadn't retained anything. With that he resigned effective immediately. His retentive brain never returned. Over the next couple of years, he slowly lost his sight. Today he practices massage therapy in California.

When it finally became clear that Lisa Kantor could not bear children, they chose to adopt. We were asked to write a letter in support of their application. As they were our next door neighbors and close friends, we were delighted to help in any way possible. In January, 1977, they collected a beautiful baby boy from the hospital and named him Isaac. Although they never identified the birth parents, they were both college students. The mother was at Butler University, the father at IUPUI.

As anticipated, Lisa and Sheldon were excellent, and devoted, parents. Having taught at Shortridge, I had had ample opportunity to observe how well Sheldon interacted with young people. Isaac was a delightful toddler peddling over on his tricycle, to visit us. Lisa's sister, and brother-in-law, lived a block away with kids of their own, producing a ready-made extended family. This made it possible for the Kantors to join us in France, unencumbered, for a short vacation. The final night of that trip, the four of us were strolling along the Seine when the two of them stopped, locked in each other's arms, and rested against the embankment wall. It being a romantic moonlit evening, Ambrose and I discreetly walked on, leaving them alone.

Two days later, back in Indianapolis, they came over to talk to us. We were completely unprepared for their announcement. Sheldon was moving out of the house, because he had finally come to the realization that he was gay. He had not met a man, but once he had a place of his own, he was confident that he soon would. I'm sure that they had come over expecting our support, but, I'm ashamed to say they didn't get it. In retrospect, we were mad at ourselves. Had we foreseen this development, we would have never have supported their adoption of Isaac. I had always thought that Sheldon was an attractive man but, my "gaydar" was *hors de combat* this time.

Lisa stayed on in the house for many years, bringing up Isaac as a single mother. She was a heavy smoker and, a few years ago, died an early death after her son had nursed her through a long terminal illness. He is a fragile personality. The loss of his mother put him over the edge, into drugs, culminating in a number of incarcerations. Oddly enough, he's also gay.

Once divorced, the first thing Sheldon did was to change his name to Josh. I like the name Sheldon, but he says he never did, so gradually, we got used to calling him Josh. After a number of brief liaisons, he settled down with a lover who soon developed AIDS. That was in the days before any drugs had been developed to manage the disease. I must admit that Josh did everything possible to ease his friend's misery. By nursing him with love and compassion to the end, he totally redeemed himself in my eyes. Soon Josh was in love again. They bought a house with a large yard, as gardening had always been one of his passions. In due course, they decided to move to California where everything grows better. Josh stayed behind in Indianapolis, to sell the house, while the boyfriend went shopping for one in the golden state. He found the perfect house in Carmichael, near Sacramento but, by the time Josh arrived, he'd absconded with another guy. Dearie me, whatever happened to old-fashioned fidelity? Fortunately, it wasn't long before Josh met Denny. So far, they are living together happily ever after.

# Chapter Twenty Seven
## *Ambrose Rocks*

Frank Halliburton Smith, Ambrose's father, had always been interested in English local politics. Ambrose inherited that interest, and rose to be president of the Mapleton Fall Creek Neighborhood Association. Being one of the largest neighborhoods in the Indianapolis metropolitan area, it runs the gamut from attractive enclaves, to pitiful slums. More or less triangular in shape, it is bounded on the north by 38th Street, on the west by Meridian Street, south to Fall Creek, and thence, up the Creek to the east end of the Fairgrounds, on 38th Street.

Ambrose believed that an annual parade and festival would go a long way towards bringing neighborhood folks together. He was right, and it wasn't long before the Mapleton Fall Creek parade was second only to the Indianapolis 500 parade. With his bullhorn, he became a pro at rounding up all the marching bands, floats, police and fire departments, and convertibles with city VIPs and other worthies on board. A stroke of genius was enlisting the aid of a much-feared black motorcycle gang called the Naptown Riders. Not only did Ambrose always have them in the parade, but he managed to persuade the Mayor of Indianapolis to ride on the back of one of their motorbikes.

Each year, the parade took a different route so that no area should feel slighted. Wherever the ensuing festival was to take place, was where the parade ended. On one occasion, the festivities were held on the Fall Creek river bank. As things were winding down, the Naptown Riders were running around, with garbage bags, picking up the inevitable discarded junk. One of them laughed, as he cleaned up around me, and said, "Hey, we're having a great day."

When we moved to the Cottage Home neighborhood, in 1988, Ambrose became involved in the new association and in the overwhelming problems of the badly-depressed near eastside. By then, he was retired and devoted much of his time working on behalf of various organizations, such as the Boner Center. Always believing that a good deed is its own reward, he worked tirelessly to improve dilapidated properties, and to help organize such essentials as a local health clinic. One of Ambrose's many admirable qualities is his modesty. It came as quite a shock to him, when the governor of Indiana honored him by creating him a Sagamore of the Wabash, in September 1993. Britain has many levels of recognition to bestow on those who have done much to leave the world a better place, from the MBE to knighthoods. In Indiana, the governor is limited to one. The Sagamore of the Wabash is it. As you could imagine, I was thrilled for him, though I teased that I should be made a Squaw of the Wabash.

Louise Craske, Ambrose's younger sister had given birth to twin sons within a month of our arrival in Indianapolis. To celebrate turning seventeen, in 1974, Mark and Clive flew over to spend a couple of months with us. We met them in New York for the usual first-time sightseeing before returning, to Indianapolis, via Sid and Dorothy Kweller, in Pittsburgh. With encouragement, and introductions, from Liz Fortune, we headed down to Beaumont, Texas, to stay at her brother Bill's, ranch. It consisted of a rambling, creaky, old wooden house with a motley assortment of hunting trophies looking down from the walls. The so-called, "in ground" swimming pool, had surfaced during recent floods. He grew rice. The twins spent a blissful day riding in an air conditioned harvester listening to the latest pop music.

In Houston, we were entertained by Harry Masterson and his wife. We remembered him from a party at Liz Fortune's, where he'd obviously tried some funny stuff with Matilda Gray. She was a substantial lady, from New Orleans, who collected Fabergé eggs. They were standing next to us, when she snapped, "Quit that, Harry, or I'll knee you in the balls!" We had also made note of his moth-eaten hairpiece with its crudely stitched parting. Even in its salad days, it could never have accomplished a smooth transition with whatever nature had left growing out of his scalp. In an effort to compete with his wife's mind-boggling suite of pink diamonds, his belt was gold, studded with umpteen large emeralds. Now, with Mark and Clive in tow, we were invited to Rienzi, their house in River Oaks.

Set in acres of manicured gardens, at first glance, the house seemed surprisingly modest. It was a spacious ranch, probably dating to the nineteen fifties, well before the days of McMansions. We were welcomed by the Mastersons in a pleasant family room overlooking a formal terrace, and swimming pool. The twins were soon in the latter. Apart from the rug, Harry was casually attired, as was his wife, though both sported ostentatious rings. Following the usual pleasantries, we were led through the house as Ambrose and I noted a number of pieces of fine antique English silver, much of it by Paul Storr, goldsmith to the king and some of Britain's wealthiest early nineteenth century aristocrats. Beyond the dining room, at the end of a hall, Harry opened a door. We gasped, as we entered a room that would have been *de rigueur* in Versailles but certainly not in a ranch house, no matter how sprawling.

That room, which they had recently added at a cost of four million dollars, was for dancing and to house their collection of antique Worcester porcelain, the finest in the world, our host assured us. Our attention was also drawn to a suite of Georgian furniture, the likes of which could be seen nowhere else except for an identical one in New York's Metropolitan Museum of Art. The next moment, its Scalamandré silk was caressing our behinds, as a butler handed us silver beakers of delicious frozen mint juleps. Slowly, we took in the environment. The sprung floor was all done in marquetry using a variety of woods with an elaborate design based on the Mastersons' entwined initials. The walls alternated between large, multipaned, arched windows and lighted showcases to display the Worcester.

Soon after our visit, Rienzi went on the market and, if my memory serves me, at an asking price of fifteen million dollars. Unsurprisingly, there were no takers. In their wills, the Mastersons left the place to the Houston Museum of Fine Arts. Today, it is open to the public as the Department of European Decorative Arts.

While in Houston, thanks to Harry Masterson's good offices, we were given a special tour of Bayou Bend. With the exception of Winterthur, it houses some of the finest examples of antique American furniture, in the nation. It had long been the home of Ima Hogg, whose parents deserved to have been hung, drawn and quartered for choosing such a name for their only daughter. By the time she died, well into her nineties, she was still a spinster though she claimed to have turned down thirty suitors. The problem could have been that none of them had the name of "Saint." Like the Mastersons, she gave Bayou Bend, and its spectacular collection, to the Houston Museum of Fine Arts.

The summer of the twins' visit coincided with the abdication of President Richard Nixon. His resignation was the spur Ambrose needed to apply for citizenship. The day it was reported, Ambrose made his decision. As he put it to me, "I'm finally convinced that the U.S. system of government actually works." Following his naturalization ceremony, early in 1975, we had a party for all our friends at which he was presented with two flags, one to fly at our front door, the other as a cake to be eaten.

By the mid seventies, almost everybody we knew had given up smoking. Those who continued to do so, would ask permission before lighting up in somebody else's house. Since Ambrose had quit some four years earlier, we kept our house smoke free. This brings me to the problem of weight. Ambrose had always weighed about a hundred and sixty pounds. Once he stopped smoking, his weight began to climb. At his heaviest, he tipped the scales at two hundred and five pounds. In an ongoing effort to keep our weight in check, we began to weigh each other first thing every Friday morning, and recorded it on a sheet of paper. By 1976, there were several such sheets so, for Christmas that year, we bought a blank book for the purpose. We used it constantly through October 19, 2012. That Friday, Ambrose was so unsteady that it took several false starts to weigh him in at a hundred and eighty two pounds. The next week, he entered hospice care.

As I continue writing my journal, that book is invaluable. Whenever there is a missed week, or two, there is a written explanation. For example, in 1977, September 9th was a Friday. The twenty fifth anniversary of our living together was the next day. Ambrose and I celebrated by splurging with a weekend at the Ritz Carlton, in Chicago. We'd hardly settled into our sumptuous accommodations, than we received an apologetic call from the management who needed to change our room. Believing Ambrose to be a lady, they had put us in a king-sized bed, so please, would we not unpack as a porter would be right up to move us into a twin-bedded room. What management's face looked like, when we said that a king size bed was exactly what we'd ordered, and wanted, is best left to the imagination. That evening, prior to going to the theater, we were dining in the hotel when I remembered that I'd left my glasses in the room. On opening our door, I found a spotlight illuminating an ice bucket containing a bottle of fine champagne. Any idea that management might be making amends, by demonstrating tolerance for kinky behavior, was quickly dispelled when we read the card. It was a gift from our gang of friends, in Indianapolis, bearing the words, "Congratulations for twenty five years in the business!" What a lovely thought. Truth be told, we did feel somewhat self-congratulatory.

When heterosexual couples married, as often as not they were showered with gifts, love and goodwill from both their families and throngs of encouraging friends. Even then, many faced marriage-on-the-rocks within a few years. In the case of homosexuals, if they were lucky, they escaped arrest, but were quite likely to be ostracized by the family. We felt fortunate to have reached such a milestone still in love with one another. Today, as we look back over sixty years together, the only time we can recall quarrelling was over how best to prune a pear tree.

The first anniversary which we celebrated publicly was our fortieth. For that, we took over the Garden on the Green restaurant, in the IMA grounds, for cocktails, dinner and a cabaret. Jeanie Logan, a popular nightclub performer, was recommended to us by Ben Solomon. About a month before the event, she came to our house, with a notebook to meet us and hear our story. Next, she got together with Brad Luther. He and his partner, Kerry Ferguson, came over to sort through boxes of photographs. They departed with whatever they needed to plan the roast. James Benn, who had been my student both at Shortridge and Herron, was to be Master of Ceremonies. Ray Lahr, Jeanie Logan's piano accompanist, rounded out the list of entertainers. The event, of necessity, was limited to one hundred. Most of those attending were friends from Indianapolis or other parts of the States, though several crossed the Pond, and one even showed up from Australia. Brad had designed mischievous invitations which were sent far and wide. We included many, who, for one reason or another, would be unable to attend. In fact, had we not received thirty or forty refusals, we could not have held the event where we did. Kudos goes, in large measure, to Brad for masterminding a party that is still remembered with the utmost pleasure. For the post-dinner cabaret, he had arranged, or morphed, slides of us from childhood on, timed to interact with Jeanie's songs and entertaining dialogue. He had found a friend to make a movie of the evening which starts, prophetically, to Vivaldi's *Autumn Concerto.* All in all, it was a night to remember.

Many celebrations of occasions, such as birthdays and anniversaries, are soon forgotten. For the most part, I only remember the ones that involved an element of surprise. Such a one was when I turned fifty. Both Ma and Sheila were staying with us. As I was teaching an evening class, we planned to celebrate the next day. My dinner would be left in the oven for when I returned at about nine fifteen. Soon after 8:00 p.m., while I was lecturing and the students were taking notes, there was a knock at the classroom door. On saying, "Enter," the door flew open and a singing stripper rushed in with at least a dozen helium balloons, attached to a gondola, announcing the occasion. The students were at least as astonished as I by the riotous intrusion. Finding the solemnity of the lecture too seriously disrupted to be resumed, I dismissed class early and drove home. I was unaware that a spy, at Herron, had alerted Ambrose to my departure. My dinner was in the oven, so the family told me to sit down while they got it out for me. On entering the dining room, I noticed that the double doors into the hall were closed. Which of us was more surprised when I opened them, is debatable but, standing in the hall was a gentleman who had never been in our house before. I merely knew him as the man who played the carillon at the Scottish Rite Cathedral. His wife sometimes attended my IMA lectures. Needless to say, my opening of the door had scuttled carefully laid plans, and in no time dozens of people emerged from every possible nook and cranny to head for our garden pavilion where champagne and birthday cake awaited. As for my dinner, by the time the party was finished, so was I.

312

A couple of Ambrose's birthdays come to mind. On one occasion, he thought we were off to a good restaurant together. In those days, Cynthia was married to David Rohn. Their bungalow style house was hardly out of our way and, as we had promised to loan them a book, we stopped by to drop it off. On their front door was a scrawled sign saying, "Come on in, we're in the back." Their backyard had been transformed into a Persian garden of delights. The lawn was covered with oriental rugs, cushions, and a sea of friends. Seduced, as we were, by the exotic music and scent of joss sticks, the steak restaurant was quickly forgotten. Tray after a tray of morsels, fit for a sultan, were washed down by, as Herb would say, "Amusing little wines which unfortunately die on the middle palate!"

Another time, we were vacationing in Spain with Brad and Kerry. We happened to be staying in the village of Consuegra, in Castille, on Ambrose's birthday. The countryside hasn't changed much since Cervantes was there conjuring up Don Quixote. Barren hills are still surmounted with windmills, in varying stages of decay. All of them had been scoped out by the boys, while we lolled by the hotel pool. Just before sundown, they collected us and, at their casual suggestion, happily agreed to drive over and check out the windmills. Spotting one with an open door, that had lost its sails and conical top, we decided to explore. Imagine our surprise, and delight, on reaching the upper room, to find it reduced to a parapet wall affording three hundred and sixty degree views, plus a stone banquette for sitting, and a hamper conveniently filled with the makings for a party! That was a never to be forgotten sunset.

A cocktail, Ambrose always maintains, should be a clarion call to dinner. On that occasion, the promise which it engendered remained unfulfilled. Having decided that the predictable hotel dinner, following our windmill wonderland, would be a letdown, we set off, map in hand, to explore several nearby small towns in search of a local taverna. Nada. It seems as though towns in parts of rural Spain are totally devoid of restaurants of any description. Eventually, we found a bar where the owner said that he could fry up some calamari. While we waited, hungry and impatient, the locals eyed us with undisguised mistrust. In due course, the promised dish arrived. It was inedible. Had it not been for the color, it could have easily been mistaken for shredded bicycle tire. It's probably just as well that we went to bed hungry that night. If we had been trenchermen and ingested the proffered mollusk, we might have well have ended our days right there in Consuegra.

On that same Spanish vacation, we had a delightful serendipitous surprise thanks to a tip from a pianist friend in Indianapolis. John Kozar is both a concert pianist and impresario for what he calls "monster concerts." They can involve as many as two hundred and fifty pianos in one performance. He's organized the types of events that Berlioz merely dreamed of staging. At some point John had been living in London where he had become friends with Michael Cox who was English and Aart van Kruiselbergen, who was Dutch. They had bought the ruins of a priory in Spain. Called Cortijo Puerto Llano, they had just finished turning it into a guest house. There was no phone, but John had an address to which I wrote asking if they could accommodate us and, if so, please would they give us directions. There being insufficient time to hear back, before leaving for Spain, I gave them the name and address of a hotel in Barcelona. We didn't stay in that hotel but we did get their letter.

What a find. It is located on a lonely plateau, some fifteen miles, by minor roads, from Ronda, in the province of Malaga. Apart from cloister arches beside the swimming pool, there were few hints of its ecclesiastical past. We were housed in charming rustic cottages, a few steps away from the main house, where we were invited to make ourselves completely at home. We discovered that our multitalented hosts were both artists and gourmet chefs. Each evening, after a sumptuous dinner, we would relax in their drawing room, enjoying liqueurs and wide-ranging conversations.

Following Aart's directions, we walked a couple of miles, along foot paths, till we came to an abandoned Roman city. Within living memory, some excavations had taken place. The well preserved theater was the only building where the archeologists had finished their work. A number of half-exposed columns indicated the location of the forum, basilica and temples but, for the most part, one could only guess what lay beneath the lumpy countryside. During the time we spent exploring the place, we saw no other human beings, hardly surprising as it wasn't even marked on our Michelin map. Is it any wonder that museums, like the Getty, acquire so many treasures with a murky provenance?

On an IMA trip to Italy, we had reserved lunch at a restaurant, just off the main road to Ravenna. When the owner found out that our shared interest was of an antiquarian nature, he asked me if I knew about the Etruscans. Realizing he'd pushed the right button, he dispatched his wife to fetch a box of assorted Etruscan pots, any of which were mine for a very reasonable price! When I asked where they came from, he said they'd dug them up in his brother's vineyard, a few kilometers from where we were lunching. I've seen a number of very convincing Italian forgeries, and I am fully aware that without thorough laboratory testing, nobody can be certain whether a pot is authentic. In this case, I believe they were genuine. They were light in weight, with signs of ancient grime which wouldn't easily clean off. Modern fakes are heavier and, generally, in better condition. We didn't get as far as discussing price, because, without a government permit, it's illegal to take such artifacts out of Italy.

# Chapter Twenty Eight
## *The Pauline Chapel*

Mary Wagner was to be one of the students for my second summer school in Italy. Unlike the French summer schools, the main emphasis in Italy was on Renaissance and Baroque art. Mary's father was a close friend of the Roman Catholic bishop of Indianapolis. He kindly agreed to write to the Vatican for permission to visit the Pauline Chapel. For those who may not know its significance, an explanation is called for.

The Pauline Chapel is the Pope's private chapel. It is never open to the public, which is unfortunate, as it contains two fresco masterpieces by Michelangelo, *The Crucifixion of St. Peter,* and *The Conversion of St. Paul.* As a young man, Michelangelo had painted the ceiling of the Sistine Chapel in four years. In middle age, he took five years to paint *The Last Judgment* on the altar wall of the same chapel, though it is barely a third as extensive as the ceiling. In area, the frescoes in the Pauline Chapel are about a third as large as *The Last Judgment.* He spent seven years painting them. When he had finished, he was seventy five years old and laid down his brushes for the last time. The so-called *Terribilita,* for which he is famous, reaches its apogee in these profoundly moving works. The prospect of being able to study them, *in situ,* would be the highlight of our time in Rome.

The bishop of Indianapolis gave me the name, and telephone number, of a priest in the American college in Rome who would facilitate the visit for us. Senator Lugar had been able to open all kinds of doors for us, such as the Carracci frescoes in the French embassy, but, the Vatican was more than he could manage.

On arrival in Rome, I phoned the contact priest. He said that he'd made inquiries on our behalf, as requested by the bishop of Indianapolis. He was sorry to tell me that visiting the Pauline Chapel was out of the question. As one who's never inclined to take "no" for an answer, I asked him the name of the person who gives or refuses that permission. He said that the name was Monsignor Monducci, but when pressed as to where I might find him, I was told that the only way to make an appointment would be through his secretary Fratello MacCarty.

A call to the Vatican switchboard got me through to the Irishman. He held out little hope of accomplishing our goal, so I told him that I had a letter, from the bishop of Indianapolis, which I would like to show him. As I had a map of the Vatican, I figured out whereabouts I might find him, grabbed my briefcase and set off. I'm sure that what I did next, I could never get away with today. The Bronze Door is at the east end of the right hand Bernini colonnade. It stands open but is always guarded by a matched pair of Swiss Guards. They are there to stop everybody who enters, to check their credentials. I walked up the steps with a brisk "Buon giorno" to the guards, and continued on as though I had been in and out of there every day of my life. As I walked straight ahead down the hall, I was aware of an office, on the right, of the "passport control" type. I ignored the man who made a feeble attempt to halt my progress. Next, I was climbing the long *scala reglia,* well aware that suspicious eyes were watching from below. Having reached the top, I turned east down a spacious marble hallway, through a glass door where I spotted a flock of nuns. They happily directed me to Fratello MacCarty's office on the right. His door was open. Outside his window, was one of those large stone saints that surmount the Bernini collonnade. He waved me to a chair while he laboriously finished typing something, painfully slowly, with two fingers on an ancient typewriter. I was reminded of Pope John XXIII's reply when asked how many people work at the Vatican. "About half," he said.

MacCarty was almost a cartoon of a wizened old Irishman, with a few haphazardly arranged ochre teeth, sunken cheeks and thin lips. When I produced the Indianapolis bishop's encouraging letter, he studied it for a long time with ill-disguised skepticism, made a note of my name and Rome telephone number, said he'd mention our request to the monsignor but held out little hope of it being granted.

Convinced that I was barking up the wrong tree, I phoned the American priest again. This time, I asked him if there were any fellow countrymen at the Vatican. "Well," he said, "there's Bishop Foley in the Department of Social Communications." Having located that on my map, I had to face another pair of Swiss guards at the Arch of the Bells, just to the left of the flight of steps up to St. Peter's Basilica. This time a guard came with me to an office with a man behind a grill. When I admitted that I didn't have an appointment with Bishop Foley, he was about to dismiss me but, hesitated, as I produced the Indianapolis bishop's letter. It was evident that he understood not a word but, as it looked suitably ecclesiastical, he made a phone call. Having no idea what I wanted, he passed the phone through the grill to me. I found myself talking to Marjorie Weeke who, at that time, was Bishop Foley's secretary. She was about to be promoted to be head of all the Vatican's international social communications. As soon as I mentioned Monducci, she told me to pass the phone back to the man behind the grill, and I soon had a pass in my hand.

That part of Vatican City is all free-standing buildings of assorted sizes and ages with Palatine guards milling about outside. In a waiting room, I was joined by Marjorie Weeke. She turned out to be a true friend. Monsignor Monducci had, in her humble opinion, grown too big for his breeches, and she would see what could be done to bypass his jurisdiction. With that she gave me her phone number with instructions to call her the next afternoon. When I did, I was told to bring all my students, with their passports, to the Bronze Door at noon the following day and to tell the Swiss Guards that we had an appointment with Archbishop van Lierde.

On this occasion, we were issued with passes at the office which I had brazenly scooted by two days earlier. Then, led by a Swiss Guard, we ascended the *scala reglia,* through a carpeted hall, to the door of the Archbishop. Three firm knocks, and the guard marched off leaving us waiting. After what seemed an age, van Lierde appeared and couldn't have been more friendly. He hoped we liked the magnificent red carpet because he had ordered its installation to honor our visit! After a little more banter, he led us through the hall into the *sala reglia.* From there, we could see into the noisy silence of the Sistine Chapel, off to our right. Straight ahead was the closed door to the Pauline Chapel. Before opening it, the archbishop opened a small panel, and turned on all the lights.

Finally we there, standing in awe of Michelangelo's masterpieces. Hardly daring to look, we gathered around the kind prelate. He had arranged for us to come at noon, he said, because the chapel, being oriented north-south, at other times of the day light streams in through the windows, making one or other of the frescoes difficult to see. Now that we were here, he planned to leave us as he had work to do before lunch and, yes, the students could stay as long as they liked and take pictures and please, Professor Fraser, would I kindly put out the lights and close the door when we leave.

After all we had been through, I could hardly believe we were there alone with two of the world's greatest art treasures; treasures that have been seen by few and appreciated by even fewer. An hour later, we left, albeit reluctantly. As a follow up, I sent one lot of flowers to Mrs. Weeke and another lot for the Pauline Chapel altar, care of Archbishop van Lierde. In due course, they also received thank you letters from Indianapolis.

Having finally found a way to gain admission, to those frescoes, I certainly wasn't going to blow it.

Over the years, Marjorie, Ambrose and I became friends, and I got to know the archbishop fairly well. Marjorie was from San Francisco, where her adult married son worked for a television station. When the first grandchild was born, they brought him to Rome for Pope John Paul II to be godfather. Marjorie's husband had a travel agency in Rome, but died of cancer soon after I got to know her. Following his death, the Pope gave Marjorie a lovely flat, for her lifetime, across the street from St. Anne's Gate.

During a dinner together, in a restaurant near her flat, I mentioned that we had just been to see the Galleria Doria Pamphili. She knew the family and had recently been a guest at one of their over-the-top banquets. In case you are unfamiliar with the name, a brief background is in order.

How much money they are worth is anybody's guess, but their collection, in excess of six hundred paintings, is estimated in the billions of dollars. Though they trace their lineage at least to the Middle Ages, Andrea Doria, the famous Genoese admiral who lived from 1466 to 1560, laid down the foundation of their wealth. Within a hundred years of his death, the Dorias had joined up with the equally prosperous Pamphilis, of whom Pope Innocent X is the best known. Today, the Palazzo Pamphili, which occupies half of one side of the Piazza Navona, houses the Brazilian Embassy. The Villa Doria Pamphili, on the Janiculum hill, is Rome's largest park. The family still lives in the Palazzo Doria Pamphili on the Via del Corso. Much of it is open to the public. While all of this is common knowledge, it was thanks to Marjorie Weeke that I know what I know of the family's more recent history.

Prince Filippo Doria Pamphili and his wife only had one child, born in the nineteen thirties. As Italian patronage requires male succession, it was a serious blow that their only child was female. But worse was to follow. Princess Orietta was a lesbian, totally unwilling to allow even artificial insemination. She was what's commonly known, in gay parlance, as a bull-dyke. The problem was solved in 1958 when a flaming English gay, by the name of Frank Pogson, happily agreed to change his name to Doria Pamphili and marry Orietta. It was to a dinner given by Prince Frank and Princess Orietta that Marjorie had recently gone. According to her, Frank had allowed his exalted status to go straight to his head. He couldn't keep his beringed hands from fondling footmen's buttocks. Anyway, to keep the family name going, they adopted two English babies, one of each sex, in the early nineteen sixties.

Princess Gesine married, produced four daughters but, a desperately desired male heir eluded her. Prince Jonathan, Frank and Orietta's adopted son, is gay. He, and his Brazilian lover, Elson, managed to get a civil union. With mixed sperm, they produced two surrogate children. By the year two thousand, both Princess Orietta and her nelly husband were dead. The ensuing lawsuits, pitting Princess Gesine against Prince Jonathan, are not likely to be settled for many years. The last time I read about it in the news, Gesine was winning with the argument that whoever fathered or mothered either of Jonathan and Elson's children is anybody's guess. Without DNA tests, she has a point. At the same time, it must be remembered that both she and Jonathan were adopted, so neither is likely to share DNA with either of their homosexual parents. With billions at stake, the future looks bright for a number of lucky lawyers.

Apart from facilitating all my students' visits to the Pauline Chapel, whenever I was in Rome, Marjorie would shower me with special tickets or passes for Vatican events. In Indianapolis, after I had retired, she suddenly sprang into my mind. I hadn't been in touch for about a year so, on an impulse, I phoned her. When she heard my voice, she said, "What a coincidence you should call at this moment. I've just stepped into my flat as I've been attending the memorial service for

Archbishop van Lierde." He had died the week before at eighty five.

As well as letting me take students into the Pauline Chapel, he had invited me to visit him in his Vatican suite. As his name suggests, he was Dutch. His particular post at the Vatican had lasted most of his life. He was the Pope's confessor. Every time that the Pope felt guilty about something that he might have done, or failed to do, he would send for van Lierde to hear him out. I asked the Archbishop if he had learned anything over the years from these confessions. "Yes," he said, "having been confessor to five Popes, I have discovered that every one of them had different besetting sins that they wanted to talk about."

A final memory of the kindly Archbishop concerns Linda Wittkowski, now senior paintings conservator at the Indianapolis Museum of Art. Of Polish descent, she had been a young artist in Chicago when Pope Paul VI visited, and had designed the cover for the Papal service. Now she and her friend, Monica Radeki, were going to Rome and, as Roman Catholics, hoped to catch a glimpse of the Holy Father. She gave me a copy of the old Chicago program. I sent it, with a covering letter, to Archbishop van Lierde asking for, but hardly expecting, a private audience with the Pope. The old Dutchman turned up trumps and she got exactly what she asked for.

Chapter Twenty Nine
*Planning IMA Tours*


When I was asked to conduct international tours for members of the Indianapolis Museum of Art, my hope was to plan the kind of trips which I would enjoy doing with a few friends. With that in mind, I would go with Ambrose, and sometimes with Emma Lou and Gayle Thornborough, a year ahead to scout everything out and make bookings. As the years passed, such planning became increasingly difficult, and by the time I retired in two thousand, it was impossible. In the early years the problems was with hotels. I came face to face with the difficulty as I was planning a Provence and Riviera tour.

The four of us were staying in Mougins, a little hill town near Nice. The delightful forty five room hotel, Le Mas Candille, was owned and managed by a Dutchman. The hotel had a dining terrace with a panoramic view over the Mediterranean. When I mentioned booking twenty to twenty five rooms for the following year, our friendly Dutch host turned nasty. "Absolutely out of the question," he said, "we never take tour groups." I tried to explain that although we would be traveling together, we would not sit, or be fed, as a group. Each couple, or family, would select from the menu and settle their own bar bills, etc. The IMA wouldn't even ask for a group discount. It was all to no avail. Having admitted defeat, I asked if we might arrange a special luncheon on the terrace. "Certainly not," he said. What came next, clarified the picture and was a salutary lesson for me. In the twenty some years he'd had the hotel, he'd built up a clientele who stayed there regularly. Many clients came for certain weeks every year, and liked a particular room or suite. People who go on tours, he explained, never come back. The same would be true of his faithful regulars, if they spotted a coach in the parking lot. Charming and unusual hotels and restaurants, I quickly realized, view the approach of a tour bus with almost as much apprehension as a tsunami.

A sighting, in Mougins, led to one of those curious coincidences that make life such fun. Ambrose, the Thornboroughs, and I were imbibing a nightcap. We were the only customers in an upscale cognac lounge, when in walked the owner of the next door restaurant with Julia Child and her diminutive husband. As I was facing the door, and have a nasty habit of blurting things out with a loud carrying voice, Julia Child gave me a withering look as I announced her arrival. When the restaurateur asked her where she would like to sit, she said, "If it's all the same to you, let's go somewhere else." With that, they departed. End of story? Not quite.

Less than two months later, I was attending the annual Mid-America College Art Association convention in Detroit, Michigan where I was giving a paper on a recently-discovered sixteenth century Flemish portrait. I was the only passenger in a Renaissance Center elevator when the door opened to pick up a passenger. It was Julia Child, pushing a cart laden with culinary equipment. I pressed the "hold open" button, to let her on, but she backed away. Her expression said it all: "I've seen that man's face before, though I don't remember where or when. I didn't like it then, and I still don't." As we must have been staying in the same place, I expected that I would run across her again, and planned to tease her that she must have been following me from France! It was not to be. She's long gone to her just rewards without affording me another sighting. No matter, we treasure her two-volume magnum opus, *Mastering the Art of French Cooking.*

Before returning to Mougins and making plans for another IMA tour, forgive me if I digress again. It was toward the end of October 1978 when I was attending that Midwest convention in Detroit. A lady I'd never heard of, and whose name I've long forgotten, was giving a talk on Picasso's painting *Guernica.* Only

324

two or three people were in the audience, hardly surprising in view of the fact that most art historians believed that everything there is to say, about that work, had already been said. Just in case you are among the benighted few who are not familiar with the painting, here's the skinny. Guernica, a small Basque town of no strategic importance, was almost obliterated by German bombers on April 27, 1937. It was during the middle of the day. Hundreds of men, women and children were killed for no reason other than to show support for the would-be dictator Franco. News of the wanton massacre horrified the world. Picasso, though Spanish, had been living in France for thirty six years. He had been asked to paint a large picture, to be hung in the Spanish pavilion, for the 1937 Paris World's Fair. The enigmatic picture he produced is the one he called *Guernica.*

Books, papers, and lectures *ad nauseam* have been presented in an ongoing effort to explain the artist's iconography. Picasso himself refused to discuss it, except to stipulate that it should eventually be given to Spain, but not until after Franco's death. Most of those years, it hung in the Museum of Modern Art, in New York. What is almost universally agreed upon is that it is the single most important painting of the twentieth century, as well as the greatest indictment of war ever created by an artist. But where did all the ideas, for this fractured abstraction, come from? The lady who gave the talk had found the key and, in half an hour, explained everything. Just as Leonardo's design for a modern bicycle was lost in a library for hundreds of years, so the lady, talking to an empty ballroom, has left it to me to enlighten the world.

Picasso's *Guernica* is entirely based on Rubens' painting of 1637 called *The Horrors of War.* How the art historians failed to spot the connection is astonishing, in view of the fact that it is well known that Picasso frequently used old master paintings for inspiration. New York's Museum of Modern Art staged a major Picasso retrospective, in 1979. At that exhibition, the top floor was devoted entirely to works derived from paintings of such masters as Velazquez and Delacroix. Though *Guernica* was still in New York City, the connection to Rubens was not recognized. Peter Paul Rubens' *The Horrors of War* hangs in Florence, in the Pitti Palace, and would, almost certainly, have been unknown to Picasso. However, when he was about nineteen, young Picasso worked, briefly, at the Prado in Madrid. It has a replica of the Florentine painting. Until the nineteen sixties, that replica, hung in the Prado as an original.

Picasso must have had a print of the Rubens painting, which, like other prints of the period, would have been reversed (i.e., a mirror image). Rubens' picture, which is roughly the same size as *Guernica,* is based on Roman mythology. Mars, the god of war, is leaving the temple of Juno goaded on by the Fury, Alecto, while Venus tries in vain to intervene. The woman, with both arms raised, is Europa who bewails the tragedy, along with monsters representing plague and famine. At the bottom of the painting, are downtrodden symbols of peace represented by Charity, Maternity and Fecundity. As soon as you see the Rubens painting in reverse, the source of Picasso's masterpiece, of exactly 300 years later, is undeniable. If any other proof were needed, look no further, than the many surviving preparatory drawings which Picasso made. Bill Tinker, a talented New York artist, son of Sid and Dorothy Kweller, looked into the matter. He created a brilliant, and amusing, amalgam of the two master paintings which he gave to us. It remains a treasured possession.

Faced with my failure in Mougins, I resolved to pursue a devious course with regard to a Michelin 3-star dinner in Les Baux. Ambrose's godfather, Richard Walker, who lived in Nice, knew Monsieur Thuilliers, who owned L'Oustau de Beaumaniers. For readers unacquainted with Les Baux, it is a medieval Provençal stronghold, wonderfully situated on a rocky promontory. The ascent on foot is fairly easy. The less adventurous can descend, after a short hike to the cafés and souvenir shops. Others can continue on to the ancient ruined castle. The coach park is at the base, close to hotels and restaurants, including L'Oustau de Beaumaniers.

Aware that booking a dinner for a coach load of touring Americans would never fly, I crafted a letter which Ellen Lee, a much-loved colleague, translated into flowery French. After bringing Monsieur Thuilliers the warmest of remembrances from Richard Walker, I explained that the enclosed check in French francs, equivalent to about five thousand dollars, was my down payment for about forty friends who would all be meeting me there for dinner. I needed to reserve ten or twelve tables. Obviously, they would be arriving in dribs and drabs but, would ask for me so, perhaps he would be so kind as to have them shown to the terrace for preprandial drinks, etc. Naturally, I continued, when everybody had finished their various dinners, I would settle up the balance. The ruse worked! The museum members explored Les Baux, at their leisure, and walked to the restaurant when they were ready. They greeted me there as a long lost friend, to the obvious mystification of the staff. When pricing the trip, we had built in the cost of that dinner with cocktails, but not drinks with the meal. Knowing that some people might choose a rare bottle of wine and others nothing, we asked everybody to reimburse us later.

I love to stay in hotels that have been beautifully converted from old palaces, or castles. They are far more interesting than standard modern ones. However, I soon learned to eschew them in favor of boring Hilton types. The problem is this. The old castle offers a variety of interesting rooms, of which no two are alike. Most people are enchanted with their accommodations. If however, one couple gets a splendid room with an antique tester bed and a view to die for, they tend to show it off to another couple whose low-ceilinged room overlooks a courtyard. As both couples paid the same, for the tour, the ensuing complaints are understandable. To further complicate the matter, single travelers pay a premium, but in converted palaces, their room is often little more than a converted broom closet, too small to accommodate a large bed. I always had an understanding, and sympathetic, museum employee traveling with us who would do her best to change rooms where necessary to avoid friction. Most hotels assigned me, as tour leader, a lovely room which I would gladly vacate, rather than have anyone disgruntled.

By the time I retired from tour guiding, the worst problem had become the museums. Each country now trains, and licenses guides, and insists on all tours using them. On the other hand, the IMA members signed up for my tours, in the perfectly reasonable expectation that I would be talking about the works of art in the European museums. Most of the major museums have works that, in one way or another, relate to works in the IMA. If you are obliged to have one of the licensed guides, you are going to be taken to see twenty or thirty world famous masterpieces, which of course, everybody wants to see, but lesser works, which often have a special connection with something in Indianapolis, are simply not on their radar.

I dealt with the problem in two ways. Number one was to have no guide. Before reaching the museum, I would explain that more than four people talking in front of a work of art, was forbidden. Therefore, I would stand close to a painting that I would like to draw to their attention, and would say a few words to anyone who stopped by. Then I'd move to another work, or into the next gallery. That way, in twos, or threes, they could hear my whispered spiel or ask me a question.

The other method, oddly enough, was worse. It involved hiring the required guide, with the understanding that I decide which works of art we are going to see and, that I plan to do much of the speaking. Susie Orso was our facilitator on my last Spanish tour. At several museums, plead as she might, she could not get permission for me to guide, even accompanied by one of their own.

On arrival in Madrid, Susie sensed trouble in the ranks, if I was forbidden from guiding our group around the Prado. She and I went together to the museum to talk to the authorities. Finally, it was agreed that one of their guides would accompany us, for double the usual fee, while I gave the talk. Susie came on that tour with us. Afterwards, she told me that she could observe the other guides looking with disdain at ours. He clearly lost status, in the eyes of his colleagues, by failing to give the talk. That tour finally brought home to me the truth that the days of museum curators conducting meaningful tours for their members were finished.

At the Thyssen-Bornemisza Museum, when I produced my credentials, I was issued a one-time permit to guide. For that privilege, I paid a fee. Frankly, it wasn't worthwhile. Every time I started to talk, I was accosted by a guard who insisted on reading every word of my official document before I was allowed to continue. In one instance, I had to wait while he checked its authenticity with his superior. After that Spanish tour, I decided that the time had come for me to hang up my hat, as far as conducting overseas tours were concerned.

For the most part, IMA tours were carefully planned and went off problem-free. I only recall two nasty scares. The first one was in France. It was raining cats and dogs. I was sitting in a recessed seat, beside the bus driver. He could barely see the road though the wipers were at full speed. Suddenly, a lady tapped me on the shoulder, saying she thought one of our tour members had died. I looked round to see a man lying in the aisle with another passenger, who happened to be a doctor, giving him mouth-to-mouth resuscitation. Fearing the worst, but anxious not to sound alarmist, I switched on the mike, and spoke to everyone. Noting the impossible weather, stopping in Villandry to visit the gardens, as planned, was pointless. Instead, we would go straight to our hotel in Tours. That would give everybody a relaxing afternoon, before returning to Paris the next day for our flight home.

Praise be, we were close to Tours, which has a school of medicine and several hospitals. The doctor, who was desperately working on the gentleman, later told me that he had technically died as he had stopped breathing. Whatever the case, he was back in his seat by the time we reached the hotel. With assistance, he got off the coach and into bed. Then I discussed the situation with his visibly shaken wife. She told me that he'd had two similar episodes, years before and, after a good night's sleep, had been none the worse for wear. She said that he was stubborn and would not go to hospital. I pointed out, that in view of the fact we were due to fly home in thirty six hours, we absolutely needed a doctor's certificate of approval, before I could allow him to fly with us. She saw my point and, after a French doctor had checked him out, he was cleared for flying.

The other incident occurred on our arrival at JFK, in New York, where we landed after a long flight from Mumbai, India. As we had only twelve participants on that trip, I was the only IMA employee. We were flying TWA, which had both national, and international, flights out of the same terminal. In order to ensure that everybody had found their luggage and cleared customs, I needed to be the last to leave the restricted area. I asked everyone to stay as a group, until I joined them. When I did, Mig Wildhack was missing. Her luggage had been off first, and nobody knew what had become of her. The airline paged her several times, to no avail. Finally we needed to find the gate for the flight to Indianapolis. I phoned the museum before we departed. They contacted Mig's sister, Patti Cochran, who had planned to meet the plane. Mig's luggage was soon located, abandoned at the TWA terminal, but it was three days before Mig was found, out of her mind, wandering about Manhattan! Patti flew to New York to collect her, but tragically, her mind was gone forever. We had all noticed signs of flakiness, during our three weeks in India, but nothing had prepared us for such a sudden degeneration into dementia.

On a lighter note, during a trip to Scotland, we visited St. Andrews. One of our ladies informed me that her husband, who was not on the tour, was a member of the Royal and Ancient Golf Club. "So," I said, "I expect you've both been here many times?" "Not at all," she replied, "we've never been here. He only joined so he can have it in his obituary!"

I remember a story my Dad, who was a golfer, told me. As a young man, he was taken by a member to play a round at the Royal and Ancient. In the locker room was a sign which read, "Members are respectfully requested to refrain from scrubbing their balls with the nail brushes." Scots are hardy.

Though I had every intention of making the Spanish tour, with Susio Orso, my swan song, I did one more. It was for members of the British National Art Collections Fund. They came over to see what Cincinnati, Indianapolis and Chicago had to offer. From the many letters I received following their visit, it's clear that, to coin their own expression, they were "gob-smacked."

Some years earlier, I took an Aegean tour that was unlike any others. A couple of wealthy brothers, from Rhodes, had built two small luxury ships called *Aurora I* and *Aurora II.* Each accommodated ninety six passengers. Our museum produced about half the complement. The rest of the passengers were members of two other cultural organizations, including one from Chicago.

We set off, for a couple of weeks of Greek island hopping, starting at Piraeus and ending in Istanbul. There was a small theater on board where I gave daily talks, to the passengers, to tell them about the treasures to be visited next. The talks could be attended, or watched on the individual's stateroom TV. I would tease the absentees that roll call was being taken and full attendance would be required for examinations.

Among the Chicago passengers were Carl Horn and his wife, Carol Linné. Though barely fifty, he had recently suffered a debilitating stroke. It had forced him into early retirement from AT&T where he had been senior vice-president, for development. Courageously struggling to get about, aided by Carol and a cane, he was almost paralyzed on his right side. We took to one another from the first day, and remained friends with Carl until his death, about eight years later.

No sooner had we returned to Indianapolis, than they invited us to spend a weekend with them at their home in Glenview, north of Chicago. We were to meet their best friends, Bob and Barbara Michael, and to attend a picnic concert at Ravinia. The Michaels were both in aviation. He was manager of the airport in Louisville, Kentucky, while she designs airports. All six of us became firm friends, frequently staying with one another and taking turnabout to organize an annual long weekend to some mutually interesting destination.

The rotational planning for these mini-vacations worked alphabetically. As my first name is Alastair, along with Ambrose, we were the As. Bob and Barbara followed as the Bs, with Carl and Carol completing the ABCs. We each elected to take the other four to places of our choosing. For example, one of our selections was New Harmony, Indiana, a town of less than a thousand souls. Founded in 1810, as an unorthodox German religious settlement, it was sold ten years later, to Robert Owen as a center for scientific experiments and free thinking. One of Bob and Barbara's choices was to stay in Shakertown, Kentucky, where we got an in-depth look at how the Shakers lived, and ultimately died out. With Carl and Carol, we went to Spring Green, Wisconsin, where Frank Lloyd Wright, and his sisters, lived. That town boasts several of his buildings which are open to the public.

As all six of us shared a passion for music and theater, we joined up for longer vacations to attend the Bernard Shaw Festival, at Niagara-on-the-Lake, and the Shakespeare Festival, at Stratford, Ontario. In addition, every summer, Carl and Carol would treat us to a weekend of music at Ravinia. Though we all saw its inevitability, Carl's death saddened us all. It was especially hard on Carol, who had borne the brunt of so many years of his declining health.

There is a happy ending to that story. She met a truly wonderful guy, online, who had finally escaped from a miserable marriage. His name is Paul Irvin, which means little, or nothing, to most people, but everything to those whose passion is the harpsichord. Not only, does he hand-craft them, you'd need to try another planet to find a better master of his craft. In 2012, the Chicago Symphony Orchestra became the proud owners of an instrument they had commissioned several years earlier.

I have an ignominious story to wind up the Aegean cruise on the *Aurora I.* Those two delightful little ships failed to make money for the Rhodian owners. After one season, they were sold to a Thai investor who brought them to Bangkok, where they were turned into brothels.

# Chapter Thirty
## *Wacky* Saints

Much of our personal traveling has been to see or check out places that might enlarge my understanding of works of art, in Indianapolis, or to research a subject that I planned to teach. Among other things, I've long been interested in improbable saints. Ambrose was driving on a Spanish country road while I was map reading, and checking in the guidebook, in case any town, along the way, had something of not-to-be-missed interest. As lunchtime was nigh, I checked out the next town, Siguenza, which happens to be the birthplace of St. Librada.

This saint enjoys great popularity throughout the Roman Catholic world, especially among women, who turn to her to intercede on their behalf when they have troublesome husbands. The north transept of Siguenza cathedral is dedicated to St. Librada. A large multi-paneled retable, illustrating miracles associated with her, surmounts the altar. Of all the events that shaped her miraculous life, two are remarkable enough to warrant mentioning. Born, as she was, centuries before fertility drugs, it must have astonished the entire population of Siguenza when her mother delivered Librada along with eight sisters, all on the same day. History doesn't relate what became of the rest of the litter, but Librada must have had what it takes to make the world her oyster. Saddled with nine nubile daughters, the harried father was surely overjoyed when the Prince of Portugal asked him for Librada's hand in marriage. Imagine his rage, when she tried to decline with the feeble excuse that she wanted to devote her life to Jesus. Dad would have none of that nonsense so, the day of her nuptials dawned, as planned. As the Prince of Portugal approached, to claim his weeping bride, she prayed fervently to be spared. Guess what? Before she could say, "Thank you, Jesus," the Almighty caused her face to grow a thick black beard. The prince's advance, turned into a rapid retreat. I doubt he paused for breath before reaching the Portuguese border. Librada's thwarted father was so angry that he had her crucified. By doing so, he gave rise to the legend of St. Librada, patron saint of women's lib.

As Christianity stands alone among religions in choosing torture for its symbol, it should come as no surprise to discover that, like Jesus, she is almost always shown crucified. When visiting Spain, the uninitiated can be forgiven for mistaking her for Christ. The latter is generally depicted naked, but for a loincloth, with blood oozing out of bodily wounds. Librada however, wears a beach towel, demurely covering all three points of male heterosexual lust. Otherwise, as both sport black beards, it's a challenge to distinguish one from the other.

In France, where topless women grace every beach or swimming pool, Sainte Liporata, as she's known there, does likewise, leading some to wonder if the Son of God was an hermaphrodite. Should you have the occasion to visit the French city of Beauvais, check out a chapel in the south aisle of the church of St. Etienne. There you'll find a particularly impressive, almost life-size, painted wood sculpture of her, complete with an identifying label under her feet.

Of all the off-beat saints that I've collected over the years, my favorite is to be found in Conques, a tiny town in the mountains of south-central France. There, pious monks had established a monastery in the eighth century. That early church was replaced in the eleventh. It survives as the smallest of the great pilgrimage churches, erected between Tours, on the Loire in France, and Santiago de Compostella, in northwestern Spain. The reason for the building of the existing church dates back to the ninth century, a time when Conques was devoid of pilgrims. Pilgrims were the tourists of the middle ages, and can be compared with Islam's Hajj. Monasteries attracted visitors who brought much needed money. However, nobody detoured to a monastery unless it had the remains of an efficacious saint. Conques didn't have one.

To rectify the matter, about 855 CE, a monk left Conques for Agen, near Toulouse, dressed as a peasant. Begging admittance to the monastery there, as a novice, he spent ten years before the opportunity arose for him to steal the remains of Sainte Foy. She was a little girl who had been martyred in the fourth century, for her Christian beliefs and refusal to worship the Roman emperor. As soon as the mole monk made it home to Conques, with his ill-gotten gains, miracles started happening. The most famous one was verified, after a thorough investigation by the Bishop of Châtres, on orders from the Pope in Rome.

The entire population of Conques testified as to what had happened. With the exception of what kind of black bird had been responsible, there was total unanimity. One of the villagers, who had been blind for twenty years, had instantly regained his vision after praying to Sainte Foy. He had lost his sight in the following remarkable manner. All the villagers had been working in a field, during the harvest when, out of the sky, a large black bird swooped down and plucked out one of the man's eyes. Evidently, human eyeballs were the flavor of the day, for the bird returned for a second helping. With eyeballs missing from both sockets, there could be no doubt that the unfortunate guy was blind. Now, thanks to the good offices of Sainte Foy, his new eyes worked perfectly though, he admitted that, for the first week or two he'd suffered mild headaches. As there are few of us who don't have a loved one with poor, or failing, eyesight, it should come as no surprise to learn that, from then on, thousands of pilgrims made their way to Conques. If their fervent prayers went unanswered, a more generous donation might help.

Over the centuries Sainte Foy's reliquary has been frequently, and lavishly, embellished to the point that now it stands supreme as the most valuable tangible testament to medieval devotion. Curiously enough, the gold head on her enthroned effigy is that of a late Roman emperor.

Ambrose and I have several magical places that we've visited a number of times and Conques is one of them. Whenever I taught summer school in France, we stayed there two nights in order to give everybody a free day to roam the hills, or swim in the river by the ancient bridge. At a reunion party in Indianapolis after one such summer school, we were all given tee shirts with "Je voudrais être à Conques" which roughly translates as "I'd rather be in Conques" printed on them. Soon thereafter, we were at a London party given by Yanie and Ann, for all our British friends. We announced that we planned to stay for three nights at the Hôtel Sainte Foy, in Conques, the following June. We then gave everybody the necessary information and promised to pay for dinner, at the hotel, on the second night for any of our friends who showed up. In those days, the hotel boasted a Michelin one star restaurant. To our surprise, and delight, more than Twenty friends were there so, the management set up a long table in the courtyard to accommodate us all. Ambrose and I dressed for dinner wearing our Conques tee shirts, much to the proprietor's amazement. She could hardly believe it, when informed that we had acquired them in the United States. She rushed off to fetch her husband, from the kitchen, to have a look. On an impulse, we both took them off and presented one to each of them. That modest gift paid for itself several times over. When the bill came, all our drinks and wine were on the house!

Our most recent visit to the village was in 2011. On that occasion we were with our son Ryan Messer, of whom more will be written in a subsequent chapter, and three other young friends. Ambrose and I had Conques tee shirts printed for the six of us. As it became a World Heritage Site in 1998, the savvy locals were underwhelmed by our flattering attire. After dinner, we found the abbey church open with organ music playing. On entering, the tribunes were illuminated and could be visited. We were all still up there, marveling at the many beautiful Romanesque sculpted capitals, when the music abruptly stopped. Chad Neilson hurried down the stone stairs ahead of the rest of us. At the door was the organist who happened to be a monk, in his white habit. Thinking that the church was empty, he was surprised to see Chad, in his cute pink tee shirt. Stopping him, the man of God suggested that they go back inside for some monkey business or, not to put too fine a point on it, a lapse in the apse. Before our nonplussed friend could find his voice to protest, the remaining five pink tee shirts joined the astonished monk. The evening ended with a photo shoot, rather than a gang bang!

## Chapter Thirty One
### *Interesting Connections*


Indiana University's school of music is generally acknowledged to be among the best in the nation. For many years Joseph Gingold was revered as their greatest violin pedagogue. He was the teacher of Joshua Bell and countless other masters of the bow. After several years of planning, an Indianapolis organization known as Cathedral Arts, directed by Tom Beczkiewicz, decided to launch a major violin competition chaired by Joe Gingold. It was to be quadrennial beginning in 1982. Today it continues as one of the most important, and certainly the most valuable violin competition on the planet.

As long time friends of Tom and Ania, we became involved and offered to host one of the participants. That first year, we were assigned a twenty nine year old Chinese American student from Julliard. A month before he was to stay with us, he backed out citing lack of practice time. Our disappointment was short lived. A call from Tom, asked us to host an observer, from London, by the name of Virginia Harding. Not only did she share a friendship with some of our British friends, but she was to become a lifelong friend of ours as well. It transpired that she held a comparable position to Tom. In London, she ran the Karl Fleisch annual violin competition. We learned that in the world of top flight fiddlers, everybody knows everybody else and thanks to Virginia we enjoyed meeting several of them.

Of the few violinists we knew well, Louis Kaufman was the most distinguished. He hailed from Portland, Oregon where he was born in 1905. In those days, to all intents and purposes, singing was the only musical career option for women. An outstanding exception, was Maud Powell, born in 1867, in Illinois. She is, arguably, the first female violinist to gain international fame. After giving a recital in Portland, in 1918, she graciously agreed to listen to Louis perform. So impressed was she by what she heard, that she persuaded his father to send him to New York, to study with Dr. Franz Kneisel.

Fast forward seventy six years to the 1994 Indianapolis International Violin Competition. The Maud Powell Foundation, in Washington, chose to honor her memory by making a posthumous presentation to the artistry of Louis Kaufman. It was accepted by his widow, Annette, who was staying with us. To celebrate the occasion, the Children's Museum mounted an exhibition of Maud Powell's memorabilia. Among the exhibits was her violin. It was owned, at that time, by Muriel Mickelsons, herself a gifted violinist, living in Indianapolis.

Fast forward another sixteen years. Two old men are pushing a bascart around a big box Costco, in Pompano Beach, Florida. A woman looks up from a freezer chest, and says, "Well, I never. It's Ambrose and Ian. Hi. I'm Muriel Michelsons." We had all moved to Florida and lived about twenty minutes apart. To shrink the world still further, we were about to have a visit from our beloved Annette Kaufman, now ninety seven years old. A delightful reunion was arranged right there and then. Such unexpected serendipity is one of the wonderful pleasures of life.

When we were not hosting either Virginia, or Annette, for the quadrennial competition, we twice opened our house to contestants. In both cases they were young Korean women. In fact, Yon Joo Lee, at seventeen, was the youngest entrant. Though she won no prizes, she was a sweetheart, and obviously loved all the meals that Ambrose cooked for her. After she returned to Julliard, in New York City, we found a large unopened box, in the closet of her room. It was full of all kinds of Korean foods that her mother had packed for her! For years she kept in touch to let us know how her career and love life were shaping up. The last time we heard, she was off to

Spain to become concertmaster of a newly formed orchestra in Segovia.

The other Korean was Joan Kwuon, from San Diego. She was about twenty six, charming and sophisticated. Sadly, she also failed to win a prize, and within a year developed breast cancer. The good news is that she survived, and annually gives a recital, at the Metropolitan Museum of Art, to raise money for the cure. Her husband is Joel Smirnoff, longtime first chair of the Julliard String Quartet. We're blessed that she also has kept in touch with us over the years.

As well as IUPUI committee work, I enjoyed volunteering for assignments where I might be helpful. Such a one came my way from the School of Social Work. Under the leadership of Dr. David Metzger, some thirty, or forty, aspiring social workers, from many different countries, would converge on Indianapolis, for the summer. They came for a hands-on experience, of social work, within an American metropolitan area. City residents offered hospitality and housing to the international visitors. One of David's jobs was to match the incoming students with appropriate families, who could speak the guest's language. About a week after their arrival, the School of Social Work would have a welcome party, for all the participants, to meet one another and some of the faculty.

Possibly on account of my peripatetic life, I was invited to the party. I spotted a young man who looked utterly miserable, so I sailed up glass in hand, bent on cheering him up. That he spoke excellent English was no surprise, when I learned that Einar Thorliefson hailed from Reykjavik, Iceland. At first, the cause of his unhappiness was hard to fathom, as he was staying with the Andersons, an Icelandic family. They had moved to Indianapolis many years before and were living the 'high life' on a fortune made in the construction business. Realizing that I was his only chance of a confidante, he steered me away from other people, before telling me that they kept slaves in the basement.

Frankly, I was naïve enough to believe that slavery in the United States had been abolished during the Lincoln presidency. Convinced that his English was at fault, I explained that wealthy people often kept live-in servants and sometimes they treated them badly, but they couldn't possibly be slaves. Einar was not about to be put off. He knew perfectly well the difference between servants and slaves. The Andersons had two of them, both Mexican girls who spoke no English. Einar spoke Spanish. When his hosts were out, he had gone down to talk to them. They told him about a man, in Mexico, who promised them good jobs in the States, and that he would have them safely brought here with no money. All they had to do, was sign a piece of paper and, as soon as their employers had paid his fee, they would make a good living for themselves. That had been more than two years ago and to date, they had been paid not a penny and had never been allowed out of the house.

With Einar's permission, I brought the matter to David Metzger's attention. Ambrose and I were leaving for Europe the next week, but we offered Einar a room in our home. The move was arranged and he showed up on our doorstep the following day.

Two or three years later, a notice appeared in the Indianapolis Star, detailing Anderson's arrest on charges of tax fraud and a number of other unspecified crimes. I didn't follow the case, but do recall that he wound up in prison, bringing one hopes, freedom for his slaves.

During the years of my French and Italian IUPUI summer schools, friends in both countries gave hospitality to all of us. Philip LeBas is the only friend who knew both Ambrose and me before we met each other. He bought a farm in France in the valley of the Cher River about three miles from the lovely château of Chenonceaux. After leasing out the fields to a local farmer, he sold off portions of the old farm buildings to Michael and Yanie, his siblings, and to a cousin. The four of them transformed the place into a vacation Shangri-La where we have all shared many happy times. For a nominal fee, they allowed me to house all the summer school students at the farm for an entire week. Everybody would help with cooking, or cleaning up afterwards. In the barn, there was a farmhand's trestle table, and benches, that could seat twenty. After the noise and bustle of Paris, the students found *Les Rosiers* to be hog heaven. Best of all, the farm's location was perfect for a week's worth of field trips.

In Italy, we were friends with Nunzio Daniele, his wife Tina, and sons Gianpiero and Luca. Nunzio was born and raised in Paestum, the best preserved ancient Greek city on the Italian mainland. After graduating from the university in Salerno, he became the resident archeological historian, in Paestum. As with the Le Bas', we have been their guests a number of times. Twice, when Nunzio was lecturing around the States, he was our guest in Indianapolis. Once, Gianpiero accompanied his father. I remember Nunzio complaining that his new shoes were impossibly uncomfortable, so Ambrose took him to Stouts to buy another pair. Seeing something suitable, he told the salesman to wrap them up, till Ambrose stopped him with "Wait a minute. You haven't tried them on." It then transpired that he'd never tried on new shoes. Since marriage, Tina had bought them for him; before that, his mother did! My guess is that Tina was miffed that he'd brought Gianpiero, instead of her, and too tight shoes might teach him a salutary lesson.

Tina Daniele is a feminist. Having dinner with them, she was complaining about the treatment of women in Italy. Nunzio, defending the status quo, argued that they have exactly the same rights as men. I got into the fray, pointing out that no woman could even get a job as a waiter in a Paestum restaurant. Nunzio responded, "She certainly could. The only reason women don't work as waiters, is because they object to having their bottoms pinched!" It may come as no surprise when I tell you that his politics are to the right of Attila the

Hun. If you belong to the NRA, and read Italian, you will enjoy a book that he authored, about the American Revolution. Its title is, *Il Trionfo Della Ragione.*

More to the point, Nunzio's brother Mario built a large guest house, surrounded by fields of artichokes, about two miles out of Paestum. There he, his wife and daughters would house and feed all the students for next to nothing. From there, we could manage a day trip as far as Reggio di Calabria, in Italy's toe. Among my mementos I have a Greek bronze nail, given to me by Nunzio. He found it, following a rainstorm, in the temple of Poseidon. Dating from 450 BCE, it was originally used for nailing a tile on the temple's roof.

August 1986 was the occasion for a partial family reunion, at our house, to celebrate Ma turning eighty. Why we humans calculate milestones based on Earth's laps around the sun, which we incorrectly describe as 'a year,' is one of those mysteries which keep me guessing about our collective sanity. Sane or not, celebrate we did. Sister Sheila was there, as was sister Mary along with husband number three, who happened to be Roy number two. It was only the second time that we three had been together since childhood; it gave me a chance to assess our similarities and differences. Most people see a strong physical family resemblance, but I see little else. Mary and I have both made conscious efforts to look our best before facing the world each day. Sheila, on the other hand, with a more extensive wardrobe than either of us, has always seemed oblivious to her appearance. She's never demonstrated any aesthetic interest either in dress, or furnishings. Ma, and Sheila, were mentally joined at the hip, almost always knowing what the other was about to say. Both were fervent adherents to the standard, upper middle class, form of British Christianity, of the "Onward Christian Soldiers" variety.

Unlike me, all of my closest female relatives were good at crafts. In some respects, Mary and Ma were exceptional. Ma's knitting was so perfectly even that it looked machine done. Her embroidery and crochet work were also superb. Mary preferred tatting, to crochet, but her forte was crafting one-of-a-kind large birds' eggs. Though less costly, her masterpieces rivaled those of Carl Fabergé.

In many respects all three women have had hard lives. Ma's childhood has already been discussed. Once married, she became the devoted wife of a self-righteous bully whose decisions, whether right or wrong, she never challenged. Mary, as Dad's favorite, grew up spoiled and manipulative with scant regard for truth. One tended to overlook the most flagrant falsehoods on account of her singular ability to keep any audience merrily entertained. She had a great sense of fun, which stood in stark contrast to her sister's earnest piety. Family was paramount for Mary. Unlike her siblings, she was fecund. She produced three sons followed by two daughters, all fathered by Oliver Robinson, her first husband. Being single when her first son was born, she surrendered him for adoption, to avoid the anticipated condemnation of our bible-thumping parents. As far as our family is concerned, his fate is unknown.

Alistair, the elder of her legitimate sons, is a tragic figure with many mental and physical problems. His life is one of professed Christianity, brought low with alcohol and cigarettes. He and his girlfriend survive on welfare. Christopher, born with brains and good looks, has spent most of his fifty years living on his wits as a petty criminal, enabled by his always forgiving mother. After an early run-in with the British police, he joined the French Foreign Legion, trained in Corsica and served time in Djibuti. Since that period, he's led a nomadic and elusive existence estranged from his family.

I'm happy to report that neither son showed up to celebrate their grandmother's birthday. Both daughters did. Miranda brought Ian Cutler, her boyfriend. With such a last name, if you guessed he came from Sheffield, famous as a center for the manufacturing of cutlery, you'd be right. As we had run out of beds, they stayed nearby with an ex-student of mine. Belinda, the last of Mary's children, was also with us. One thing all three generations had in common was a chaotic childhood as our families moved about the globe.

Mine was the last generation to be educated in what the British call "public" schools. Today they should be more descriptively called "elitist" schools. Less than five per cent of the population attends them. Brits are unique in recognizing a class system based on one's accent. To be sure, other countries can judge from correct, or incorrect, grammar what level of education a speaker has achieved. That's not the same thing. By attending what we would call a "private" school, in Britain, you emerge speaking with an upper class accent, devoid of regionalism. Sheila, Mary, Ambrose and I are all graduates of that system. Mary's children and Ian Cutler are not. The place that houses a car is pronounced "gah-RAJ," by me. Miranda calls it a "GA-ridge." So varied are British regional accents that neither Ambrose nor I could understand more than an occasional word that came out of Ian Cutler's mouth. Let me add that, since 1986, he's become a citizen of the great US of A, and speaks with a transatlantic accent that is both pleasant and readily understood by all.

As I looked at the family members gathered together for the great eight oh! Miranda stood out as different from the rest of us. For generations, on both sides of the family, we've all had blue eyes and mousy brown hair. Miranda alone has dark brown eyes and almost black hair. She's also very different in character from any of her siblings. Unlike the other three, she can be relied upon to decide what's the right thing to do, and then do it. Honest, almost to a fault, she's smart as a tack, kind, and totally reliable. There can be no doubt that Mary's her mother, but a paternity DNA test might surprise us all.

Sensing the possibility of a closer bond between Miranda and me than I enjoyed with any other family members, I determined to see her again on our next visit to England. We did just that, and found Ian and Miranda the proud owners of a retired police boat called *The Original Brahms.* As most of the interior seemed to be occupied with their mattress, we sat in the stern, being royally entertained. I say "royally" because they had secured a mooring at Hampton Court Palace. By the time we saw them again, Ian had custom built a miniature house for themselves on an island in the river Wey, just where it joins the Thames. With Miranda heavily pregnant, they flew to Florida for a private wedding and honeymoon before returning in time to welcome Thor into the world.

Multitalented Ian Cutler made his living selling, and installing, software. Speedboats were his passion, securing him a goodly share of International prizes. He was fortunate to survive the explosion of his vessel, when it hit some submerged flotsam as he was traveling at great speed in the Solent. Miranda started working for l'Oréal supplying cosmetics for resale in duty-free shops. Unfortunately she developed an aggressive and crippling rheumatism that could incapacitate her for weeks at a time. The treatment took the form of painful gold injections into her joints. Whether the cause of her illness could be traced to living constantly exposed to the damp of the river, is impossible to tell. What we do know is that when Thor was eight, Ian's work brought them to Florida, where Miranda's health has improved markedly.

A phone call from a mutual friend in St. Louis alerted us to the fact that Raymond Leppard was heading our way to discuss his anticipated appointment to replace John Nelson as conductor of the Indianapolis Symphony Orchestra. With no friends in Indianapolis, the hint was dropped that a little TLC might be appreciated. When he accepted the post, almost everybody was thrilled. He was the first conductor Indianapolis had had of international acclaim. Not that we hadn't had good conductors in the past; we certainly had, but Raymond was to raise the symphony to a whole new level. As a person, he wears his scholarship lightly, never puts on airs, has

347

.

a great sense of the ridiculous, and shares our values. We were soon firm friends and enjoyed many good times together.

Raymond still had a home in Connecticut, at the time of his Indianapolis appointment. It was within striking distance of Tanglewood, where we were enjoying the summer festival with Desmond and Janet Tivy. We were all invited over to lunch, and had fun recalling blissful memories of Dartington Hall, in Devon. At one time, or another, we had all been seduced by that artistic oasis. We were introduced to, but hardly enchanted by, Jeffrey Engel. He was Raymond's significant other, a sometime cellist in the Paris Garnier opera. Apart from belittling Raymond and playing tennis, his time was occupied by two curious interests. The first was frogs. He collected frogs made of anything, and of sizes that ranged from a grain of rice to that of an ottoman. One of his rooms must have contained at least a thousand. Like the amassing of frogs, his other stated goal could hardly be realized in his lifetime. Even if it were completed, it's hard to believe that the planned encyclopedia would be an invaluable tool for more than a handful of people. Regardless, he was attempting to obtain detailed information on every musical group, irrespective of its significance or size that had ever been formed in France. No town or village library was exempt from his letters of inquiry intended to galvanize tens of thousands of desiccated librarians to delve tirelessly, and ever deeper, into dusty archives in the hopes of unearthing evidence of eleventh century minstrels, or jongleurs, who might have performed to a background of alpenhorns, or pipes of Pan, on a cart in the village square. The good news is that when Raymond sold the house, Jeff went with it.

## Chapter Thirty Two
### *From Ambrose's Retirement to Mine*


Soon after the family gathering for Ma's birthday, PR Mallory offered Ambrose early retirement. The company had long since ceased to be owned by the Mallory family. It had changed hands several times till it finally came to rest with Black and Decker. Meantime, almost all the operations had moved out of Indianapolis. Much of Ambrose's work had been for the space program, designing and miniaturizing specialized capacitors capable of functioning flawlessly while being subjected to enormous temperature and gravitational fluctuations. While his expertise in the field was well-recognized and appreciated, his being gay precluded security clearance to work at top secret government plants. Under the circumstances, he chose to hang up that hat and throw his energies into neighborhood development. After twenty five years in our Delaware Street house, we decided to move.

Several young friends were renovating houses in a dilapidated downtown neighborhood called Cottage Home. The Hostetters had bought a double designed by Bernard Vonnegut, grandfather of the novelist, for five hundred dollars. When, in next to no time, Bruce Baird and Ed Norman paid fifteen hundred dollars for an identical double, albeit badly fire damaged, our curiosity was aroused. As a frustrated architect, Ambrose had designed a solar-powered dream home. To build it, we needed a sizable lot with access on the north side. We found one that suited us to perfection. It was owned by a long-time Cottage Home resident. Clearly it was going to take time, and perseverance, to convince the owner to part with his land. He had long cultivated it as a vegetable garden.

While we were involved in preliminary negotiations, an 1894 gingerbread cottage, in the same neighborhood, came for sale. We bought it for seventeen thousand dollars with the idea that we could live there, while Ambrose spent two or three years executing the plans for our environmentally friendly home. As the address of the cottage was 1215 Polk Street, we called it *Runnymede.* An explanation is in order.

1215 is the year that King John signed Magna Carta, the great-granddaddy of the US Constitution, on an island in the Thames, called Runnymede. The assassination of President John F. Kennedy so affected the British that one square yard of this almost sacred island was ceded to the United States in perpetuity. As ex-Brits, who share a love for both the slain president and for the constitution, we couldn't resist naming the cottage as we did.

Our second reason for deciding to move from Delaware Street concerned the conservatory. Over the years, I had developed an allergy to scratches from the thorns on bougainvillea. We had an abundance of it. Of course we could have rooted it all out and replaced it with something non-toxic, but it was so spectacular that we were loathe to do so.

Our friend Ann Ryder had recently married John Groot, so while our plans were fluid we let them have *Runnymede.* The arrangement worked perfectly. By the time we were ready to take possession, they had found a house to buy. With me as his 'go-for,' Ambrose gutted, and totally rebuilt, the inside. Once completed, the fourteen hundred and fifty square foot, one bath cottage, had two and a half baths and almost two thousand square feet of living space. It took him ten months, but the result was so delightful that, we decided to move in permanently and abandon Ambrose's plan for a solar house. As soon has he had completed the finishing touches, we sold 3678 North Delaware street and moved. The job had taken him all day, and almost every day, but the silk purse he had created quickly caught the attention of the media. Our house was featured on TV programs and in newspapers and local magazines. In June of 1988, it made the cover of *Better Homes and Gardens.* The resurrection of Cottage Home was underway.

During the sixteen years that we lived there, we rehabbed the houses on either side of ours, one being a double, a house across the street, that was about to be bulldozed, and another house in the neighborhood. With the exception of the double, Billy Vantwoud, a brilliantly creative ex-student of mine, did all the work.

Of all the neighborhoods that make up the city of Indianapolis, Cottage Home stands alone in its diversity. When first developed in the second half of the nineteenth century, it consisted almost entirely of blue-collar workers' cottages. All that changed in the nineteen sixties with the construction of the interstate system, designed to put Indianapolis at the junction of Interstates sixty five, sixty nine and seventy. When completed, interstate sixty nine should link Canada to Mexico. While the other two roads have long been finished, acrimonious lawsuits over segments of the planned routing of sixty nine through Indiana, remain unresolved. As originally envisioned, Cottage Home neighborhood was to be razed and replaced with a complex spaghetti-junction involving all three interstates. In anticipation of its destruction, much of the housing stock was demolished and replaced with businesses such as garden supplies, signage companies, lumber and roofing contractors. Plans for the triple interstate interchange were abandoned in the nineteen eighties allowing for a change in zoning.

Artists, musicians and other creative souls, along with aging flower children, saw the neighborhood's potential and began buying and fixing up cottages. With no restrictive historic designation in place, the houses were transformed into rainbows of eye-popping candy colors, offsetting black-barned businesses. The few old residents, generally very poor, were cherished by the newcomers. All neighborhoods need to resolve conflicts from time to time, but as neighborhoods go, Cottage Home enjoys, to this day, a *laissez-faire* lifestyle that sets an example well-worthy of emulation.

On the subject of fixing up old houses, Jock and Pam Bevan bought one in the Var, in France, in 1992. They lived in Scotland, but Jock, whose work, as an artist, revolved around architectural renderings, was getting many French commissions. He needed a French studio. His nephew Tim, who is in the movie making business, had married into the Richardson- Redgrave family. They owned a compound of houses near La Garde Freinet, a small ancient village in the hills above St. Tropez. On Tim Bevan's recommendation, Jock and Pam bought a decaying house with potential, at the intersection of three tiny streets, in the heart of the village. Like all such restoration projects, expenses exceeded expectations, so Ambrose and I chipped in to help bring it to completion. As they were our oldest and dearest friends, we agreed that, rather than repay us, we could vacation there free, whenever they didn't need it. In fact, Jock had a self-contained studio with kitchenette on the ground floor. He could live there independently while others occupied the rest of the house.

When Ambrose and I first visited La Garde Freinet, in December 1992, the house was still uninhabitable. We stayed in the village hotel, where the creature comforts included cold showers. Fortunately, a couple of the restaurants were open during the winter. Had they, like the hotel, lacked heat, I might not have survived to write this account. In spite of the cold, we fell in love with this special place. Dating back to the Romans and Saracens, most of the village was a monastery during the middle ages. Today, many of the buildings, including the Bevan house, date from that era.

From La Garde Freinet, we drove into Nice, to have lunch with Uncle Richard Walker, Ambrose's godfather. The trip takes about an hour and fifteen minutes. Having bundled up against the cold in every garment we'd brought, we were back to shirtsleeves by the time we reached sea level. We quickly discovered that whatever climate you fancy, within reason, is a short drive away. Best of all, this village of fourteen hundred souls, so close to cosmopolitan St. Tropez, is still authentically French. The climate is temperate, with window boxes of geraniums and begonias. Ten minutes drive down a corkscrew road, through forests of cork, chestnut and olive trees brings you to the little town of Grimaud with palm trees and cascading bougainvillea.

A number of the world's rich and titled glitterati have luxury villas in the hills around La Garde Freinet. They descend on the village for the farmers' market on Sundays and Wednesdays to shop, and to enjoy the cafés, before vanishing until the next market. For almost twenty years, Ambrose and I were to spend time there annually. The length of our sojourns varied from as little as five days to as long as three months. Indeed, we were in the midst of a three month stay when Sid Kweller, in Pittsburgh, phoned to tell us of planes crashing into the twin towers. Those who hold the French in contempt should have been with us at that time, to witness the genuine concern of all the good folks of La Garde Freinet.

Back teaching in the fall, we heard from Helen Pilgrim-Minor. She had moved to Montreal from Paris a couple of years earlier. Now she had decided to return to Indianapolis in about six weeks. Of course, we invited her to stay with us while she looked for a permanent place. Within a few days, a large trunk with her name on it arrived at our house from Canada. A couple of days after that, she walked into the Herron lecture hall just as I was dismissing a class. Her long, heart-felt embrace was delivered in silence. It was my first experience of someone's speech being severely impaired by a stroke. At first, we wondered if so many years of speaking French, had affected her ability to access the English words. When we suggested that she speak French, she seemed equally tongue tied. Clearly, there was something wrong.

Helen rented an unfurnished apartment in Riley Towers. Before she moved in, we helped her buy some essential furniture, including a reclining chair, the operation of which seemed to be beyond her. We made an appointment for her to see her former doctor. As she had never driven a car, we took her shopping and to her various appointments. Once installed in her high rise, we determined to check on her daily and take her out for meals. We also found that she was eligible for Meals on Wheels. They were delivered, but remained uneaten. Within days, she became incapable of pushing the appropriate button to allow us entry to her building, when we rang from the street door. Giving her instruction on what to do seldom worked, so we'd walk in on the coattails of an arriving resident.

When we found out that Helen had a life-long friend in Atlantic City, whom she dearly wanted to see, we arranged to take her there. She had lost the address, but she knew where the house was, so off we set. En route, miles from any filling station, cries from Helen brought us to a stop on the shoulder of the road. Jumping out of the car, she fell and rolled about fifty feet down the grassy embankment. Thankfully, she seemed to have escaped injury and was unfazed by the indignity of peeing, there and then, while we steadied her, or by the fact that her wig had been dislodged by the fall, revealing an almost hairless head. About 8:00 p.m. we stopped for dinner and booked rooms at the adjoining motel. Just as well that we'd paid before retiring. Helen started knocking on our door, every few minutes, starting around 11:30 p.m., urging us to get going again. Sensing the futility of getting any sleep, we dressed and drove through the night to reach Atlantic City by 7:00 a.m.

A strip of gambling casinos almost persuaded Helen that we were in the wrong city, and without an address to go by, we decided to drive slowly around in the hopes that something would look familiar. Luck was on our side. On Helen's excited urging, we headed up a hill on a twisting road to an unassuming white-painted clapboard house. Enough time elapsed between our knock on the door and any sign of life, that we feared the worst. In due course, an old black lady, clad in a nightdress and slippers, opened the door. The two women fell into each other's arms amid tears of joy. Once we were all seated in a little parlor, a middle-aged daughter appeared and, in no time, Helen was being given news of various people of whom we'd never heard. The daughter took Helen off to the bathroom before returning to rustle up some breakfast, in the kitchen. Grabbing the opportunity, while Helen was out of the room, the old lady did her best to fill in the missing pieces for us.

During the course of a travel lecture that Helen was delivering in Montreal, a couple of months previously, she had suffered a stroke. In the hospital, she refused treatment and checked herself out. Evidently, that's when she'd contacted us. We were astonished to learn that, not only had she been married and produced a daughter, but that they both lived in Indianapolis. When Helen had taken early retirement and moved to Zaire, she determined to never have contact again with either of them. Believing her to have money, they had run her to ground several times, so whenever she heard from them, either by mail or phone, she would move to another country. Most recently they had found out her Montreal phone number, but when the daughter phoned, Helen recognized the voice and hung up. Apart from her friends in Atlantic City she trusted nobody but Ambrose and me and a gay black teacher, who had taught with her at Crispus Attucks High School. His name was David. The old lady wrote down his phone number, as well as her own, so that we could keep in touch.

Over breakfast, Helen allowed us to discuss plans for her future. She realized that she might soon need full time care and, if so, she wanted Ambrose to have legal power of attorney. Above all, she wanted her whereabouts to be kept from both her divorced husband, who had another wife, and her loathsome daughter. Helen's words of so many years before came back to haunt me, to wit, that we got on so well because we never asked her prying questions.

Back in Indianapolis, we contacted her friend David. He agreed to share responsibility, for her care. We would alternate days. We would see to her food intake, he would clean her apartment and do the laundry. The arrangement was short lived. After a thorough medical examination, the doctor recommended that she move to a nursing facility called The Cambridge. The time had come for Ambrose to assume power of attorney. We arranged for our old lawyer friend, Reno Freihofer, to draw up the paperwork. Helen was barely capable of answering the necessary questions to make it legal, but with occasional prompting from Reno it was finalized.

By an unlucky coincidence, a nurse seeing Helen's name on a chart put two and two together and phoned her daughter. In as little time as it takes to tell, ex-husband and daughter were at her bedside, causing the dying woman considerable distress. Armed with his recently acquired power of attorney, Ambrose had them banned from visiting. However, they could not be budged from a waiting area, where I had a chance to meet and talk to them. The daughter struck me as furtive and thoroughly untrustworthy. Within minutes, I understood why she and Helen had long been at loggerheads. The ex-husband turned out to be a carefree and somewhat amusing old roué. I enjoyed talking to him but realized that his unapologetic philandering lifestyle would be anathema to his erstwhile wife.

Ambrose's responsibilities ended with her death, which occurred within three weeks of her family running her to ground. We had been housing all her belongings from the Riley Towers apartment. The Christian Church, to which she belonged, was happy to receive her clothes, furniture, books and papers. When The Cambridge informed the bank of her death, it transpired that only weeks before she had made them trustees and liquefied as much money as possible, to be divided equally between her old friend in Atlantic City, David, and us. In short order we received a totally unexpected windfall of about forty thousand dollars. Thank you, Helen Pilgrim-Minor for enriching our lives in so many ways. Whether her death made me suddenly more aware of the fragility of life or not, I can't say, but it was about that time that I began volunteering at the Damien Center.

We had met the Rev. Howard Warren at a party on Brookside Parkway. He stood out in a crowd as he usually wore a baseball cap encrusted with a gay rainbow of sequins and, sometimes, an ecclesiastical stole to match. As an unrepentant gay HIV-positive minister, he constantly needled the Presbyterian Church, which bitterly regretted having ordained him. What's more, they failed dismally in their futile attempts to silence and defrock him.

The Damien Center, housed in a building south of 16th Street, on Pennsylvania Street, was part of a Roman Catholic enclave behind the cathedral. Its only *raison d'être* was to help people who were struggling with HIV and AIDS. It was a lifeline for those diagnosed with this devastating, and almost invariably fatal disease. The building housed a doctor, a food pantry, various lounges with helpful literature, and meeting rooms, on the first floor. Upstairs were offices for counselors and social workers along with other meeting rooms. Mary Z. Longstreth, who had been denied ordination in the Methodist Church because she lacked a penis, trained and coordinated the volunteers. In my case, I was to be a buddy.

Infected people who came to the Center for help were referred to as clients. Most clients, when first diagnosed, were justifiably terrified. Usually, either too sick to work, or fired from their jobs for the false, but stated, reason that they were contagious, they were in despair. As often as not, they were ostracized by their own family, and had nowhere to live. There was also the problem of frequently changing medications, aimed at keeping the client's t-cell count high enough to prevent opportunistic infections from making a bad situation worse. Costs could easily run a thousand dollars, or more, a month.

As a buddy I was matched with a man who had requested me. We had met once or twice, in happier times, at Museum social events. The idea was to form a bond and to be available for whatever eventuality might happen. At that time, most people died within months of their diagnosis. While the client enjoyed reasonable health, we could expect to meet up, once or twice a week, for a meal or perhaps a movie or sporting event. As death approached, the buddy might sit by the client's bed, to help in any way or, just to bring comfort. After the client had died, Mary Z. would not reassign a buddy to another client for three to six months, to allow for a period of mourning. During training sessions we were well prepared for the anticipated stages of decline.

My pairing started out well. My client quickly accepted his situation, and was enjoying surprisingly good health, when he suddenly moved to Phoenix, Arizona, where he had friends. Anxious to become more involved, I joined the Damien Center's pool of drivers, to transport clients from wherever they lived, for medical appointments, and home again. I found myself driving through parts of Indianapolis that I had never even heard of, let alone visited. When not chauffeuring clients, I got in the habit of dropping into Parkview, the AIDS hospice. The small building had seen better days, but the dedicated staff did their best to bring as much joy as possible to the thirty or so patients.

At first, I would join a group in the all-purpose living area for a chat, or a board game. Gradually, I got to know most of the patients. They ran the gamut from a small girl, who was born infected, to a sixty-something-year-old grandmother. As their health deteriorated and they could no longer manage a wheelchair, I would spend time visiting by their bedside. I seemed to be always welcomed as one of very few people, other than a doctor, who came into the place. So far as I remember, I never saw a patient being visited by a relative. I would estimate that five out of six patients were men. Half of them were white. Most of the black patients and some of the white ones were drug addicts. They got AIDS through shared needles. On the other hand, most of the whites and some of the blacks were gay. They became infected as a result of unprotected sex.

One patient stood out from the rest. Tall and good-looking, Tom Edens was a country and western singer and songwriter. He'd grown up as one of several children in a poverty-stricken Midwestern community. Childhood centered on his family's fundamentalist church. There he graduated from treble to tenor, as lead gospel singer. At eighteen, he took a bus to Los Angeles where he had an aunt. Unlike his immediate family, she'd been around the block a time or two. She recognized both his singing potential and his sexual orientation. Following a few dead-end leads, and a brief affair with an aspiring young actor in West Hollywood, he was selected to join a singing theatrical group in Branson, Missouri. Within months, Tom heard from his erstwhile boyfriend that he had full-blown AIDS. The shocking news galvanized Tom to be tested. Unfortunately, the test was positive, and the initial flu-like symptoms followed soon afterwards. The diagnosis should have been confidential, but Branson was a community where gossip flourished. His secret was soon brought to the attention of the faith-based couple who owned and ran the theater. He was summarily fired.

Tom Edens won a lawsuit and, with the settlement, started his own country and western musical ensemble which he called "Deep River." It was an instant success with a gratifyingly long list of future gigs, and several CDs under their belts, when AIDS struck with a vengeance. Deserted by everybody, Tom came to the Damien Center, in Indianapolis. He wound up at Parkview. Sometimes, when his health permitted, he would play his guitar and sing songs, in the common room, to cheer everybody up.

He told me that he had written an autobiography. He had hoped to have it printed, but had been rejected by several publishers. The story, entitled *Singing My Song,* was compelling but both spelling and grammar would have been the despair of a sixth grade teacher. With Tom Edens' permission, Ambrose and I edited it just enough to leave the simple language intact, while correcting the most egregious errors. We also added *Pursuing a Positive Life with AIDS* as a subtitle. We had the modest book printed, with pictures, and sold copies, as Tom wished, to make money for the Damien Center. He lived long enough to attend an inaugural signing party at Indianapolis' gay bookstore.

A couple of years after I had started to volunteer at the center, Doug Shoemaker joined us. He bears a striking resemblance to the cartoon advertising character known as "Mr. Clean." With an enviable muscular physique, a head shaved bald, laughing eyes and a generous smile, I saw in him a lifelong friendship, even before we'd been introduced. Once in a long while, as we journey through life, we meet somebody whose goodness shines and never tarnishes. Doug is one of those rare individuals.

Once on board, he became the hardest working and most valuable volunteer of all time. On Saturdays and Sundays the Damien Center was closed. That's when Doug went to work. The task he undertook was invaluable and monumental. The records were in turmoil, so he set about bringing order out of chaos. Realizing the importance of the Buddy System, he spent an inordinate amount of time contacting buddies, and clients, to ensure that the latter's needs were being met, and to facilitate changes if they were not. With a key to the center's office, he labored alone, almost every weekend. Modest to a fault, it was many months before he shared with me the reason for his passion.

Some years earlier he had visited his best friend from school days who, by then, was living in Los Angeles. Soon after Doug returned to his family in Zionsville, Indiana, he got the chilling news that his friend had AIDS. Putting his own future as a student of architecture on hold, he returned to L.A. to care for him. Anybody who has ever undertaken the fulltime responsibility of nursing an AIDS patient knows full well the toll it can take on the caregiver. Many good people look after their significant others as they are dying, but it's a measure of Doug's humanity that he didn't hesitate to do it for a school chum. Naturally, the full horror of such a miserable death made a profound impression on Doug. He vowed to do his part to help, in any way possible, to alleviate the suffering of others. First however, he needed a degree in architecture. He did that at the University of Illinois, in Champagne.

Recalling the annual costume ball, known as "The Revels," at the College of Art and Architecture in Edinburgh, Scotland, I suggested something similar as a fundraiser for the Herron School of Art, in Indianapolis. Called "The Janus Ball," it soon became a popular annual affair. Each year a different theme was chosen and, as it had been my suggestion, Ambrose and I always dressed in appropriate costumes.

The final Janus Ball, before my retirement in 1995, had the theme of "Limbo." What exactly the committee had in mind is debatable, but we settled on Adam and Eve in Limbo. We acquired flesh-colored body stockings from a ballet supply shop in London. I was to be Adam. A bald wig and long, moth-eaten, white hair took care of my head. On the chest of the body stocking, I painted nipples, a bellybutton and glued on white hair. The penis presented problems. A furtive visit to an adult shop proved fruitless, if you'll excuse the pun. Even the least aggressive member looked more suited to Superman than dear old desiccated Adam. In the end, we found a plastic toy in a "Farts Are Funny" shop on the St. Tropez waterfront. By drilling a few strategic holes in the scrotum, I was able to sew it onto the appropriate spot, and by the time I'd finished adhering gray pubic hair, it looked remarkably convincing. It seemed a shame to cover it up with a fig leaf but, being cognizant of historical precedent, that's what I did. We found a floor-length wig for Ambrose, as Eve. We partially braided it, before adding a floral chaplet. As we had no pockets, Ambrose carried a basket for our mundane essentials, plus a wriggly green serpent and an apple. The effort paid off. We won first prize, which took the form of a week's vacation on the Caribbean island of St. Maarten.

It wasn't long before the Damien Center saw the wisdom of such fundraising costume balls. "The Grand Masquerade" as it's called, has proved an important annual source of revenue. Unlike the Janus Ball, the seriousness of the AIDS epidemic is not forgotten. Along with dinner, dancing and costumes, an invited keynote speaker gives a reality check reminding everybody that the war against this deadly disease is far from over.

I taught my last class at IUPUI in June, 1996. The Indianapolis Museum of Art threw a lovely retirement party for me, even though I was to remain curator of the Clowes collection for another two years.

Ambrose and I celebrated by leaving for Europe on our own. We spent almost three weeks exploring Apulia. It is southeastern Italy, including the heel and instep. It's the only part of the country that we had never visited. After a couple of nights with Nunzio and Tina Daniele, in Paestum, we headed to Alberobello, a town renowned for it curious domestic architecture of ancient, but unknown origin. Called *trullo* houses, they are more or less circular with conical limestone roofs laid in mortarless courses, and finished with individualized stone finials. Inside, the perfectly fitted and finished stonework creates a parabolic dome. Often several *trulli* are interconnected to become a larger house. For historical precedent, these homes can be compared with the so-called beehive tombs of the Mycenaens, dating to about 1400 BCE, the largest and best preserved of which is the *Treasury of Atreus,* at Mycenae, in Greece. So far as is known, the Mycenaens were never in Italy, so one is led to conclude that almost identical building techniques were developed independently.

We found a small hotel and settled in for ten days of fascinating field trips. During the four centuries leading up to the Christian era, waves of Greeks from diverse islands settled in Apulia. Most museum goers are familiar with black and red figure Greek ceramics, but for total exposure to the works of tribes such as the Gnathians and Canosans, you need to spend time in Apulia. Canosan ceramics tend to be large wheel-turned pots, encrusted with full relief sculpture. Typical would be a large-bellied vase surmounted by a graceful neck, dull-glazed over all in a soft pink. Bas-relief figural decorations, in white and cream, around the handles and body of the vase, might culminate in a fully three-dimensional quadriga defying gravity as it heads into space. Gnathian ceramics, on the other hand, are elegantly understated. For the most part, they conform to the size and shapes of Corinthian ware. Overall they have a black eggshell finish with restrained decorations, often in the form of a single encircling band of tiny leaves and flowers, culminating in a small cameo picture of people working, dancing, or fighting.

Even the smallest Apulian towns boast a museum, usually full of treasures stacked up higgledy-piggledy in unkempt dingy cabinets. I recall one such showcase that contained no less than a dozen shallow Greek drinking cups, of the *kylix* variety, in nigh perfect condition. With the aid of a detailed map, you can find Greek and Roman remains within a few miles of wherever you happen to be. Chances are, when you reach your destination, you'll find the site devoid of people.

Another marvel of the area is the Norman legacy. Magnificent castles and semi-fortified Romanesque churches dot the landscape. The latter sometimes have the entire floor in mosaic pictures illustrating the world's creation.

While the surviving works of mankind have always been a major interest of mine, we discovered one natural phenomenon that needs to be seen to be believed. It is in the small seaside town of Polignano a Mare, a few miles southeast of Bari, the final resting place of Santa Clause. That part of the coast consists of high cliffs. Once inside a modest hotel, called The Grotto Palazzese, you take an elevator down through the cliff. Emerging, you find yourself on a natural stone bridge spanning a vast cavern that opens to the Adriatic Sea. The breakers come rolling in, a hundred feet beneath the bridge, which has been adapted for use as a restaurant. While lunching there, I had to pinch myself, for reassurance that we had not become experimental specimens in a science fiction novel.

Nicola and Susie Orso, had recently bought a country home south of Florence, off the main road to Siena where they were living for the summer. Generous to a fault, they gave us the keys to their comfortable flat on the south side of the Arno, between Santo Spirito and the Pitti Palace. As if the wonders of Apulia weren't sufficient for one trip, we settled into the Orso home where we could come and go like the natives. Though we had stayed many times in Florence, we'd only once been in a pensione on that side of the river. On that occasion, we had been close to the Piazzale Michelangelo. Now we had the opportunity to spend time exploring lesser known nooks and crannies of this endlessly fascinating Renaissance city. Having just come from Lecce, in Apulia, which is nicknamed 'the Baroque Florence', it was a treat to be back where it all started. All too soon, our seven-week second honeymoon was over. It was time to go home.

# Chapter Thirty Three
## *Ryan*

While tidying up around the house wondering what the future would bring, there was a ring at the front door. What happened next was destined to change our lives forever. On the porch, I found a clean cut young man dressed in a neat black suit, perfectly polished black shoes, a plain black tie and a spotless white shirt. Instantly sensing Mormon missionaries, I scowled but looked in vain for the customary clone, expecting to get rid of them with dispatch.

"Hi," he said, with a disarming smile, "I'm Ryan Messer. Judy O'Bannon sent me." Frank, Judy's husband, was Lieutenant Governor of Indiana. A couple of years earlier, during a Cottage Home house tour, the O'Bannon's had come by and we'd heard Judy enthuse to her husband that she could happily settle into our house. As thoroughly decent Hoosier Democrats, we held the O'Bannons in high regard so, of course, I threw open the door and welcomed Ryan in as I called for Ambrose to join us.

We learned that, having graduated from Purdue University, he had started working for the O'Bannons. He had mentioned to Mrs. O'Bannon that he'd like to buy a house, but admitted that he had no money to do so. She promptly referred him to us, saying, "The only people I know who buy houses with no money are Ambrose Smith and Ian Fraser." What we didn't discover, until much later, is that Judy had a more important reason for sending him our way. Recognizing his sexual orientation, Ryan had been about to enter Our Place, a gay bar on 16th Street, to check out the scene, when he was savagely attacked by homophobic hoodlums who left him brutalized, and unconscious, in the street. Two good

Samaritans got him to hospital. By the time he'd regained consciousness he was out of surgery. Once released from hospital, the young men who'd found him nursed him, at their home, till he'd recovered sufficiently to return to work.

The attack had occurred on Saturday. On Monday morning, Ryan phoned the O'Bannon office, to report what had happened, but lied about the location. He said that he'd been beaten up in Broad Ripple, a trendy north side neighborhood of restaurants, and bars, popular with socially mobile young couples. His fib was ill-advised. When Judy O'Bannon phoned the police, for the report, she learned that it had taken place at 16th and Delaware Streets. She put two and two together and came up with the right answer. Once Ryan returned to work, Judy's enquiries confirmed her suspicions. The young man had told nobody of his homosexuality, least of all his parents in southern Indiana. Ambrose and I might be able to offer the help he needed. While she may have been right about that, she couldn't possibly have envisioned the ensuing lifelong bond that was to form between us.

At this point, a précis of the twenty-two years before Ryan stepped into our lives, is in order. His parents, Gerald and Joyce Messer, have a small farm near Rising Sun, a tiny town on the Ohio River in southeastern Indiana. They have three sons, of whom Ryan is the second. Nearby lived a family whose son Billy is Ryan's age. Neither can remember a time before they were best friends. As luck would have it, both boys were uncommonly bright. From kindergarten on, they competed in school.

As a farmer's boy, Ryan was adept at helping his father with all the varied chores that are involved in mixed farming. Before his eighth birthday, he was in 4-H and regularly taking the first prize in the county fair, showing his goat. Whether or not he deserved the annual award is debatable, but Ryan knew how to wow the judges by making sure that the animal's hooves were as shiny as his own shoes and that his tie, and leash, matched. At the last moment, he would highlight the goat's coat with just a hint of sprayed sparkle.

By the time the boys graduated from the Rising Sun High School, it was clear to all that they were the cream of the crop. They both went to Purdue University, where Billy, a born mathematician, majored in science and engineering. Ryan was largely responsible for reorganizing their fraternity which set a new scholastic standard for the university. As homecoming King, the posters listed an abbreviated sampling of his twenty seven extra-curricular activities. Majoring in business and social studies, Ryan is first and foremost a born people person and a consummate politician. Beyond that, his gifts are so varied that it's hard to think of any job beyond his capabilities. He absorbs and processes everything he's told. In due course, when his opinion is called for, his suggestions are often brilliant and original. Whatever the goal, if Ryan can't achieve it, he'll die in the attempt.

He spotted a dilapidated double at the end of our street, and determined to make it his. Doing so proved more of a challenge than he expected. He discovered, to his chagrin, that the cows in Rising Sun could not be used as collateral. In the meantime, we had bought, and renovated, a double next door to our house. In order to acquire it from an unscrupulous slumlord, we had paid top dollar. The builder we hired to rehab the place was a delightful incompetent. After he had finished "remuddeling," Mary Jo Showley faced the problem of selling the house for what we had invested in it. On her suggestion, we rented one side for about the same amount as the buyer's mortgage.

Ryan had some nice pieces of furniture, so we offered him the other half on the understanding that he'd have to move as soon as Mary Jo found a buyer. Thanks to him, that was sooner rather than later. When prospective buyers came round, he allayed their fears about the dangers of living in Cottage Home. He was adept at pointing out charming details in the house

367

while skillfully ignoring its shortcomings. Ryan's infectious enthusiasm, coupled with the attractive way he'd arranged his belongings, rendered him homeless soon after he'd moved in.

Mike Quinn, a delightful banker friend, had a nearby cottage, with an available attic where Ryan could stay while negotiations for his own double ran their course. The thoroughly obnoxious realtor tried every trick in the book to prevent Ryan from acquiring the property. In the end, he surrendered when we joined the fray and co-signed the paperwork. In short order, Ryan had transformed one half for himself and found a tenant for the north side. With his rapidly growing circle of friends, he was soon throwing parties for upwards of fifty of the closest of them.

By this time, we had got to know Ryan's mother, Joyce. What's not to love about that woman. From seeing the best in everyone, (she even calls Charles Manson, 'a gentleman') to her invariably sunny disposition, she's an inspiration to all who would complain of life's problems. We are eternally grateful to her for her friendship and especially for raising a son she so generously shares with us.

Aware that the time to choose the direction his life should take was fast approaching, Ryan opted to visit Europe alone. With only a backpack, he flew to London. After touring the Tower, he spent the rest of the day in the company of a Beefeater, absorbing the old man's reminiscences of London's rich history. In Paris, where he lodged in a youth hostel, he met an Argentinean student of agriculture who was there for an international exposition. As a farm boy himself, Ryan was eager to learn how things were done in other countries. All in all, his six-week adventure was anything but run of the mill. He returned mentally enriched and well prepared to face the future.

With no medical background, Ryan answered a Johnson and Johnson advertisement for salesmen of pharmaceutical products. Despite lacking all relevant credentials, the company gave him a stack of textbooks and three months to study them, to be followed by an exam. If he passed, he would be employed as a sales representative. Hitting the books without delay, he passed the exam with flying colors, in half the allotted time. Assigned northern Indiana as his territory, he racked up more sales in the remaining six months of the fiscal year than all but one of the seasoned sales force had done in all twelve months. Needless to say, his remarkable achievement did not go unnoticed by top brass in New Jersey. His stint as a salesman in Indiana was to be short lived.

# Chapter Thirty Four
## *Key West*

With Ambrose retired, and me partially so, we decided to check out Key West, Florida, as a possible escape hatch during the worst of the winter. We had visited there once in 1983 for a few days, liked what we saw, so we returned for a longer look. Phoning Vacations Key West, I found myself talking to Vanessa McCaffrey. She noted that we would like to stay for a couple of weeks in a small, gay-friendly bed and breakfast inn. Bananas Foster, at Simonton and Caroline Streets, worked perfectly and was exactly what we expected from Vanessa's description.

Once there, we set about finding an apartment that we could rent for a couple of months the next winter. Vanessa kindly gave us a number of leads but, for various reasons, we came up empty handed. To repay her kindness, we invited her to dinner on our last Saturday, and asked her to choose her favorite restaurant. Called Square One, it was unknown to us, but was soon to become our Key West favorite. By an odd coincidence during the course of dinner, we learned that Vanessa and my sister Sheila had both attended Roedean School for Girls in Johannesburg, South Africa. Bemoaning our failure to find a rental apartment for the following winter, Vanessa had an idea. Had we met Patrick Hayes, a.k.a. Patticakes? No, we'd never heard of him. Having finished dinner outside, we went in to meet Mr. Hayes, the bartender. Between pouring drinks, he explained that he and Les Boatwright, his partner, had just fixed up an efficiency on Seminary Street that they might consider renting. Sunday being his day off, we arranged to stop by at noon.

Stepping through the front door, it seemed less than stellar. It was one fairly small, gloomy room, with a trundle bed, a pokey kitchen in the far corner, and a barely adequate bathroom. In the middle of the floor were Patticakes and a tiny baby gurgling with delight. What business he had with a baby, I don't know, but I was soon to discover that for sheer kindness, Patrick has few equals. We decided that we could manage, in the place, and as the rent was within our budget, we agreed to a lease for the winter of 1998. When we opened the kitchen door, we knew we'd made the right decision. Our efficiency was the middle section of a single story triplex. Two sections opened out to a totally private back deck and swimming pool. The dining area, which included a sink and refrigerator, was roofed over. Attractively furnished sundecks were on either side. Beyond one deck, there is a sizable kidney-shaped swimming pool and a laundry area. A gate, through the fence enclosing the pool leads to two cottages. One was Les and Patti's, the other they rented to John , a.k.a. 'Ma' Evans, the senior drag queen at the 801 bar on Duval Street. Ray, a chef, lived in the first section of the triplex, and Randy Roberts, a gifted female impersonator, occupied the other.

By the time we returned to Key West for our first extended visit, I had retired from the Indianapolis Museum of Art and we had established a symbiotic relationship with Doug Shoemaker. His home, in Zionsville, is about fifteen miles from Indianapolis. At the time, he was working for an architectural firm in the city, so was delighted to avoid the winter driving by staying in our house. He could be relied upon to shovel the snow and forward mail. Even better, he willingly house sat for us in the summer as well, as we were sometimes in La Garde Freinet for months at a time.

On arrival at 1220 Seminary Street, in Key West, we found that our landlords had gone overboard to make us welcome. Unwanted furniture had been replaced with a useful tilt-top desk. There was a new TV and state-of-the-art sound system, and the kitchenette was piled high with goodies and vases of fresh flowers. In no time we felt completely at home and, in consultation with Les and Patrick, made plans for the future. The mutual agreement was that we would come down every winter for the next ten years, for a very reasonable rent, on the understanding that, on our return to Indianapolis, we would free up the cash to pay the entire amount up front. The result was that, by the time our lease expired in the winter of 2008, we had been to Key West during twelve consecutive winters. During those winters, we had made a number of good friends who knew our names. The remaining inhabitants knew us simply as "the Aunties." Unless you are a pitiful nonentity, you can't be in Key West for long before acquiring a nickname, with naming rights the undisputed purview of Patticakes.

Each year, we'd see the New Year in with Ina Mohlman, and a group of friends. Dinner would be followed by an Indianapolis Symphony Orchestra concert, ending with the Radetzky March, amidst descending balloons and traditional noisemakers. Next day we'd usually drive as far as Chattanooga, Tennessee, or Atlanta, Georgia. After a second night on the road, we'd reach Key West, park the car, and hardly ever use it again till it was time to head home.

Between our visits the boys markedly improved the place. After one year, the awkward trundle was replaced with a state-of-the-art Murphy bed, which allowed for easy transition from day to night use. The best news was when we arrived to find an entirely new bathroom with a party-sized shower.

With less than thirty thousand inhabitants, Key West must be one of the smallest places on earth to have its own symphony orchestra. It was started in 1998, with Key West maestra Sebrina Maria Alfonso. At first the orchestra was about forty strong, but over the years we watched it double in size. Sebrina is a first class, and highly respected, musician with the audacity to program composers from Anton Bruckner to Ellen Zwillich. With a pool of some three hundred professional musicians to call on, she has no problem persuading her friends in Detroit or Chicago to head south for music making and to bask on the beach.

On Sundays, we would attend a chamber series of concerts given in St. Paul's church on Duval Street. Known for nearly forty years as the Impromptu Concerts, they are anything but. Distinguished musicians, from all over the world, are booked years in advance and might consist of anything from a single piano recital to the full Moscow Chamber Orchestra.

No sooner were we settled in on Seminary Street, than we'd head off to the various theaters and cultural venues, calendar in hand, to buy tickets for all the concerts and plays. In order to justify our hedonistic lifestyle, we became volunteers on Tuesdays and Thursdays at Nancy Forrester's Secret Garden. Many Key Westers are oblivious to its existence, though thanks to publications such as the Michelin Green Guide, Europeans would seek us out. Little more than an acre in size, it can only be reached down an unpaved path, off Simonton Street, called Free School Lane. Completely surrounded by houses, it has been justifiably described as the only piece of tropical rain forest to be found on the continental United States. Nancy Forrester, an aging free spirited artist, bought the lot, as well as an adjoining old Bahamian house, on Elizabeth Street, some forty to fifty years ago. The underlying structure of the Keys is coral. In prehistoric times, the center of Nancy's garden collapsed. The resulting sinkhole gradually filled with soil capable of growing large trees. In due course, a canopy formed over the top creating a dark and mysterious forest that seems considerably larger than it is. Sadly, recent hurricanes have removed the canopy.

Our job was to greet people, charge them an entry fee, and hopefully, persuade them to become sustaining members. Nancy, a poster child for starving artists, seldom knows where the next penny is coming from. The value of her land has soared since she acquired it, resulting in a formidable annual tax bill. On top of that, she has a deep love and understanding of birds. She will take in any that their owners can no longer care for. Each large animal needs two cages, one in the garden, and another in the house. She has so many that most of her time is occupied cooking and feeding them their favorite treats, or driving them to Marathon, fifty miles away, to see the vets after the treats backfire.

Among the many people we met, at the toll gate, was Patti Rodriguez. She, along with her husband Bubby, had just moved to Key West from New Orleans. He looks remarkably like a larger than life Ernest Hemingway and, like the writer, is a dedicated and accomplished fisherman. His quiet speech and gentle manner belie his size and powerful physique. In contrast to Bubby's laid back demeanor, Patti's effervescent enthusiasm is infectious. She can pack more into twenty four hours than most of us can accomplish in a week. To make pin money for her busy travel schedule, she caters dinners, and parties, of all sizes and, when not catering other people's affairs, she's entertaining Big Easy type parties at their home. Over the years, we have become dear friends in spite of our political views being diametrically opposed. Since our lease on Seminary Street ended, we are always welcome to stay with them. The same thing holds true with our English friends Jeff and Rosie Ware, as well as our erstwhile landlords Les and Pattycakes, who are happy to have us as house sitters when they are away on vacation. We are greatly blessed to have so many good friends in Key West.

Through attending some of the many worthwhile fundraisers for which the city is renowned, we met a number of interesting people. Among them were Joe and Beth Pizzo who invited us to a forthcoming costume party at their home. When we informed Patticakes, he said that we were lucky to get such an invitation, but that it was always obligatory to dress appropriately depending on the theme. In this case, the theme was to be "military." For most costume parties, we had it made, living as we did, in an enclave of drag queens Sadly, military uniforms, we decided, were unlikely to be part of our neighbors' wardrobes. "No problem," Patrick assured us, "I've got the perfect thing for each of you." When party time arrived, Patticakes came over with two exotic hats. The flower and fruit confection, which he'd created for me looked for all the world as though it belonged to Carmen Miranda. Ambrose was to be crowned with a fluffy stovepipe hat, in gay rainbow colors. Before we could protest, he said that as soon as the shocked Pizzos pointed out the error of our ways, we should apologize while claiming that we thought the theme was "millinery!" Needless to say, we got away with it, and stood out like a pair of flamingoes in a cave full of bats.

In my spare time, I caught up with correspondence. Many years earlier, as nonbelievers, we had quit supporting Hallmark, and the others, who make money through the sale of Christmas greetings. In spite of the fact that all of our friends know that they'll get no seasonal card from us, we continue to receive between a hundred and twenty and two hundred cards every Yuletide, often accompanied by a form letter, replete with news of family accomplishments. Once read, they worked their way via a large salad bowl into a grocery bag, for re-appraisal in Key West. During the first culling, cards with only printed greetings would be trashed. The same fate befell cards from friends, or acquaintances, who were seen on a regular basis. Should we run into such friends, we'd try to remember to acknowledge their kind thoughts. Finally, we'd be left with greetings from those we care about but seldom see. That number tends to be about eighty. Until 2012, I hand wrote a two or three page letter to each of those friends, usually at the rate of four or five a day. Before retirement, when I had less spare time, Ambrose would print all the addresses ahead of time, for me to send postcards from Europe.

Time in Key West would fly, with friends from Indianapolis visiting most weeks. The general pattern of our lives there varied little from year to year. On Saturdays,

Patticakes would often have a garage sale to raise money for a worthy cause. Naturally, we'd be cajoled into buying something. A couple of weeks later, he'd be over to collect what we'd bought, to sell at his next garage sale, with the simple and logical explanation that we clearly didn't need it, as it was still in its wrapping paper!

Spotting Ambrose emerging from a fairly radical session in the barber's shop, Patrick said, "Oh, my God, Auntie, you look ten minutes younger!" On another occasion, he advised a visiting friend of our neighbors, who said he was celebrating his fiftieth birthday, to "Go and knock on the Aunties' door and have Ian show you his birthday suit so you can see what you've got to look forward to!"

During our stay in 1999, the phone rang while we were in the throes of entertaining a number of friends. It was Ambrose's sister Charlotte to say that their mother had just died. We don't do funerals, but we arranged to go to England that March for some closure, and to sprinkle her ashes into the same rose bed as she had sprinkled Frank's, eighteen years earlier. Oddly enough, my mother also survived Dad by eighteen years.

A sour orange tree grew by the back deck on Seminary Street. Prue Smith had taught Ambrose how to make marmalade. Ma Evans, who lived in our next door cottage, had a couple of enormous pots, so every year days were spent marmalade making while I did my best to keep abreast of cleaning the kitchen floor. In the end, even after sharing the spoils with Ma, and giving away most of the rest, we still had plenty to see us through the next year's breakfasts. Strange to report, right after our lease expired in 2008, the tree died.

At a number of charity fundraisers, Ma was the auctioneer. We gave him an enormous photograph taken by Mark Lee, an Indianapolis photographer. The subject was of Ambrose and me, in profile, rubbing noses. It had been taken, to be included in a photographic exhibition devoted to depicting the lives of gays, lesbians and their families. Though Mark had kindly given us an original print, we had no use for it. We hoped that Ma Evans could make some money by selling the thing. The Key West auction was scheduled for after our departure, so we were sorry to be greeted by the picture on our return, next winter. On inquiry, we discovered that a bidding war at the auction had ended when a vacationing couple from Boston had placed the highest bid. At the end of the affair, as they were settling up with Ma Evans, they asked him if he had any idea who the two men might be. By the time he'd finished embellishing his version of our lives, they decided they wanted to pay for it, but chose to return it to us as a gift! We all approve of gifts that keep on giving, so back to the auction block it went, and we understand, did very nicely the second time around.

The success of the Indianapolis photographic exhibition encouraged Mark Lee to make a documentary movie, to be included in the 2009 Heartland Film Festival. The subject of the movie centered on discussions with ten homosexual couples who had been together for at least ten years. He managed to line up a diverse group of people of both sexes ranging in age from the thirties through the eighties. Some were inter-racial. Several had children through adoption, artificial insemination, or by conventional means during a marriage which had been consummated before the person was aware of their sexual orientation. We were the oldest couple, and, after fifty seven years together, we also had had the longest relationship. The film was called *Ordinary Couples/Extraordinary Lives.* We never saw it, but doubt it lived up to its title.

We make no secret of our homosexuality, but we've never been rainbow flag twirlers. The one time that I can remember coming out publicly was in 1995. I was visiting my cousin, James Irvine Robertson, in Scotland. In those days, he did a weekly public affairs program from a broadcast studio in Perth. As his guest, I was interviewed for half an hour on my life as a gay. He told me that he received a lot of positive feedback from people who had heard the program.

In contrast to our two night drive down to the Keys, we generally spent up to two weeks on our return to Indianapolis, visiting friends en route. Peter and Sabine Sehlinger were sometimes our first stop. They have a condominium half way up the Keys where they spend six months each year. A couple of years after we started wintering in Key West, my niece Miranda and her husband Ian moved, with eight year old Thor, from The Shack on the River Wey, in England, to Coral Springs, Florida. Once they were *in situ* we made a habit of spending a night visiting them. We would zigzag north through Florida, visiting such friends as the Kwellers, who often took a rental in St. Petersburg. In Thomasville, Georgia, we would stay with Leila Holmes who had briefly been married to Allen Clowes. By the time we reached Indianapolis, we would have caught up with many dear friends and the city would be ablaze with yellow forsythia, and pink magnolias. Of more immediate concern, our garden would be screaming for attention.

Chapter Thirty Five
*Totally Retired*


By the time I retired from the Indianapolis Museum of Art, in 1998, I had been with the Clowes Collection for thirty eight years. A generous outpouring of money, from members, enabled the museum to buy a fine seventeenth century Dutch painting entitled, *The Battle Between Carnival and Lent,* in my honor. I was overwhelmed and, for once in my life, speechless. The painting by the genre painter Jan Molenaer, was an inspired choice. Bear with me and I will tell you why.

Molenaer, born in the Dutch city of Haarlem, became a pupil of Frans Hals, the foremost local artist. Judith Leyster was also from Haarlem. She was born in 1609, making her a year older than Jan. Although there is no documentary evidence that she was also a pupil of Hals', most art scholars agree that she must have been. Her style of painting is so like that of Frans Hals that, from her death until 1893, all her paintings were wrongly attributed to him. Even today, only about twelve of her signed paintings have been identified, though perhaps twenty more are reliably attributed to her. That she was greatly admired, during her lifetime, is attested to by contemporary writers, even as early as 1621, when she was only twelve. By the age of twenty four, she was a member of the prestigious Guild of St. Luke. If there is some doubt that Leyster was Hals' pupil, there's documentary evidence that he purloined one of her students, for she sued him, and won a small settlement. However, there can have been no lingering hard feelings for she became godmother to his daughter, Maria.

At age twenty six, Judith Leyster married Jan Molenaer. In the hopes of selling to a wider audience, the newlyweds moved to Amsterdam. They were there for eleven years and produced five children. By the time they returned to live near Haarlem, their loveable old teacher, Frans Hals, would have been sixty seven years old.

The Clowes Collection has a most intriguing portrait of Frans Hals dating from about that time. It's first recorded in the 1722 inventory of the Royal collection in Dresden, Germany, where it is described as a "Self-portrait" by Frans Hals. Apart from the Indianapolis painting, and some inferior versions of it, we know of only one likeness of the artist. In 1639, Hals had been commissioned to paint a group portrait of the Company of St. Joris, to which he belonged. His self portrait appears in the background of that picture. Unlike his younger contemporary, Rembrandt, he seems to have been totally disinterested in painting himself, so how do we account for the Clowes portrait?

Most of today's scholars consider the Clowes painting to be either a contemporary portrait of the artist, by an unknown painter, or a copy of a lost self portrait. I believe in the former theory and argue that the artist was Judith Leyster, a.k.a. Mrs. Jan Molenaer. If I still have your attention, here's my reasoning, supported by a couple of facts.

Jan Molenaer, who survived Judith by eight years, died in 1668. An inventory of his belongings showed that he had three portraits by Hals. Extrapolating on the facts, here's my explanation. When his young friends married in Haarlem, Frans Hals painted a portrait of each of them, as a wedding gift. More than a decade later, when they returned with five children, the old man would have been delighted, as he had ten children of his own. My sense is that he wanted to paint a portrait of the now matronly mother, and that she would have agreed to pose again on condition that he allow her to paint a portrait of him in return. If that happened, from what we know of Hals' character, he would have found it an embarrassment. Later, a visitor in Hals' home who admired the portrait would have been given it, thus starting the old tradition that it's a self portrait.

A final thought. There is no documentary evidence that Judith Leyster continued to paint after she started a family. That somebody so talented laid down her brushes, flies in the face of reason. In fact, she was a much better painter than her husband. A cursory glance at Jan Molenaer's *Battle Between Carnival and Lent* draws one's attention to the superior draftsmanship in the two brawling foreground figures, compared with the rest. I believe that she improved on most of his paintings. Naturally, he signed them. After all, it's a man's world.

Having hung up both my working hats, we had the time to explore further afield. An extended Grand Circle tour to Australia and New Zealand was the first tour we had taken without me as the guide. At Ayres Rock we recalled the travel advice offered many years earlier by a droll old gentleman. "Mountains," he said, "from below, churches from the outside, pubs from within." Heeding his words, we walked around the base. In Alice Springs, we visited a game reserve where we witnessed something that needed to be seen to be believed. When a ranger spotted an eagle on a distant rock, he told us to sit down and not move. Then he attracted the bird's attention by twirling a stone, attached to a string, around his head. The eagle took the bait and he swiftly flew at us. At the last moment, the ranger ducked. Having teased the bird, who returned to his rock, the ranger put an emu's egg at our feet. The eagle swooped back and started pecking at the egg, to no avail. Looking around, he soon spotted a suitable-sized stone, picked it up with one foot, flung it at the egg and flew off with the unhatched chick, so fast that we could scarcely take in what had happened.

In Melbourne, we were entertained by John Junner, an old friend from our dancing days, in London. He had traveled with his parents, as a boy, to England from his native Australia. He was an only child. While still a young man, his parents died, leaving him well set for life, with nothing to do but play bridge with his affluent boyfriends. In middle age, he suffered a devastating stroke from which he never recovered. He sold his charming Kensington house and returned to Melbourne, Australia, where a devoted gay cousin nursed him into an early grave. I'm inclined to think that we were his last guests.

In Auckland, New Zealand, we had the chance to spend the day with my niece Belinda Riddle. Her husband, Stuart, had inherited a lumber supply business on the south side of London. When Belinda produced their second child Claudia, she arrived without thumbs. A thorough examination revealed that, in every other department, the baby had been delivered with a full complement of parts. The question was, should something be done about it and, if so, what and at what age? As soon as my sister Mary phoned me with the unwelcome news, I had an idea. Dr. James Strickland is among the most respected hand surgeons on Earth. He's the author of the standard text on the subject. As he lives and works in Indianapolis, I suggested that the family should fly over for a consultation and possible surgery.

Belinda wasted no time in calling Jim Strickland. He told her to meet him at the Savoy Hotel, as he would be flying to London, next day. She was to bring Claudia and the x-rays. After his examination, and ascertaining which hospital was involved, he asked Belinda to return a few days later. When she did so, Dr. Strickland told her that he'd discussed the case with the hospital surgeons. They planned to operate in exactly the same way as he would, in Indianapolis. Both Claudia's index fingers would be removed and relocated as thumbs. When Belinda tried to pay him for his time and wise advice, he laughed and said, "It was my pleasure, and in any case, I never charge when I'm on vacation." What a prince! The bottom line is, Claudia is growing up normal in every way except that she gives you a "high four."

A fire destroyed Stuart Riddle's business. Rather than start over, they used the insurance to relocate to New Zealand. By the time we visited, they had acquired a large house and yacht near the town of Kerri Kerri, some two hundred miles north of Auckland on the north island. Belinda collected us first thing in the morning, so we enjoyed the trip in her car. When we reached their house, we had no difficulty understanding why they had left England. It sits on a cliff, at the head of an inlet on the east coast. The view east, towards many pristine islands, is unsurpassed. The climate is delightful, hovering as it does between temperate and subtropical. The house and adjacent guest house were in the process of remodeling, in anticipation of tourist rentals. Stuart planned to use the yacht for chartered excursions. Belinda was investing in inflatable playhouses, and castles, to rent out for children's parties.

I'm glad that we have the memory of seeing it in the planning stages, for everything was about to collapse like those inflatable playhouses. While Stuart, Belinda and the children all continue to live in the Kerri Kerri area, the couple is divorced, living with new partners, in different houses.

After a final few days spent in Fiji, we were hardly adjusted to the time change in Indianapolis, before Jane Jack arrived for a visit. She'd had a long and distinguished career, at Oxford University, teaching courses on the lesser English seventeenth century poets. For forty years she'd had a house within shouting distance of the Bevans', in La Garde Freinet, where she had retired. Since we had been spending time there, every summer and fall, we had not only become good friends, but had introduced her to all our visitors from the states. Above all, she'd fallen in love with Ryan. He'd missed no opportunity to join us, for a few days' vacation, most years.

The previous summer we'd had to play the heavy father with Ryan. He'd arrived with his nose thoroughly out of joint. Expecting to be in La Garde Freinet for a week, he was thwarted when Johnson and Johnson insisted he return for an interview, in four days. Having recognized his outstanding abilities, the company had moved him, in rapid succession, from Indianapolis to New Jersey for proximity to their global headquarters, in Trenton. He'd bought a charming eighteenth century farmhouse on a large lot in Frenchtown, overlooking the Delaware River. Once installed, he was as happy as a sand-boy. Now, to his obvious chagrin, the company wanted to move him to Pittsburgh, the subject of his upcoming interview. He told us that he had no intention of moving there. It was a city that, so far as he could ascertain, had nothing to recommend it. We pointed out that, dump or no dump, that's where he was headed. The good news was that we had friends there with whom he was certain to fall in love. The reason he had to move to Pittsburgh, we pointed out, was because J and J were fast-tracking him up the corporate ladder. From day one, we never doubted that, provided Ryan jumped whenever they asked him to do so, he would wind up their youngest CEO, ever. In particular, we looked forward to his multi-million dollar salary. We estimated that it would be ample to maintain all four of his doting parents in the lap of luxury, terminating in funerals fit for queens. Since those heady days, we've revised our predictions, because our boy, wise beyond his years, has seen how soul-destroying the race can be. If the top job is your goal, you can refuse to move once; do it a second time and you're doomed.

Ryan did climb on the Pittsburgh rung, and within days Sid and Dorothy Kweller were among his closest friends. Now, with Jane Jack in tow, we headed there for a visit. We stayed in his sizeable house, where we were joined by Carol and Paul and the Michaels. After a few days of fun, the seven of us left Ryan, in an RV, for Canada. Our first stop was Niagara-on-the-Lake for the Bernard Shaw festival. Then it was on to Stratford, Ontario for some Shakespeare. After visits to Chicago, Cincinnati and New Harmony, the time came for Jane to return to France. Before doing so, she told us that she had just enjoyed the best holiday she could ever remember. That's a joy to recall for, within a year, she was to be felled by a stroke.

Allen Clowes had become bed-ridden while we were in Australia so it came as no surprise when he died. What did surprise everybody was the size of his estate. By the terms of his will, almost everything was earmarked to establish the Allen Whitehill Clowes Foundation. It is worth twice as much as the Clowes Fund. His foundation was to be used exclusively to fund arts related organizations in Indiana, with the exception of the Indianapolis Symphony Orchestra. He'd never forgiven the Symphony board for moving to the Circle Theater from Clowes Hall. Though the move had occurred during John Nelson's tenure, as conductor, salt was rubbed into the wound when he discovered that Raymond Leppard would never have succeeded Nelson if Clowes Hall had still been the venue.

Allen left almost nothing to family, friends, or servants. The largest legacy went to Betty Roberts, his bookkeeper and wife-wannabe. When she heard that the amount was forty thousand dollars, she sued the estate, which settled out of court to avoid publicity. At five thousand dollars each, Ambrose and I did as well as anybody else. We gratefully used the money for a Grand Circle tour to Egypt, Israel and Jordan. In August, we joined all the Clowes family in Woods Hole to inter Allen's ashes in the churchyard, next to his parents' graves. He bequeathed Westerley, his Indianapolis home, and its contents to the Indianapolis Museum of Art. The house would be adapted for use by future museum directors.

Among the pictures which were to join the Clowes Collection is a charming small Madonna and Child with a bird, described as *School of Raphael*. It had been left to Allen by his mother. In the early nineteen sixties, a scholarly paper had attributed the painting to a sixteenth century Perugian artist, in the circle of Perugino. I had visited Perugia to study that artist's works and concluded that Allen's painting was far superior. It had to be by another hand. I visited John Sherman, the noted Raphael scholar, with photographs of the Clowes picture, at the Courtauld Institute, in London. He was at a loss, saying that it had all the hallmarks of an early Raphael, but he suspected it was a forgery.

Raphael's life and work is well documented, especially his wonderful series of Madonnas, painted during the years 1504-8 when he was living in Florence. The Clowes painting, at eight and a half by six and a half inches, is far smaller than any of them. During one summer, while Allen was at Wood's Hole, I took the painting to David Miller, the IMA's chief painting conservator, for study. Testing showed that the paint was all nineteenth century, giving credence to Dr. Sherman's suspicions. The panel however, was old, possibly sixteenth century Florentine. Further examinations and x-rays revealed an exquisite silverpoint drawing on the gessoed panel which carried all the hallmarks of the High Renaissance. When David produced a catalogue from a recent exhibition of Raphael drawings, there were two, in Her Majesty the Queen's collection, which stopped us dead in our tracks. Dated about 1504, they were both Madonna and Child compositions. Though neither was identical to the Clowes picture, there were telling similarities. All three drawings are in silverpoint. As that is a medium that resists erasure, alterations are visible. Evidently, Raphael tended to elongate baby's legs because in all three drawings he shortened them slightly, leaving a double image of the foot. As a keen observer, the artist had a habit of drawing the big toe slightly curled up. Beyond that, there were striking similarities in the arrangement of veiling around the Madonna's head.

If, as I suspect, the drawing hidden beneath the nineteenth century painting, is an autograph work by Raphael Sanzio, we have a rare treasure. Further research revealed that a small drawing, on a panel, attributed to Raphael of a Madonna and Child with a bird had been sold in London about 1830. As drawings in those days were dirt cheap compared with paintings, I believe that the Clowes painting covers up that London drawing. A drawing by Raphael, of the head of an apostle, was sold at a New York auction in December 2012. It realized over forty seven million dollars!

One day I hope that it will be possible to transfer the nineteenth century painting to another panel, or canvas, to reveal the underlying drawing, undamaged. In the meantime, the IMA's Madonna and Child with a bird, in the manner of Raphael, is keeping a secret.

Following the opening of Circle Center Mall in the heart of downtown Indianapolis, almost all the derelict factories, and warehouses, were being transformed into condominiums or rental lofts. At the same time, townhouses were springing up on almost every available lot and downtown throbbed with all kinds of night life, restaurants and new hotels. The already sizeable convention center was expanding in every direction. Clearly, it was an exciting time to be living in the heart of the city. To mitigate the effects of harsh winters and hot summers, much of the downtown area has been imaginatively interconnected so that pedestrians can walk miles without stepping outdoors.

As we were now in our seventies, the idea of living in an interconnected condominium for the rest of our foreseeable future had its appeal. Much as we enjoyed Runnymede and so many of our Cottage Home neighbors, digging the garden was becoming a chore. The same could be said for raking leaves and shoveling snow. To date, no residences were linked to the indoor mall, but as we rightly guessed, it was only a matter of time. While waiting, we continued traveling.

The Cunard Line had just launched the *Queen Mary 2.* Aware that it was almost half a century since we boarded the *Italia,* in Southampton, bound for New York, we resolved to do the trip in reverse. Setting sail from New York at sunset, with martinis in hand, we sat in a window watching the glow reflected off Miss Liberty's torch. Poignant memories of our arrival, so long ago in the mist of dawn, came flooding back. It may have been alcohol induced but, as I fought back the tears, I noticed them rolling down Ambrose's cheeks. What other people in the lounge were thinking was immaterial. This was one of those unplanned moments when lifelong lovers fall wordlessly into each other's arms.

# Chapter Thirty Six
## *Santa Fe*

Keith Jameson was starting a nine summers' long series of contracts to sings in the Santa Fe, New Mexico, opera. As opera buffs and fans of Keith, we regularly attended, with Annette Kaufman, toward the end of each season. Louis and Annette had attended together, for many years, always staying at the St. Francis Hotel. It's a charming old hostellery, conveniently located steps from the Governor's Palace, shops and galleries. Sometimes, we would stay with Annette in the St. Francis. In more recent years we have been guests of Louis Bixenman and Sterling Zinzmeyer. They have a gracious hacienda just south of the city. We'd attend four or five operas each season and were seldom disappointed. The spectacular setting for the partially-enclosed opera house in the hills five miles out of the city is surely unrivaled.

Each year, we could be sure that a number of opera-loving friends would overlap with us. Matthew Tivy would fly out, and we would always enjoy a dinner party at whatever house Keith had been assigned for the summer. Jim Rogers and Cynthia Snowden had moved near Albuquerque, from the Sea Ranch in California, to be near her son David and his family, so we'd rendezvous with them.

Whether we were living in Indiana, or Florida, we were in the habit of driving to Santa Fe. We would spend up to a week, on the road, visiting friends along the way. One year, after staying with Phil Mischler and John Luttig, in Overland Park, Kansas, we decided to drive west on the nearly abandoned Route thirty six towards Denver. Realizing that finding a motel anywhere along that road would be difficult, we consulted the AAA handbook. Evidently, there was a tiny motel in a place called Oberlin, Kansas. With nothing to be seen for miles in either direction, we couldn't miss the down-at-heel strip of rooms on the left. Humming along the empty road at eighty miles per hour however, we overshot it. Slowing down, and turning left, a road led down to the old railroad station and a small village.

Oberlin's one block main street had roofed boardwalks connecting a handful of withering shops, terminating on one side with a substantial red brick building bearing the inscription of a 1904 bank. A crisp striped awning alerted Ambrose to the possibility that it was a restaurant. We stopped to look. Not only was he right, but a cursory glance at the embossed menu, in the window, gave every indication that we'd struck gold. An arrowed sign directed us to a door inviting us to enter the 'bed and breakfast.'

We were greeted by a youngish man, sitting at a large mahogany desk, in a plush office. As he had no other customers, he suggested that we start at the top of the four-story building to check out all the rooms before choosing the one that we'd like for ourselves. While no two of the ten or so rooms were alike, they were all furnished in Victorian antiques and so over-accessorized with knick-knack covered whatnots, and dressers, that, apart from the section of bed that was free of lace and satin-beribboned cushions, there was no where to put anything larger than an *étui.* Under the circumstances, we were not surprised to find the first sheet of every roll of toilet paper folded to a perfect point, but the method used by our fastidious host to ensure continuing compliance, was totally original. Each point was held in place with an adhesive label depicting Raphael's playful *putti* from the lower section of his *Sistine Madonna,* to be found in Dresden's Gemäldgalerie.

We settled for a room on the second floor because it adjoined a comfortable lounge. Since only two or three people were expected in the restaurant, our host suggested setting a candle-lit table for us in the lounge. We both started with *escargots* in their shells accompanied by a modestly-priced burgundy. Ambrose followed with a succulent rack of lamb. I had duck *à l'orange* with *haricots verts* and wild rice. To conclude an evening that, an hour earlier, had had dismal prospects, we shared desserts of tiramisu and crème brulée, with some cognac. Both dinner and breakfast next morning were stellar.

Before departing next day, we had a chance to visit with our host. He was more than happy to confide his story to a couple of sympathetic queens. He and his brother had grown up on their parents' farm. Unlike his sibling, he found everything about farming thoroughly distasteful. Following their deaths, a few years earlier, the boys inherited the farm. His brother, who was married with a family, bought him out. With his share of the inheritance, our host bought this abandoned bank building. He had just finished turning it into his idea of a world class inn. The following year, we phoned ahead planning to stay there again. To our astonishment, he was fully booked. Evidently we had chosen to be there on the weekend of the county fair.

# Chapter Thirty Seven
## *The Block*

We were keeping a close tab on downtown developments. The buzz was that two Cleveland, Ohio, businessmen had bought the William H. Block department store with the intention of turning it into condominiums. It was to have an indoor connection to Circle Center Mall. On the face of it, this seemed to be exactly what we were waiting for. Wasting no time, we contacted one of the partners who kindly supplied us with particulars and floor plans. We reserved the most desirable apartment in the building.

Because it is on the register of historic places, the developers took advantage of the option to finance the rehabbing with tax credits. This required that they rent the apartments for five years, before they could be sold as condominiums. Our twelve hundred square foot apartment, we were told, would be sold for about two hundred and fifty thousand dollars. In the meantime, the rent would increase annually by five per cent which worked out at about a hundred thousand dollars, for the five years. Ambrose figured that, once we owned the place, we'd need to spend another fifty thousand dollars for various desirable improvements. That grand total of four hundred thousand dollars was just manageable, so we became the first tenants to sign on.

From Ryan's point of view, the timing of our proposed move was perfect. Having fallen in love with Marcus Adiutori, a Cincinnati restauranteur, he cajoled Johnson and Johnson to relocate him to the Queen City, from Pittsburgh. He was lucky. The headquarters of Ethicon Endo-Surgery, a major company within J and J, is in Cincinnati. It meant changing from pills to medical devices but, he was up to the challenge. In due course,

Ryan became Director of Strategic Initiatives. He sold the Pittsburgh house and bought a bargain-priced mansion in Western Hills, overlooking the city of Cincinnati. The spacious living rooms included one for billiards, and a winter garden, as well as a dozen bedrooms. The estate boasted an orchard and swimming pool. Our necessary downsizing meant that Ryan and Marcus came in for half a lifetime of accumulated stuff. What they couldn't take found its way to Goodwill.

Ambrose and I got in the habit of donning hard hats to wend our way among the workmen who were converting Block's into apartments. We noticed that they were sealing up all the large sash and casement windows. One smaller window, in each apartment, was to be left unsealed, in case of fire. Once sealed, it would be a costly undertaking to reverse the damage. Our corner apartment had twelve windows, all of which we had every intention of opening, at will. Recalling my early professional life, as a commercial artist in London, I produced a dozen official-looking signs saying, "This window is to be left unsealed." Having checked that the builders broke for lunch daily at 11:30 a.m., leaving the building locked, I parked at the back five minutes later. Finding the fire escape accessible, I high-tailed it to the seventh floor and, avoiding all hazards, made my way to our future apartment. Once there, I firmly attached one of my notices to each window. Still unobserved, I left the way I'd entered. The twelve signs, clearly visible from the street, indicated to all our friends the exact extent of our future home.

As work continued on Block's, Doug Shoemaker moved into our house while we went to France for two months. During our absence, Marilyn Solomon rebuilt the party table that we had bought in 1958. It had served a useful purpose in every home we'd had, since the Meadows. In Polk Street, it had been our library table but, now that we were downsizing, it was going to have to double as a dining table. At fifty four inches in diameter, it could seat eight. The disadvantage was its

393

being five inches lower than a conventional table. With laudable ingenuity, Marilyn's cabinet makers created a central spindle, enabling one to raise or lower the top in a matter of seconds.

Alec Clowes, Allen's nephew, was building a new home in Seattle. His new dining room turned out to be the perfect setting for our dining room furniture. A few other antiques, for which we would no longer have space, we traded to Ben Solomon for a breakfront and a pair of Venetian mirrors. Mary Jo appraised Runnymede, Ambrose's seventeen thousand dollar re-hab of sixteen years earlier. When she sold it for two hundred and twenty thousand dollars, a new benchmark was established in the Cottage Home neighborhood.

With the help of several friends, including Ryan, Marcus and Doug, we moved into the Block in October 2003. The smaller of the two bed rooms became our office and TV room. With a fourteen foot ceiling, nine enormous windows and spectacular views, our great room was all that we had hoped for. In the basement, next to the elevators was our assigned parking space. Once settled in, we were confident that the next time we moved, it would be to the crematorium. For the likes of us, it was the perfect retirement home. One could hole up for months, in the Block, without ever stepping outdoors. It offered at least as much indoor walking as a large airport albeit with considerably more things to see and do.

We found ourselves connected to both the Indiana Statehouse and all the state office buildings through to the canal. Another route took us to the convention center and as far as the baseball stadium or, by forking left, to the Union Station. We were attached to the Indiana Repertory Theater, with its three stages, and to the fake Mediterranean village of the Indiana Roof Ballroom. For other entertainment, the mall's top floor contained a fully-equipped gym, nine movie houses and an amusement arcade. The accepted wisdom was that, within the complex, there were in excess of two hundred food venues. At the time of our move, Circle Centre joined into six hotels, though that number was about to increase. With hundreds of stores, including Nordstrom and Parisian, we had it made.

Looking to the future, we were only a few blocks away from one of the nation's largest, and best equipped, medical centers. While we continued to enjoy good health, we could lock our door and travel, with the assurance that, should a problem occur in our apartment, there were custodians to take care of the matter. In fact, the halcyon days of living in the Block lasted less than three years. News came that the Cleveland developers had decided to maintain the building permanently as rental apartments. Anticipating long lives for ourselves, we now faced the real possibility that we'd run out of money, paying an ever escalating rent on a fixed income. Winding up as vagrants under a bridge, we wouldn't wish on our worst enemy and, for queens, it's simply not an option.

Well before we heard that unwelcome news, we faced a crisis on Seminary Street, in Key West. Florida real estate was booming. Consequently, Les and Patrick decided to put the triplex, which included our time share, on the market. They told us not to worry. They planned to use money from the sale, to remodel the cottage inhabited by Ma Evans, and make it available for us, to see our lease out.

We discussed the matter with Ian and Miranda during a weekend visit to Key West. As their own house in Coral Springs had appreciated in value, they had begun investing in rental properties with considerable success. Frugal Ian Cutler lives by his own adage that "You're never too rich to save a buck." With the stock market in the doldrums, we asked them to look out for a small condominium, near them, for us to buy. Hopefully we would sell it at a profit when the time came to buy our Indianapolis apartment. Not only did this plan offer a better chance at capital gains than we were getting from our stocks, but it also would ensure that we could continue as snowbirds, even if the boys' cottage was uninhabitable.

By the time we had unpacked back at the Block, the Cutlers had found what was described as a two-two. Outside of ballet, we'd never heard of such a thing, but we learned that it refers to a dwelling with two bedrooms and two baths. On their advice we bought it sight unseen and drove down for the closing. By the time Ian and Miranda had skillfully rectified a few minor problems we were delighted with their choice. Apart from good beds, we bought a few inexpensive pieces of furniture. The Cutlers gave us some hand-me-downs to complete the picture. Job done, we drove north again.

Back in Indianapolis, Patticakes contacted us with the good news that they had decided not to sell the triplex, after all. What you gain on the swings, you loose on the roundabouts. Several months later, back in Key West, we were informed that the Block would not be converted into condominiums. It was to remain a rental property. We did not want to leave Indianapolis. As we had lived there for nearly fifty years, it was our home as well as being home to almost all our dearest friends. Condominiums were for sale within our budget, but not one of them was connected to Circle Center Mall. A few were just across the street. The problem, as we saw it, was that it would only take one fall on the winter ice to end one's mobility for life. The few condos that were within the complex were well beyond our means. The least expensive was over eight hundred thousand dollars. Under the circumstances, we decided to move south permanently.

We decided against Key West for two reasons. At the time, it was prohibitively expensive and it lacks good medical facilities. The latter, in the light of our advancing years, was becoming a consideration. In March, as we departed Key West, we stopped to look at housing opportunities in Coral Springs. We contacted Jim Price, the realtor who'd sold us the condominium, asking him to show us three bedroom houses in the range of three hundred and fifty thousand dollars, or less. Little was available at that price, as the bursting of the housing bubble was a year in the future.

After a fruitless day, we were almost ready to admit defeat when we drove into an enclave of sixty four similar cottages called Ramblewood Villas. A three bed, two bath house was for sale there, at our maximum price. It had curb appeal, so we made arrangements to see inside next day. Our hopes were dashed when we found the interior to be dark and the floor plan inconvenient. We felt thoroughly dispirited as we re-entered the realtor's car. Then he mentioned that there was another house for sale in the same neighborhood, but he doubted it would suit us as it only had two bedrooms. We walked in, did a rapid tour and decided to buy it. The house had been built in about 1980. While small, the clever "H" plan made it seem larger than it is. Having downsized to one car, we figured out how to carve a small but adequate office out of the two-car garage. While the kitchen left much to be desired, the living room was the same size as our one in the Block. The one here had the added bonus of a clerestory-lit cathedral ceiling. A good sized screened in porch at the back overlooked a bucolic canal and wildlife refuge.

Merill Edelstein, the current owner, was sitting on a bar stool, one of the few remaining pieces of furniture, wearing nothing but a gossamer thin shift. In view of her advanced age, the sight of all but entrails, struck us a gross. Her story, we cobbled together later. Evidently, she had moved to Coral Springs, from San Diego, California, a few years earlier as a 'cougar'. Terrified of storms, she wasted no time in making the house as hurricane-proof as possible, even to cutting down the surrounding trees. That done, she turned her sights to attracting a man. Angelo, the youngish bachelor next door north, looked promising. From his kitchen, he could look straight into her bedroom where she made a habit of prancing about in the altogether. Far from turning him on, he was terrified. Once she discovered his attractive young girlfriend, she checked out the house to the south. That household consisted of two widowers. Their wives, who had predeceased them, had been sisters. As they backed out of the garage, she could hardly have failed to notice that neither gentleman was on the right side of eighty. She might even have glimpsed their walkers, in the back seat. It must have been a blow to her hopes when, by gradual degrees, she came to the realization that the remaining houses in the circle, with one exception, were inhabited by families or single women. The exception was a gay *maison à trois.* The final blow came in 2005 with Hurricane Wilma. It was the worst storm to hit Coral Springs in seventy five years. Her preparations paid off. Hers was the only house in the neighborhood to emerge totally unscathed. The house was fine but Merill had had enough. Deciding to return to California, she sold it for three hundred and fifty thousand dollars, and had shipped her furniture when the buyers' financing fell through. At that moment, Ambrose and I walked in with two hundred and ninety five thousand dollars. She took our offer and fled. The next week we sold our Coral Springs condominium for a hundred and eighty nine thousand dollars. That was fifty four thousand more than we had paid for it less than a year earlier.

## Chapter Thirty Eight
### *Florida, With a Side Trip to Ghana*


Ambrose and I spent much of the next two months driving between Indiana and Florida, transporting small and breakable items to our new home. As we were locking up on one occasion, prior to heading north again, a neighbor hailed us. Anxious to be on our way, we requested a rain check for the proffered bubbly, but gathered some hopeful information during our few minutes of conversation. Anne Mitchell's principal recreational interest was theater with music a close second. She looked forward to introducing us to the local venues. Turning out to be as good as her word, she became our first friend.

Anne was long since divorced from her gay husband. Her daughter, son-in-law and two grandsons also lived in our neighborhood. Connor, the younger boy, was not yet five, and gay as a lark. Austin, at eight, was all boy, into baseball and other sports with his cap on backwards. Connor loved ballet and walking in his mother's high heels. When gay friends in Indianapolis were concerned that we would be the lone gays in Ramblewood Villas, we could truthfully reassure them that in our sixty four houses the average age of our gay population was about forty, but that we run the gamut from five to eighty!

On a Sunday afternoon, once our furniture arrived, we invited all our neighbors over. With help from Miranda, we had a jolly party with a chance to take one another's measure. Dorrie Butler, a good looking lady in her middle eighties, lived diagonally across our circle. Her back garden was next to busy Riverside Drive. With all the conversation abuzz with what had happened to her two nights earlier, I asked her to tell me the story.

Before retiring on Friday night, Dorrie was enjoying a snack in her kitchen when all hell broke loose. A seventeen year old boy was driving a pickup truck north on Riverside Drive. His girlfriend had put one of her legs through the steering wheel, for reasons unexplained in the Karma Sutra. Whether or not her provocative position tempted coition on the part of the driver is mere speculation. What happened next is not. He struck the median with such velocity that the truck became airborne, sailed above the southbound traffic, over the Butler's protective bank and hedge, between two substantial trees, to demolish in turn the Florida room, dining room and kitchen. Finally halted by the refrigerator, the truck hit that appliance so hard that the ejected contents flew out with sufficient force to smash through a cabinet door, dislodging the sink's garbage disposal. Neighbors, hearing the noise, rushed into to rescue Dorrie, fearing that the whole house might collapse. The boy was unscathed and, as the son of a judge, remained unpunished and the incident unpublished. The girl suffered a minor fracture.

Nancy Butler, who normally lived with her mother, was due to return from Italy in a week. Along with the demolition of half her house, Dorrie had lost a lifetime's collection of antique Wedgwood china. When I attempted to commiserate, she laughed and said, "Oh, come on, we were all young once, and best of all, nobody got seriously hurt!"

Dorrie died in 2012. Ambrose and I feel fortunate to have enjoyed several years of her nonjudgmental friendship. When I asked if she had told Nancy about the disaster, she said, "No. I don't want to spoil her vacation, but I'll have some fun when I pick her up at the airport." "How so?" I asked. "Well," said Dorrie, "before she left, she said the time was ripe for the kitchen to be remodeled, so I think I'll tell her that I've started the job and that my enthusiasm got the better of my judgment!" Nancy later reported that her mother said nothing at the airport, but spilled the beans, over a pub drink, before they reached the remains of their home. With neighbors like that, we could already see a silver lining to leaving Indiana.

Though we had lived in the states for half a century, our knowledge of legal matters was limited to Indiana. We had long had wills, living wills and other legal documents necessary for the specialized protection of gay couples living in a straight world. Our punctilious lesbian lawyer, Jean Oswalt, had worked tirelessly to close all legal loopholes that avaricious relatives might try to get through should one, or both, of us succumb or become incompetent. All too soon we were to discover from Dom Bisignano, another gay Hoosier transplant to the Sunshine State, that Indiana law would not hold up in Florida. Arthur Smith, a gay attorney in Ft. Lauderdale, undertook the job of solving that problem for us. We enrolled with the Cremation Society of Florida, and made arrangements for our ashes to feed fish. Before we could become bone fide Floridian residents, various documents had to be produced, or completed. We also needed Florida driving licenses. With everything accomplished, we reckoned that we were marginally better off financially living in Florida, where there is no state income tax. In Indiana, our combined state tax was annually about seven thousand dollars. Conversely, we pay a slightly higher sales tax and about two thousand more in property tax, than we did on Polk Street. In all honesty, there's no great difference between the two.

Thanks to recommendations from neighbors, we found excellent doctors. Just as well, because it wouldn't be long before Ambrose would be in need of them. I've spent almost no time writing about health issues for two reasons. Number one is that, for the most part, we've lived our lives enjoying good health. The second is that only the most exotic, and improbable, ailments are of interest to any but the sufferer. Nevertheless, as we are a couple of crumblies well north of eighty, perhaps you will indulge me if I briefly refer to health problems as they occur? Even before our departure from

Indianapolis, Ambrose was often in pain when he walked. A definitive diagnosis was a long time in coming, but when it did, a hip replacement solved the problem.

On Ryan's suggestion, the three of us spent a couple of weeks in November 2007 in Ghana. My cousin James Fraser has a small house there in the coastal town of Winneba. Like many, we were in the habit of corresponding by email but, in view of our anticipated trip, I asked him for his street address. I wonder if, as I do, you consider that a reasonable request? In reply, James almost accused me of elitism. His house has no address. "When you get to Winneba, a city of about ten thousand, anyone will direct you to the home of the white man!" Of course, how silly of me. What could be simpler?

There is a direct flight to Ghana from Kennedy, in New York, so we planned to meet Ryan in the departure lounge. Experience has taught me that, if you plan to arrive on the same plane as your baggage, especially if there's a change involved, you'd better make it carry-on. Now this is a lesson which we have attempted to teach Ryan, over the years, with limited success, so when he joined us from the Cincinnati plane, wearing an enormous backpack and carrying a shoulder bag, we greeted him with heartfelt congratulations. We spoke too soon. Another bag had been checked through to Ghana. What in the world, I wondered, could be the need for that much stuff for a tropical fortnight? Ryan is one of those people who pays the closest attention to what he's told, and then does what he wants!

Cousin James and his driver Joe met us on arrival in Accra and settled us all into the Shangri-La Hotel for two nights. That afternoon, they drove us to Akosombo to see the Volta dam. Built under President Kwame Nkrumah, it has played a vital role in Ghana's economic success. James had arranged a tour of Achimota, where I had spent much of the first four years of my life, for the following morning. Never having returned, I was excited and wondered if anything would look familiar. Having seen photographs, and listened to stories all my life, I suspect much of what we saw that day resonated more as a result of those secondary sources than from direct experience.

We began with a visit to the headmistress. Her bright and spacious office had been Grandfather's. An excellent portrait of the old man hung behind her desk. It dated from when he and Granny had paid the college a final visit, in 1957. Starting in 1924, Achimota Hill had been cleared in order to realize the master plan for the College. Saplings planted at that time had grown into impressive avenues of beautiful trees. While I was taking a photograph of the little tin roofed hospital, a happy mother emerged with babe in arms. "You've got a lovely baby," I said. When she replied that he'd been born there eight weeks previously, I said that I too had been born there nearly eighty years earlier. She looked incredulous, so I added that I was the first white baby to be born there, to which she replied, "I guess you were the only one!"

Thanks to an inquiry from Ryan, James had got the address of a needy orphanage in Accra, so after lunch we drove there. It was a sobering experience to be taken around overcrowded and dilapidated buildings, with mud floors, full of hopeful smiling faces. When it comes to children, Ryan is a modern Pied Piper. By the time we got back to the car, he had a child hanging on to each of his fingers. It was then, that the reason for his oversized luggage became apparent. When Joe and Ryan heaved it out of the trunk, and opened it, the kids' excitement was worth the whole trip. It was packed with goodies, toys and fun things. As we drove off, Ryan was inflating brightly colored rubber balls, trying to keep pace with demand. I'm sure that the afternoon he spent with those children will long be remembered. It is one of the many reasons we love Ryan as we do.

After visiting James in Winneba, he kindly loaned us his car and driver to explore some of the country. Joe was an amazing young man. What Jesus did for Lazarus, Joe did for that automobile. He resurrected James' broken down jalopy, time after time, from almost certain death. Mind you, even a healthy car would be challenged to survive, for long, on what passes for roads in Ghana. The better highways are described as mettled, but even they are replete with axle-breaking chuckholes which must be circumnavigated, if the car is to continue on its way.

We spent time in the teeming city of Kumasi. Its marketplace is said to be the second largest in all of Africa. All thirty acres are sunken below the surrounding streets. Consequently, one can look over it to spot which area is devoted to hardware, fish, vegetables, clothes or whatever, expecting that once down there, you'll find what you want. You won't. Without Joe to guide, you would soon be hopelessly lost in the labyrinth of tightly packed stalls.

With a population exceeding a million, Kumasi is the capital of Ashanti, Ghana's largest and most respected tribe. The king of the Ashantis is known as the Ashantehene. The grounds of his palace are encircled with a wall which includes a greatly enlarged facsimile of the revered "Golden Stool." For those benighted souls who don't know what I'm talking about, I'll explain. African stools are traditionally carved out of a single log of wood. The curved seat is separated from a flat base with abstract designs or, for tourists, with elephants. Every man has his own stool. He carries it from place to place, because it is a serious breach of etiquette to sit on another man's stool. When somebody becomes chief of a tribe, there is an elaborate "enstooling" ceremony. The European equivalent is "enthroning."

In the case of the Ashantis, nobody knows when the Golden Stool dropped out of the sky. We do know that the great Ashantehene, Nana Osei Tutu, was enstooled on it in the late 1600s. Evidently on arrival, it hit the ground with such force that a sword was needed to pry it loose. Known as the Okomfo Anokye Sword, it remains, to this day, stuck in the same spot.

One of the most beloved Anshantehenes was Prempreh II who reigned from 1931 to 1970. My grandfather, Alec Fraser, had the unique distinction of being created an honorary chief. When he left the Gold Coast, as it was then known, Prempreh II had his royal goldsmith create a small replica of the stool, in pure African gold, as a gift. In due course, I inherited it from Dad. The stool that dropped out of the sky is actually gold-plated wood. By now it is too fragile to be used. It is only seen in public during the enstooling ceremony, which takes place on a replica, with the treasured original resting on a cushion.

Ryan, Ambrose and I gained admission to the Manhyia Palace, in Kumasi, by producing a photograph of Prempreh II's gift. We were entertained, and given a tour by the Ashantehene's chief of staff. Unfortunately, His Majesty was in Nigeria till the following Monday, by which time we would be on our way home.

Before leaving the subject of the Golden Stool, honesty requires that I admit to a disgraceful transgression. At a cocktail party, Rosemarie Carolan, a devout Roman Catholic, was asking about our Ghanaian trip. She interrupted my account of the unexpected delivery of the stool, by saying, "Are you trying to tell me that a stool dropped out of the sky?" When I admitted that that's what happened, she said, "I've never heard of anything so ridiculous in my life." I'm ashamed to report that, before I could hold my tongue, I replied, "It's no more ridiculous than the Virgin Mary shooting straight up there." With that, our conversation, and her feigned interest in Ghana, came to an abrupt conclusion.

Traveling around the central part of the country, between the villages of Ho and Hohoe, near the border with Togo, we happened upon a group of Kente cloth weavers. The craft, which is practiced in very few places, is unique to Ghana. The fabric is woven in long strips about three inches wide, in a bewildering array of colors and designs. Once woven, the strips are sewn together to make large wraparound togas. We watched fascinated, as the young men worked out elaborate patterns flawlessly, on narrow looms, at a dizzying speed. Looking on, it was evident that it must take a full day to create a six-foot strip, yet they were happy to sell it for five dollars, or less. Ryan talked to a man who was working in black and white. Did he have any, like that, made up into a large enough size to cover his dining room table, in Cincinnati? He did not. What he was working on was all he had but, with his helpers, could make him one in a few days. When Ryan said that we'd be at the Shangri-La Hotel, in Accra, on Sunday night, he said he'd have it there for him. The man made a note of Joe's cell number and called daily to report progress. Working all hours, he completed the job on time, hitched a ride on a "tro-tro" and delivered it as promised, all for eighty dollars!

We stayed in Elmina, a large fishing village with an impressive castle built by the Dutch in 1482. Like Cape Coast castle, a few miles farther east, it was the departure point for millions of slaves. In my childhood, the castle was for the use of Sir Gordon Guggisberg, the governor, as a vacation retreat. He loaned it to my parents for their honeymoon. The harbor is full of fishing boats. Resembling enormous canoes, each one is carved from the trunk of an odum tree. As one drives through Ghana, the majestic trunks of the odum trees soar above the forests like vast umbrellas. While Ambrose and I enjoyed a siesta, Ryan made friends with some fishermen who allowed him to join them as they went out to sea. All in all, it was, for me, a curiously satisfying return to my roots.

Returning to Coral Springs, we read about, and joined, an organization called The Ghanaian Association of South Florida. They meet monthly, in a Fort Lauderdale library, where news is exchanged, and plans formulated for annual picnics, parties, and festivals of one kind or another. Ghanaians are delightfully outgoing and fun loving. Every member is accepted as part of their extended family. They care deeply about the well-being of all. Despite being the only white members, we have never felt out of place.

Before you go off with the impression that Ghanaians are paragons of virtue, I should mention an almost universal shortcoming. Time. They seem to have no conception of it. Our last Christmas party is only the most recent example of what happens regularly. It was scheduled from 6:00 till 11:00 p.m. The caterers were starting to set up trestle tables, when Ambrose and I arrived at 7:30 p.m. Nobody else was there so, we rolled up our sleeves to spread tablecloths, napkins and decorations on twenty, or more, tables. By the time we finished, it was eight o'clock and about half a dozen people had shown up. We shared a bottle of wine while wondering if anybody else would appear. By 9:00 p.m., we were up to about twenty people including Bismarck, the president. He asked how long we thought he should allow before he delivered his invocation, prior to eating? At that, I said that Ambrose and I were hungry and planned to eat now, before all the food was stone cold. He kindly gave us the go-ahead but decided to delay his invocation, until more people were there. A few minutes later, the sluice gates opened, and by 10:00 p.m., a hundred, or more, people were having a ball. We were ready for bed.

# Chapter Thirty Nine
## *Honorary Conchs*

Having left the cultural life of Indianapolis behind, we set about finding replacements in Coral Springs. To our surprise and delight, we discovered the Coral Springs Museum of Art with the inspired acronym of CSMART. It shares a complex of buildings with other arts organizations in spacious well-landscaped grounds. The founding executive director, Barbara O'Keefe, has worked diligently, since 1997, to create a facility that is the envy of the surrounding cities. What she has accomplished on an ever-diminishing budget is impressive. With a population where more people are under the age of five than over sixty five, CSMART has seen its mission as one of education first, with special exhibitions a close second. Hundreds of young students enroll in a wide-ranging choice of art, and craft, classes taught by practicing artists.

Over the years, Barbara has brought in artists-in-residence from many parts of the world. They create a work of art watched by, and often assisted by, the students. These works cover the media spectrum, paint, fiber, mosaic, or sculpture. The latter may be cast, fired or carved and many of the completed pieces have been placed throughout the museum's grounds. The small permanent collection is displayed in beautifully lighted galleries alongside changing exhibitions. An outstanding collection of *fin de siècle* French prints, from a Chicago collection, exhibited in 2012, received a good review in the *New York Times.* Annette Kaufman has twice loaned us exhibitions from her extensive holdings, including one devoted to the work of Milton Avery.

When Barbara O'Keefe asked me to join her board of directors, I accepted with alacrity. During the course of the several years since then, I have come to appreciate her extraordinary ability to maintain the high quality of the Coral Springs Museum of Art on what appears to be an impossibly meager and ever-diminishing budget. In large measure, that success is due to having only one other full time member of staff. Sheri Adanti happens to be both multi-talented and hard working. Along with a couple of excellent part time employees, the Museum's high standards have been maintained throughout the recession. Barbara retired in the fall of 2012, to be replaced by Bryan Knicely, lately director of the Stonewall Library and Museum.

Friends of Music is a Coral Springs organization which was started to do fundraising for the Florida Philharmonic Orchestra. The modest amount of money which it raised did little to save the orchestra's bacon. It went belly-up in 2003. By the time Ambrose and I joined, the money was going to help finance music programs in the schools. They sponsor a few recitals and musical groups who perform from time to time at varying locations in the city. In addition, we have seasonal fund raising parties and dinners. As a committee member, my job is to phone all the members to alert them of forthcoming events.

In 2009, when Sebrina Maria Alfonso met, and fell in love with, Jacqueline Lorber, of Fort Lauderdale, a new era began for the Key West Symphony Orchestra. Ambrose and I became office volunteers, as it became the South Florida Symphony Orchestra. Along with Key West, the orchestra presents concerts in Palm Beach, Broward, Dade and Monroe counties. We made ourselves available, whenever possible, for such jobs as mailings, putting together packages, or phoning subscribers. Sadly, Ambrose can no longer help, due to health issues, to be discussed later.

Raising money for the arts is always hard work. This is especially true in south Florida, where so much disposable income is spent on the body beautiful that little is left to nurture the mind. Jacqueline, against all odds, works tirelessly to squeeze blood out of stones. To our astonishment, she often succeeds. Her determination to ensure that the orchestra doesn't suffer the same fate as the Florida Philharmonic is laudable. Sabrina is, by any measure, an excellent conductor and, if for no other reason than that, we attended her first Key West concert in 1997. We are excited to watch her moving up to the next level.

Our other volunteer work has been at the local hospital which is called the Coral Springs Medical Center. Ambrose was placed in the office of Quality Control, where sheets of figures are in constant need of tabulation. My assignment was in the Outpatients department, as a general dogsbody, which provided the variety I enjoy. One minute, I might be at the copy machine, and the next pushing a patient in a wheelchair to a hospital bed. In February 2010, Ambrose was the wheelchair-bound patient being transported, for surgery, to replace his right hip.

Just after the conclusion of our ten year lease on the Seminary Street apartment, in Key West, my cousin James Fraser came to visit. We took him down to Key West where Patti and Bubby Rodriguez had invited the three of us to dinner. Settled into a bed and breakfast, we get a phone call inviting us for preprandial drinks to Les and Patticakes' so, naïve as ever, we did as bidden. A handful of friends were there to meet James and enjoy a drink. After answering the phone, Patrick said that the woman who had moved into our apartment was home from work and wondered if we'd like James to see it? With that, we left the boys' cottage.

Patticakes opened the gate, in the fence, and we were instantly blinded by the paparazzi's' flashing cameras! Following the initial shock, we realized that dinner chez Rodriguez had never been in the cards. An elegantly decorated buffet dinner had been organized, right there, for at least fifty people. First we were to be subjected to a short ceremony. A "conch" is a person born, and raised, in Key West. Framed documents, signed by the Mayor of Monroe County, and accompanied by much flowery language, ended up by declaring that henceforth, we were honorary Conches, with all the appropriate rights pertaining thereto. Along with our artistically embellished certificates, we were presented with a pair of coffee mugs labeled The Key West Aunties on one side, and with our pictures in feathered costumes on the other.

Key West has always been a special place, but imagine James' astonishment when, during the course of dinner conversation, he discovered that the guy sitting next to him was from the town of Winneba in Ghana!

Keith Jameson, who now sings regularly in New York's Metropolitan Opera, was born and raised in a small town called Greenwood, South Carolina. Anxious to give back to his home town, he and his parents started a small annual music festival there, at about the same time as we moved to Florida. The festival was scheduled during the winter. Much as we love Keith and his family, I regret to say that our love doesn't stretch to northern forays during winter months. However, once the festival was moved to summer, we wouldn't miss it for the world. Nor were we alone. Annette started flying in to Atlanta, from Los Angeles. We would pick her up for the four hour drive to Greenwood. Herb and Bonnie would join us from Indianapolis, and Bob Michael drove down from Louisville. Even cousin James flew in for it one year. He enjoyed the music immensely, but what really impressed him was the genuine warmth of southern hospitality, exemplified to perfection by Carol Richard, Keith's mother. Oh! Happy days.

Chapter Forty
*Cruising*


The winter of 2009 was the first for thirteen years that we would not be in Key West. Instead, we booked ourselves on a seven-week cruise around South America, starting in Ft. Lauderdale and ending in San Francisco. With Ian and Miranda Cutler's help, we had bought the furnishings to redo our kitchen. They generously offered to do all the work during our absence. Had we ever been on a Carnival cruise, I doubt we would have embarked on this one, which lends credence to the saying that "there's no fool like an old fool."

Aware that we'd have time on our hands, we armed ourselves with six new books. On a visit to Barnes and Noble, we each chose three which we hoped would be of interest to both of us. On board ship, we planned to read one book at a time. We would each read the same two or three chapters and then, the one who had chosen the book would pose questions over content to the other. Worried that our memory was deteriorating, we hoped that these mental exercises would have a salubrious effect on the old noggin. Sad to report, I can't for the life of me remember whether the outcome was what we'd hoped for. What it did achieve, was escape from the stultifying monotony of hedonistic cruising. Before starting a book however, we needed to board the ship.

We were set to sail at 4:00 p.m. on a Saturday. Susan Harner, a Ramblewood Villas neighbor, kindly drove us to Port Everglades and deposited us among some four thousand fellow travelers. Official-looking people began herding us into some semblance of a line. Next, a tiny lady with a bullhorn asked passengers without Brazilian visas to follow her. Doing as requested, we found ourselves, among two or three hundred others, being taken past the front of the line and packed into a cage elevator which brought to mind the Black Hole of Calcutta. Emerging on the second floor of the terminal building, we were escorted to a holding area and told to await further instructions. No sooner had the bullhorn lady departed than deafening alarms sounded, followed by instructions to leave the terminal building immediately as indicated by the flashing arrows.

The next couple of hours were spent, along with most of the passengers, under relentless sunshine, hemmed in by police. Shortly after noon, a hush fell over the crowd as a loudspeaker delivered the scoop. The makings for a bomb had been found in some luggage, rendering the terminal unsafe. Furthermore, all the baggage that had already been taken aboard was being unloaded for further inspection. While Carnival apologized for the delay, we must understand that concern for our safety was paramount. Now please would we follow the uniformed officers into another building? We did as bidden and found ourselves in an erstwhile customs shed devoid of furniture, but with a row of five or six conveyor belts for screening luggage. Ambrose and I sat on one of them with nothing to lean against and our legs dangling. Within minutes all the inspection tables were covered with people pressed buttock to buttock, like vultures on a tree waiting patiently for a Parsee to die. Not a word of further explanation was forthcoming so there we remained, with nothing to eat or drink, for over seven hours. Those of us perched on the inspection belts were comparatively lucky. Everybody else sat on hand luggage or the filthy concrete floor. On one side of the shed was a water fountain in front of totally inadequate toilets. The latter, quickly degenerated into third world horrors.

At 7:30 p.m., we were finally to make a move. The loudspeaker instructed us to line up with boarding cards, and passports, in hand to begin the embarkation process. As we emerged into the tropical moonlight, there at last was the

Carnival *Splendor,* aglow with welcoming lights. At the foot of the gangway, we were summarily turned away because we lacked Brazilian visas. Our pleas that we would stay on board at every Brazilian port fell on deaf ears. We needed visas and could join the cruise at a later date once we had obtained them.

As we still had our cell phone, we called the Cutlers. They thought that, by then, we would have been well into the Caribbean. Dropping whatever they were doing, they drove over to rescue us and get us fed before we crumbled away to dust. We always travel light, so fortunately we had all our luggage with us. Ambrose was sufficiently demoralized to cut our losses and forget the whole thing. Over dinner however, we realized that that was not an option. Ian and Miranda had already put in a full day's work in our kitchen. The appliances, and all the contents of the cabinets, had been moved into the now unusable living room. They'd emptied the Florida room of its furniture, to free it up as a temporary carpenter shop. Finally, they had demolished the old kitchen. That was the bad news. The good news was that our bedroom remained untouched, along with our bathroom, so we certainly had somewhere to sleep that night. After such a day, we were soon comatose.

While we were in la-la land, Miranda was hard at work. Sunday morning she came over with the fruits of her labors. She had printed out copies of the required forms to obtain Brazilian visas, plus all the necessary instructions. The first order of business was to get photos taken to precise specifications. We drove into Miami to locate the Brazilian consulate, on an upper floor of a high-rise building adjacent to a fast food breakfast joint. Noting that the consulate would be open the next day at 10:00 a.m., we decided to get there by eight. That way, one of us could stand in line while the other had breakfast. It did not work out as planned.

Monday morning on arrival, we found the building open. The information desk informed us that we could take the elevator, to the floor of the Brazilian consulate, and wait up there. When the doors opened on the twenty-something floor, we could hardly get out for the crowd of Carnival passengers who had arrived ahead of us. They were sitting on the carpet, whiling away the hours until 10:00 a.m. One passenger had taken charge. Holding a writing tablet, she had everybody sign in, as we exited the elevator, to ensure being interviewed in the same order. Shock and awe is the only way to describe the effect it had on the Brazilians, when they arrived for work, to discover some two hundred people sprawled all over their lobby floor. Never before had so many people needed visas at one time. Under normal circumstances, a week was required between the application being accepted and the visa being issued. This time, they would bend the rules and call us individually as they got through.

We lucked out, got our visas next day and, thanks to Miranda, caught a plane to Barbados that evening. At the airport, we were greeted by a Carnival agent who had a bus, and hotel bookings, for passengers who were in our predicament. Unlike the rest of the passengers arriving on that flight, we were not on the list. You would think that, by now, we would have admitted defeat. We didn't. Miranda had booked us into a hotel, at half the advertised rate, so we hailed a taxi and settled in for a Barbadian night. Before joining the ship, next morning we bought some local rum, only to suffer another indignity when we were forbidden from taking it onboard.

By the time we joined the four day old cruise, a debilitating bronchial infection which soon came to be known at "Carnival cough" was rapidly spreading from stem to stern. As new arrivals, we survived several days before our turn came. We both came down with the complaint. Night time was the worst. For weeks, neither of us got a good night's sleep. When one wasn't hacking, the other was. Ambrose recovered in about a month, but my cough lingered till after we returned to Coral Springs. In a matter of days, the ship's supply of medication was exhausted. Seasoned passengers complained that the Carnival *Splendor* was the first cruise ship that they had traveled on without sanitizers at the entrance to the dining rooms. To make matters worse, at dinner every night the maître d'hôtel would go from table to table shaking hands with whoever was well enough to be there. We tried to explain why handshaking, under the circumstances, was a bad idea, to no avail. By the time we were half way up the coast of Chile, three elderly passengers had already succumbed. A fourth went into hospital at Valparaiso where he also died. The last I heard about that case, was from the newspaper. His widow was suing Carnival who were balking at paying for his body to be flown home to Atlanta.

A sixty three year old gentleman may, or may not, have been suffering from the cough but, whatever the case, he'd had enough and jumped overboard. For some unknown reason, it took four hours to establish what had happened. Every five minutes, starting at 6:30 a.m., the PA had been urging him to report to the Purser's Office. At 10:30 a.m., the ship turned around and returned to where he was thought to have jumped. There we remained, going round in circles until dark. His body was never recovered. The delay played havoc with the plans of a number of passengers who had paid megabucks for a two-night, three-day, side trip to Macchu Picchu. How that problem was resolved, I don't recall.

As our only experience of a large ship had been the *Queen Mary 2,* we were astonished and, I may say, appalled by the over-the-top interior decorations of this Carnival behemoth. The hallways, and elevator lobbies, were done in Pepto-Bismol pink with silver blobs. A bewildering variety of mismatched decorative schemes quite overwhelmed the senses, as one battled one's way in search of the next feeding trough. Speaking of feeding troughs, apart from a couple of swimming pools, the entire acreage of deck nine was devoted to them.

Fully half the passengers were obese, or morbidly so, several to the point of being permanently wheelchair-bound. Almost all could be found, at any time of the day, on the ninth deck polishing off endless platters of food with the dispatch of industrial vacuum cleaners. One couple in their thirties, who together must have tipped the scales at a ton, traveled about on vehicles that resembled small farm tractors. Once or twice a day, they would interrupt gourmandizing, drive poolside and, with help from a posse of sun baked athletes, plop into the pool. The ensuing water displacement sent pantywaists scurrying to avoid the tsunami.

For dinner we were assigned to one of two huge dining rooms. Ours was called the Gold Pearl. The pseudo-Baroque wall decorations were so intrusive that, in spite of the *Splendor* being almost brand new, there was evidence of damaged plasterwork, revealing underlying chicken wire which had fallen apart when a satiated customer had carelessly reversed his chair. The equally intrusive overhead decorations, were supposed to represent vast oyster shells, with golden pearls. Were it not for the restaurant's name, I would have mistaken them for sunny side up fried eggs. As our table was on the upper level, we noticed that even those decorations had sustained a modicum of damage. We were mystified as to the cause because, at their lowest, they would clear the heads of all but the loftiest of basketball players. All became clear when stewards emerged from the kitchen with trays, at shoulder level, stacked high with a pyramid of covered dishes. After a couple of disasters, the staff became skilled at ducking to avoid the edge of an oyster shell. Sometimes, they would miss by microns.

During days at sea, activities were scheduled nonstop from dawn till midnight. Most of them held little interest for us. The main lobby, where capsule elevators were in constant motion, was the venue for semi-classical music twice daily. The pianist and three young string players were all Polish. Though they played passably, their repertoire was decidedly limited. We were subjected to their transcription of Ravel's *Bolero* at least once, and often twice, a day. As the voyage dragged on, their smiley faces became increasingly surly. Their recitals became briefer and briefer, with longer and longer rest periods between the hackneyed pieces.

It was at these musical offerings that we made friends with two recently-retired couples. Kathy and John Digits, from Boston, had moved to Georgetown, near Austin, Texas to be near an unmarried daughter. They had built a lovely house in a retirement community, to find themselves lone Democrats, surrounded by Tea Party Republicans. We greatly enjoyed one another's company and, the following year, spent a delightful and interesting couple of nights as their houseguests, en route to Santa Fe.

Pam and Ray Cook are English with a well honed sense of fun. They live in a small town near Chester, with Pam's mother nearby. His hobby is toy trains. They attend swap meets in the hopes of unloading a duplicate caboose in exchange for a rare mail carriage. Having finished putting Kirsty, their only offspring, through college, they bought a canal boat for weekends, and vacations of a peculiarly English type.

A number of years ago, with Brad and Kerry, we rented a canal boat in Worcester for ten days. Kerry, an ex-sailor, was soon the intrepid master of the craft. On rare occasions, when I steered, within minutes, everybody would fall over as I rammed into the bank. Dear Ambrose was pushing us off when he fell in, onto a bloated dead sheep. Had it been me, I would have freaked out and suffered nightmares for weeks, but Ambrose was barely fazed.

At a place called Tardibigg there is the longest flight of locks in England. In the space of a mile, one has to descend about four hundred and fifty feet through manually operated locks. According to the guidebook, it would be an eight hour undertaking. Kerry accepted the challenge. Never have I seen anybody put in such a sustained performance, as he did that day. Each lock has double hung gates at either end. Unless they are closed, you can not walk across the top of the gates. The standard method is for one person to be on each side of the canal, turning the wheels that open the gates, allowing water to fill the lock. The problem was that, the weight of water pressing against the gates was too much for weaklings like us to get them started. Kerry to the rescue. He would get one wheel started, jumping over the widening gap, he'd start the other one. While Ambrose and I finished that job Kerry, breaking all the rules, would run to the next lock to start opening the entry doors for that one. In short, by always keeping one lock ahead, we made it through the entire flight in just over three hours. At the end, Kerry looked triumphant. We were exhausted.

Another day called for crossing a deep valley, on an aqueduct, just wide enough for our boat. Looking down hundreds of feet, the cars resembled ants. Suddenly, the wind carried Kerry's jacket overboard and he leaped off, in frantic pursuit. That he retrieved it, and returned to tell the tale, is tantamount to a miracle. We even went through the longest tunnel in England. Its length I forget, but there's a three mile stretch where nary a pinpoint of light was visible in either direction. Brad chose the tunnel to treat us to a tea party on the poop deck. The thought was appreciated, but the event was marred by unwelcome drips of icy water from above. Between such adventures, we tied up in Stratford-on-Avon, for a Shakespeare play, in Gloucester, for a serendipitous cathedral concert, and Droitwich, recognized by the Romans for its efficacious briny waters. But I digress.

The year after circumnavigating South America, Pam and Ray Cook flew over, from England, to spend a vacation with Ambrose and me, in Coral Springs. After using us as a base to explore south Florida, we joined them on a Caribbean cruise. I'm happy to report that it went off without a hitch.

Before concluding our Carnival *Splendor* tale of woe, I feel constrained to comment on the cruising phenomenon. For those who want to say, quite simply, that they've been to Montevideo, or Rio, then cruising is perfect. We find it frustrating. Buenos Aires, for example, is an enormous city which bears comparison with Paris. On a cruise, you disembark after breakfast. Next, you either get herded onto one of a fleet of waiting buses, for an overpriced tour which includes shopping time, in selected tourist markets, or you hail a taxi, to escape the dock area and head into the city. Needless to say, the latter, in our opinion, is the lesser of two evils. In the case of Buenos Aires, we took a swift tour of the downtown, admiring its wide avenues and tree-lined boulevards, before winding up at the Museo National de Bellas Artes. It deserves a full day. As it was, with the ship sailing at 6:00 p.m., we were constantly checking our watches rather than allowing the art to entrance us.

No doubt, Ambrose and I are odd fish, but our recipe for a perfect vacation is to drive independently, stopping for a day, or a week, whenever we happen upon somewhere that promises rewards for further exploration.

The penultimate stop for the *Splendor* was Long Beach, California, where Annette Kaufman met up with us. We visited the local art museum which boasts an important collection of twentieth century ceramics, including pieces by Bernard Leach. He had been the leading ceramicist at Dartington Hall, in Devon. With a pang, we remembered our two large platters by him, abandoned in London in 1957, for lack of packing space. During lunch, Annette contacted two friends of hers that she wanted us to meet when we arrived, the following day, in San Francisco. They were long time gay partners who had married in Massachusetts and recently relocated to the Bay area, from Boston. We arranged to meet them for lunch.

Finally disembarking from our seven week odyssey, we were greeted by Josh Kantor and Denny, who live in

Carmichael, near Sacramento. They had married, during the brief window of opportunity, in California. Also there to meet us, was Ed Kelley, who had taught modern art at Herron and been divorced because he is gay, and his partner, Bart Casimir. They had also married during the same period. As the eight of us sat down to lunch, the curious paradox of Ambrose and I being the only unmarried couple at an all gay luncheon struck home. We had been a couple for many years longer than the other three combined. Would we consider getting married after six decades of living in sin? At the time, our answer would have been a resounding, "Yes, just as soon as the Federal Government recognizes the legitimacy of same-sex marriages, we'll be first in line for our certificates." Now it's too late. My lifelong love has lost his mind. Scar tissue, following a number of small strokes, is to blame.

Nothing would make me happier than for Ryan to enjoy the same conjugal bliss as we have had. Unfortunately, his life with Marcus Adiutori came unstuck when, after a few years, Marcus strayed. For several years we hoped for reconciliation, but in vain. Early in 2012, via the internet, Ryan met Jimmy Musuraca. To those who believe that life begins at forty, I hope you're right. That year, Ryan turned thirty nine and Jimmy forty one.

While we have never met a friend of Ryan's whom we didn't like, Jimmy is the only one who, in our opinion, deserves Ryan. Had Jimmy fallen for someone else, the fact of him having a four year old son, could present problems. As it is, Anderson and Ryan bonded immediately. Jimmy and his ex-wife remain on good terms. She lives in Columbus, Ohio, caring for their son during the week. On most Fridays, Jimmy picks him up for the weekend in Cincinnati. Many readers may consider this to be a recipe for disaster. We don't. Although these are early days, gaydar tells me that they have found their life partners.

## Chapter Forty One
### *La Garde Freinet.*


On returning to Coral Springs, at the end of the South American cruise, we were met by Ian and Miranda Cutler. They had finished the kitchen for us. Though we have never set foot in most of the sixty four houses that constitute Ramblewood Villas, I'm confident that ours is by far the best kitchen in the neighborhood. We felt like those deprived people you see on TV who are astonished by the fabulous transformation of their pitiful hovel by some world class design company. We are greatly blessed to have two such devoted relatives.

The Cutlers live about five miles from us. We talk on the phone every few days, but see surprising little of one another. At the same time, if there is anything that we need, they will be right over. In the few years that we've lived in Florida, though we share few interests, we've come to love them dearly. Most of their friends are British ex-pats, of about their age. On Fridays, they often meet up at an English pub, for a few drinks, while watching a ball game. They also keep up with old friends from England, several of whom fly over for visits. At weekends, whenever possible they drive to State parks, with their camper. On a few occasions, they have accompanied us to the Opera, in Fort Lauderdale. Though they appeared to enjoy it, none of the arts is given high priority in their lives.

Ian shares our taste for cocktails, wine and good food. He will sample anything. Thor, on the other hand, is about the most conservative consumer of food, and drink, that I've ever met. As far as I can ascertain, his only drink is diet Coke which he imbibes by the quart. Miranda is much the same though she also drinks tea. She eats salad but, hold the avocado. Thor will have none of it. He considers all green vegetables to be highly dangerous, if not lethal. He survives, almost exclusively on chicken nuggets, French fries and pasta, so far with no ill effects. We seldom invite them to our house for a meal, as most of the food we consume with gusto, they would refrain from trying. Very trying.

Speaking of food, like most of our friends we find gourmet meals to be one of life's great pleasures. Whenever possible, Ryan joins us for special occasion dinners. A few days before our fifty-fifth anniversary, he asked us how we planned to celebrate. We said we'd made no plans but might drive down to Key West. That year, September tenth fell on a Monday, a day that Patrick Hayes is off work. You may remember that he is the bartender at Key West's Square One restaurant. He knows our anniversary date, so we would avoid eating there, were he on duty, for fear of him picking up the tab. Under the circumstances, we slipped into Key West, booked into a bed and breakfast and had a romantic dinner at Square One. When we called for our bill, Ryan had taken care of it! In retrospect, we realized that just telling him our possible destination was all he needed. Knowing that Square One is our favorite restaurant there, doubtless he zeroed in on the first phone call.

Three years later was another occasion when Ryan could not be with us. He visited us the previous week, taking pains not to tip his hand. Casually asking about any forthcoming plans, we said that we would be driving up to Greenwood, South Carolina, next week. Keith Jameson would be having a fund raising concert, to support his festival there. As we planned to reach Greenwood late on Saturday September the eleventh, we would leave Coral Springs on Friday. For fear of arousing suspicion, Ryan left the matter there. He knew that we generally stay in Macon, Georgia, at a bed and breakfast called, "The 1843", and that we have two special restaurants in that town. For once in his life his two plus two addition made five. Whenever we attended the Greenwood festival, we did exactly what he expected us to do. What he failed to take into account is that, the reason for going via Macon was to collect Annette Kaufman, from Atlanta airport. This time there would be no Annette, so we would save a couple of hundred miles by another route.

Back in Cincinnati, Ryan called the 1843. He drew a blank. Recognizing his mistake, he rightly figured that we would take a more direct route. Noting the mileage between Coral Springs and Greenwood, he concluded that, regardless of which road we took, the mid-point would be in southern Georgia. Knowing that we favor historic hotels or bed and breakfasts, he wasted no time in calling every conceivable place, with no luck. What he didn't know was that Ambrose had a doctor's appointment at noon on the Friday, so we would not be departing Coral Springs before 2:00 p.m. Because of that, we had done our own research and found a bed and breakfast called, "Chalet Suzanne." It is near Lake Wales, in Florida, and boasts a gourmet restaurant. It was a fair distance out of our way but, being our anniversary, we made the detour.

Reaching dessert, at the end of a memorable meal, Ambrose asked the waiter to bring us a half bottle of good champagne. "Is this a special celebration?" he asked. "Yes," said Ambrose, "it's our anniversary." Evidently, he informed the chef, for when we asked for our bill, it came accompanied by a gift-wrapped can of their signature soup, with a congratulatory note. When we opened the bill, we found a card saying, "Hope you had a wonderful dinner? Love from your son, Ryan."

At first, we were totally flummoxed. We hadn't told a soul where we were going. Then we twigged. While we were getting dressed for dinner, our cell phone had rung. It was Sid and Dorothy Kweller, in Pittsburgh. They sometimes call on our anniversary. They assumed, they said, that we were celebrating in Coral Springs. We were caught completely off guard and spilled the beans. Ryan had put them up to it. He wasted no time in calling the Chalet Suzanne to tell them that his parents were staying there and that he wanted to pay for their dinner.

When he gave them our names, management asked which of us was his father. "They both are," he replied.

I'm reminded of the first time that Ryan was with us in La Garde Freinet. The best restaurant there is owned, and run, by Jean Paul and Jean Louis, two gays. Philippe, the waiter who always attends to us, is also gay. As the saying goes, "It takes one to know one." A mixed group of us were having dinner one evening, at La Faucado, with me sitting at one end of the table. As he delivered a dish, Philippe asked who the young man was at the other end. "Oh!" said I, "that's my son, Ryan." Philippe looked startled, having assumed that I was gay. "You're his father?" "No, I'm his mother," I replied. "His mother?" he echoed incredulously. "Yes," I answered, with as much matter-of-fact nonchalance as I could muster. "And that's his other mother," I continued, pointing at Ambrose. "Mon Dieu," he wailed, as he went indoors. Moments later he reappeared, with the owners, gesticulating towards the unsuspecting Ryan. "C'est lui," he informed them. "Il y a deux mères!" Poor Philippe, he had the hots for Ryan. His unrequited passion has never abated. C'est la vie.

While on the subject of La Garde Freinet, our beloved old friend Jock Bevan, who bought the house there, died while we were circumnavigating South America in 2009. On our return home, we had long talks with Pam about the future of the place. She mentioned selling but, as she was a lifelong procrastinator, we didn't expect prompt action. Aware that its sale was a possibility, we went there in September with Ryan and a few friends, to look the place over more carefully. While there, we checked out the local housing market to get a handle on what the Bevan house might be worth. Subsequently, we told Pam that, at the right price Ryan would be interested. During the next few months, Pam put the house in the hands of a realtor, in La Garde Freinet.

Meanwhile, the grim reaper spotted Ambrose and started sharpening his scythe. We were cleaning up in the kitchen when Ambrose said, "What would you like for dinner? I thought we might have either------." "Either what, or what?" I asked. Realizing that his mind had gone blank, we made a doctor's appointment. It was the first of a number of little strokes. Every known test was administered, followed by the best available therapy. Nobody could have worked harder than Ambrose. When he wasn't having sessions with Sarah Porter, his first rate and utterly devoted speech therapist, he was slogging away at his homework. I believe that we both realized simultaneously it was a lost cause. About a year after the incident, and about a year before he could no longer speak, he held me tight as he said, quite simply, "I'm losing my mind." How long we stood there sobbing with our arms around each other, I don't know. What I do know is that once we'd pulled ourselves together, I promised to take care of everything going forward.

Oddly enough, from my perspective it was not all doom and gloom. Almost all our lives he's looked after our financial affairs, done our taxes and most of the cooking and driving. Payback time has its rewards. I've learned to do our banking on line and Ryan does our taxes. For his part, Ambrose accepted his limitations with commendable grace. Not once, did he allow his frustrations to get the better of his good humor. My cooking is mediocre at best but, he never complained and happily ate whatever I put on his plate. For a while, he attempted the word games, puzzles and sudoku, published in the daily newspaper, with ever diminishing cognition. Eventually, even the simplest games were beyond him. We found solace, just sitting on the sofa holding hands, while listening to music or watching television.

We still know so little about the working of the human brain. Dr. Goldschmidt, the neurologist who worked with Ambrose, feels that his dementia is caused by scar tissue from all the strokes. As for me, having to deal with the gradual decline of his once incisive mind helps to mitigate the inevitable pain of bereavement, which is the lot of us all when we lose our life's partner.

After Ambrose's hip replacement, in February 2010, he was assigned an outstanding therapist in the form of a Dutchman, Richard van Pelt. Not only did he get Ambrose off a walker, in record time but, he and his wife, Lisa, have become devoted friends. Thanks to Richard, Ambrose was fit enough to fly to Scotland cane free within three months of the operation.

We flew into Glasgow with Ryan and his mother, Joyce. Ryan had met Jock and Pam some years earlier in La Garde Freinet, but not their children. Joyce was meeting them all for the first time. It's a beautiful drive from Glasgow, via Loch Lomond, up the west coast to Ardfern, the tiny village where Pam, her eldest son, Simon and Namaste, his wife, live. Knowing that we were coming, other family members and friends had shown up to give us a great couple of days. In between parties and sightseeing, we broached the subject of Ryan buying their house in La Garde Freinet.

The price which Ryan had in mind, and which we considered reasonable following our survey of properties the previous September, fell far short of what the realtor had told Pam, that he could sell it for. Under the circumstances, we agreed that he should handle the sale. Should he fail to secure a buyer, the Bevans could always fall back on Ryan's offer. That settled, we drove off for a short vacation to visit some of our favorite Scottish haunts and friends. In Oban, Ryan had himself measured up for a Fraser tartan kilt plus all the formal appurtenances. While adjusting the sporran, he enquired as to where it should hang? "Right in front of yer meat and two vegetables!" was the curt response.

A year later, the Bevans had not had a single prospective buyer for their house in France. In September, we went over to give the place a further look. As well as Ryan, we were joined by three of his closest friends. We usually fly in to Nice and pick up a rental car there. On this trip, we flew to Paris, to enjoy a couple of days sightseeing, before driving south. Philippe Delcourte, the gay waiter from La Faucado, built his own house outside the village. Knowledgeable about French building codes, he came over to the house and quickly spotted signs of rising damp and spauling plaster. Ryan and Philippe went over the place, with a tooth comb, documenting all the problems. There seems to be little doubt that the main objection to the Bevan house is because it shares a party wall with another house which can only be described as a wreck. That house has been abandoned for decades. Eons ago, when the owner died it was inherited by innumerable descendants. Under Napoleonic law, all of them have to agree on the disposition of the property. As none of them is local and all attempts, over the years, to get them to agree to anything have come to naught, that situation is unlikely to be resolved any time soon. Ryan is young enough to bide his time till the heirs agree to sell. Should he acquire it, the added space would allow for a garage, a greatly expanded living room and a roof terrace.

While Ryan and I were walking around the village, we dropped into a real estate office. He was seeking information about Americans buying French properties. Terry Bourke, the realtor, is English. He was most cordial, and promised to have a whole lot of pertinent information the next day. As it happened, Ryan and his friends were off to the beach that day, so I went to Terry's office to see what he had found out. Not knowing that Ryan was only interested in the Bevan house, he took me off to see another property that was for sale. After touring the place, I told Terry that it was too large a place for Ryan. He looked surprised and said that he assumed that Ryan was my boyfriend and that we were looking for a love nest for the two of us! Now it was my turn to be surprised. When I pointed out that Ryan is young enough to be my grandson, Terry was unfazed. He had recognized the age difference, but figured that I had just got lucky! With that, he told me that recently he'd been dumped by his boyfriend, fifteen years his junior, in favor of another guy who was fifteen years younger still. Somehow, that saga conjured up a vision of painted Russian dolls.

Since Pam had had the house on the market for fifteen months, without so much as a nibble, she decided to accept Ryan's offer. Unfortunately, she could not find the deed. Gay Terry Bourke to the rescue. As a realtor dealing with French law, he knew how to get a duplicate. When it arrived, it bore only Jock's signature, opening a can of worms. While his Scottish will had left everything to Pam, Napoleonic law being what it is, his French property could not be included. Pam needed to complete some paperwork to satisfy the French government that Jock was dead and she was his widow. That done, she discovered, to her surprise, that she was only entitled to half the house. The other half had to be divided between her four children. As Katie, their eldest, had died, her eighth share had to go to her son, Aaron. All five had to agree to sell the house at the proposed price. Fortunately, the members of the Bevan family were all on the same page of music. Had they not been, the house could easily have deteriorated like its abandoned neighbor.

Ryan became the owner of the house in La Garde Freinet in July 2012. With a fresh coat of paint, some new furniture, including beds and linens, this charming old gem is now available as a rental. For anyone who yearns to escape, even briefly, the hurly burly of twenty first century life, this ancient French village could be the answer.

Chapter Forty Two
*A Diamond Celebration*


Just before meeting up with Pam Bevan, in France, for the house closing, Ryan flew down to us to discuss the possibility of our joining him and Jimmy in Cincinnati, to celebrate our diamond anniversary. The neurologist had advised that Ambrose should not be away from home overnight. Under the circumstances, I was reluctant to undertake such a trip. It soon became clear that Ambrose wanted to go so we agreed to a six day celebration.

In February 2012, Ryan had bought a sound, but abandoned nineteenth century brick Italianate building across a corner of Washington Park from Cincinnati's beloved Music Hall. With help from an architect, it has been transformed into two dwellings. A door at one end of the building opens to stairs to a rental apartment on the third and fourth floors. The basement and first two floors have been skillfully remodeled into a home for Ryan and Jimmy. As of January 2013, the household has expanded to include Jacques, a French bulldog. He's black and white to match Ryan's Kente cloth.

Originally scheduled for occupancy on June 1st, 2012, the building was still an uninhabitable work in progress when we flew in on September sixth. Mercifully, friends of the boys loaned the four of us a house across the Ohio River. By 8:00 a.m. on Friday September seventh, Ryan had some fifty men choreographed to grout, hang doors, install appliances and staircase handrails etc. before the furniture was delivered. While Ambrose and I enjoyed a leisurely day at the Art Museum, Ryan was overseeing the miraculous transformation of his erstwhile building site into a gracious home ready to welcome thirty guests for cocktails and dinner, at 7:00 p.m.

On Saturday, some seventy friends and relations arrived in Cincinnati for a celebratory evening, arranged by Ryan, in a soaring semi-raw space in the northeast corner of Music Hall. The ten circular tables sported floor length satin tablecloths in the form of Union Jacks. They were illuminated with sparkling diamante centerpieces. Surrounded as we were by so many treasured friends from as far away as Canada and the west coast, we hardly registered the fabulous food. My niece, Miranda, and several friends, read anecdotes based on this book interspersed with skillfully selected arias sung by a soprano and a tenor, accompanied by a pianist. Both are gifted young opera singers. Tom Beczkiewicz who, with Ania, had cut short an Aegean odyssey in order to attend, read a poem he'd written for the occasion. Titled, "Old Men Cry a Lot," it certainly worked on these two old men. Kerry and Brad documented the event with photographs set to beautiful music for us to enjoy in the future.

A number of the guests were staying at a converted bordello, now called The Symphony Hotel, just around the corner from Music Hall. We took over their dining room for Sunday brunch. Afterwards, Jimmy and Ryan began an all day open-house for us to visit with friends who still had time to linger.

Monday September tenth being our sixtieth anniversary, Ryan's parents, Jerry and Joyce came over from Rising Sun for the six of us to enjoy a quiet dinner, cooked by the boys, in the new house. Quiet, it was not. The merest whiff of smoke from the cooking sent the newly installed smoke detectors into paroxysms of ear-splitting unstoppable shrieks. Opening all the windows, while it did nothing to lower the decibels, must have alerted the entire Over-the-Rhine neighborhood that Armageddon was at hand.

Earlier in the day, Ryan took us to visit the Creation Museum. A sizeable place, and beautifully done, it is situated near Cincinnati airport in a veritable Garden of Eden. As we learned God's truth, I realized that, along with most people, our idea of how things began is almost totally wrong. The entire universe was created six thousand years ago, so the notion that the Colorado River took millions of years to gouge out the canyon is patently false. For evidence, one needs look no further than Mount St. Helens where God radically altered the landscape in the blink of an eye. As for dinosaurs, they survived the great flood of circa 2200 BCE. No less a man than Noah was there to explain that he rescued two each of the fifty species of dinosaurs by selecting baby ones to save space on the ark. Along with other benighted people, I had had questions about the continuation of the human race after Cain had killed Abel. In my Bible, it says that, after a nasty dust up with God, Cain settled in Nod where his wife gave birth to Enoch. Where my Bible falls short, the Creation Museum kindly fills in the details. Cain, I was surprised to learn, married his sister. In fact, for many generations God condoned incest. Before repairing to the museum restaurant for lunch, we had an encounter with Methuselah who, at nine hundred and sixty nine years old, looked remarkably spry. He seemed a very nice fellow. I wonder why his grandson Noah left him to drown? Well, you can't expect the Creation Museum to answer every silly question.

In retrospect, it seems almost miraculous that we were able to fly up to Cincinnati to enjoy six blissful days of celebrating sixty years together with Ryan, Jimmy, and so many dearly loved friends. Within days of our return to Coral Springs, Ambrose's health, both physical and mental, began a rapid decline. Forgive me for not going into details of how precipitously our lives changed. I haven't the heart to do so.

Saturday October 27, 2012 began as possibly the most painful day of my life. Only two days earlier, Ambrose had returned home, from five days in hospital, in an ambulance. The verdict was in. Henceforth, he will be in hospice care. In the misguided belief that I could nurse him, I had a hospital bed installed in our bedroom. Sadly, the task proved to be beyond my strength and capabilities.

Ernie Ospina, a prince among princes, who lives two houses away from ours, got us through the days and nights that Ambrose was home. Without his selfless help at all hours I could not have managed. Miranda and Ian took charge. They devoted all their time to finding a home for Ambrose. In the end, we settled on a place only two minutes by car from our house.

That Saturday, Miranda and Ian stayed with us awaiting the call that a hospital bed had been delivered so that we could take Ambrose over. It was cold comfort to know that he understood nothing of what was happening. I knew full well the wrench in store. At my lowest point, as the sun went down, Bubby Rodriguez's daughter, Danni, and Patti arrived. They had been shopping on the mainland and planned to return to Key West next day. First they would help us get Ambrose safely moved. Then they would take me out for a lovely dinner. Finally, they stayed the night with me. Such dear friends.

As the weeks turn into months, we are finding contentment in the new reality. I visit Ambrose daily, usually twice. Most often, I bicycle over. It takes no more than five minutes. I suspect that it does more for me than it does for him. He likes holding my hand, though I sometimes wonder if he knows who I am. In any case he soon falls asleep. His once lively mind has all but gone. The unbelievably dedicated Jamaican nurses cheerfully wash, shave and feed him. They sing songs and try to make him smile. Bless them.

For my part, I'm adjusting to living alone. Ryan keeps in touch by phone every day or two. He and Jimmy come to stay as often as their busy lives permit. In addition, I enjoy frequent visits from friends and family. Several, including Ina Mohlman and Brad Luther, nagged me to write an account of my life. For years, I resisted. Frankly, I didn't think that my story would hold much interest for anybody but me. Then, I got a letter from Herb Budden. He listed several reasons for me to embark on this project. I was finally persuaded, and began writing in 2012. Here's hoping that you, dear readers, have found something of interest between the covers? As for Herb, I'm eternally grateful to him for putting my nose to the grindstone and for all the editorial work that he continues to do to bring this book to completion.

Whatever we thought to the contrary, during our salad days, I've discovered to my surprise, and delight, that old age has much to recommend it. As youths, the farting of the elderly may have repulsed us, but, by the time one has lost both senses of smell and hearing, loud ones can be helpful when adjusting hearing aids, while the formally dreaded silent ones pass unnoticed. An added bonus is that, thanks to failing eyesight the craggy face facing you in the mirror, looks as smooth as a baby's bottom.

With your life of cutthroat competition behind you, you dress to suit yourself. Many people open doors, carry parcels and vacate their seats for you. When you speak they listen but, when they do so, you don't have to. Now that you are old, almost everybody cuts you plenty of slack. You're indulged to the hilt. Don't breathe a word about this to a soul but, very frankly, you can get away with bloody murder.

Life in the "Troisième âge," as the French call it, is a blast. True, acrobatic sex terminating in wild screams of delight, may have morphed into gentle snuggling. That could be a good thing. I still have visions of Bonnie and Herb, in their youth, disporting themselves with such enthusiasm in the bathtub, that the commotion dislodged a potted mother-in-law plant from the shelf above, to join in the fun.

We finally have time to re-read the books we were crazy about years ago but can no longer remember what they are about. After a good night's sleep, it's enormously satisfying to wake up aware that you're still on your perch with marbles intact. My breakfast is predictable but the view from where it's eaten never is. I overlook a canal full of turtles, fish, ducks and otters. Seldom is the lawn bereft of large tropical birds foraging for food. The far side of the canal consists of a forest designated as a wildlife refuge. There a family of raccoons have set up housekeeping. But I digress. Here's wishing you all a blissful old age.

# AFTERWORD
*The Case for the Peerage*


Under Scottish law, both titles and entailed estates can only be inherited by the eldest son of the eldest son. While it's not quite as simple as that, the well-known problem of establishing paternity goes a long way towards making the law's enforcement well nigh impossible. Until the discovery of DNA, locating the man responsible for fertilizing the egg generally relies on the testimony of the woman who delivers the baby and, depending on the circumstances, her word may be totally unreliable.

Diligent genealogists can frequently trace a person's last name back for many generations, but such research is an exercise in futility if you hope to trace your roots. If your father's name is McLeod, yours is generally the same even though your mother, whose name is Campbell, is equally responsible for your creation. By carrying this unassailable logic back a mere thirty five generations, we may be astonished to discover that we are all related because the number of our direct ancestors, by that point, exceeds all the human beings who have ever lived.

Nevertheless, absurd as it may be, people continue to trace Dad's name. In my case, the name is Fraser and many people believe that, under the law, I should be Lord Lovat. Whatever the merits of the case, I hope that you will find the evidence entertaining, if not convincing.

Here I must make a disclaimer. Having no personal desire to establish the claim, I have done no research into primary sources. The timeline I use is entirely based on the research of others, especially that of the "claimant," as well as generally accepted tradition. Many of the suits and countersuits, replete with convoluted and often unverifiable claims, I have ignored in the interest of simplicity. Even the secondary accounts, which I have consulted, vary somewhat from one another especially with regard to ages and dates. For example, Simon, the eleventh Lord Lovat, claimed to be eighty at the time of his execution, in 1746, whereas he was almost certainly ten years younger. Also, there are two ways of numbering the Lords Lovat. In England, the current one is number sixteen whereas in Scotland he is considered number eighteen. As a Scotsman myself, I will use the latter system. Where I know dates to be uncertain, I will give them as "circa."

The name Fraser seems to be an Anglicization of "fraise," the French word for "strawberry" and to this day, the Lovat coronet includes strawberry leaves. Accepted wisdom is that among William of Normandy's invading army of 1066 CE, so delightfully depicted in embroidery on the misnamed "Bayeux Tapestry," were a number of his vassals whose day job was to tend the ducal strawberry fields. Following his successful conquest of Britain at the Battle of Hastings, William gave lands to all his faithful Normans. They were destined to become the French-speaking aristocracy. This accounts for the difference, in wording, so often noticed in English, between the word used to describe farm animals and the word used by the time they are prepared for milord's table. For example, the English word "chicken" becomes French "poulet," "sheep" becomes "mouton," and "deer" becomes "venison." In the same way, Normans who grew "fraises" would become "Frasers." Indeed, some branches of the family still spell the name "Fraiser." As strawberry-picking serfs, the Frasers who did battle for William the Conqueror would have been near the bottom of the pecking order, so it should come as no surprise that they made their way to the North of Scotland where they settled near modern day Inverness.

Apart from a lot of begetting, the semi-barbarous Frasers didn't amount to much before 1458. That year a certain Hugh

Fraser was created Lord Lovat. At the same time, the Scottish king gave him a sizeable serfdom. For the next nine generations, the title and ever-burgeoning estates descended predictably from father to eldest son.

The ninth Lord Lovat was another Hugh. He died in 1696, at thirty without a son. The title went to his great uncle Thomas, who died three years later. Thomas was succeeded by his twenty three-year-old son, Simon. He became eleventh Lord Lovat at the turn of the eighteenth century, and his colorful life terminated with his decapitation in the Tower of London, in 1746, when he was seventy. Because my claim to the peerage dates to his generation, a few key points in his deceitful and chaotic life must be mentioned. Scullduggery had been his forte since his youth with two main goals: to become powerful and to return the Stuarts to the Scottish throne while kicking the hated English back to England.

An early attempt to satisfy his first goal ended in his fleeing to France, dressed as a woman, to avoid execution. He had kidnapped, married and possibly raped the widow of the ninth Lord Lovat, Lady Amelia Murray. She was the daughter of his erstwhile ally, the Marquess of Athol. As a result of that debacle, he hid in France for a number of years biding his time. He took John , his youngest brother, my direct ancestor, with him.

Though a lifelong Jacobite, on returning to Scotland, in 1715, he grabbed the opportunity to raise an army of Frasers, to help the English put down the Jacobite uprising. For his supposed English patriotism, his death sentence was revoked and, fifteen years later, he won a lawsuit to reclaim his title and estates.

Had he settled down to tending these estates, which at 250,000 acres were the largest land holding in Britain, the subsequent family history might not have been so contentious, but he didn't. He was legitimately married to Margaret of Grant who bore him three sons, Simon, Alexander and Archibald.

Meanwhile, the wily "Old Fox," as Simon Lord Lovat was nicknamed, was conniving to bring Charles Stuart (Bonny Prince Charlie) back from French exile to be crowned King of Scotland. At the Battle of Culloden, in 1745, many Frasers perished at the hands of the English who won a resounding victory. A search for the Old Fox, whose army was defeated, ended on an island in Loch Morar where he was caught, wrapped in a blanket, hiding in a hollowed-out tree trunk. As a prisoner, he was taken down to London where he was tried before the House of Lords, found guilty of treason and sentenced to beheading.

It was at that time that William Hogarth painted his portrait from which he created the well-known print. The painting entered the Clowes Collection, of which I was curator, in Indianapolis, Indiana. At Mrs. Clowes' death, it passed to her son, Dr. George Clowes of Dover, Massachusetts. In 1968 it was stolen and, as of this writing, has never been found. A replica, albeit with white, rather than orange gaiters, hangs in London's National Portrait Gallery.

Hogarth was no piker where money was concerned. When bleachers were built at the Tower of London to accommodate the crowds assembled to witness the grisly affair, Hogarth was "Johnny-on-the-spot," hawking his prints at one shilling each. Such a crowd had shown up that one bleacher collapsed under the weight killing several people. In the meantime, Hogarth had run home to collect a different batch of prints which he sold to the survivors as they left. That print depicted Lord Lovat, with his severed head under his arm, haunting the Tower's battlements. Simon was the last person to suffer this method of execution in Britain. The chopping block is usually on view at the Tower, but the last time I saw it, it was part of a travelling exhibition at the Cincinnati Museum of Art!

For his crime, the Lovat title and estates were forfeited to the Crown. His eldest son, Simon, though also attainted, was pardoned by King George II in 1750 on account of his youth at the time of the rebellion. This Simon later distinguished himself by leading a regiment of Frasers who fought in the first American War of Independence. As a result, George III restored the peerage and estates to him in 1774. When he died, childless, six years later, because his brother Alexander had predeceased him without an heir, Archibald, the youngest of the Old Fox's sons, became the thirteenth Lord Lovat. For those who believe that thirteen is an unlucky number, I have evidence to support your theory. He married Jane Fraser, a distant cousin, who bore him five sons, all of whom died without issue. Poor old Archibald Campbell Fraser died in 1815 having outlived the last of his sons by over ten years.

This is the point were many legal experts argue that the peerage should have shifted to my direct ancestor, John Fraser. But here we come to another bit of illegal skullduggery that, in the eventual outcome, is pivotal.

Simon, twelfth Lord Lovat, had the peerage restored to him in 1774 by George III in gratitude for his distinguished service in America. He then hired lawyers to draw up papers to ensure that, if his brother Archibald were to die without a surviving son, the order of succession should revert to the descendants of his grandfather Thomas, tenth Lord Lovat. What he did would appear to be illegal under Scottish law, but why he did it one can only guess. True, his uncle, John Fraser (my fifth great grandfather), had died a decade earlier, but he must have known that his cousin, John's son, Dr. James Fraser (my fourth great grandfather) was alive and well in South Carolina. Possibly, his uncle John's cowardice at the time of the Battle of Culloden was the reason. I doubt we will ever know the answer.

At any rate, John Fraser, born circa 1688, was the youngest brother of Simon, the Old Fox, and thanks to him being the only brother to have male descendants, this story is being written. John's father, Thomas, the tenth Lord Lovat, died when John was about eleven, followed by his mother a couple of years later. Brother Simon, who was about twenty four, brought him up and took him to France in 1702 when he was fleeing the wrath of the Athols. The brothers were back in Scotland in 1715. Unfortunately, John, now about twenty seven, was another brawler. Near Inverness he got in a fight with Amelia's son, Hugh, who had started an illegal claim to the title and estates. In the ensuing melee, he killed Hugh's servant, Chisolm. Fearing the consequences, he fled to America.

Foxy Simon claimed that John had died but in fact, he several times sent money across "the pond" to him, using a clansman by the name of William Fraser, of Dalcraig, as a go-between. Thanks to the Lovat's powerful ally, the Duke of Argyle, John was granted land in South Carolina near Beaufort, which happens to be the name of the family castle, in Scotland. He was soon in business trading with England, and by 1740, he is recorded as "living with his wife and children" under the protection of the Duke of Argyle, on the Isle of Islay, in Scotland.

John's eldest son to survive childhood was James (my fourth great grandfather), born circa 1745. Evidently, the capture and beheading of John's brother, Simon, sent the family scuttling back to South Carolina, where they remained till 1752. That year, he returned to Scotland with his family. They settled in Greenock and, ultimately he died there circa 1764.

Meanwhile, son James studied medicine, first at St. Andrews and then in Edinburgh, where he became a doctor, before returning to Beaufort, South Carolina, to open a practice and to marry. His wife, Mary Ashe, was descended from the Ashes of Ashville, North Carolina. Dr. James Fraser was a Tory loyalist and found himself exiled, following the defeat of the British, in 1782. For ten years, the family lived in England where Dr. James worked for the House of Fraser, a family business that later included Harrod's department store.

Nine years into his exile, word came from Beaufort that his best friend, Dr. Alexander Garden, for whom the gardenia is named, had died. Simultaneously, their first son to survive childhood (my third great grandfather), was born. They named him, Alexander Garden Fraser. Due, in part no doubt, to Mrs. Fraser's political connections back home, as well as an acute shortage of doctors, James received a pardon and returned to South Carolina for the rest of his life. Both he, and Mary, and several young children are buried in St. Michael's Episcopal churchyard in Charleston.

Alexander Garden Fraser was twelve when his father died but not too young to have been told that he was the rightful Lord Lovat. He took religion in school, and graduated as an Episcopalian minister to be known as the "Reverend Alexander Garden Fraser, M.A." In view of the fact that he had his eldest son christened with the same name, and that he also took holy orders, from now on I will refer to the father as "the claimant."

Circa 1828, at the age of thirty seven, the claimant went to Scotland, intent on pursuing his claim to the peerage. His uncle Archibald, thirteenth Lord Lovat, had died about thirteen years earlier and, owing to a number of circumstances, including his uncle Simon's questionable transfer of inheritance, the peerage was to remain in limbo while both sides fought it out, at first in the lower courts, and later in the Scottish court of sessions. The claimant's adversary was Thomas Alexander Fraser, of Strichen, who lived from 1802-1875. Just what his relationship was to Thomas, the tenth Lord Lovat, is unclear. However, in 1824, he had petitioned King George IV to recognize him as the fourteenth Lord Lovat on the grounds that John Fraser had died without a son!

Not only had Dr. James Fraser been John's son but Thomas was soon to meet John's grandson, the claimant. Meanwhile, King George IV hedged his bets and never gave an answer. From all accounts, the dice were heavily loaded in favor of Thomas, a Roman Catholic, who had lived his entire life in the Scottish Highlands and was well known by all. The claimant, an

Episcopalian, was a slave owner who grew indigo on Daufuskie Island, South Carolina.

In 1837, King William IV granted the peerage to Thomas. Undeterred, the claimant spent the next eight years amassing evidence and, on July 25, 1845, submitted his claim to Queen Victoria who promptly referred the matter to the House of Lords in London.

Meanwhile, his son (my second great grandfather) Alexander Garden Fraser, who had been born and brought up in the U.S.A., had earned a doctorate in divinity at the University of New York, and gone to Edinburgh, Scotland, for ordination, in 1845. While his father moved to London to press his claim before the House of Lords, the Reverend Alexander Garden Fraser, D.D. got his first living as a minister to the English congregation in Bombay, India, where he met and married my second great grandmother. As a man of God, he was totally disinterested in his father's pursuit of the peerage. He spent his life, which lasted ninety healthy years, attempting to convince reluctant Indians to dump Krishna in favor of Christ.

His dad, in the meantime, finding that the battle for the peerage would be long and costly, had to return to South Carolina to sell real estate. Luck was against him. While in Charleston he died, and with him, all attempts by our side of the family to pursue the matter further.

Back in India, Rev. A.G. Fraser and his wife produced a bouncing baby boy in 1848. They broke with tradition by christening my great grandfather Andrew Leith Henderson Fraser. He was to enter the civil service where he rose through the ranks to wind up head honcho of Bengal, the largest province in the British Empire.

My partner Ambrose and I visited Belvedere, his home in Calcutta. Today, it houses the National Library of India. The only piece of furniture, from Sir Andrew's day, that remains in situ, is the banqueting table which can seat 150 people! One can only imagine the splendor of bejeweled Maharajas and Maharanis seated with turbaned attendants behind every chair during the Durbar to celebrate Queen Victoria's diamond jubilee. Sir Andrew Fraser's eldest son (my grandfather) was another Alexander Garden Fraser.

To return briefly to what might have been. Had the Scots defeated the English at the Battle of Culloden, there would have been a Stuart on the Scottish thrown. He had already invested the Old Fox with some impressive titles. Under those circumstances, it's on the cards that today I would be living in a hideous nineteenth century red sandstone castle in the north of Scotland with the following name: Alastair Ian, Duke of Fraser, Marquess of Beaufort, Earl of Stratherrick and Upper Tarf, Viscount of the Aird and Strathglass and seventeenth Lord Lovat of Beaulieu! How 'bout them apples? Mind you, you wouldn't be expected to rattle that lot off every time you addressed me. Just remember to inject "Your Grace" into every utterance.

Before closing this Foreword, I must give you a brief summary of what subsequently happened to the title and the estates. In 1854, Thomas Alexander Fraser of Strichen was finally recognized, by the British government, as holder of both the title and the estates. He had married Charlotte Georgina Jerningham in 1823. As a wedding gift, her father, Lord Stafford, had given them a splendid tea urn bearing the Lovat crest by Matthew Boulton. It is now in my possession.

At Thomas' death in 1875 he was succeeded by his son Simon as fifteenth Lord Lovat. His son and grandson, sixteenth and seventeenth, were also Simons.

The seventeenth Lord Lovat was a brigadier who fearlessly led his troops on to the beaches of Normandy on D-Day during World War II, preceded by his piper! Sir Winston Churchill described him as "the handsomest man who ever slit an enemy's throat." He had two sons, Simon and Andrew. Unfortunately, Simon had no business sense. He and his father

445

had little in common but, Scottish law being what it is, the title and estates would eventually be his. However, under British law, the only way to avoid "death duty" is by deeding the estates over to your heir at least seven years before you die.

In 1970, following a heart attack, the seventeenth Lord Lovat deeded the estates to his elder son who was twenty five at the time. Known as "The Master of Lovat," he started selling off land and investing huge sums in one harebrained scheme after another. Within twenty years, he was drowning in debt. At a sale, where he was unloading some family treasures, Matthew Stephanich, a silver dealer from Winnetka, Illinois, bought the tea urn which we now have.

Disaster struck big time in 1994. By then, the seventeenth Lord Lovat was too frail to leave his room when he got the news that Andrew, his beloved younger son, had been killed by a buffalo in Tanzania. Andrew was forty two. The following week, the Master of Lovat, who was fifty four, suffered a fatal heart attack while riding his horse. Their forlorn father was to linger on for another year, but the government and creditors had everything in receivership well before then.

In the end, a distant family connection, in the person of Brian Souter, who had started as a bus driver and wound up making a fortune in tourism, bought Beaufort Castle and the remaining sixteen thousand acres for his daughter, Ann Gloag. Along with his debts, the Master of Lovat left a son called Simon who was seventeen at the time. When Simon, seventeenth Lord Lovat died in 1995, the eighteen-year old grandson Simon inherited the title of eighteenth Lord Lovat but with almost nothing to show for it. Today, he's in business vowing to make enough money to buy back the castle and estate from Mrs. Gloag. Stay tuned.

# Index of Names

2834535R00257

Made in the USA
San Bernardino, CA
12 June 2013